Macroeconomics for developing countries

Raghbendra Jha

London and New York

First published 1994
by Routledge
11 New Fetter Lane, London EC4P 4EE

Simultaneously published in the USA and Canada
by Routledge
29 West 35th Street, New York, NY 10001

Typeset in Garamond by
Goodfellow & Egan Phototypesetting Ltd, Cambridge
Printed and bound in Great Britain by
Biddles Ltd, Guildford and King's Lynn

British Library Cataloguing in Publication Data

A catalogue record for this book is available from the British Library

Library of Congress Cataloging in Publication Data
Jha, Raghbendra.
  Macroeconomics for developing countries / Raghbendra Jha.
    p.   cm.
  Includes bibliographical references and index.
  ISBN 0-415-10025-9. – ISBN 0-415-10026-7 (pbk.)
  1. Developing countries–Economic conditions.
  2. Developing countries–Economic policy.   3. Macroeconomics
  I. Title.
HC59.7.J5 1994
330.9172'4–dc20
                                                    94–4394
                                                    CIP

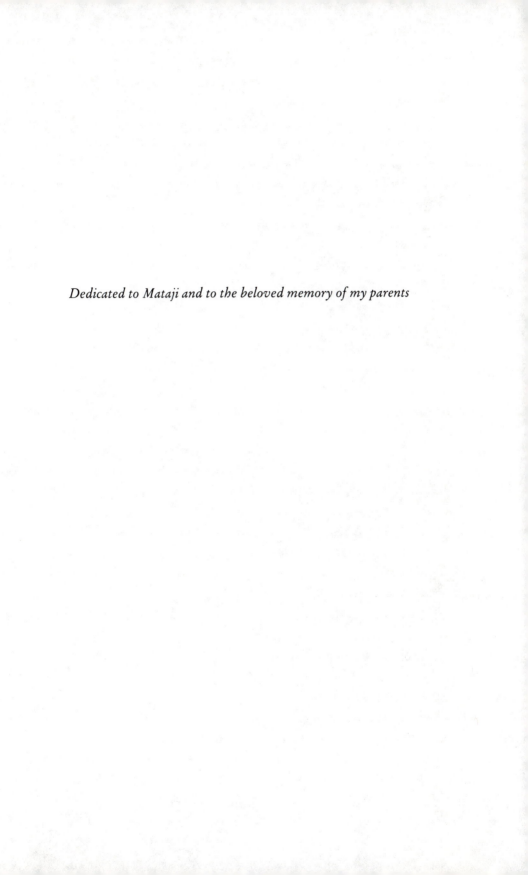

Dedicated to Mataji and to the beloved memory of my parents

Contents

List of tables

Preface

Macroeconomics for developing countries has recently become important in the curricula of many universities. This subject, however, is usually taught at an advanced level either in graduate school or in a 'Topics' course at the senior undergraduate level.

The rationale for this philosophy seems to be twofold. On the one hand, it is felt that students should have a thorough grounding in the basic tools of economic analysis before they study specialised topics such as less developed country (LDC) macroeconomics. Second, most of the material on LDC macroeconomics is available in esoteric papers in specialised journals and is therefore inaccessible to undergraduate students.

In writing this book I have tried to bridge both these gaps. Students working through this book should be able to pick up the tools of modern macroeconomic analysis at the same time as they learn about the special macro issues confronting developing countries. It then becomes possible to present the advanced material pertaining to LDC macroeconomics as relatively straightforward extensions of the tools of analysis already learnt.

In doing this I have tried to make the treatment of both the macroeconomic analysis and the special problems of developing countries exhaustive. We begin with elementary tools of macro analysis. In Part I of the book we develop the tools of analysis of the closed economy, and in Part II the open economy is studied. A good part of this material is common to 'standard' intermediate macro courses. However, issues of relevance to developing countries are brought up in key instances.

In Part III we study some alternative views of LDC macroeconomics that have gained considerable prominence and respectability of late. We follow this up in Part IV with a review of some key policy questions confronting developing countries. The material in this part harks back to a long-held belief of LDC macroeconomic theory that long-term growth rather than short-term stabilisation is the key question facing developing countries.

This book can be used in a variety of courses on macroeconomics. Parts I and II can be used for a 'standard' one-semester course on intermediate macroeconomics. In a one-semester 'Topics' course, Parts III and IV and some sections of Part II can be used as material for studying 'special macro-economic problems of LDCs'. Finally, the whole book can be used for a two-semester course on intermediate/advanced macroeconomics with special reference to developing countries.

The prerequisites for reading this book are a first-year course in economics and a first-year course in mathematical analysis. I have relied primarily on graphical methods, and advanced mathematical tools, wherever they appear, have been fully developed and explained in the text. There is an exhaustive bibliography at the end to help students plan additional reading.

In writing this book I have been the recipient of the help of several people. The economics department at Queen's University has provided a congenial and stimulating environment for my work. Professors Robin Boadway, Martin Prachowny, Dan Usher and Isao Horiba have been especially helpful to me during my tenure here. (The late) Professor Douglas Purvis provided critical encouragement and a number of ideas when this work was in its infancy. The comments of an anonymous referee provided absolutely critical input in restructuring and extending the original manuscript. The consistent and unflinching support of Alan Jarvis, economics editor of Routledge, throughout the three years over which this book was conceived and written is a pleasure to acknowledge. Dr Bagala Biswal was immensely supportive throughout and helped with the diagrams. Parts of this book were tried on students in a 'Topics' course at Queen's University. Their forthright appraisals of the manuscript have been invaluable. I am deeply indebted to all these people for their help, patience and friendship. My greatest debt, however, is to my wife Alka and our son Abhay. I shall not be so presumptuous as to thank them.

Raghbendra Jha
Kingston, Canada

Part I

Mainstream macroeconomics
– the closed economy

Part II

1

Macroeconomic problems of developing countries
An introduction

This book is about *macroeconomic* problems of developing countries. Until quite recently, there was scarcely any independent analysis of such problems within the purview of mainstream macroeconomics. There were several reasons for this and two of them may be mentioned here. First, it was generally perceived that a traditional concern of macroeconomic theory – counter cyclical stabilisation – was not very relevant to developing countries. It was felt that the most important concern of policy makers in developing countries was medium- and long-term growth and not short-term stabilisation. Second, there was a perception, almost up to the late 1980s, that the developing countries were not very different from developed countries except for levels of per capita income and the like. The developed country presented to the developing country a mirror image of its future.[1]

To be sure, so far as macro problems of developing countries are concerned, there was a significant and distinguished line of theory called *structuralism* that had always challenged this point of view. It argued that the problems of developing countries were *qualitatively* different from developed countries and, therefore, required separate treatment. Structuralism provided alternatives to the received doctrine. More recently, structuralism has been enriched by significant contributions from economists such as Sweder van Wijenbergen and Lance Taylor.

The most significant impetus to structuralism, however, was provided not by concerted intellectual debate (although that certainly played a role) but by a historical turn of events in the 1970s. The price of fuel oil quadrupled overnight and the whole trading world was dealt a very significant shock. Developed and developing countries alike faced ever increasing bills for imported fuel oil. Developed countries were more able to deal with this shock for several reasons. First, they produced goods that the Organization of Petroleum Exporting Countries (OPEC) needed and the prices of these goods could be increased to compensate for the sharp deterioration in the terms of trade. Second, OPEC placed much of its revenues from fuel oil exports in the banks of the developed countries. Third, developed countries had the technological capacity to develop fuel efficient processes and substitutes.

None of these conditions was satisfied in the case of developing countries. The prices of less developed countries' (LDCs) exports could not be increased substantially; LDCs faced adverse balance of payments positions and their technological abilities were and are limited. The LDCs therefore faced a sharp deterioration in their terms of trade as the prices of fuel oil and goods imported from developed countries went up (see Gilbert 1987). This led to a sharp drop in output potential which the LDCs tried to counteract by increasing domestic money supply. The ensuing inflation and large balance of payments deficits sent LDC economies into deep crisis. They borrowed from international banks, since borrowing in home markets could only be very limited, and from the International Monetary Fund (IMF).

The IMF imposed severe conditions on loans advanced to LDCs. They were required to devalue currencies, reduce import and other indirect taxes and reduce government expenditure at home. The rationalisation for these policy measures came from the *monetary approach to the balance of payments* – a theory developed to analyse the balance of payments problems of more developed economies.

The logic behind this approach, to be spelt out in some detail in Chapter 11, was as follows. Devaluation was necessary to make the price of foreign exchange better reflect true scarcity of foreign exchange. In most LDCs it was felt that at the 'official' exchange rate the home currency was overvalued. Devaluation was often made a precondition for granting of assistance.

Devaluation was to be followed by reduction in credit and reduction of indirect taxes and imported goods. The former, by controlling aggregate demand, would reduce inflationary tendencies. Reduction in indirect taxes would lead to a more efficient allocation of resources which would, in turn, improve aggregate supply. This step and devaluation would increase exports. Hence, inflation and the balance of payments deficit could be brought under control.

This is the premise on which IMF conditionalities are based. The record of the performance of countries that had agreed to the IMF conditionalities, however, is somewhat mixed. The immediate impact was to cause hardships to LDC populations as social programmes and employment were sharply curtailed to accommodate lower ceilings on government expenditure. It was hoped that the set of policy measures advocated by the IMF would result in LDC economies becoming more competitive and efficient in the medium run. In some cases this did turn out to be the case but, in other instances, LDC economies experienced sharp stagflation – high unemployment and high inflation – for protracted periods.

The crisis due to the oil shock helped to focus attention on the theoretical underpinnings of the IMF policy prescription. The IMF had been following the point of view that it is not necessary to develop a separate theory to understand the macroeconomic problems of developing countries. The structuralist school, with a completely different theoretical perspective, had been arguing that the IMF stabilisation would only exacerbate stagflationary tendencies in developing countries. The qualified success of the IMF stabilisation package gave the structuralists considerable support. The debate about whether a different theoretical approach was needed for studying the macro problems of developing countries gained credence. That debate is, as of now, still unresolved.

In this book we do not adhere to one point of view or the other. We present the received macroeconomic theory and point out the differences, in key areas, brought about by considering the special characteristics of developing countries. This is true of the first eight chapters of this book. In this section of the book, then, the implicit assumption is that refinements to the received macro model are enough to understand the macro issues confronting the developing countries. We then study a variant of structuralism and point out the differences that this makes to the analysis of key policy questions. The model, as laid out, is aggregative and could be said to be representative of the experiences of some Latin American countries. It is then argued that an aggregative model may not be representative of the experiences of all, even most, LDCs. Many LDCs, particularly African ones, have very significant agricultural sectors. Typically, the agricultural/rural sector is qualitatively different in these countries from the nascent industrial sector. It would, then, be inaccurate to study the macroeconomic problems of these countries within the context of an aggregative model. We consider, therefore, a *dual* economy along these lines. We also consider a model of an LDC which is definitely dual but where the industrial sector is fairly important. These characteristics can be claimed to be true of South Asia.

The layout of this book is as follows. The first part, entitled **'Mainstream Macroeconomics – the Closed Economy'**, begins with national accounts and elementary Keynesian economics. We then proceed to the classical–Keynesian synthesis with the IS–LM and aggregate supply and aggregate demand models. Real balance effects are also studied. We then generalise the IS–LM model to a variable inflation rate model.

In the second part of the book, entitled **'Mainstream Macroeconomics – the Open Economy'**, we move to the open economy model within both the standard and generalised IS–LM frameworks. Current account and asset market approaches to the balance of payments are studied. A number of important policy issues such as demand management and the assignment of policy to target are also taken up. When dealing with these policy issues the special circumstances of developing countries are also taken into account.

The third part of the book is entitled **'Alternative Approaches to Less Developed Country Macroeconomics'**. We first study an eclectic and representative structuralist macro model of the 'Latin American' LDC. This is followed by two dualistic macro models which may be said to be representative of the experiences of some African and South Asian countries. We

then review the structuralist–monetarist debate with regard to LDC inflation. The structuralist critique of the IMF stabilisation packages for LDCs
is also reviewed.

The last part of the book, entitled **'Special Policy Problems of
Developing Countries'**, takes up some key questions of relevance to LDCs
and international economic institutions. We study economic repression and
liberalisation, as well as problems of LDC domestic and international debt.
We also study long-term policy problems with a review of the implications
of financial repression for economic growth.

NOTE

1 Sah and Stiglitz (1989) present a useful analysis of the profound technological differences that exist between developed and developing countries.

2

Aggregate accounts and balance sheets

INTRODUCTION

Aggregate income accounting is the centrepiece of Keynesian macroeconomics. A key element of this analysis is the distinction between stocks and flows. A *stock* is a value at a point in time. The value of the money supply on 9 August 1992 or the capital stock of a nation are both examples of stocks. A *flow* measures a rate per unit time. National income during the calendar year 1992 or additions to a country's plant and equipment during 1991 are both examples of flows.

AGGREGATE INCOME, OUTPUT AND EXPENDITURE

There are three sets of economic actors in the macroeconomy: firms, households and the government. The financial flows that take place between them are depicted in Figure 2.1. On this basis, economists often make distinctions between three different measures of aggregate economic activity.

National product

The sum of value added during an interval of time at various stages of production is a measure of a nation's output. Value added at any stage of production is the value of output produced at that stage of production minus the cost of intermediate inputs. Value added at the bakery is the value of bread minus the cost of flour and other inputs used in the production of bread. The sum of all value added is sometimes called the gross domestic product (GDP) of a country. The adjective *domestic* is used here because all value added within the geographic boundaries of the country are considered *irrespective* of whether these values are produced by foreign or domestic firms. In measuring gross national product (GNP) we deduct from GDP the value added by foreign-owned firms and add to it the value added by domestic firms working in foreign countries.

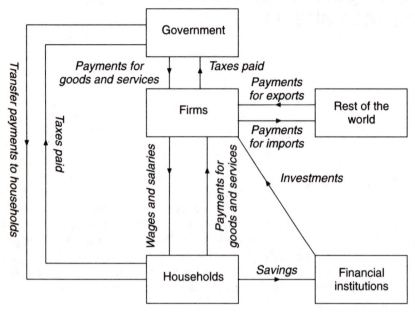

Figure 2.1

National income

This is the sum of all factor incomes generated during an interval of time. Thus we add up all wages, salaries, profits, interest, rent, dividend income and the like, i.e. all remuneration received for productive economic activity by all factors of production. This is called net national income at factor cost. If we add to it indirect taxes and subtract subsidies we get national income at market prices. If depreciation is also added we get gross national income.

National expenditure

A third way of measuring aggregate economic activity during an interval of time is by summing up final expenditures. Hence we add up consumption, investment and government expenditures. To this we add net exports, i.e. exports minus imports.

These three measures of aggregate economic activity are usually calculated for a year. When the year closes national income must equal national product which in turn must equal national expenditure. This is because they are realised magnitudes. Desired magnitudes, however, might differ systematically from realised ones.

Each of these magnitudes can be measured in real or nominal terms. When the GNP for 1992 is measured with the prices of 1992 used to evaluate output, then we have measured GNP in current prices. This is also called nominal GNP.

If, however, we wish to compare GNP figures of 1992 with those of 1970, we realise that there are some difficulties. Comparing nominal GNP for 1970 with nominal GNP for 1992 may not be such a good idea, because during the period 1970–92 the price level would have risen and the structure of relative prices would have undergone several changes. One way of getting around this difficulty is to calculate real GNP. Let $P_1^0, \ldots, P_n^0$ be the year 0 (or base year) prices of all n goods produced in the economy. The corresponding quantities transacted in the base year are $X_1^0, \ldots, X_n^0$. We may evaluate current year quantities in terms of base year prices. Let the current year quantities traded be $X_1^1, \ldots, X_n^1$. Real GNP for year 1 (with year 0 as base) can be written as

$$\frac{\Sigma_{i=1} P_i^0 X_i^1}{\Sigma_{i=1} P_i^0 X_i^0}$$

This measure has obvious disadvantages, such as the fact that the same bundle of goods may not be produced in year 1 as in year 0, but in macroeconomics we must learn to be pragmatic rather than fussy.

We can similarly compute an index of how prices may have moved during the period. One such indicator is

$$\frac{\Sigma_{i=1}^n P_i^1 X_i^0}{\Sigma_{i=1}^n P_i^0 X_i^0}$$

Similarly one can define a GNP deflator (a measure of price change) as nominal GNP/real GNP. Let P_{1992} be the value of the GNP deflator in 1992 and P_{1981} be its value in 1981. The rate of inflation between 1981 and 1992 was

$$\frac{P_{1992} - P_{1981}}{P_{1981}} \times 100$$

Price index numbers and GNP in real and nominal terms are some of the most important macroeconomic variables. Another important macroeconomic variable is the aggregate rate of unemployment. This is defined as the aggregate number of people unemployed and actively searching for work during a period of time divided by the total size of the labour force during that period. Unemployment data are also collected annually but are available for shorter durations of time as well.

We have so far examined some key flow macroeconomic variables. Let us now look at some important stock variables.

Table 2.1 An example of a personal balance sheet

	Assets ($)	Liabilities ($)
Notes and coins	500	
Balance in savings account	1,000	
Term deposits	5,000	
Credit account		500
Bank loans		3,000
Total financial assets and liabilities	6,500	3,500
House	100,000	
Car	10,000	
Total real assets	110,000	
Total assets and liabilities	116,500	3,500
Wealth		113,000
Totals	116,500	116,500

ASSETS, LIABILITIES AND BALANCE SHEETS

An asset is simply something you own. A liability is something you owe. There are two types of assets: financial and real. A real asset is something tangible: cars, plots of land, mines, airplanes, apartments and steel factories are all examples of real assets.

Financial assets are different. They are pieces of paper which constitute an asset for one person and a liability for another. In other words they define a debt relationship between two economic agents. An example is your savings account in your neighbourhood bank. The amount of money in your account is your asset – you own the money. It is the bank's liability – they owe that money to you. A $5 currency with you is your asset – the corresponding liability is that of the Federal Reserve Bank of the USA.

The balance sheet of an economic agent is a comprehensive statement of that agent's assets and liabilities. An individual's balance sheet may look like Table 2.1. The balance sheet drawn here follows the principle that the sheet must balance. Hence wealth is shown as a liability. One can think of it as what the individual owes to herself.

MONEY

Money is anything that is generally accepted as a medium of exchange. What precise assets constitute the medium of exchange varies from one society to another and has varied over time. Gold, silver and several other precious metals have served as mediums of exchange. In developed countries personal cheques are accepted as mediums of payment. In several developing countries payment by personal cheques is often unacceptable. The use of cash is much more common.

In modern societies money is typically a financial asset which is the liability (most commonly) of the central bank of the country. There are several definitions of money but two are most common. Narrow money (M_1) consists of currency in circulation plus demand deposits in commercial banks. Broad money (M_2) consists of M_1 plus time deposits in commercial banks.

Money does not include 'plastic money' such as credit cards. These plastic cards are convenient identification tags that enable the holder to create two debts. One debt is between you and the bank issuing the credit card and the other is between the credit card bank and the seller whose goods you have bought.

BALANCE SHEETS OF SIX AGENTS

We may now examine the balance sheets of six major economic actors: households (H), commercial banks (B), central bank of the country (C), the government (G) and the rest of the world (R).

Their balance sheets are represented in Table 2.2. A plus (+) denotes an asset and a minus (–) a liability. An explanation of the terms used in the table is given below.

1 *Commercial bank deposits with the central bank* are the commercial bank's accounts with the central bank of the country. These are the central bank's liability and the commercial bank's asset.
2 *Currency* consists of all the notes and coins held by (and, therefore, assets of) households, firms and commercial banks. The corresponding liability is that of the central bank.
3 *Demand deposits* are accounts from which funds may be withdrawn on demand. They constitute a liability of the commercial banks and are assets of firms, households and the government.
4 *Other (term) deposits* are held at commercial banks by firms and households. They may not be withdrawn immediately.
5 *Government securities* are loans issued by the government and held by many agents; in a typical developing country they are held principally by the central bank of the country.
6 *Bank loans* are personal and business loans which form an asset for the commercial banks and are a liability of the people who have borrowed the funds.
7 *Equities* are issued by funds to raise capital for their activities. An equity holder in a firm is in fact an owner of the firm, i.e. the householders and foreigners who own equity shares in a firm really own a share of the firm's capital stock. Actually, of course, the owner of a share can only sell the share. The firm has a liability and the households and firms own the corresponding asset.

Table 2.2 Structure of financial indebtedness

	Sector					
	H	F	B	C	G	R
Commercial bank deposits with central bank			+	−		
Currency	+	+	+	−	−	
Demand deposits	+	+	−		+	
Other (term) deposits	+	+	−		+	
Government securities	+	+	+	+	−	+
Bank loans	−	−	+			
Equities	+	−				+
Corporate bonds	+	−				+
Foreign securities				+	+	−
Foreign exchange				+	+	−
Net financial assets	+	−	0	0	0	±

8 *Corporate bonds* are held by bondholders in a corporation. A bond-holder, unlike an equity holder, is not an owner of the corporation. Rather such a patron has simply made a loan to the corporation. A corporate bond is a liability to firms and an asset to those advancing the loan (households and foreigners).

9 *Foreign securities* can in principle be held by the households, domestic firms, commercial banks and the government. In practice, however, in most developing countries foreign securities are held by the central bank and the government.

10 *Foreign exchange reserves* in developing countries are typically assets of the government and the central bank and the liabilities of the foreign governments that have issued them.

NET FINANCIAL ASSETS

If we add up the elements along any column of Table 2.2 we shall get the net financial assets of that sector. Those for the commercial banks and the central bank will approximately add up to zero. This is because although the absolute size of the real assets owned by these institutions is very large, in comparison with the size of their financial liabilities it is minuscule.

Households and firms have positive net financial assets. The government, on the other hand, typically has a net financial liability referred to as the national debt. The net financial asset position of the country *vis-à-vis* the rest of the world may be positive or negative.

REAL AND FINANCIAL ASSETS

Real assets are owned primarily by households, firms and government, and the total of all these constitutes the non-human wealth of the economy

Table 2.3 Net asset positions of economic agents

Item	Sector						Economy
	H	F	B	C	G	R	
Net financial assets	+	−			−	±	
Real assets	+	+			+		Non-human wealth
Future tax liabilities	−	−			+		
Undistributed profits	+	−					
Human wealth	+						Human wealth
Wealth	+	0	0	0	0	±	Wealth

If the government has liabilities which exceed its real assets then it is the household and firms which will be responsible for meeting these liabilities. The government will have to levy taxes on them which equal in value the excess of its liabilities over its assets. This might be thought of as an implicit financial asset.

Households are the ultimate holders of wealth. Firms can be regarded as owing to households net undistributed profits, which are exactly equal to the difference between the firm's real assets and net financial liabilities. In the case of firms that have issued equity, undistributed profits are already taken into account provided that the equity has been valued correctly. The value of the future income of individuals constitutes the economy's human wealth.

The net wealth or all the real assets plus human wealth is the economy's wealth. This is the same thing as the household sector's wealth. The reason why all the wealth is owned by the households is because of the implicit asset/liability items which take into account future tax liabilities and undistributed profits. Government has no wealth of its own. It owes any excess of assets over liabilities to households who are liable for its net debts. Similarly, firms have no net wealth because they owe to households any undistributed profits. These ideas are summarised in Table 2.3.

THE NATIONAL ACCOUNTING FRAMEWORK

Aggregate demand in an economy can be written as the sum of consumption expenditure C, investment expenditure I, government expenditure G and net sales to the rest of the world (exports X less imports Z). We know that *ex post* aggregate expenditure equals national income y. Thus we can write

$$y = C + I + G + X - Z \tag{2.1}$$

Domestic expenditure $C + I + G$ is often referred to as domestic absorption A and $X - Z$ is called the balance of trade, so that we may write

$$y = A + X - Z$$

or

$$y - A = X - Z \tag{2.2}$$

In other words the balance of trade is equal to the difference between national income (which in equilibrium equals domestic supply) and domestic demand (absorption). Realise that if net factor payments from abroad are zero then $X - Z$ also equals the current account balance. Now any current account surplus (CAS) is equal to the net acquisition of foreign assets (ΔNAFA). Thus

$$\Delta\text{NAFA} = X - Z = y - A = y - C - (I + G)$$

upon substitution for A. Now $y - C = S$ (savings). Hence we have

$$\Delta\text{NAFA} = X - Z = S - (I + G) \tag{2.3}$$

Hence the trade account can be improved only by increasing net savings. Equivalently the trade account can only be increased by increasing national income or reducing absorption.

SIMPLE MULTIPLIER ANALYSIS

Our analysis so far has been conducted in terms of the accounting framework. In the simple Keynesian framework these relationships have been used to predict causal linkages between aggregate demand and national income. Let us dwell on this somewhat.

Consider an economy in which the absolute price level, the nominal wage rate and the interest rate are fixed. The price level and the nominal wage rate may be assumed fixed because we are considering only the short run – a time period too short for any significant wage and price adjustments. We abstract from interest rate effects by assuming that the monetary authorities keep the interest rate pegged. The rate of interest is allowed to vary in the IS–LM model, which is discussed further in Chapter 3.

Desire consumption C depends on disposable real national income y_d. Keynes hypothesised that with higher disposable income people consumed more. But part of every additional dollar of disposable income is saved. The consumption function relates desired consumption in the aggregate to disposable income. A particularly simple example would be

$$C = a + by_d \tag{2.4}$$

where b is often referred to as the marginal propensity to consume (MPC). The average propensity to consume (APC) is defined as the ratio of consumption to income, C/y_d, and varies inversely with y_d.

Real national income equals disposable income plus direct (restricted to income) taxes T: $y_d + T = y$. Hence if T is a relatively simple magnitude it is easy to convert the consumption function from the (C, y_d) plane to the (C, y)

plane. We shall assume that this is the case.

Desired investment I is treated as exogenous. The rate of interest is fixed. Other factors such as expectations of profitability that might affect desired investment do not depend on y.

Government expenditure G is treated as exogenous since the government's expenditure is affected by factors other than y. Finally exports X are exogenous and imports Z depend on imports. However, the marginal propensity to import (the additional import following an increase in income of \$1) is assumed fixed and less than one.

Total desired aggregate expenditure E is the sum of desired consumption, investment and government expenditure:

$$E = C + I + G + X - Z \tag{2.5}$$

I is fixed at $\bar{I}$, X at $\bar{X}$ and G at $\bar{G}$. Algebraically, let

$C = a' + b'y$ be the consumption function in terms of real national income,

$I = \bar{I}$ be exogenous investment,

$G = \bar{G}$ be exogenous government expenditure,

$X = \bar{X}$ be exogenous exports, and

$Z = zy$ be the import function with z as the marginal propensity to import.

The equilibrium condition is

$$E = a' + b'y + \bar{I} + \bar{G} + \bar{X} - zy = y$$

Hence equilibrium national income is

$$y^* = \frac{a' + \bar{I} + \bar{G} + \bar{X}}{1 - b' + z} \tag{2.6}$$

This equation expresses equilibrium national income as a function of exogenous variables and parameters of the system.

Suppose we wish to model taxes explicitly. Let $T = t_0 + t_1 y$, $t_0 > 0$, $0 < t_1 < 1$. Then we would have the consumption function $C = a + b(y - t_0 - t_1 y)$. The other components of aggregate demand are as before. Equilibrium national income would be given as

$$E = C + \bar{I} + \bar{G} + \bar{X} - Z = a + b(y - t_0 - t_1 y) + \bar{I} + \bar{G} + \bar{X} - zy = y$$

or

$$y^{**} = \frac{a - bt_0 + \bar{I} + \bar{G} + \bar{X}}{1 + bt_1 + z} \tag{2.7}$$

where y^{**} is equilibrium national income with taxes.

The *multiplier* is defined as the change in equilibrium national income consequent upon a change in some exogenous component of aggregate expenditure. From equation (2.7) we get

$$\frac{dy}{dI} = \frac{1}{1 + bt_1 + z} \qquad \text{investment multiplier}$$

$$\frac{dy}{dG} = \frac{1}{1 + bt_1 + z} \qquad \text{government expenditure multiplier}$$

$$\frac{dy}{dX} = \frac{1}{1 + bt_1 + z} \qquad \text{export multiplier}$$

$$\frac{dy}{dt_o} = \frac{-b}{1 + bt_1 + z} \qquad \text{tax parameter change multiplier}$$

In the simplified model,

$$C = a + b(y - T) \qquad T \text{ fixed}$$
$$I = \bar{I}$$
$$G = \bar{G}$$

we get $y = [a + b(y - T) + \bar{I} + \bar{G}]/(1 - b)$, $dy/dG = 1/(1 - b)$ and $dy/dT = -b/(1 - T)$ so that $dy/dG + dy/dT = (1 - b)/(1 - b) = 1$, i.e. if G and T change by the same amount (say \$1) output would increase by \$1. This is often referred to as the *balanced budget multiplier*.

There is another interesting interpretation of the equilibrium condition

$$E = C + I + G + X - Z = a + by_d + I + G + X - Z$$

Savings S are the surplus of disposable income over consumption,

$$S = y_d - a - by_d = -a + (1 - b)y_d = -a + (1 - b)(y - T)$$

Now $S + Z + T = -a + (1 - b)(y - T) + zy + T$. Now if

$$S + Z + T = \bar{I} + \bar{G} + \bar{X} \tag{2.8}$$

we get our equilibrium condition that aggregate income equals aggregate expenditure. Now $S + Z + T$ is the sum of leakages from the income stream whereas $I + G + X$ are the injections. Hence equilibrium is attained when injections into the income stream equal leakages.

In the analysis in this chapter changes in demand drive the macroeconomy. A higher exogenous demand always leads to a higher income. Other critical macroeconomic variables like the price level, real wage and interest rate do not adjust. More output always means more employment from the production function. More workers are always willing to work at the prevailing wage rate. Output demand constrains labour demand which constrains demand.

The labour market equilibrium is depicted in Figure 2.2. The labour supply curve is horizontal at the going wage rate. Employment is constrained by the demand for labour. The modelling of the labour market is very simplistic here. A more sophisticated analysis is definitely possible. However, it needs to be remembered that in most developing countries

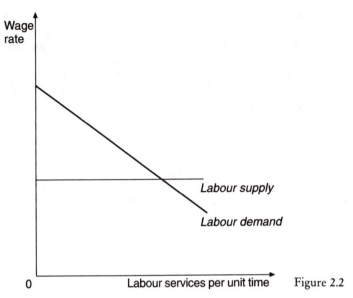

Figure 2.2

labour is plentiful. Output is constrained not by labour so much as by availability of foreign exchange and capital. The assumption about the labour market made in this chapter, therefore, may not be as outlandish as it may seem at first glance.

CONCLUDING REMARKS

The analysis in .this chapter is the starting point of almost all texts on macroeconomics, *even those* which have the more developed countries as their focus. Does this mean that the same analysis can be used for developed and developing countries?

This question is rather complicated and controversial. Complicated because there are many differences in the economic structures of developed and developing countries. To name just a few of these differences: developed countries, apart from the fact that they enjoy much higher living standards than developing countries, also have much more developed financial and banking institutions, their currencies enjoy much more confidence than the currencies of developing countries in exchange markets and they have much better supply responses than developing countries.

Many economists believe that these differences are *quantitative* rather than *qualitative* in nature. In other words the same economic model with different values of the parameters can be used for developed as well as developing countries. The aggregate supply curve, for instance, is upward sloping in developed as well as developing countries. The slopes might be different.

Several other economists, however, argue that the differences between developed and developing countries are so deep that they amount to being *qualitative* rather than merely *quantitative*. They argue that models used to study the macroeconomic problems of developed countries are inapplicable to developing countries. A whole new approach has to be developed.

This debate is controversial because, after all, the economic policy measures that one advances would depend on the model used to study the economy. The approaches of the two groups of economists to economic policy are fundamentally different. Given the severe economic predicament in which many developing countries have found themselves since at least the mid-1970s, this controversy assumes significance.

The approach taken in this book is agnostic. We do not necessarily subscribe to the point of view of any school. We shall develop both approaches and, whenever possible, resolve differences by appealing to the facts.

3

Keynesian aggregate demand and aggregate supply

INTRODUCTION

In this chapter we shall further develop the Keynesian analysis initiated in the last chapter. We begin with an IS–LM analysis with fixed prices. We then relax the assumption of fixed prices and study output and price level determination in a model of aggregate demand and supply. We then generalise the model to include wealth effects in aggregate demand. Finally we study Phillips curves and the natural rate of unemployment.

IS–LM ANALYSIS

In the previous chapter we developed the Keynesian model for, the case where both the interest rate and the price level are fixed. In this section we relax the assumption of a fixed interest rate but keep the price level fixed. This is called IS–LM analysis.

The IS schedule

To develop the IS curve, consider the model developed in Chapter 2. Equilibrium national income is given by

$$y = E = C + I + G + X - Z \tag{3.1}$$

In the model presented in the previous chapter I, G and X were treated as exogenous. Hicks, and later Hansen, in an attempt to generalise this model to include some concerns of the classical economists, allowed investment to depend negatively on the rate of interest, r. Thus

$$I = I(\underline{r}) \tag{3.2}$$

We shall inquire more carefully into the rationale for the investment function in equation (3.2). Suffice it to say here that the higher the rate of interest the greater is the cost of borrowing funds for investment, *ceteris paribus*, and the lower, therefore, will be investment. The price level is still kept fixed. Equilibrium national income is then given by

$$y = C + I(r) + \bar{G} + \bar{X} + Z \tag{3.3}$$

or, equivalently,

$$S + Z + T = I(r) + \bar{G} + \bar{X} \tag{3.4}$$

Equation (3.4), or equivalently (3.3), is the equation of the IS schedule. This schedule gives us the r,y combinations for which leakages from the stream of national expenditure $S + Z + T$ equal injections $I + G + X$. Totally differentiating equation (3.4) gives

$$S_y dy + Z_y dy = I_r dr$$

for fixed T, G and X. A subscript denotes a partial derivative: $S_y \equiv \partial S / \partial y$ etc. Hence the IS schedule in the r,y plane is downward sloping,

$$\left. \frac{dr}{dy} \right|_{IS} = \frac{S_y + Z_y}{I_r} < 0 \text{ since } S_y, Z_y > 0 \text{ and } I_r < 0.$$

The intuition behind the IS schedule is rather straightforward. The lower the rate of interest, *ceteris paribus*, the higher is going to be aggregate demand. With higher aggregate demand, equilibrium national income is going to be higher.

We depict the IS curve in Figure 3.1 as the locus of combinations of combinations of r and y. To the left of the IS schedule at any level of income the rate of interest is too low to give us commodity market equilibrium. If the rate of interest is 'too low' then the rate of investment will be too high. Correspondingly, aggregate demand will be too high. This last step in the argument follows from the 'Keynesian' assumption retained by Hicks and Hansen that output and employment respond to aggregate demand changes in the commodity market. All points to the left of the IS schedule then denote r,y combinations that are associated with excess demand (ED$_G$) in the commodity market. Analogously, at any point to the right of IS, at the relevant level of income, the interest rate is 'too high' to maintain equilibrium in the commodity market. This implies that investment is too low and so will be aggregate demand. All points to the right of IS then denote r,y combinations that are associated with excess supply (ES$_G$) in the commodity market. This is shown in Figure 3.1. Horizontal arrows in the diagram denote pressures on y. When there is excess demand for goods there is pressure for y to rise. Conversely, when there is excess supply in the goods market there are pressures for y to fall.

The IS curve gives a relationship between r and y that must obtain to have equilibrium in the commodity market. As is obvious, the IS curve, by itself, cannot determine equilibrium r and y. To do this we have to introduce another equilibrium relation between r and y. To get this other

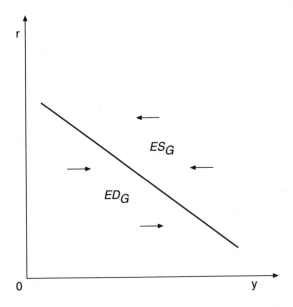

Figure 3.1

relation let us dwell a little on the general equilibrium underpinnings of the Keynesian model.

We have four aggregate markets: the labour market, the commodity market, the bond market and the money market. Keynes simplifies the analysis by assuming that the wage rate is fixed in the labour market. Employment, then, is entirely dependent on the demand for labour, which is derived from the demand for goods. Thus employment rises when demand for goods rises and, correspondingly, falls when the demand for goods falls. Hence the labour market's behaviour is entirely explained by the commodity market. We exclude the bond market by Walras' law (which says that excess demand in any market in an n market system is the sum of the excess supplies in the other $n - 1$ markets). Hence, we get the other relationship between r and y from the money market.

The LM Schedule

Keynes had made a spirited departure from the classical tradition by assuming that monetary influences determine the rate of interest. In the classical tradition, r is determined by the equality of real saving and investment, and monetary influences primarily affected the price level. Keynes' major departures from classical thought (at this level of aggregate general equilibrium analysis) are

1 that the price level and nominal wage are fixed and national income adjusts to clear the commodity market,

2 that monetary influences determine the rate of interest.

Keynes visualises the demand for money (real cash balances) as rising from the transactions, speculative and precautionary motives. Although we shall discuss them in some detail later a word about the transactions, speculative and precautionary motives are in order. People hold cash balances for transactions purposes because of the immediate liquidity of money and because of the non-synchronisation of payments and receipts. People get salaries at discrete intervals of time, usually a month, whereas expenses have to be incurred more or less continuously. These expenses have to be paid for with cash. Hence people hold money balances for transactions purposes. We might reasonably expect that the higher a person's income the higher would be her expenses and the greater would be the transactions demand for cash. For the economy as a whole the higher the national income the greater would be the transactions demand for cash balances.

People often hold cash for precautionary purposes – for an unforeseen contingency which requires extra expenses, an illness in the family for example. We would reasonably expect that the higher a person's income the higher would be his demand for cash for precautionary purposes. For the economy as a whole the higher the national income the greater would be the demand for cash for precautionary purposes.

People demand money for speculative purposes as well. Suppose that people can hold their money in two forms: a riskless asset (cash) and a risky asset (bonds). For simplicity the bond is assumed to be an annuity – the bond pays an interest of r and the principal is never paid. The price of the bond, therefore, is $1/r$. The higher the rate of interest the lower will be the price of bonds. If we assume that at high interest rates people will expect the interest rate to fall (bond prices to rise), it would be rational for an investor to buy more bonds and reduce demand for money. Analogously when interest rates are low (bond prices are high) investors will expect interest rates to rise (bond prices to fall) and will therefore tend to sell bonds to make capital gains. In this process they will increase their demand for money. Hence the demand for money for speculative purposes depends negatively on the interest rate. Hence we may write the aggregate demand for money as $L(r,y)$. When the interest rate rises, *ceteris paribus*, the demand for money will fall. When y rises, *ceteris paribus*, the demand for money will rise. Equilibrium in the money market is given by

$$L(r,y) = \frac{M}{P} \tag{3.5}$$

where M is the nominal stock of money and P is the aggregate price level. M/P, therefore, is the real value of cash balances. Equilibrium in the money market is shown in Figure 3.2.

If the real value of existing money supply is $(M/P)_0$ and the national income is y_0, the equilibrium rate of interest in the money market would be

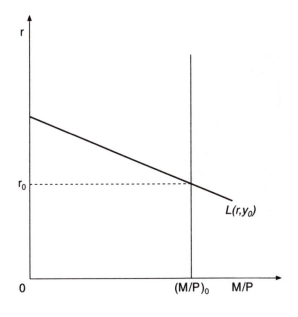

Figure 3.2

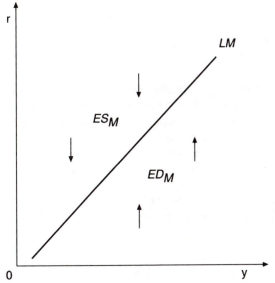

Figure 3.3

r_0. At a lower rate of interest, *ceteris paribus*, demand for money would be too high and at a higher rate of interest it would be too low in comparison to the existing money supply.

Equation (3.5) is the equation of the LM schedule – the locus of r,y combinations giving us equilibrium in the money market. Totally differentiating we have (for fixed M/P) $L_y dy + L_r dr = 0$, so that

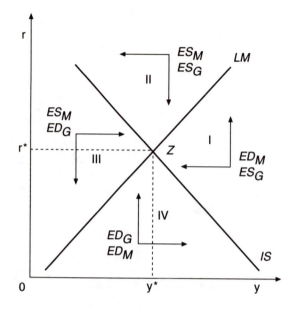

Figure 3.4

$$L_y dy + L_r dr = 0, \text{ so that}$$

$$\frac{dr}{dy} \bigg|_{LM} = \frac{-L_y}{L_r} > 0$$

since $L_y > 0$ and $L_r < 0$

In Figure 3.3 we have drawn the LM schedule. Above the LM schedule for a given y the interest rate is too high. This means that the demand for money will be too low relative to money supply. This is labelled as ES_M in Figure 3.3. If, along with Keynes, we assume that monetary factors affect r (primarily) then there will be pressures for r to fall in this region. This is denoted by vertical arrows in Figure 3.3. To the right of the LM schedule at any level of income the rate of interest is too low to maintain equilibrium in the money market. There will be excess demand for money (labelled as ED_M) in Figure 3.3 and there will be pressures for r to rise.

Equilibrium in the commodity and money markets

At point Z in Figure 3.4 the interest rate is r^* and the level of national income is y^*. At this point there is simultaneous equilibrium in the goods and money markets. Students should satisfy themselves that the bond market equilibrium schedule will go through quadrants I and II and pass through Z, by Walras' law. In any event, the bond market schedule is redundant and we shall work with the IS and LM schedules.

Shifting the IS schedule

Assume we have equilibrium at Z in Figure 3.4 with rate of interest r^* and national income y^*. A rise in any exogenous component of aggregate demand would shift the IS curve to the right. To see this, suppose government expenditure goes up. Now totally differentiate equation (3.4) with the understanding that $dG > 0$. This gives $S_y dy + Z_y dy = I_r dr + dG$. At any fixed r we have $dy/dG = 1/(S_y + Z_y) > 0$. Similarly for fixed y we have $d_r/dG = -(1/I_r) > 0$. With higher government expenditure aggregate demand is higher, *ceteris paribus*, at every rate of interest. Hence every rate of interest is associated with a higher level of national income (correspondingly at every level of income the interest rate required to give us equilibrium in the commodity market is higher). Consequently the IS curve shifts outwards. The analysis here is not confined to an increase in government expenditure: an increase in any component of aggregate demand would shift the IS curve outwards. Conversely, any fall in any exogenous component (an increase in T) will shift the IS curve inwards.

Shifting the LM curve

A change in the money supply will shift the LM curve. Totally differentiating equation (3.5) with the understanding that $d(M/P) > 0$ gives $L_y dy + L_r dr = d(M/P)$. Hence for fixed r we get $[d_y/d(M/P)] = 1/L_y > 0$. Hence with an increase in the money supply every interest rate is associated with a larger value of real national income. In other words, the LM schedule shifts outwards.

Policy analysis in the IS–LM framework

In this section we analyse economic policy. However, the kinds of policy issues that can be addressed within the IS–LM framework are rather limited: it is difficult to analyse price level changes.

Within this framework we can say that expansionary fiscal policy (any increase in exogenous expenditure which, as we know, shifts outwards the IS schedule) will most likely increase output. So will expansionary monetary policy (an increase in the money supply in real terms). Totally differentiating equations (3.4) and (3.5) and writing in matrix form gives

$$\begin{bmatrix} S_y + Z_y & -I_r \\ L_y & L_r \end{bmatrix} \begin{bmatrix} dy \\ dr \end{bmatrix} = \begin{bmatrix} -dT + dX + dG \\ d(M/P) \end{bmatrix} \quad (3.6)$$

Setting $d(M/P) = 0$ and solving by Cramer's rule we get

$$\frac{dy}{dG} = \frac{L_r}{S_y Z_y L_r + I_r L_y} > 0 \tag{3.6a}$$

$$\frac{dy}{dX} = \frac{L_r}{S_y Z_y L_r + I_r L_y} > 0 \tag{3.6b}$$

$$\frac{dy}{dT} = \frac{-L_r}{S_y Z_y L_r + I_r L_y} > 0 \tag{3.6c}$$

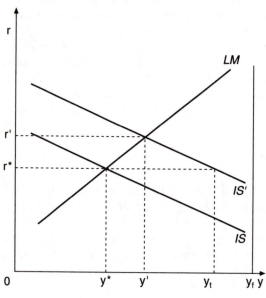

Figure 3.5

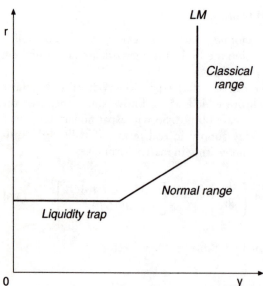

Figure 3.6

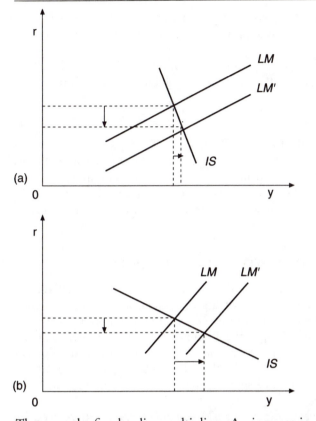

(a)

(b)

Figure 3.7

These are the fiscal policy multipliers. An increase in exogenous exports or government expenditure or a reduction in taxes shifts the IS curve outwards without disturbing the LM schedule. It can be checked from equation (3.6) that in all these three cases r also rises. This is shown in Figure 3.5. Clearly the magnitude of these multipliers depends upon the sizes of the coefficients L_y, I_r and the like. In particular we realise that as (the absolute value of) L_r rises these multipliers drop. In extreme cases the LM is nearly vertical, L_r is very large and the multipliers are nearly zero. This is the so-called 'classical case'. In another extreme case L_r is very small and the LM schedule is nearly horizontal. In this case the multiplier is large (the so-called liquidity trap case). Classroom expositions of IS–LM analysis often depict a schedule as in Figure 3.6. This shows a LM schedule with three distinct ranges. At low rates of interest everyone expects the interest rate to rise so that the LM schedule is horizontal (the liquidity trap case). At moderate rates of interest the LM schedule is upward sloping. At very high rates of interest the LM curve becomes vertical. Any increase in exogenous expenditure simply raises the rate of interest and 'crowds out' private investment with no effect on equilibrium output. This last situation has often been used by some economists to argue against expansionary fiscal policy.

If the LM curve is neither completely inelastic nor perfectly elastic, then the effect of an increase in the supply of money will depend on the slope of the IS schedule.

To analyse the effects of expansionary monetary policy we go back to equation (3.6). Setting $dX = dG = dT = 0$ and solving by Cramer's rule gives

$$\frac{dy}{d(M/P)} = \frac{I_r}{S_y Z_y L_r + I_r L_y} > 0$$

(3.6d)

It can similarly be checked that $dr/d(M/P) < 0$. We depict the situation in Figure 3.7. An increase in the money supply (from $(M/P)_0$ to $(M/P)_1$) leads to a drop in the interest rate (from r_0 to r_1) and an increase in equilibrium national income (from y_0 to y_1). Clearly, for any given shift of the LM schedule, the flatter the IS schedule the greater will be the increase in equilibrium y.

AGGREGATE DEMAND WITH VARIABLE PRICES

In the IS–LM analysis developed in the previous section, we integrated asset markets into the Keynesian model of aggregate demand. However, we had kept the price level fixed. In this section we relax this assumption.

When the price level changes the IS curve will not shift, nor will the money demand schedule. However, the value of the money supply will change with a change in the price level. In particular, higher values of the price level will lower the money supply and shift the LM curve upward. We depict this in Figure 3.8.

In Figure 3.8(a) we have drawn the LM schedule for four different values of the price level, P_0, P_1, P_2 and P_3 with $P_0 < P_1 < P_2 < P_3$, everything else remaining unchanged. With higher price levels the real value of the existing stock of money drops and the LM schedule shifts upwards. Equilibrium y, therefore, falls. The first thing we realise is that if we allow the price level to vary, the IS–LM apparatus is insufficient to determine equilibrium y. What we get from the demand side is a relationship between P and y as plotted in Figure 3.8(b). For each price level (P_0, P_1, P_2, P_3) we get equilibrium y (y_0, y_1, y_2, y_3) from Figure 3.8(a). The locus of all such points is the aggregate demand schedule plotted in Figure 3.8(b).

Aggregate supply

To determine equilibrium P and y we now have to define another relationship between them. The natural candidate for this is an aggregate supply schedule. Our modelling of the supply side has been very simplistic so far. We have assumed that the nominal wage and the price level are fixed. Hence employment is constrained by demand (not supply) of labour which, in

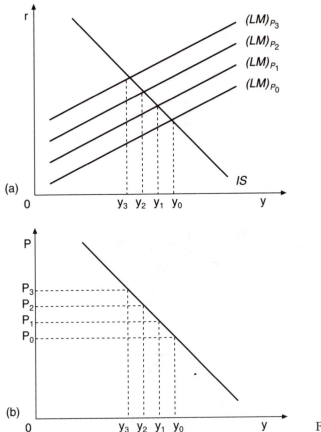

Figure 3.8

turn, is constrained by the demand for goods. Correspondingly, the aggregate supply schedule in Figure 3.8 can be thought to be horizontal at the existing price level. With a variable price level, however, this reasoning is untenable.

So we must think more deeply about the supply side. We visualise a labour market where the nominal wage rate is fixed but the price level is variable. In Figure 3.9(a) the nominal wage is fixed and labour supply is perfectly elastic at this wage. If the price level is P_1, $N_{P_1}^d$ is the demand for labour schedule as a function of the nominal wage. Profit maximising firms will equate the marginal product of labour to the real wage. With the nominal wage rate fixed, a higher price level corresponds to a lower real wage and, therefore, a higher demand for labour. At the higher price level P_2 the demand for labour would shift out to $N_{P_2}^d$. Employment rises (to N_2) and so does output (to y_2). The logic, restated, is that when the price level rises, the real wage falls and profit maximising firms increase their demand for labour. Since employment is constrained by labour demand alone, employment and

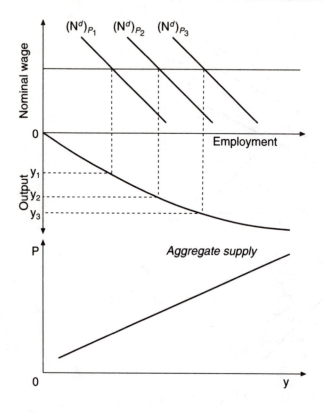

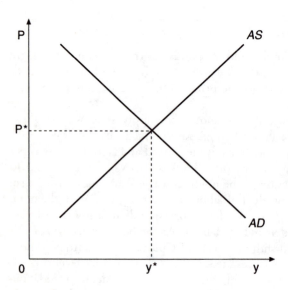

Figure 3.9

Figure 3.10

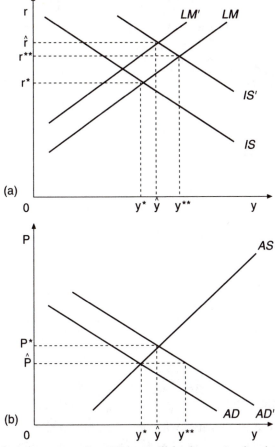

Figure 3.11

hence output rise. With a still higher price level (P_3) labour demand would be N_3 and output y_3.

In Figure 3.9(b) we have plotted these price levels and the associated levels of output. The locus of all such points has been labelled the labour supply schedule. It shows the optimal supply responses of competitive profit maximising suppliers to changes in the aggregate price level. Thus *given* price level P_3 output would be y_3 and so on.

The aggregate demand schedule of Figure 3.8 and the aggregate supply schedule of Figure 3.9 jointly determine equilibrium P and y. In Figure 3.10 they are labelled P^* and y^*.

Policy analysis

The emphasis now shifts to aggregate demand and aggregate supply policies. A fiscal policy change will shift aggregate demand. The effects of an increase in (exogenous) government expenditure are worked out in

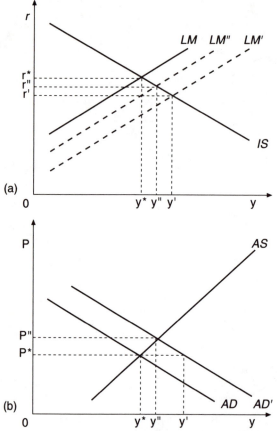

(a)

(b)

Figure 3.12

Figure 3.11. Initially we are at equilibrium with (less than full employment income) y^*, interest rate r^* and the price level P^*. When the government increases its expenditure the IS curve shifts outwards to IS'. The impact is to shift the aggregate demand schedule to AD'. Had the price level remained unchanged output would have risen to y^{**} and the interest rate to r^{**}. But the feasible equilibrium is where aggregate supply (AS) intersects the new aggregate demand schedule, i.e. at $\hat{P}, \hat{y}$. In Figure 3.11(a), as price rises from P^* the LM schedule starts shifting upwards until, with price level $\hat{P}$, it intersects the new IS curve (IS') at interest rate $\hat{r}$ and output level $\hat{y}$. In final equilibrium the output level is $\hat{y}$, interest rate is $\hat{r}$ and the price level is $\hat{P}$.

We now trace the effects of a change in the nominal supply of money. This is considered in Figure 3.12. We are initially in equilibrium at price level P^*, output level y^* and interest rate r^*. An increase in the nominal supply of money shifts the LM schedule to LM'. The impact of this is to shift AD to AD' so that with a constant price level output would have risen to y' and the interest rate would have fallen to r'. But more output (along the supply curve) can only be had at a higher price level. As the price level rises

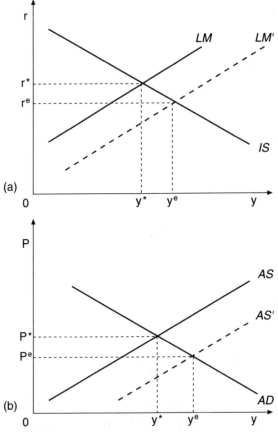

Figure 3.13

LM starts shifting back. It rests at LM" with price level P". In this situation, the rate of interest would have risen to $r"$ (from r') but it is still below the old equilibrium rate of interest r^*. The level of output is $y"$. Apart from monetary and fiscal policies, which may now more appropriately be called demand management policies, the government may also pursue policies of aggregate supply management. Assume that government helps the economy absorb new technology. This reduces costs and shifts out the AS schedule. In Figure 3.13 equilibrium in the economy occurs at income y^*, price level P^* and interest rate r^* before the technological improvement. When technical progress occurs, costs are lowered and aggregate supply shifts to AS'. The price level falls – which means that the real supply of money increases and the LM curve shifts outwards. Final equilibrium occurs at income y^e, price level P^e and interest rate r^e. A critical assumption underlying the analysis so far is that nominal wages are fixed. Clearly this is an extreme assumption. Let us take up the case of another extreme assumption – workers are interested only in their real wages and that real wages are perfectly flexible. We analyse the implications of this in Figure 3.14. In Figure 3.14(a)

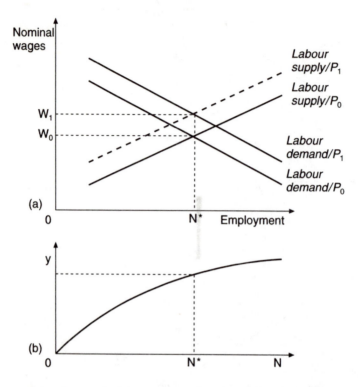

Figure 3.14

we have drawn the labour demand and supply schedules under the assumption that workers are interested only in their real wages and that these wages are flexible. With price level P_0, the lower the nominal wage the lower will be the real wage and the higher will be the demand for labour. (Profit maximising firms will equate the real wage to the marginal product of labour to determine the demand for labour.) Hence the demand curve for labour is downward sloping in the nominal wage, employment plane. Furthermore, with the price level fixed at P_0 the lower the nominal wage the lower will be the supply of labour. Hence the supply of labour in the nominal wage employment plane will be upward sloping. When the price level rises to P_1 every nominal wage will correspond to a lower real wage. The demand for labour, therefore, will shift outwards whereas the supply of labour will shift inwards. Equilibrium nominal wage will rise from W_0 to W_1. However, real wages and employment are unchanged: $W_0/P_0 = W_1/P_1$ and employment is still N^*.

The implications of this for aggregate output are traced in panel (B). We have drawn the production function relating employment to output. With employment unchanged at N^* output is unchanged at y^*. At any price level output would be y^* and the aggregate supply curve would be vertical. When the supply curve is vertical aggregate demand expansion will raise prices and have no effect on real output. Output is completely supply determined.

Correspondingly we come to the conclusion that Keynes-type effects of aggregate demand changes on real output are possible only when nominal wages do not respond immediately and completely to price level changes. So long as an increase in the price level leads to a drop in the real wage an increase in aggregate demand will lead to an increase in output and employment. The assumption that nominal wages are completely fixed is rather extreme and unnecessary.

Tobin (1947) has argued that labour supply depends on real as well as nominal wages. It is argued that the current price level will be known only one period later, but the nominal wage to be paid today has to be agreed upon today itself. In a monetary economy, workers bargain for a real wage but what is set is the nominal wage. Suppose, argues Tobin, that workers expect a certain (normal) price level to prevail. If the price level is below this then it is expected to rise up to its normal level and if it is higher it will be expected to drop next time period. Suppose now that the price level falls below the normal level. Should the workers accept a nominal wage cut? It would be irrational for them to do so because when the price level goes back up to its normal level next time period they would lose doubly: lower nominal wage and higher price level. So the nominal wage would be rigid.

The above explanation is in terms of a fixed expected price level. Tobin demonstrates that this analysis would go through so long as the elasticity of the future expected price with respect to the current price level is less than unity: in other words, when the current price level goes up by x per cent expectations of the future price are revised by less than x per cent. Casual empiricism suggests several other reasons for nominal wage sluggishness. It may be argued that in a situation of high unemployment, firms might be tempted to cut the nominal wage of the existing work force because the (unemployed) workers are willing to work for less. But firms spend considerable time and effort in their recruitment efforts and want to develop a stable and committed work force. An easy way to lower the morale of the existing work force is to cut their nominal wages. The gains from reducing these wages will be more than made up for by the losses suffered on account of higher employee turnover, costs of recruitment, loss of efficiency on the shop floor and so on. In short, there are rather compelling reasons to believe that workers and employers will resist nominal wage cuts. Hence there are good reasons to suppose that the short-run aggregate supply schedule is not vertical.

SOME REFINEMENTS OF AGGREGATE DEMAND AND SUPPLY

The Keynesian analysis developed in the previous section can be faulted on one count. Suppose the economy currently has unemployment. This amounts to an excess supply of labour and goods. Suppose commodity prices fall in the face of this excess supply. This will raise the real value of all forms of nominal wealth held by consumers. If people's consumption expenditure depends positively on real wealth, then, in response to the aforementioned increase in real wealth, consumers should increase consumption expenditure. As this happens aggregate demand will rise and employment and output will increase. This is the Pigovian *real balance effect* after A.C. Pigou who first developed this idea. Thus Pigou would write the equation of the IS schedule as

$$S(y, M/P) + Z(y) + T(y) = I(r) + \bar{G} + \bar{X} \tag{3.7}$$

When real cash balances rise (M/P goes up) savings fall and consumption rises.

This is depicted in Figure 3.15. In this diagram we have drawn the IS–LM schedules for three different values of the price levels, P^0, P^1, and P^2 with $P^0 > P^1 > P^2$. As the price level falls from P^0 the LM curve shifts to the right because the real value of the money supply has risen and the IS curve shifts to

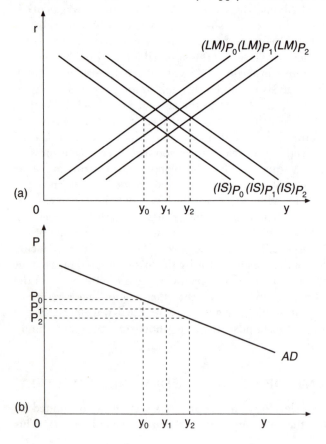

Figure 3.15

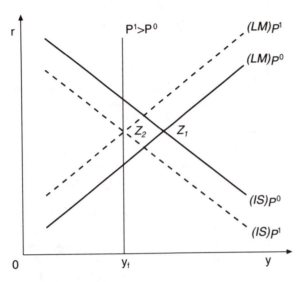

Figure 3.16

the right because of the real balance effect. Correspondingly, the aggregate demand schedule is more price elastic than it would be without the real balance effect. In other words, the AD schedule of Figure 3.15 is more price elastic.

Pigou then goes on to argue that with the real balance effect the economy must always be in full employment equilibrium. To see this, refer to Figure 3.16 where full employment income is denoted by y_f. Suppose, for a moment, that the IS–LM schedules intersect at Z_1 with price level P^0. Can this position be sustained? Clearly not. Z_1 represents a position of excess demand in the commodity market since national income at Z_1 is higher than y_f. This will lead to inflationary pressures in the commodity market. As the price level rises, the IS schedule will shift leftward and the LM will shift up. The new equilibrium will occur at Z_2 with a higher price level P^1. From this it may be argued that whenever there is unemployment (excess supply in the commodity and labour markets) the price level will fall. This will raise aggregate demand and, therefore, output and employment.

Thus, argues Pigou, full employment will automatically result if the price level is fully flexible. How credible is this claim? Tobin (1982) has made special efforts to address this issue and neatly summarises Keynes' rebuttal of Pigou's position.

Suppose we are in a situation of less than full employment. Will Pigou's real balance effect automatically lead us to full employment? As the price level falls the real value of all debt (not just the government's through M/P) goes up. Lenders and borrowers are affected asymmetrically. Lenders gain and borrowers lose. Pigou is obviously assuming that in the aggregate these effects cancel each other out. But, argues Tobin, borrowers are usually younger people with higher marginal propensities to consume, and lenders are usually older people with lower marginal propensities to consume. With a price fall the relative wealth position of borrowers deteriorates, *ceteris paribus*. Hence, on this count, aggregate demand should fall.

Furthermore, argues Tobin, even if this effect is negligible there is a still more powerful reason to believe that the Pigou effect will not work. Suppose that from a position of less than full employment the price level starts to fall. The rational consumer would find it in her interest to *postpone* purchases until prices have fallen. This will lead to a collapse of aggregate demand and a serious exacerbation of the problem of unemployment! Keynes, argued Tobin, was doing the classical economists a favour by assuming that the price level does not fall in the presence of excess supply in the commodity market.

Keynes did talk about a real balance effect, but in a manner different from Pigou. He said that if we start from a position of less than full employment a fall in the price level may stimulate demand for two reasons. First, a lower domestic price level would make imports less attractive than domestically produced goods. By the same token exports should pick up. Moreover, the lower price level would increase the real value of money and, therefore, lower the interest rate and stimulate investment demand. Keynes, however, deliberately underplayed the real balance effect because of the potential dangerous consequences of a fall in the price level.

In sum, the Pigou effect talks about the automatic attainment of full employment equilibrium in a model with flexible prices. If the Pigou effect works smoothly there would not be any need to provide monetary or fiscal stimulus to the economy during a recession. However, the operation of the real balance effect is fraught with pitfalls.

One last point before we close this section. When the demand for money is perfectly elastic (the liquidity trap region) an increase in the supply of money will not alter the interest rate and, hence, will not be able to affect aggregate demand. A drop in the price level will shift the LM schedule as before but since we are in the liquidity trap range the intersection of the IS schedule with the LM schedule is unaffected if there was no real balance effect. With the real balance effect in consumption the IS schedule will shift outwards. This enables the economy to move to a higher level of real national income and, ultimately, toward full employment. Thus it is theoretically possible to think of the real balance effect as encouraging employment.

While such theoretical possibilities exist it cannot be stressed too much that reliance on the real balance effect to get the economy out of a recession is fraught with too much danger. It is much better to pursue expansionary fiscal and monetary policies.

THE PHILLIPS CURVE

In 1958 Phillips published an empirical study of British data about the relation between unemployment and the rate of change of nominal wages. He discovered that there is a negative relation between the rate of change of nominal wages and the rate of unemployment. This is shown on Figure 3.17. On the abscissa we plot the rate of unemployment, u, defined as the number of people unemployed, U, divided by the total size of the labour force, N. On the ordinate we plot the rate of inflation of nominal wage, i.e. $(dW/dt)/W = \dot{W}/W = \mu$. The observations on μ and u for the various years (Phillips covered the period 1861–1957) are clustered fairly close to this Phillips curve. Phillips' analysis was purely empirical. He did not provide a theory or explanation for this negative relation between u and μ.

The link between u and the rate of price inflation is fairly easy to establish. Let η be the marginal product of labour. Remember that in competitive equilibrium firms would equate the marginal product of labour to the real wage rate:

$$\eta = \frac{W}{P} \text{ or } \frac{\dot{\eta}}{\eta} = \mu - \frac{\dot{P}}{P}, \text{ so } \frac{\dot{P}}{P} = \mu - \frac{\dot{\eta}}{\eta},$$

i.e. we obtain the rate of price inflation by subtracting the rate of growth of productivity of labour from the rate of wage inflation. Once we do this we can define a Phillips curve between the rate of price inflation and the rate of unemployment much like that we described in Figure 3.17. Thus if we write the equation of the Phillips curve in Figure 3.17 as

$$\eta = \alpha(u - u^*) \qquad \alpha > 0$$

where u^* is the rate of unemployment consistent with wage stability, we can write

$$\frac{\dot{P}}{P} = \alpha(u - u^*) - \frac{\dot{\eta}}{\eta}$$

We have said nothing so far about the theoretical underpinnings of the Phillips curve, this problem being addressed in an important contribution by Phelps (1969). Suppose that the labour market is characterised by pure not perfect competition. This means that there are many employers and many workers. However, the labour market is not characterised by perfect knowledge. Workers do not know the going market wage, nor do firms. Workers search for jobs and firms make wage offers to workers. Workers expect wage inflation to be say 5 per cent over the previous period. If a worker is offered a wage that is more than 5 per cent higher than the previous period's wage it is likely that the job offer would be accepted. By this reasoning, the higher the rate of wage inflation, given the expected rate of wage inflation, the greater would be the number of people accepting jobs and the lower, therefore, would be the rate of unemployment. We show this

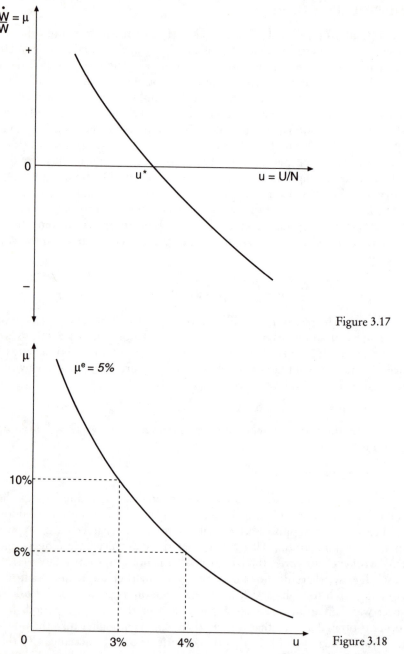

Figure 3.17

Figure 3.18

in Figure 3.18. Given expected inflation of 5 per cent, if the actual inflation turns out to be 6 per cent unemployment would be 4 per cent of the labour force. If the rate of inflation was higher, say 10 per cent, unemployment

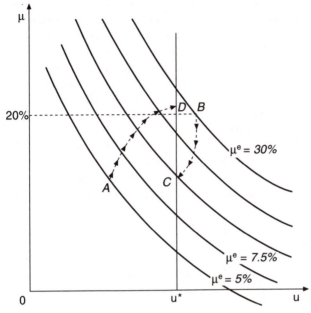

Figure 3.19

would have been 3 per cent. Suppose that the current inflation rate is indeed 10 per cent. Next time period people realise that their expectations were wrong: they expected inflation at the rate of 5 per cent whereas the actual inflation rate turned out to be 10 per cent. Rational economic agents would revise their expectations. Suppose they revise their expectations of inflation by a fixed fraction of the gap between the actual inflation last period and the expected inflation in that period – the so-called adaptive expectations hypothesis. Suppose the fraction of adjustment is 0.5. Hence expected inflation this period would be 5 per cent + 0.5(10 – 5) = 7.5 per cent. When the expected rate of inflation is 7.5 per cent it will not sustain 3 per cent unemployment with 10 per cent inflation. With higher expected inflation fewer workers will accept jobs when the actual inflation rate is 10 per cent. In other words the Phillips curve will shift upwards. Expected inflation will keep rising and Phillips curves will keep shifting so long as actual inflation is higher than expected inflation. When unanticipated inflation is zero the Phillips curves will stop shifting.

In Figure 3.19 we begin at point A. As expected inflation rises the Phillips curves starts shifting upwards. In the medium run we move along a path like the one indicated by the arrows. At rate of unemployment u^* there is zero unanticipated inflation. A couple of points about this should be made clear. First, it is argued that no matter where the process of expectations adjustment starts we shall always end up at the unemployment rate u^* in the long run. At point B in Figure 3.19 expected wage inflation is 30 per cent whereas the actual rate of wage inflation is 20 per cent. Hence inflationary expectations have to be adjusted downwards. We trace a path from B to C as shown by the arrows – once again to a level of unemployment u^*. It is hypothesised that u^* is unique. It does not matter whether the long-run (fully anticipated) rate of inflation is 5 per cent, 10 per cent or 30 per cent – the rate of unemployment will be u^*. It denotes a kind of long-run equilibrium unemployment in the economy. It has been called *the natural rate of unemployment*. In the medium term, unemployment and inflation can both rise as in the movement from A to D or fall as in the movement from B to C. This is the so-called *accelerationist hypothesis*.

An important conclusion that emerges from the analysis is that in the long run the economy will supply the natural rate of output – one that is consistent with the natural rate of unemployment. In the short run output can deviate from the natural rate by a factor that depends upon the magnitude of unanticipated inflation:

$$y_t = y^* + \beta(\mu - \mu_t^e). \qquad \beta > 0 \tag{3.8}$$

Actual output at time t (y_t) is equal to the natural rate of output (y^*) plus a factor that depends on the magnitude of unanticipated inflation. This equation is often referred to the Lucas supply function.

AN ALTERNATIVE INTERPRETATION OF THE NATURAL RATE OF UNEMPLOYMENT

We have interpreted the natural rate of unemployment as a situation in which the actual and the expected rates of inflation are equal to each other. There are other possible interpretations. We outline one now.

Consider the labour market depicted in Figure 3.20. The demand for labour is a decreasing function of the real wage. The supply of labour is drawn as an upward sloping function of the real wage. Equilibrium in the labour market is denoted by J where the demand and supply of labour are the same.

Now labour demand consists of actual employment and vacancies. In every economy there are some vacancies that are unfilled *coexisting* with workers who are searching for work. We can then define a *labour use* schedule ($\hat{N}$ in Figure 3.20) which shows actual employment. The gap between labour demand and labour use is unfilled vacancies. The higher the real wage, it is reasonable to expect, the smaller will be the number of unfilled vacancies. The lower the real wage the greater the number of workers looking for work.

With labour market equilibrium at J in Figure 3.20 actual employment is ON_1 whereas labour demand is ON_2. The distance N_1N_2, therefore, represents unfilled vacancies. Since labour demand equals labour supply unfilled vacancies must equal quits to search for jobs. An alternative interpretation of equilibrium in the labour market is, thus, a situation where the number of vacancies equals the number of quits. If this is the case there will be no pressures for the wage to change. Expectations of inflation will, therefore, also be fulfilled. The distance N_1N_2, therefore, represents the natural rate of unemployment.

CONCLUDING COMMENTS

In this chapter we have analysed various variants of the static Keynesian model. A variant of inflation has also been studied. However, this has not been built into the IS–LM apparatus studied here. This theme is picked up in the next chapter.

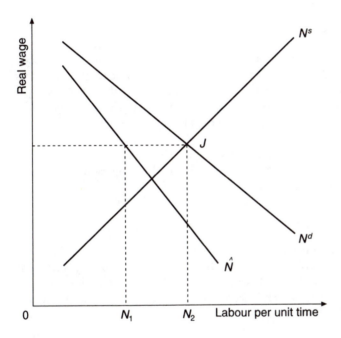

Figure 3.20

4

A generalisation of aggregate supply and aggregate demand

INTRODUCTION

The basic macro model we have studied so far is cast in terms of aggregate supply and aggregate demand in the Py plane. It is possible to generalise this to the case where the rate of inflation (π) rather than the price level (P) becomes the important endogenous variable. This generalisation pays additional dividends since it is possible to model the effects of expected inflation in a straightforward manner.

We did not study inflation dynamics comprehensively in Chapter 3. We want to do so now. Our basic tools will be an IS–LM apparatus along with an aggregate supply (AS) schedule.

THE IS SCHEDULE

Define V as the natural log (henceforth written as ln) of saving plus taxes and J as the ln of investment expenditure plus exogenous government expenditure. Let Y be the ln of real national income, i the nominal rate of interest and π^e the expected rate of inflation, so that $(i - \pi^e)$ denotes the real rate of interest. We can write

$$V = \beta_0 + \beta_1 Y \tag{4.1}$$

$$J = \beta_2 + \beta_3 Y - \beta_4 (i - \pi^e) \tag{4.2}$$

Savings and taxes are assumed to depend on real national income alone whereas investment depends on real national income and the real rate of interest. β_1 and β_3 are, respectively, the income elasticities of savings and investment. β_4 is an interest semi-elasticity. (Remember that $i - \pi^e$ is in terms of levels not logs.) All parameters are positive.

What is the difference between the real and the nominal interest rate? Suppose you lend out $100 at an interest rate of 5 per cent for one time period. You expect to get back $100(1 + 0.05) = $105. If there is no inflation your real rate of return would be 5 per cent or, in this case, $5. Suppose, however, that the price level was expected to rise at 6 per cent? How much

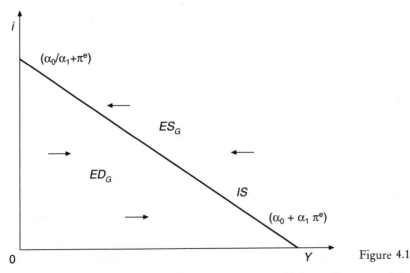

Figure 4.1

should you get back in order for you to get a real rate of return of 5 per cent? The answer is $100(1 + 0.05)(1 + 0.06)$. In other words, if r is the real rate of return and π^e is the expected rate of inflation you should get back $\$1(1 + r)(1 + \pi^e)$ for every dollar you lend out. Now $(1 + r)(1 + \pi^e) = 1 + r + \pi^e + r\pi^e$. Now $r\pi^e$ is a very small magnitude and can be ignored. Hence the gross of inflation rate of return or the nominal rate of interest, i, can be written as

$$i = r + \pi^e \tag{4.3}$$

This is the famous Fisher equation after Fisher (1930). Sometimes it is implied that $di/d\pi^e = 1$ so that r is impervious to monetary disturbances. This, however, is not always true. See, for example, Jha *et al.* (1990).

To derive the IS schedule we set leakages from national expenditure equal to injections into national expenditure. In other words, we set savings plus taxes equal to investment plus government expenditure. This gives us a relation between Y and i which can be written as

$$Y = \alpha_0 - \alpha_1(i - \pi^e) \tag{4.4}$$

where $\alpha_0 = (\beta_2 - \beta_0)/(\beta_1 - \beta_3)$ and $\alpha_1 = \beta_4/(\beta_1 - \beta_3)$. Since the coefficient of i is $-\alpha_1$ the slope of the IS equation in the (i, Y) plane is $-1/\alpha_1$. However, the IS will be negatively sloped only if $\beta_1 > \beta_3$.

The intercept of IS on the i axis is $\alpha_0/\alpha_1 + \pi^e$ whereas its intercept on the Y axis is $\alpha_0 + \alpha_1 \pi^e$. This curve is shown in Figure 4.1. Disequilibrium zones are also labelled in the diagram. An increase in expected inflation will leave the slope of the IS schedule intact and shift it outwards. α_0 is a summary measure of the exogenous components of aggregate demand. A change in α_0, therefore, may be taken as a change in fiscal policy. Thus an increase in government expenditure will increase J and shift outwards the IS schedule without changing its slope.

THE LM CURVE

Whereas the IS curve deals with the market for goods and services as flows per period of time, the LM curve deals with asset markets as stocks at a point in time. Let us write the demand for real cash balances as

$$m - p = \alpha_2 Y - \alpha_3 i \tag{4.5}$$

where m is the natural log of the nominal supply of money, p is the log of the price level and α_2 and α_3 are positive parameters. Notice that the opportunity cost of holding real cash balances depends on the nominal (not real) rate of interest.

Now let μ be the rate of growth of nominal money and π the rate of inflation. Thus real cash balances grow at the rate $\mu - \pi$. Thus we can write the equation for the LM schedule as

$$\mu - \pi = (m - p) - (m - p)_{-1} \tag{4.6}$$

$(m - p)_{-1}$ is money demand last period so that the right-hand side of equation (4.6) denotes the growth of real cash balances from the demand side, whereas the left-hand side gives the equivalent expression from the supply side. Upon substituting from (4.6) for $m-p$ we have the final form of the LM equation

$$\mu - \pi = \alpha_2 Y - \alpha_3 i - (m - p)_{-1} \tag{4.7}$$

Let us examine it in the steady state where real cash balances are constant. The intercept of this schedule on the i axis occurs at $-(m - p)_{-1}/\alpha_3$ and on the Y axis at $(m - p)/\alpha_2$, its slope is $di/dy = \alpha_2/\alpha_3$. This curve is shown in Figure 4.2 where the disequilibrium zones are also labelled.

In Figure 4.3 we plot both the IS and LM schedules. If we make the 'Keynesian' assumption that the interest rate responds primarily to pressures from the money market and national income responds to pressures from the goods market we can label i, Y movements in the disequilibrium zones as shown.

With expansionary fiscal policy and unchanged inflationary expectations, the IS schedule in Figure 4.4 would shift outwards. Both i and Y would rise. With expansionary monetary policy LM would shift outwards leading to a drop in i and a rise in Y. This is shown in Figure 4.5. However, both these policy experiments can be misleading if we keep π^e constant in the face of changes in the actual inflation rate. Therefore, Figures 4.4 and 4.5 should be used only to show how macro policies are incorporated into the model and not to show their final effect on the economy. We shall encounter this later.

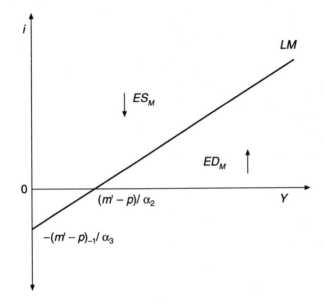

Figure 4.2

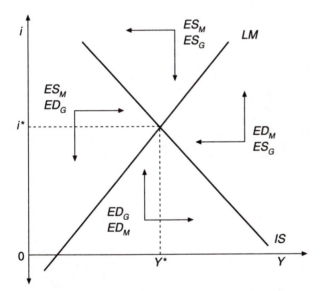

Figure 4.3

THE AGGREGATE DEMAND SCHEDULE

Just as in Chapter 3, we can use the IS–LM schedules to derive an aggregate demand (AD) schedule. To derive the AD schedule we rewrite the IS curve as

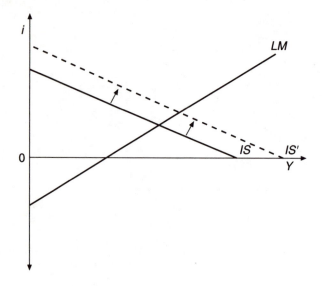

Figure 4.4

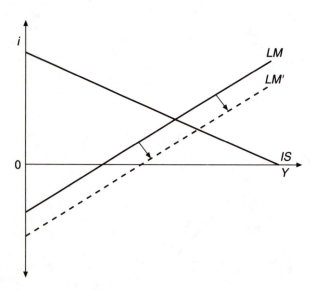

Figure 4.5

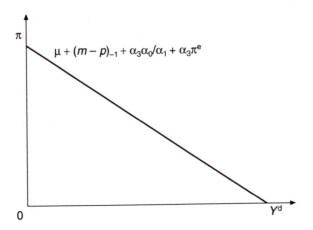

Figure 4.6

$$i = \frac{\alpha_0 - Y}{\alpha_1} + \pi^e$$

and then substitute it into the LM equation to get, after rearrangement,

$$\pi = \mu + (m - p)_{-1} - \left(\frac{\alpha_2 + \alpha_3}{\alpha_1}\right) Y^d + \left(\frac{\alpha_3 \alpha_0}{\alpha_1}\right) + \alpha_3 \pi^e \qquad (4.8)$$

where Y^d stands for output demanded as distinguished from Y^s (output supplied) which we shall introduce later. We have drawn the AD schedule in Figure 4.6. Its intercept on the π axis is $\mu + (m - p)_{-1} + \alpha_3\alpha_0/\alpha_1 + \alpha_3\pi^e$ and the slope of the AD curve is $d\pi/dY^d = -(\alpha_2 + \alpha_3/\alpha_1)$ which is negative – hence the AD schedule defines a negative relation between π and Y^d. An increase in the rate of inflation reduces the real quantity of money in the economy creating excess demand in the money market. In turn, this causes the nominal interest rate to rise. With π^e held constant the real interest rate also rises which, in turn, reduces investment and aggregate demand.

Two other facets of the AD schedule should be pointed out. First, a change in fiscal policy will shift the AD schedule without changing its slope. Second, so long as the rate of growth of money and the rate of inflation are not equal to each other, $(m - p)_{-1}$ will keep changing and so will the intercept of the AD schedule. An increase in π^e will shift the AD schedule by α_3 times the change in π^e. At any given level of income this would also increase π by α_3. In that way expected inflation pursues actual inflation. However, there must be some restraint on this self-fulfilling prophecy otherwise π and π^e would chase each other without reference to μ. Students can check that the required constraint is $0 < \alpha_3 < 1$.

THE AGGREGATE SUPPLY SCHEDULE

The AD curve, by itself, cannot determine π and Y. To complete the system we introduce an aggregate supply (AS) schedule. The derivation of the AS schedule, which shows combinations of π and Y consistent with production conditions in the labour market, has two key elements: (i) an aggregate production function relates total output produced to labour input, and (ii) labour market supply and demand conditions relate labour supply and demand to the rate of inflation.

THE PRODUCTION FUNCTION

Without loss of generality we shall take a specific form of the production function:

$$Y^s = \beta_5 + \beta_6 n + \beta_7 k \tag{4.9}$$

where Y^s is the ln of output supplied, n is the ln of total labour input and k is the ln of total capital input. β_5, β_6 and β_7 are defined as positive parameters. In terms of levels, then, we have a Cobb–Douglas production function.

In the short run we shall take the amount of capital to be fixed and given exogenously so that we can write the production function as

$$Y^s = \beta_8 + \beta_6 n \tag{4.9'}$$

where $\beta_8 = \beta_5 + \beta_7 k$. This relation between Y^s and n is shown as the straight line in Figure 4.7. Its intercept is β_8 and its slope is β_6. An increase in the capital stock will shift the production function by β_7 times the increase in capital.

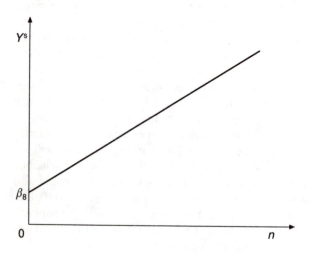

Figure 4.7

THE LABOUR INPUT

From our discussion in Chapter 3 we recall that labour demanded by firms depends negatively on the real wage rate. Let us write this as

$$n = \beta_9 - \beta_{10}(w - p) \tag{4.10}$$

where $w - p$ is the ln of the real wage rate and β_9 and β_{10} are defined as positive parameters.

In an environment where wages and prices are rising we need to write the labour demand schedule in terms of rates of changes rather than the absolute levels of wages and prices. Writing equation (4.10) for the previous period and subtracting from (4.10) we have

$$n - n_{-1} = \beta_{10}[w - w_{-1} - (p - p_{-1})]$$

or

$$n = n_{-1} - \beta_{10}(\omega - \pi) \tag{4.10'}$$

where n_{-1} is labour demand in the previous period and ω ($\equiv w - w_{-1}$) is the rate of change of nominal wages. From this perspective, the number of workers rises only if $\omega < \pi$ since, in that case, real wages would be falling over time. Only if $\omega = \pi$ is the real wage constant and $n = n_{-1}$.

THE GENERAL AS SCHEDULE

By taking first differences of the production function (4.9') we obtain

$$Y^s = Y^s_{-1} + \beta_6(n - n_{-1}) \tag{4.9''}$$

Into this we substitute the expression for $(n - n_{-1})$ from (4.10') to get

$$Y^s = Y^s_{-1} - \beta_6\beta_{10}(\omega - \pi) \tag{4.11}$$

According to this equation, an increase in the inflation rate, with ω given, would start to reduce real wages and increase the demand for labour with the extent of this adjustment given by the parameter β_{10}. Then the extra labour will produce more output, as measured by the parameter β_6, allowing Y^s to exceed Y^s_{-1}. Hence there is a positive relation between Y^s and π. The AS curve is drawn in Figure 4.8. Its intercept on the Y^s axis is $Y^s_{-1} \alpha_4\omega$ ($= \beta_6\beta_{10}$) and its slope is $1/\alpha_4$.

On the other hand, if the labour market is in equilibrium we must have $\omega = \pi$ and $n = n_{-1}$ so that output is fixed at Y^e ($= \beta_8 + \beta_6 n$) and the aggregate supply curve would be vertical.

NOMINAL WAGE DETERMINATION

The last step in the process of determining the AS curve involves the determination of the rate of change of nominal wages (ω). Again a special characteristic of the labour market is involved. A labour market is not a 'spot'

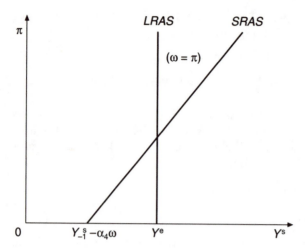

Figure 4.8

market where purchases and sales are made for current use. Labour supply and demand usually requires some long-term commitment. In an inflationary setting the rate of change in the nominal wage will be set so as to maintain equilibrium in the labour market since firms want to be on their demand curve for labour and households want to be on their supply curve. This requires a constant real wage. Given that commitments in the labour market must be made for some time in the future, and given that the actual rate of inflation to prevail is not observed today, it seems reasonable that the expected inflation rate will have to be used instead. This requirement can be written as

$$\omega = \pi^e \qquad\qquad (4.12)$$

Substituting from (4.12) we have the final form of the AS curve

$$Y^s = Y^e - \alpha_4(\pi^e - \pi)$$

THE COMPLETE SYSTEM

The complete macro model can be written as:

$$Y^d = \alpha_0 - \alpha_1(i - \pi^e) \qquad\qquad \text{IS schedule}$$

$$\mu - \pi = \alpha_2 Y - \alpha_3 i - (m - p)_{-1} \qquad\qquad \text{LM schedule}$$

$$Y^s = Y^e - \alpha_4(\pi^e - \pi) \qquad\qquad \text{AS schedule}$$

$$Y = Y^s = Y^d \qquad\qquad \text{Equilibrium condition}$$

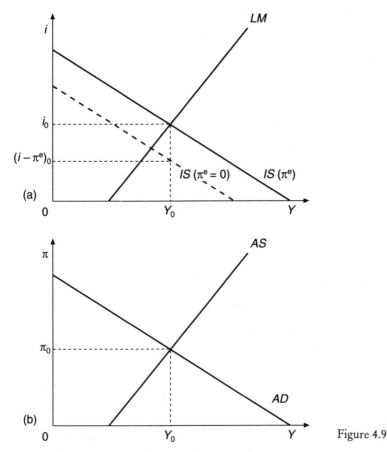

Figure 4.9

This complete system is depicted in Figure 4.9. In Figure 4.9(a) we have the IS–LM framework which is similar to Figure 4.3. Figure 4.9(b) combines the AS and AD schedules of Figures 4.6 and 4.7. Because of the connection between the IS–LM curves and AD curve the equilibrium level of income in part (a) cannot be different from that in part (b).

The intersection of IS (π^e) and LM determine Y and i and from IS ($\pi^e = 0$) we can read $i–\pi^e$. Then from the intersection of AD and AS we can derive the equilibrium values of π and Y.

LONG-RUN EQUILIBRIUM

If left to itself the economy would settle down to a particular combination of i, Y and π, and would replicate itself year after year. Keynesians and New Classical economists argue about the time it would take to reach this equilibrium. Keynesians argue that it would take a long time for the economy to reach its long-run equilibrium so that it would become necessary to

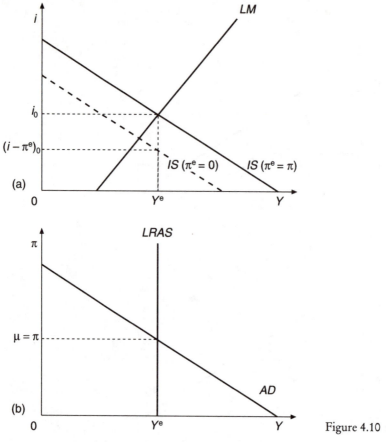

Figure 4.10

intervene in the operation of the economy with suitably designed fiscal and monetary policies. New Classical economists argue that the economy is quite resilient and would settle to its long-run equilibrium quite quickly. Both sides agree on the notion of equilibrium but the term 'equilibrium' means different things to the two camps. Let us, therefore, define two notions of equilibrium: short-run or temporary equilibrium exists when

$$Y = Y^d = Y^s \tag{4.13}$$

while long-run equilibrium requires, in addition, that

$$\pi = \pi^e \text{ or } Y = Y^e \tag{4.14}$$

We can see that the goods market is in a position of rest under both concepts of equilibrium. If output demanded was different from output supplied there would be unwanted movements in inventories and further changes in output and employment would occur. This process is assumed to be completed every time we observe the goods market in short-run equilibrium. Equation (4.13) also requires that asset markets be in equilibrium all the time since the position of the AD curve would not remain constant if μ or $(m - p)_{-1}$ were changing over time. However, it is clear that the labour market may not be in equilibrium in the short run although it must in the long run. Only if equation (4.14) is satisfied is the real wage constant at the level required to set supply equal to demand in the labour market. When expectations of inflation are fulfilled, there is no incentive to make further adjustments and the economy can settle down to a stationary state. If $\pi^e \neq \pi$ this will not be known until the end of the current period during which no adjustment takes place, but after which a new estimate of π^e will be made.

In long-run equilibrium $\pi = \pi^e$ and the macro model of this chapter becomes even simpler. The AS schedule becomes vertical and is shown in Figure 4.10. Output is determined independently of demand. Second, given Y, the IS schedule can be written as $i = (\alpha_0 - Y^e)/\alpha_1 + \pi$. So far as the LM schedule is concerned, we must have $\mu = \pi = \pi^e$. From this we get the real money supply $(m - p)$ and finally the real rate of interest is determined as $i - \pi^e = (\alpha_0 - Y^e)/\alpha_1$.

The solutions for Y, π and i are determined sequentially not simultaneously. Output is determined by the AS schedule, the inflation rate is equal to the given rate of growth of money supply and the interest rate is determined by the location of the IS curve. In Figure 4.10(b) the AD curve plays a limited role, it intersects with the AS curve at a vertical distance of $\mu = \pi$. In summary, then, the long-run values of Y, π and i are given by

$$Y = Y^d = Y^s = Y^e \qquad (4.15)$$

$$\pi = \mu = \pi^e \qquad (4.16)$$

$$i = \frac{\alpha_0 - Y^e}{\alpha_1} + \mu \qquad (4.17)$$

It should also be understood that AD plays no significant role in determining Y. In other words demand management policies, be they fiscal or monetary policies, play no role in determining Y in the long run.

Another point that needs to be stressed is that, whereas in the simple IS–LM model expansionary monetary policy would lower the nominal rate of interest and increase output, this would not happen in long-run equilibrium. An increase in μ from μ_0 to μ_1 will shift outwards the LM schedule in Figure 4.11. But we know that in long-run equilibrium the rate of inflation must equal the higher money supply growth rate μ_1. Moreover, Y has to equal Y^e in long-run equilibrium and $\pi = \pi^e = \mu_1$. Hence the IS curve must shift to intersect the retreating LM at Y^e. i is higher by the amount of the increase in the rate of growth of the money supply. However, since IS ($\pi^e = 0$) has not changed the real interest rate will not change and the Fisher equation will apply. The real money supply rose initially when $\mu_1 > \pi$ but as the LM started retreating the rate of inflation exceeded the rate of growth of the

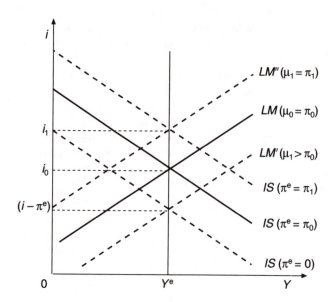

Figure 4.11

money supply. Hence although the central bank started out with a larger growth of money the economy ended with a lower value of real cash balances. However, this is the only real variable that has been affected by the increase in the growth rate of money supply.

THE LONG-RUN EFFECT OF A SUPPLY SHOCK

Suppose that at every wage rate the supply of labour falls – perhaps because of an increase in the preference for leisure or because of an increase in non-wage income. In Figure 4.12 this shifts the AS schedule to AS' and real output in the long run would drop to Y_1^e. If the AD curve does not shift there would be an increase in the rate of inflation. However, since μ has not changed, π must remain as before and AD will shift to the left to intersect the AS' schedule at E''. The LM curve in Figure 4.12(a) is also affected by this exogenous event. Since income is lower, transactions demand for money must fall. This means that $\pi > \mu$ for some time in order to reduce the value of money. In final equilibrium at E' both i and $i - \pi^e$ will be higher. The higher real rate of interest would choke off some aggregate demand in the face of lower equilibrium output.

THE DESIGN OF ECONOMIC POLICY IN THE GENERALISED MODEL

What role does economic policy have in the generalised model? To conduct a meaningful analysis we must introduce uncertainty into the model. We write the IS–LM model with uncertainty as

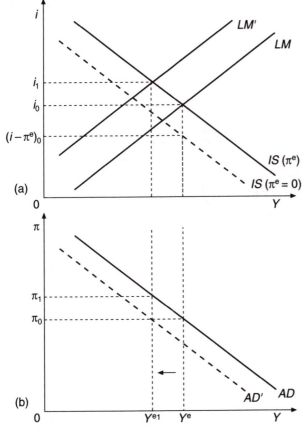

Figure 4.12

$$Y = \alpha_0 - \alpha_1(i - \pi^e) + \varepsilon_g \tag{4.18}$$

$$\mu - \pi + \varepsilon_m = \alpha_2 Y - \alpha_3 i - (m - p)_{-1} \tag{4.19}$$

Hence the error terms are merely added on to the IS–LM equations. The random terms ε_g and ε_m are assumed to be white noise processes – uncorrelated random variables with mean zero.

On the supply side we introduce productivity shocks into the labour demand equation as

$$n^d = \beta_9 - \beta_{10}(w - p - \varepsilon_s) \tag{4.20}$$

where ε_s is the shock to the real wage. This has the same effect on the demand for labour as an equal proportional decline in the real wage. In the period prior to the shock

$$n^d_{-1} = \beta_9 - \beta_{10}(w_{-1} - p_{-1}) \tag{4.21}$$

By taking the difference between the two periods, we get

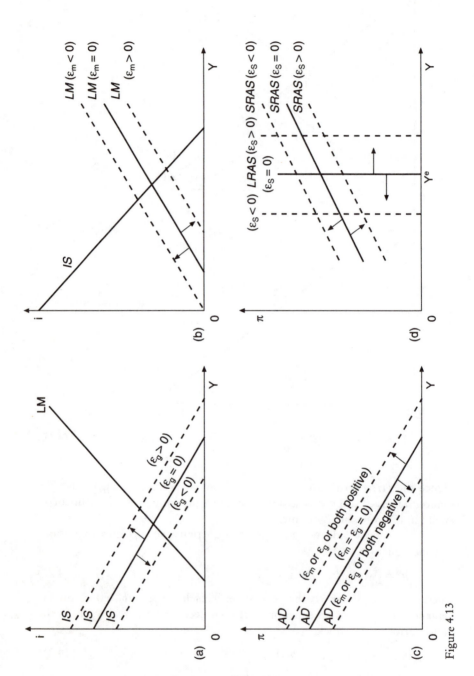

Figure 4.13

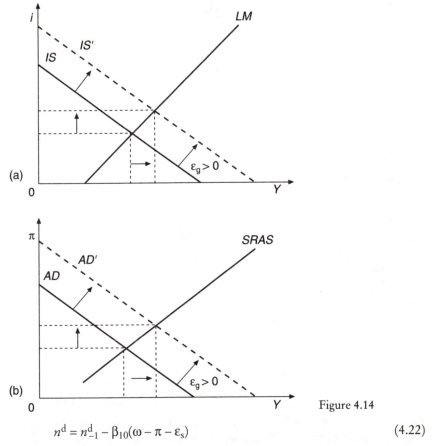

Figure 4.14

$$n^d = n^d_{-1} - \beta_{10}(\omega - \pi - \varepsilon_s) \tag{4.22}$$

where $\omega = w - w_{-1}$ and $\pi = p - p_{-1}$. Let us write the aggregate supply schedule as $Y^s = \beta_8 + \beta_6 n + \varepsilon_s$ and substitute for n from (4.22) to get

$$Y^s = Y^s_{-1} - \beta_6 \beta_{10} (\omega - \pi - \varepsilon_s) + \varepsilon_s \tag{4.23}$$

Workers set wages so that $\omega = \pi^e$. We write α_4 for $\beta_6\beta_{10}$. Hence we write the aggregate supply schedule as

$$Y^s = Y^e - \alpha_4(\pi^e - \pi - \varepsilon_s) + \varepsilon_s \tag{4.24}$$

In Figure 4.13 we depict the effects of changes in the values of these stochastic variables. In Figure 4.13(a) an increase in the value of ε_g shifts the IS curve outwards whereas a decrease will shift it inwards. In Figure 4.13(b) an increase in ε_m will shift the LM schedule outwards and a decrease will shift it inwards. Any stochastic disturbance that shifts the IS or LM curve outwards will also shift the AD schedule outwards (as in Figure 4.13(c)), and any disturbance that shifts the IS or LM schedules inwards will shift the AD schedule inwards. In Figure 4.13(d) we depict the effects of supply-side

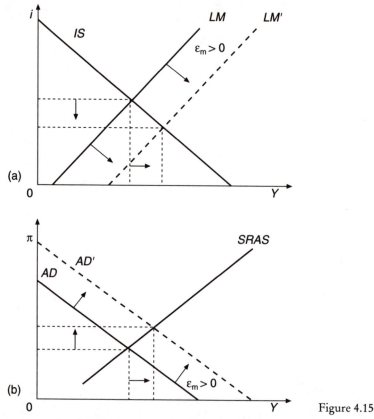

Figure 4.15

random shocks. With $\pi = \pi^e$ the long-run supply schedule shifts because of a change in the value of ε_s. When we are on the short-run supply schedule a change in π_s will change the short-run supply schedule.

The stochastic version of the AD schedule is derived by substituting the IS curve of equation (4.18) into the LM curve of equation (4.19). The AD schedule is written as

$$\pi = \mu + (m - p)_{-1} - \left(\alpha_2 + \frac{\alpha_3}{\alpha_1}\right) Y + \frac{\alpha_3 \alpha_0}{\alpha_1} + \alpha_3 \pi^e + \varepsilon_m + \frac{\alpha_3}{\alpha_1} \varepsilon_g \quad (4.25)$$

The values for ε_g, ε_m and ε_s are not directly observable even after the fact because the data do not distinguish between anticipated and unexpected events. For instance, if the growth rate of money supply is measured at 10 per cent for a current year it is unlikely that the central bank would be able to indicate that 8 per cent was expected and 2 per cent was unintended. However, from the behaviour of the three endogenous variables π, i and Y we can extract information about the behaviour of the random variables.

First let us refer to Figure 4.14. An increase in ε_g will shift the IS curve outwards in part (a) and the AD curve outwards in part (b). Thus i, Y and π

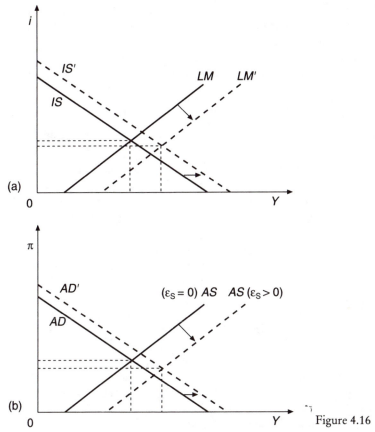

Figure 4.16

will all rise. Let us now refer to Figure 4.15. An increase in ε_g will shift the LM curve outwards in part (a) and the AD schedule outwards in part (b). Thus Y and π will rise and i will fall. Let us finally look at the effect of an exogenous supply shock. In Figure 4.16 an increase in ε_s will shift the AS curve outwards, leading to a drop in π. The lower π will, in turn, mean a faster growth of real cash balances (given μ). Hence the LM schedule will shift outwards somewhat and so will AD. Hence Y will rise and π and i will fall. We can summarise this in the following matrix:

$$
\begin{array}{c|ccc}
 & \varepsilon_g & \varepsilon_m & \varepsilon_s \\
\hline
y & + & + & + \\
\pi & + & + & - \\
i & + & - & -
\end{array}
$$

Remember, though, that these are all short-run effects.

Thus if we observe Y, i and π going up even though policy is steady we can infer that there has been a positive goods market shock (a sudden increase in consumer demand, for example). If we observe Y and π going up and i falling we can infer that there has been a positive money market shock – a sudden influx of cash as people want to buy more bonds and hold less cash, for example – even though policy is steady. If we observe that Y has gone up and π and i have fallen we can infer that there has been a positive supply shock – a sudden increase in labour productivity, for example.

FORMING EXPECTATIONS ABOUT INFLATION

In the previous analysis an important distinction was made between short- and long-run supply schedules. The difference between the two was ascribed to differences between the actual and expected rates of inflation. In the short run actual inflation may deviate from expected inflation whereas in the long run this would not occur. It therefore follows that the process of expectations formation is an extremely important ingredient in the macro model we have been studying in this chapter.

How are expectations of inflation formed? Since expected magnitudes are not observed we have to theorise about them without being able to observe them directly. In Chapter 3 we encountered the *adaptive expectations* process. However, theorising in terms of the adaptive expectations process is a thing of the past. Individuals are now expected to use all the information about the economy that they have in the optimal manner. This is what rationality would require. Such a process is called *rational expectations.*

The question that then arises is what information do individuals have and what does one mean by optimal use of information. First, they know the IS–LM–AS model that we have been working with. They know that a decrease in consumption expenditure will cause AD to fall and hence π will fall. As π falls so will π^e in the long run so that there will be a drop in the real interest rate $(i - \pi^e)$ and IS and, therefore, AD will shift outwards. Hence the drop in the inflation will only be temporary. Second, individuals have certain information about the current performance of the economy and policies in force at the current time which they would use in forecasting inflation. To formalise this process we first solve the IS–LM–AS model to obtain the determinants of the rate of inflation. This involves finding the solutions for Y, i and π from equations (4.18), (4.19) and (4.24) in terms of all the exogenous variables in the system. The solution for π is

$$\pi = \frac{1}{\alpha_1 + \alpha_3\alpha_4 + \alpha_1\alpha_2\alpha_4} \{\alpha_1[\mu + (m - p)_{-1} + \varepsilon_m] + \alpha_3(\alpha_0 + \varepsilon_g)$$

$$- (\alpha_1\alpha_2 + \alpha_3)[Y^e + (1 + \alpha_4)\varepsilon_s] + (\alpha_1\alpha_3 + \alpha_3\alpha_4 + \alpha_1\alpha_2\alpha_4)\pi^e\} \quad (4.26)$$

Each individual knows what causes inflation and to what extent. For instance an increase in consumption expenditure is caused by an increase in α_0; multiplying by the known value of $\alpha_3/(\alpha_1 + \alpha_3\alpha_4 + \alpha_1\alpha_2\alpha_4)$ permits us to calculate the effect on π. Similarly an exogenous increase in π^e increases π

by $(\alpha_1\alpha_3 + \alpha_3\alpha_4 + \alpha_1\alpha_2\alpha_4)/(\alpha_1 + \alpha_3\alpha_4 + \alpha_1\alpha_2\alpha_4)$. To ensure that π does not rise more than π^e we can impose a limit $0 < \alpha_3 < 1$ on the parameter α_3; otherwise, we would end up with an explosive cycle of inflation merely through the expectations process without an accompanying increase in μ.

Even more importantly we should remember that π^e should not be treated as an exogenous variable. If α_0 changes and π responds, π^e cannot remain at its previous level. If it did we would not be using all the information we have at hand. To get out of this vicious cycle of π determining π^e and vice versa we need to eliminate π^e from equation (4.26). However, without π^e in equation (4.26) the parameters attached to other variables in the equation would no longer be the same since the underlying model now treats π^e as an *endogenous* rather than as an *exogenous* variable. To get around this difficulty we 'invent' an equation similar to equation (4.26) but without π^e in it which means that π and other exogenous variables are connected by as yet *undetermined* coefficients (see Blanchard and Fischer 1991). This equation is written as

$$\pi = \gamma_0\mu + \gamma_1(m - p)_{-1} + \gamma_2\varepsilon_m + \gamma_3\alpha_0 + \gamma_4\varepsilon_g + \gamma_5 Y^e + \gamma_6\varepsilon_s \qquad (4.27)$$

where the γs are undetermined – undetermined because in (4.27) we have assumed that π^e is endogenous. Next, π^e is the mathematical expectation of π from this equation. Therefore,

$$\pi^e = E(\pi) = \gamma_0\mu + \gamma_1(m - p)_{-1} + \gamma_3\alpha_0 + \gamma_5 Y^e \qquad (4.28)$$

The terms $\gamma_2\varepsilon_m$, $\gamma_4\varepsilon_g$ and $\gamma_6\varepsilon_s$ have been eliminated since the expected value of each of these is zero. We can now substitute this expression for π^e into equation (4.26) and thus eliminate π^e from the list of exogenous variables. This produces

$$
\begin{aligned}
\pi = {} & \frac{1}{\alpha_1 + \alpha_3\alpha_4 + \alpha_1\alpha_2\alpha_4} \{\alpha_1 + \gamma_0(\alpha_1\alpha_3 + \alpha_3\alpha_4 + \alpha_1\alpha_2\alpha_4)\mu \\
& + [\alpha_1 + \gamma_1(\alpha_1\alpha_3 + \alpha_3\alpha_4 + \alpha_1\alpha_2\alpha_4)](m - p)_{-1} + \alpha_1\varepsilon_m \\
& + [\alpha_3 + \gamma_3(\alpha_1\alpha_3 + \alpha_3\alpha_4 + \alpha_1\alpha_2\alpha_4)]\alpha_0 + \alpha_3\varepsilon_g + [\gamma_5(\alpha_1\alpha_3 \\
& + \alpha_3\alpha_4 + \alpha_1\alpha_2\alpha_4) - (\alpha_1\alpha_2 + \alpha_3)]Y^e - [(\alpha_1\alpha_2 + \alpha_3)(1 + \alpha_4)]\varepsilon_s\} \quad (4.29)
\end{aligned}
$$

By a careful comparison it can be seen that equation (4.29) has exactly the same variables on the right-hand side as equation (4.27), the one that each individual invents when forming expectations about π^e. Since they come from the very same IS–LM–AS model of equations (4.18), (4.19) and (4.24) the coefficients attached to each variable must be the same. With this information we can now solve for the undetermined coefficients, the γs in equation (4.27), by setting each of them equal to the corresponding coefficient in equation (4.29) and solving for the γs. Thus we have

$$\gamma_0 = \frac{\alpha_1 + \gamma_0(\alpha_1\alpha_3 + \alpha_3\alpha_4 + \alpha_1\alpha_2\alpha_4)}{\alpha_1 + \alpha_3\alpha_4 + \alpha_1\alpha_2\alpha_4}$$

which simplifies to $\gamma_0 = 1/(1 - \alpha_3)$. This parameter is positive since it was shown earlier that $0 < \alpha_3 < 1$. Next we have

$$\gamma_1 = \frac{\alpha_1 + \gamma_1(\alpha_1\alpha_3 + \alpha_3\alpha_4 + \alpha_1\alpha_2\alpha_4)}{\alpha_1 + \alpha_3\alpha_4 + \alpha_1\alpha_2\alpha_4}$$

which again simplifies to $\gamma_1 = 1/(1 - \alpha_3) > 0$. Thus $\gamma_2 = \alpha_1/(\alpha_1 + \alpha_3\alpha_4 + \alpha_1\alpha_2\alpha_4) > 0$. In a similar manner we can determine the other coefficients as

$$\gamma_3 = \frac{\alpha_3}{\alpha_1(1 - \alpha_3)} > 0$$

$$\gamma_4 = \frac{\alpha_3}{\alpha_1 + \alpha_3\alpha_4 + \alpha_1\alpha_2\alpha_4} > 0$$

$$\gamma_5 = \frac{-(\alpha_1\alpha_2 + \alpha_3)}{\alpha_1(1 - \alpha_3)} < 0$$

$$\gamma_6 = \frac{-(\alpha_1\alpha_2 + \alpha_3)(1 + \alpha_4)}{\alpha_1 + \alpha_3\alpha_4 + \alpha_1\alpha_2\alpha_4} < 0$$

The undetermined coefficients are now determined and it is possible to get rid of the γs in equation (4.27) which now represents the structural relationship for the inflation rate, including the rate of expected inflation, but without having π^e as a variable on the right-hand side. By substituting for the γs in equation (4.27) we arrive at

$$\pi = \frac{1}{1 - \alpha_3} [\mu + (m - p)_{-1}] + \frac{\alpha_1}{\alpha_1 + \alpha_3\alpha_4 + \alpha_1\alpha_2\alpha_4} \varepsilon_m$$

$$+ \frac{\alpha_3}{\alpha_1(1 - \alpha_3)} \alpha_0 + \frac{\alpha_3}{\alpha_1 + \alpha_3\alpha_4 + \alpha_1\alpha_2\alpha_4} \varepsilon_g - \frac{\alpha_1\alpha_2 + \alpha_3}{\alpha_1(1 - \alpha_3)} Y^e$$

$$- \frac{(\alpha_1\alpha_2 + \alpha_3)(1 + \alpha_4)}{\alpha_1 + \alpha_3\alpha_4 + \alpha_1\alpha_2\alpha_4} \varepsilon_s \tag{4.30}$$

Taking expectations about inflation from equation (4.30) we have

$$\pi^e = E(\pi) = \frac{1}{1 - \alpha_3} [\mu + (m - p)_{-1}] + \frac{\alpha_3}{\alpha_1(1 - \alpha_3)} \alpha_0 - \frac{\alpha_1\alpha_2 + \alpha_3}{\alpha_1(1 - \alpha_3)} Y^e \tag{4.31}$$

Equation (4.31) differs from (4.30) only to the extent that $E(\varepsilon_m) = E(\varepsilon_g) = E(\varepsilon_s) = 0$. This completes our examination of the process by which expectations about inflation are formed by rational individuals who use all available information.

POLICY INEFFECTIVENESS

With the present version of the model it can be shown that policy is unable either to maintain equilibrium in the economy in the face of an exogenous shock or to reduce unemployment below the natural rate even temporarily.

From the AS schedule of equation (4.24) we know that there are two sources of change in Y: (i) a deviation of π from π^e and (ii) a non-zero ε_s. To see what policy can and cannot do we need to focus just on these two sources. Substituting from (4.30) and (4.31) into equation (4.24) we get

$$Y = Y^e + \frac{\alpha^4}{\alpha_1 + \alpha_3\alpha_4 + \alpha_1\alpha_2\alpha_4} [\alpha_1\varepsilon_m + \alpha_3\varepsilon_g - (\alpha_1\alpha_2+\alpha_3)(1+\alpha_4)\varepsilon_s] + (1 + \alpha_4)\varepsilon_s$$

$$(4.32)$$

According to equation (4.32), Y deviates from Y^e only when ε_m, ε_g or ε_s take on positive or negative values. Here ε_s appears twice, once with a minus sign and once with a positive sign. On the one hand $\varepsilon_s > 0$ improves the marginal product of labour directly and therefore increases Y, but on the other hand it also lowers π below π^e and, hence, reduces Y. The net effect, however, is positive: Y increases by $[(\alpha_1 + \alpha_1\alpha_4)/(\alpha_1 + \alpha_3\alpha_4 + \alpha_1\alpha_2\alpha_4)]\varepsilon_s$.

Let us now examine carefully the difference between π and π^e by examining (4.30) and (4.31). We observe that (i) a change in a predictable or deterministic exogenous variable such as μ, α_0 or Y^e has exactly the same effect on π and π^e; and (ii) random events such as ε_m, ε_g or ε_s affect π but not π^e. The difference between π and π^e is the error that people make in forming expectations. Our analysis suggests that there is nothing systematic about these differences. They are entirely random. In particular, policy authorities do not have any systematic advantage over rational individuals in predicting π.

SHORT-RUN EFFECTS OF POLICY CHANGES

Let us consider the case where the economy is operating at equilibrium and the government attempts to reduce the rate of unemployment below the natural rate. To do this it increases the rate of growth of money supply μ. We analyse the consequences of this in Figure 4.17. The LM schedule shifts to LM' as $\mu > \pi$. From equation (4.25) it would appear that AD would shift up by the increase in μ to AD' and, given the positive slope of the AS schedule, it would seem that output would rise which, in turn, would reduce unemployment. However, since everyone in the economy is aware of the policy and its effects and knows how the inflation rate will change because of this move, π^e will be revised upward. This will cause AD to shift still further. To measure the combined effects of the changes in μ and π^e we rewrite the AD equation with π^e substituted from (4.31) into (4.25). We then get

$$\pi = \frac{1}{1 - \alpha_3} [\mu + (m - p)_{-1}] - \left(\alpha_2 + \frac{\alpha_3}{\alpha_1}\right) Y - \frac{\alpha_3(\alpha_1\alpha_2 + \alpha_3)}{\alpha_1(1 - \alpha_3)} Y^e +$$

$$\frac{\alpha_3}{\alpha_1(1 - \alpha_3)} \alpha_0 + \varepsilon_m + \frac{\alpha_3}{\alpha_1} \varepsilon_g \qquad (4.25')$$

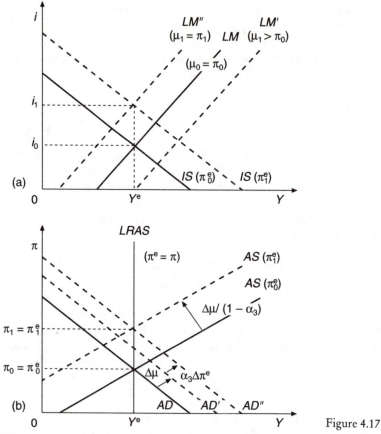

Figure 4.17

Thus the AD schedule shifts up to AD" by the amount $1/(1 - \alpha_3)$ which is larger than the change in μ itself. The AS schedule is also affected by changes in π^e. Substituting from equation (4.31) into the AS equation we have

$$\pi = \frac{1}{1 - \alpha_3} [\mu + (m - p)_{-1}] - \frac{1}{\alpha_4} Y - \left[\frac{1}{\alpha_4} + \frac{\alpha_1 \alpha_2 + \alpha_3}{\alpha_1 (1 - \alpha_3)} \right] Y^e$$

$$+ \frac{\alpha_3}{\alpha_1 (1 - \alpha_3)} \alpha_0 - \frac{1 + \alpha_4}{\alpha_4} \varepsilon_s \qquad (4.20')$$

Hence the AS schedule shifts up by the same amount $1/(1 - \alpha_3)$ so that the intersection of the AS and AD schedules will occur at the same Y^e as before. The other important variables can be deduced from this model. Obviously π and i are higher. From the IS equation of (4.18) we can rewrite the real rate of interest as $i - \pi^e = (\alpha_0 - Y)/\alpha_1 + \varepsilon_g$.

Since monetary policy cannot alter Y, it cannot alter the real rate of interest. However, the IS curve does shift up by the amount of the increase in π^e. Finally the same Y and higher i means that there will, in final equilibrium, be a lower demand for money. To make $m - p$ smaller π must be greater than μ at least for a while which, in turn, implies that LM must backtrack above its original position.

What about predictable fiscal policy? It is clear that higher α_0 will imply higher real interest rates. However, from the AS and AD equations an increase in α_0 will lead to the same shifts in AS and AD. Hence, Y will remain unchanged. The higher real interest rate will mean that investment will be lower. Higher government expenditure will 'crowd out' private investment.

So traditional monetary and fiscal policy are not very useful. We are now ready for the second question. Suppose the workers make mistakes in predicting π. In these circumstances can the government through its policy instruments help to re-establish equilibrium? To answer this question suppose that we are in equilibrium and a shock occurs, say $\varepsilon_m > 0$. This shifts the LM curve downward. This is shown in Figure 4.18. The AD curve will also shift outwards by ε_m. Neither the AS nor the IS schedules are going to be disturbed because of this. The rate of inflation rises to π_1 and the nominal interest rate falls to i_1. The economy is in short-run equilibrium but not in long-run equilibrium since π and π^e are different. Can the government use macroeconomic policy to avert this situation? The answer is 'no' since the authorities cannot anticipate ε_m any better than the people. If the government altered μ to counteract the effect of ε_m the result would be no different from the case in which the authorities do nothing.

ANTI-INFLATION POLICY

While the New Classical model renders active stabilisation policy ineffective it also enhances the effectiveness of monetary policy as an anti-inflationary measure. We understand from the above analysis that the economy can be at equilibrium at *any* rate of inflation. It is generally agreed that inflation has several costs attached to it.

To reduce the rate of inflation permanently, the central bank must reduce the rate of growth of the money supply. Assume that such a policy is announced and implemented. If such a policy is believed it will reduce π and π^e by $1/(1 - \alpha_3)$ times the change in μ according to equations (4.30) and (4.31). Therefore, in Figure 4.18 the economy will stay on the vertical line at Y^e. Reducing the rate of growth of the money supply from μ_0 to μ_2 lowers the position of the AD schedule to AD' by $(\mu_0 - \mu_2)/(1 - \alpha_3)$. As was the case before, the inflation rate will overshoot its final target and ultimately the AD schedule will have to shift to AD" where the vertical distance between E" and E is $\mu_0 - \mu_2$. Not only is credibility important for this result but so is the requirement that all market participants be aware of the overshooting. Consider a case when π^e did not adjust at all to the announcement of a lower μ. If workers did not believe this and thought that the central bank

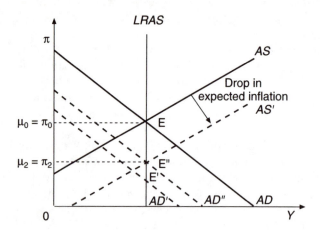

Figure 4.18

announcement was a way to get them to accept lower real wages they may continue to bargain for wages based on the current value of π. In that case the AS schedule would not shift whereas the AD would and equilibrium would be established at E'''. In general the smaller the change in π^e relative to the shift in the AD curve in the wake of a policy change, the greater is the departure of income and employment from its equilibrium level. In other words, in the ultimate analysis, not only does monetary policy influence π, it also influences π^e. The greater the credibility of the central bank of a country the greater would be its ability to reduce inflation.

THE NEW KEYNESIAN MODEL

In the New Classical model we have studied so far the guiding principle is equilibrium. Underlying this belief is the perception that all markets are like auction markets, clearing almost always and almost instantaneously. Nevertheless, we observe markets that are emphatically not auction markets. In particular the labour market is a market characterised by contracting behaviour. There are other features of the New Classical model that have been questioned by those economists who believe that stabilisation policy remains useful and effective. In their view the economy is not as self-regulating as the New Classical economists would have us believe. One area of disagreement between the New Classical and New Keynesian schools is the process of expectations formation. Sometimes the New Keynesian school argues that expectations are of the adaptive variety discussed in Chapter 3.

In terms of the current analysis μ_{-1}, $(m-p)_{-2}$, α_{0-1} and Y^e_{-1} are known today and we can use this information to calculate π_{-1}. This variable summarises all the information about the economy that is currently available and is used as a predictor of π in the current period. Thus the following expectations process is applicable:

$$\pi^e = \pi_{-1} - \frac{1}{\alpha_1 + \alpha_3\alpha_4 + \alpha_1\alpha_2\alpha_4} \; (\alpha_1\varepsilon_{m-1} + \alpha_3\varepsilon_{g-1} - \alpha_1\alpha_2 + \alpha_3)(1 + \alpha_4)\varepsilon_{s-1}$$

(4.33)

The parameters attached to the ε_{-1} variables are determined in the manner of equation (4.29) which shows how εs change π. For example, if $\varepsilon_{m-1} > 0$, π^e should be lower than π_{-1} because the inflationary shock is not expected to last.

Adaptive expectations lead to systematic errors in π^e because π^e will always be below π when inflation is rising and it will be above π when inflation is falling; only when π is steady will π^e equal π. Although individuals try to eliminate such errors they cannot improve their performance without knowing what has yet to be measured.

An economy operating with adaptive expectations as expressed by equation (4.33) can move away, although only temporarily, from its equilibrium level of output through deliberate but unknown policy changes. Starting from Y^e assume an increase in μ. Since π^e is still geared to π_0 the economy must move along the short-run AS curve in Figure 4.19. The AD curve shifts up by the increase in μ and therefore the new equilibrium is established at E'. But this cannot be a final position for the economy. Since inflation has risen to π_1, AS must shift up by $\pi_1 - \pi_0$ to AS'. Further, since the increase in π^e shifts the AD schedule up by α_3 and, since $\mu > \pi$ in the first

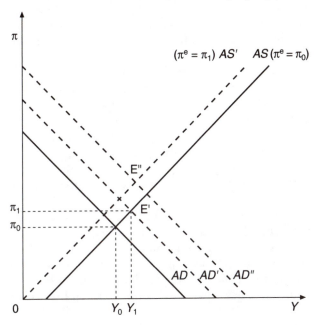

Figure 4.19

period, $m - p$ has increased and this puts further upward pressure on the vertical intercept of the AD schedule. Suppose AD" is the new position so that a new temporary equilibrium has been established at E". Here Y may be higher or lower than at E'. Subsequently the AS and AD schedules keep shifting until final equilibrium is established at E'" with income again equal to the natural rate and $\mu = \pi = \pi^e$. In the meantime, the policy change has been able to influence income and the unemployment rate by lowering the real wage when π^e responds to the change with a lag. The government's ability to exploit such situations may lead them to conceal information.

PRODUCTIVITY AND WAGE GROWTH

An important aspect of the New Keynesian literature is that labour productivity keeps changing almost continuously. Let us see what this implies for the labour market of our analysis. Our labour demand equation was written as $n^d = n^d_{-1} - \beta_{10}(\omega - \pi - \varepsilon_s)$ where supply shocks have been incorporated because increases in ε_s increase the marginal product of labour. Our non-stochastic labour supply schedule was $n^s = n^s_{-1} + \beta_{12}(\omega - \pi)$. We equate the two and calculate an equilibrium value of ω:

$$\omega_e = \pi + \frac{n^d_{-1} - n^s_{-1} + \beta_{10}\varepsilon_s}{\beta_{12} + \beta_{10}} \tag{4.34}$$

From this equation we realise two important things. First, if the labour market was not in equilibrium last period (in particular if there was an excess demand for labour), nominal wages must, today, rise at a rate *faster* than the current rate of inflation. Further, since the value of ε_s is not known today it is not possible to keep the labour market in full equilibrium in the face of supply shocks unless we find out some method of rewarding workers today for productivity gains that will occur only *ex post*.

Productivity of labour keeps changing almost continuously because of accumulation of human and physical capital. Let us suppose that such exogenous changes in the productivity of labour are captured by the term $\varepsilon_s - \varepsilon_{s-1} = \kappa_s + \zeta_s - \zeta_{s-1}$ where κ_s represents trend growth in labour productivity and ζ represents unpredictable movements around that trend. The trend is predictable and should be included in the wage increase whereas the random disturbances are not and cannot be incorporated. We may calculate the trend by taking the average value of ε_s for the past n years and then ζ is the residual.

With such growth in labour productivity the equilibrium increase in the nominal wage is $\omega_e = \pi + [\beta_{10}/(\beta_{10} + \beta_{12})] \zeta_s$. A given value of ζ_s leads to higher real wages, but not to the same extent because $[\beta_{10}/(\beta_{10} + \beta_{12})] < 1$.

However, one can never be sure whether a particular observation for ε_s is the start of a new trend or a particularly large random shock. Consider a situation where ζ_s has fallen to a new lower level: from ζ_{s0} to ζ_{s1} because of smaller growth in productivity. If this new trend is not detected nominal wage growth will be too high for equilibrium to be maintained in the labour market. We can write the difference between the actual and the equilibrium rate of growth of nominal wages as

$$\omega - \omega_e = \frac{\beta_{10}}{\beta_{10} + \beta_{12}} \ (\zeta_{so} - \zeta_{s1})$$

Since $\zeta_{so1} > \zeta_{s1}$ it must be the case that $\omega > \omega^e$. This causes the AS curve to shift up and will lead to a higher π and lower Y. In the next period the fact that $\omega > \pi$ puts pressure on ω to fall, but so long as the new trend in productivity growth is not incorporated in wage equations the actual rate of wage increase will continue to be greater than the equilibrium rate and the AS schedule shifts again. Problems such as this imply that the labour market continues to be in disequilibrium for considerable time.

LONG-TERM CONTRACTS

An important difference between New Classical and New Keynesian economists is that the latter believe that nominal wages are not set in an auction market but are set contractually. Suppose a contract lasts for two time periods. In year 1 half the workers and half the firms sign a two-year contract. They examine equation (4.34) for this purpose. Suppose expected inflation, as these firms and workers calculate it, is too high. Real wages will therefore rise by $\omega - \pi$ and excess supply appears in the labour market. In year 2 the other half of the work force begins its contract negotiation. However, it is stuck with a disequilibrium from period 1 and, therefore, must accept lower wage increases if the labour market is to clear. To be precise nominal wage increases must be lower by the amount $(\omega - \pi)_{-1}$. This is a situation of conflict between the two groups of workers. In this situation it will be possible to reduce or even remove the real wage gains of the first group of workers by increasing μ to increase π. This would increase labour demand and remove the necessity for adjustment on part of the second group of workers.

The argument for intervention by the policy authorities becomes even more convincing if the second group of workers, in the interest of wage equity, asked for still higher real wages. This would further exacerbate the problem of unemployment. In the case of long period wage contracts policy intervention speeds up considerably the adjustment to equilibrium in the labour market.

INDEXATION OF NOMINAL WAGES

The foregoing analysis points to the possibility that workers would like to protect wage gains in real terms. Workers may want to achieve a real wage

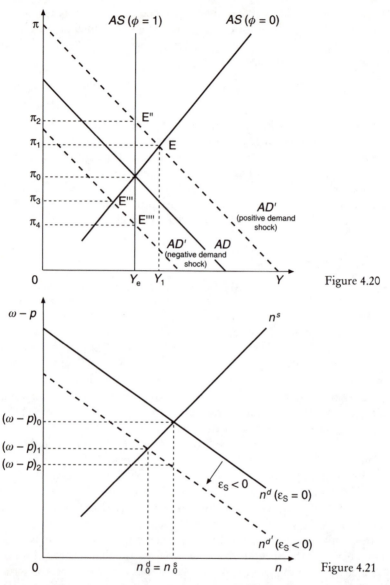

Figure 4.20

Figure 4.21

ex post rather than *ex ante*. This is possible through cost of living adjustment (COLA) of nominal wages. This aspect of the labour market can have different effects depending upon the type of shock that occurs. Our analysis here follows that of Gray (1976).

Up until now nominal wage increases were forward looking in that they were set equal to the expected rate of inflation. With COLA nominal wage setting becomes backward looking. Nominal wage increases get tied to whatever π was last period. Let us suppose that nominal wage increases are partly geared to actual inflation last period and partly to expected inflation, i.e.

$$\omega = \phi\pi + (1 - \phi)\pi^e \qquad (4.35)$$

where $0 < \phi < 1$ is the indexation factor. $\phi = 1$ means that there is full indexation, $\phi = 0$ means that there is no indexation and $0 < \phi < 1$ means that there is partial indexation.

The AS schedule is affected by the form that indexation takes. If $\phi = 0$ then the AS schedule remains as before. With indexation of the form given in equation (4.35) we get, upon substitution in the AS equation,

$$Y = Y^e - \alpha_4(1 - \phi)(\pi^e - \pi) \qquad (4.36)$$

The slope of the AS schedule is $1/\alpha_4(1 - \phi)$. If $\phi = 1$ the AS schedule is vertical and the distinction between π and π^e is unimportant.

We analyse the effects of AD shocks with and without indexation in Figure 4.20. As ε_m rises, for instance, AD floats upwards. With a positive shock and no indexation both output and inflation rise and we move to E'. With full indexation Y remains stuck at Y^e and inflation climbs up to the higher level associated with the equilibrium E''.

As we have seen, in a world which is subject to shocks it is not possible to maintain labour market equilibrium. If Y^e is a preferred level of output then full indexation ensures that output does not deviate too much from it. To that extent indexation in the labour market is desirable.

However, when the economy is subject to supply shocks originating in the labour market the optimum may be only partial wage indexation. To see this let us analyse Figure 4.21. Initially $\varepsilon_s = 0$. Now allow ε_s to take a negative value. This shifts the n^s curve down by the extent of ε_s. To move toward a new equilibrium the real wage should drop to $(w-p)_1$ but unless there is just the right degree of wage indexation this will not happen. With full indexation we remain stuck at real wage $(w-p)_0$ and there will be unemployment in excess of the natural rate. With no indexation π will rise by the amount $[(\alpha_1\alpha_2 + \alpha_3)(1 + \alpha_4)/(\alpha_1 + \alpha_3\alpha_4 + \alpha_1\alpha_2\alpha_4)]\varepsilon_s$ as indicated by equation (4.30). Let us assume, for simplicity, that $\alpha_2 = 1$ and $\alpha_3 = 0$; then $w - p$ will fall exactly by the amount of ε_s which leads us to $(w-p)_2$ which is too low for the new equilibrium. To reach the new equilibrium, therefore, we require partial indexation.

5

The process of money creation and the demand for money

INTRODUCTION

In this book we have used the demand for money and its supply without inquiring into the foundations for such relationships. It is time to dwell on these issues somewhat. Students have, no doubt, been exposed to these foundations in earlier courses in macroeconomics. The discussion here, therefore, will tend to supplement these. We begin with a discussion of the importance of the role of the financial system in economic development. We then move on to a discussion of elementary models of money supply. The discussion here includes the effects of 'financial repression' – a characteristic of many developing countries – on the money supply. We then proceed to discuss the underpinnings of the demand for money.

THE IMPORTANCE OF MONEY AND FINANCE IN ECONOMIC DEVELOPMENT

Students often begin their study of macroeconomics by appreciating the advantages of a monetary economy over a barter economy. Unless there is a 'double coincidence of wants' – the buyer wanting to buy exactly what the seller wants to sell at a mutually acceptable ratio of exchange – a barter economy is likely to be extremely inefficient, we are told. No modern economy can be based on the barter system and expect to prosper.

Most developing countries started their post-colonial phase of development as near barter economies. However, the mere introduction of money does not make for a modern monetary economy. A fully developed financial system consists of a wide range of institutions, instruments and markets. Further, a well-developed financial system is not a static system – but one that keeps changing over time. How does the growth of the financial system affect the development of the economy?

At one extreme it can be argued that if the financial system is completely underdeveloped there will be no transfers of funds from savers to investors. Savers and investors are usually different people and the financial system plays a crucial role in mediating the transactions between them.

Savers may not be willing to invest directly in the enterprises of firms and other investors but these savers may be willing to keep their funds in banks. These banks may, in turn, be willing to lend funds to investors. To perform well their role as mediators of the saving–investment relationship, banks and other intermediaries must be attractive both to savers as well as to investors. In other words, they must provide the incentive to save, increase the volume of investment and improve the efficiency of investment.

If banks perform their role well savers will find that financial investment with these banks is preferable to increased high consumption or investing directly in enterprises. Potential investors will now have access to savings other than their own. Thus the volume of investment will pick up. Moreover, the development of markets in money and financial instruments will tend to channel funds toward the more productive and profitable ventures.

Apart from facilitating the development of a productive relationship between savers and investors, a well-functioning financial system performs other roles as well. Financial instruments and institutions perform the extremely important tasks of maturity transformation and risk transfer.

Maturity transformation permits savers to save short term and investors to acquire long-term funds. Typically savers do not want to lock their funds for long periods of time. They want to have access to fairly liquid funds should they want to change their financial portfolio or consume more. But the typical investor wants long-term funds. The essential function of maturity transformation between saver and investor is performed by financial institutions.

Risk transfer is another very important role of financial institutions. Many savers do not wish to undertake the risk of physical investments themselves. Moreover, they may also be reluctant to lend to investors who can take these risks. Apart from the purely psychological factor of not wanting to take risks, savers may, quite reasonably, feel that they do not have the technical expertise to evaluate the worth of the projects being contemplated by the investors. Such savers prefer to use financial intermediaries, in which they have confidence and which they perceive to be financially sound. These financial institutions then provide funds to many investors thereby diversifying and reducing average risk to themselves.

Other important financial institutions such as stock and bond markets also perform very important roles in the development of the economy. However, stocks and bonds provide relatively quicker liquidity and, in any case, their significance is relatively limited in most developing countries.

The relationship between financial development and economic growth has been the focus of considerable empirical research. Three competing empirical hypotheses have vied for attention. One suggests that financial development must precede economic development. The second suggests that financial and economic development occur together. The third, rather extreme, view is that financial development follows rather than leads economic development.

This last view has not been supported by the facts and very few economists espouse it. For a recent statement in the case of Nigeria see Woolmer (1977).

The large empirical literature with respect to the first two views has been surveyed by Gupta (1984). He also conducts causality tests along the lines of Granger (1980) between various indices of financial development and economic growth. His conclusion was that financial development leads economic development. This was true of a sample of fourteen fairly representative developing countries that he studied.

THE SUPPLY OF MONEY AND MODELS OF MONEY CREATION

In this book and in scores of theoretical and empirical analyses it has been assumed that the money stock (M_1, i.e. demand deposits plus currency) is determined by the monetary authorities. However, in most countries it is probably more appropriate to assume that the money stock is determined by a process which results from the complex interaction of the behaviour of various economic agents, rather than as a process controlled exclusively by the central bank of the country.

In this chapter, we shall try to understand the complexities of the money supply process. To do this we shall have to make assumptions about the behavioural responses of various economic agents involved in the money supply process and the institutional setting within which they function.

Our approach in this section will be to introduce a number of simplified models to understand the process of money creation. From this it will become clear why it is inherently difficult for the monetary authorities to control the money supply.

MODEL OF MONEY CREATION I

In this model we assume that the domestic money supply consists of currency holdings and demand deposits alone and, further, that banks wish to hold no excess reserves. We can then define the monetary base (B) of the economy as total commercial bank reserves (R) plus currency in circulation (C):

$$B = R + C \tag{5.1}$$

Under our assumptions, commercial banks will be in equilibrium (in the sense of desiring no expansion or contraction of loans and deposits) only when all reserves they hold are required against their demand deposit liability.

If RR_D are reserves legally required against demand deposit liabilities, r is the average legal reserve requirements on commercial bank demand deposit liabilities and DD are demand deposit liabilities of commercial banks, then it must be the case that

$$RR_D = rDD \tag{5.2}$$

and that

$$R = RR_D = rDD \tag{5.3}$$

Substituting equations (5.2) and (5.3) into (5.1) we have

$$B = rDD + C \tag{5.4}$$

Equation (5.4) makes clear an important characteristic of the model. The monetary base is determined by the monetary authorities; however, its composition is determined by the actions of the non-bank public.

From equation (5.4) we can see that

$$DD = \frac{1}{r}(B - C) \tag{5.5}$$

Thus changes in the stock of deposits are related to the changes in the base by the equation (5.6):

$$\Delta DD = \frac{1}{r}(\Delta B - \Delta C) \tag{5.6}$$

Now we can examine the impact of a change in the monetary base. Suppose that for every dollar held in a bank account people wish to hold a fraction s as currency so that

$$C = sDD \text{ or } \Delta C = s\Delta DD$$

From equation (5.4) we can write

$$\Delta B = r\Delta DD + \Delta C = (r + s)\Delta DD$$

or

$$\Delta DD = \frac{1}{r + s}\Delta B \tag{5.7}$$

We can similarly write the increase in cash holdings as $\Delta C = s\Delta DD$ or, from equation (5.7),

$$\Delta C = \frac{s}{r + s}\Delta B \tag{5.8}$$

Total increase in money supply equals increases in currency held and deposits: $\Delta M = \Delta DD + \Delta C$. From equations (5.7) and (5.8) we have

$$\Delta M = \frac{1}{r + s}\Delta B + \frac{s}{r + s}\Delta B = \frac{1 + s}{r + s}\Delta B \tag{5.9}$$

Equation (5.9) is the final expression we want. It relates total money supply increase to an increase in monetary base. It also determines the split up of this ΔM between ΔDD and ΔC.

MODEL OF MONEY CREATION II

In this model we continue to assume that commercial banks want no excess legal reserves. They will expand or contract their outstanding loans any time total reserves differ from required reserves. We now define the monetary base

$$B = R + C$$

where

$$R = RR_T + RR_T \tag{5.10}$$

where RR_D are reserves legally required against demand deposit liabilities and RR_T are reserves legally required against time deposit liabilities. Thus $RR_D = rDD$ and $RR_T = bTD$ where TD is total time deposits and b is the average legal reserve requirement on commercial bank time deposit liabilities. Thus

$$R = RR_D + RR_D = rDD + bTD \tag{5.11}$$

Hence $B = R + C = rDD + bTD + C$. In terms of differences,

$$\Delta B = r\Delta DD + b\Delta TD + \Delta C \tag{5.12}$$

We want again to get the total increase in money supply in response to an increase in the monetary base. Suppose that the public maintains fixed proportions between time and demand deposits where the factor of proportionality is γ, i.e. $TD = \gamma DD$. Hence

$$\Delta B = r\Delta DD + b\Delta TD + \Delta C$$

$$= r\Delta DD + b\gamma\Delta DD + s\Delta DD$$

$$= \Delta DD(r + b\gamma + s)$$

so that

$$\Delta DD = \frac{1}{r + b\gamma + s} \, \Delta B \tag{5.13}$$

This gives us the increase in demand deposits. We know that $\Delta TD = \gamma\Delta DD = \gamma[1/(r + b\gamma + s)]\Delta B$ and $\Delta C = [s/(r + b\gamma + s)]\Delta B$. We know that

$$\Delta M = \Delta C + \Delta DD + \Delta TD$$

$$= \frac{s + 1 + \gamma}{r + b\gamma + s} \, \Delta B \tag{5.14}$$

Equation (5.14) then relates total change in money supply to a change in monetary base.

MODEL OF MONEY CREATION III

It is reasonable (and historically accurate) to assume that commercial banks may not act like the 'automatic dispensers of credit' pictured in models I and II. Suppose that banks wish to maintain a fixed proportional relation between their holdings of excess reserves (RE) and their deposit liabilities, i.e. $RE = wDD$, where w is the factor of proportionality. Now, as before,

$$B = R + C \qquad R = RR_D + RR_T + R_E$$

Substituting appropriately we have $B = rDD + b(\gamma DD) + wDD + sDD = DD(r + b\gamma + s + w)$, whence

$$DD = \frac{1}{r + b\gamma + s + w} B \qquad (5.15)$$

so that

$$\Delta DD = \frac{1}{r + b\gamma + s + w} \Delta B \qquad (5.16)$$

This gives us the required relation between changes in the monetary base and changes in demand deposits. To get the effect of changes in B on total money supply we add ΔC to equation (5.16) to get

$$\Delta M = \frac{1 + s}{r + b\gamma + s + w} \Delta B \qquad (5.17)$$

MODELS WITH VARIABLE INTEREST RATES

In reality the public's asset preferences may be well described only by quite complicated relationships. The interested reader is referred to Cagan (1965) for a thorough analysis of the many complexities involved. In this section, we shall give students only a minor taste of some of the richness that can be built in.

Time deposits are markedly different from demand deposits and currency because they pay fairly high rates of interest. Hence, giving up time deposits for demand deposits or cash involves a substantial opportunity cost. The higher the rate of interest on time deposits, *ceteris paribus*, the more costly it would be in terms of foregone income to hold money in the form of demand deposits or currency. Hence it might be the case that the interest on time deposits and the size of demand deposits may influence the size of time deposits. One may postulate, for example, that

$$TD = e + fDD + gi_T \qquad (5.18)$$

where i_T is the interest payable on time deposits. We can then write

$$B = rDD + bTD + RE + C$$

with $RE = wDD$, $C = sDD$ and $TD = e + fDD + gi_T$. Upon substitution we have

$$B = rDD + b(e + fDD + gi_T) + wDD + sDD$$
$$= DD(r + be + bf + bgi_T + w + s)$$

or

$$DD = \frac{1}{r + be + bf + bgi_T + w + s} B \qquad (5.19)$$

To take another example, let us suppose that the asset preferences of the banks and the public are dependent on some market interest rates. For example, the public may consider Treasury Bills an alternative to their holding currency or time deposits. Commercial banks' behaviour may also be influenced by market rates of interest. If we let i_m be a summary measure of such interest rates, we may write

$$TD = e + fDD + gi_m \qquad (5.20a)$$

$$C = a + d\,DD + \phi i_m \qquad (5.20b)$$

$$RE = V + wDD + \varphi i_m \qquad (5.20c)$$

Equations (5.20a)–(5.20c) denote the fact that the market rate of interest may affect holding of cash and time deposits by the public and excess reserves by banks. Now $B = rDD + bTD + C + RE$. Substituting from (5.20) and solving for DD, we have

$$DD = \frac{B - \lambda - \beta i_m}{r + bf + d + w} \qquad (5.21)$$

where $\lambda = be + a + V$ and $\beta = bg + \phi + \varphi$. Equation (5.21) is a reduced form equation. In this form φi_m represents the total influence of i_m on the volume of demand deposit liabilities through its effect on the preferred asset holdings of the public and the banks. Since g, ϕ and φ are negative and b is positive, β is also negative. From equation (5.21) then $\partial DD/\partial i_m = -\beta/(r + bf + d + w) > 0$, or, as the market interest rate increases, the equilibrium quantity of demand deposits increases. This is shown in Figure 5.1.

Our discussion above shows that there can be many 'money multipliers' and the supply of money can be influenced by several different interest rates. The form of the money multiplier and the choice of interest rate variables that affect the money supply depend directly on the form of the behavioural relations employed to explain the asset preferences of the banks and the public. These equations could easily be expanded to include additional variables such as income, wealth, expectations of inflation and so on. The 'best' money supply model will be the one that explains the actual data (actual past values of the money supply) and predicts future money supply better than any other model.

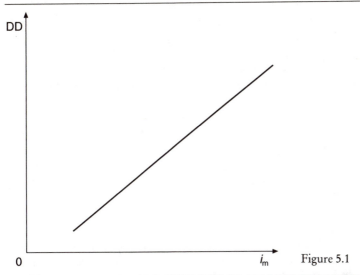

Figure 5.1

SOME SPECIAL CHARACTERISTICS OF MONEY SUPPLY IN DEVELOPING COUNTRIES

Many developing countries do not have free capital markets. These markets are often characterised by 'financial repression'. Financial repression takes many forms in developing countries – the most common being ceilings on interest rates or government-controlled interest rates – particularly interest rates on deposits or/and on loans. During periods of inflation, then, real rates of interest (nominal interest rates minus the rate of inflation) are often negative. At the artificially low rate of interest there exists an excess demand for investment. But investment must equal saving so that both saving and investment are lower.

Sometimes repression also takes the form of government restrictions on the free development of financial instruments and institutions. It is often the case that reserve requirements of commercial banks, set by central banks in developing countries, are very high. In developed countries reserve require-ments of 10–15 per cent are common. In developing countries, however, reserve requirements of 50 per cent or more are quite common. These high reserve requirements have two serious implications. First, a substantial por-tion of investible funds is directed away from potential investment. Second, the banks' interest rate structure remains distorted because they must retain a wide margin between borrowing and lending rates in order to compensate themselves for the fact that they have to retain substantial funds in the form of reserves.

Sometimes governments compound matters even further by regulating investments by banks. In many cases banks *have to* buy government bonds since there is not much of a private demand for these bonds. Over and above this, governments encourage investment by banks in certain 'priority' sectors. Bank investment then gets guided by the government's preferences which may not be an accurate reflection of true economic productivity or profitability.

Clearly, financial repression retards the development of the financial sector and, hence, of the economy. We examine these consequences of financial repression in Chapter 14, where we discuss economic liberalisation, and Chapter 15, where we discuss growth models with financial repression. In this section we realise that financial repression may have very serious implications for the money supply in developing countries.

Total money savings is roughly equal to bank and quasi-bank deposits and currency in circulation. This is the M_2 definition of money supply. Since bank deposits and cash are the principal forms of savings in developing countries these savings and M_2 are approximately equal to each other. Hence, in equilibrium, savings and the demand for money are equal to each other. Suppose now that inflation rises. With controlled nominal interest rates a higher rate of inflation means a lower real rate of interest. Savers will be discouraged from holding money balances with a low or often negative real rate of interest. They will tend to invest in inflation hedges such as gold jewellery, real estate and the like. Productive investment will therefore decline. This will have the effect of lowering the rate of economic growth. It should also be noted that investment in the inflation hedges is itself inflationary since this tends to push up the prices of these hedges and the general price level has a tendency to rise with these prices. It should also be noted that expectations of higher real inflation will tend to have the same effect as higher inflation itself.

THE DEMAND FOR MONEY

We have studied the demand for money in Chapter 3. At that level of simplification, we could distinguish between two different sources of the demand for money: the transactions motive and the speculative motive. The precautionary motive is not considered too significant.

The transactions motive

Economists believe that money is demanded, like any asset, because of the flow of services it yields. With most assets, the value of this flow of services is measurable in terms of dollars per period of time. With money, however, this flow is not measurable in dollar terms. Cheque accounts in banks pay low rates of interest and the value of these accounts gets depleted in times of inflation. The flow of benefits provided by money is implicit and recognisable in the services it performs. Money is a unit of account, a medium of exchange and a store of value. The unit of account function of money simply means that money is used as a *numeraire* in which the prices of all other goods and services are measured. In other words, the price of money in terms of itself is one and the prices of all other goods are measured in terms of money – dollars per unit. The store of value function of money is discussed with the speculative demand for money.

As a medium of exchange, money is held between the receipt and disbursement of income because of the costs of converting into and out of other, earning, assets which themselves are not generally acceptable as media of exchange. A monetary economy is more efficient than a barter economy. The amount of money demanded to finance expenditures, in principle, thus depends on these conversion costs as well as the size of the expenditures and how far in the future they will be made. Most economists, nevertheless, have emphasised the size of expenditures as the primary constraint affecting the demand for money as a medium of exchange. In fact, the transactions demand for money, associated with its use as a medium of exchange is usually depicted as varying in direct proportion with the level of expenditures. Following this tradition, the ith individual's transactions demand for money function is

$$\frac{M_i}{P_T} = \alpha_i T_i \tag{5.22}$$

with M_i/P_T being the average quantity of real transactions balances held by the individual, where P_T is the price level of all transactions, M_i is the nominal cash balances held by the ith individual, T_i is the level of the ith individual's total real expenditures over the relevant time period, say a month, and α_i the proportionality factor with a value $0 < \alpha_i < 1$ for the relevant period.

The order of magnitude of α_i relates the size of the average money stock needed to finance a flow of expenditures to the size of that total flow. For instance, suppose an individual is paid a monthly income of $3000 on the first day of each month. Assume further that she spends this income at a uniform rate of $100 per day for 30 days until she is paid again on the first day of the next month. The average transactions balance will be ($3000 + 0)/2 = $1500. Therefore,

$$\alpha_i = \frac{M_i/P_T}{T_i} = \frac{\$1500}{\$3000/\text{month}} = \frac{1}{2} \text{ month.}$$

Since our major concern is the analysis of aggregate economic behaviour we must aggregate over all individuals in the economy as a whole, and show what determines the value of α for the economy as a whole. We can define $\alpha = (M/P_T)/T$. In an economy with N individuals

$$T = \sum_{i=1}^{N} T_i$$

Now

$$\frac{M}{P_T} = \sum_{i=1}^{N} \alpha_i T_i \tag{5.23}$$

so that

$$\alpha = \sum_{i=1}^{N} \alpha_i (T_i / T)$$

The value of α for the entire economy is the summation of the individual α_i each weighted by that individual's share of aggregate total expenditures for a given time period (in our case here, a month).

It will be useful to reformulate the demand for transactions balances as a function of the level of output of newly produced goods and services (real national income) rather than the level of total expenditures. Total expenditures exceed the expenditures on new goods and services since total expenditures include expenditures on intermediate goods, second-hand goods, financial assets and the like.

Define α_0 as the ratio of real aggregate transactions balances to the level of aggregate output

$$\alpha_0 = \frac{M/P}{y} \tag{5.24}$$

where P is the aggregate price level and y is the level of real national income. Hence

$$\alpha_0 = \frac{M/P_T}{T} \; \frac{T}{y} \; \frac{P_T}{P}$$

$$= \sum_{i=1}^{N} \alpha_i \frac{T_i}{T} \; \frac{T}{y} \; \frac{P_T}{P} \tag{5.25}$$

We can now write the aggregate demand for money function as

$$\frac{M}{P} = \alpha_0 y \tag{5.26}$$

Early theorists like Fisher and Keynes pointed out that income was not the only variable affecting the transactions demand for money. But it took some time for economists to develop rigorously a theory of how conversion costs affect the transactions demand for money.

William Baumol was the first economist to formally incorporate conversion costs in the transactions demand for money. Baumol proceeded from the assumption that the stock of cash is the holding inventory of the medium of exchange. The rational individual will try to minimise the cost of holding this inventory. Suppose transactions costs are perfectly foreseen and occur in a steady stream over the month. Real income is H per month and it is assumed that the individual pays out all her $H per month at a constant rate. Thus during the month the individual will be holding an ever diminishing stock of assets.

In what form will these assets be held? If assets are held in the form of money then some interest income is foregone. If assets are held as bonds then the individual will have to pay a conversion cost every time she tries to convert bonds for money for purposes of carrying out transactions.

Suppose the individual begins the period holding all her income in bonds. She is assumed to withdraw the money from bonds in units of $C evenly spaced. For example, if the individual's income is $3000 per month then C might be $3000 every 30 days or $1500 every 15 days and so on. There will be H/C withdrawals made during the period. For each such withdrawal there is assumed to be a real transactions cost of $b. The expression $b(H/C)$ is a kind of 'inventory replenishment cost' which includes not only the explicit cost (e.g. brokerage fees) of selling assets to get cash but also the implicit cost (the inconvenience of doing so).

We assume that the individual's withdrawal of $C is expended at a constant rate. Hence the individual's average cash balance is $C/2. Hence the interest opportunity cost of holding bonds is $iC/2$ where i is the interest payable on bonds. Total cost J of holding this inventory can now be written as

$$J = \frac{bH}{C} + \frac{iC}{2} \qquad (5.27)$$

The individual will choose C to minimise J. To do that set $dJ/dC = 0$ and solve for C to get

$$C = \left(\frac{2bH}{i}\right)^{0.5} \qquad (5.28)$$

Since the optimal average balance is $C/2$ we can rewrite equation (5.28) as

$$\frac{M}{P} = \alpha H^{0.5} i^{-0.5} \qquad (5.29)$$

where $\alpha = (0.5)(2b)^{0.5}$.

This result shows that (i) the transactions demand for money does not generally vary in proportion to the level of total expenditures, i.e. since $\partial^2 M/\partial H^2 < 0$ there are economies of scale in the management of cash balances; (ii) the quantity of transactions balances is negatively related to the interest rate; and (iii) because of the transactions cost of exchanging cash for bonds ($b > 0$), it generally pays to hold cash.

This square root rule of Baumol is justifiably famous for several reasons. Two of the most important are: (i) it provides a justification for the negative relation between the interest rate and the demand for money *independent* of the speculative demand for holding cash, and (ii) it predicts that the demand

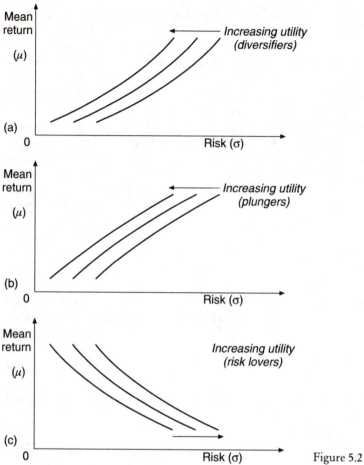

Figure 5.2

for money varies less than in proportion to variations in income. Hence, a given increase in the money supply will, *ceteris paribus*, require a larger increase in income to increase money demand sufficiently to equilibrate the money market. This means that monetary policy is a potent tool for stabilisation.

Speculative demand for money balances

Suppose we live in a world with two assets: cash M/P carries zero yield but, by definition, the distribution of returns has zero variance. The other asset, R, is a perpetuity with a mean return of μ and standard deviation of returns σ. We think of this standard deviation as a measure of the risk of holding R. The wealth holder has a utility function defined over risk and return with risk 'normally' being a bad and return a good. What do we expect the individual's indifference curves between risk and returns to look like? The possibilities are plotted in Figure 5.2.

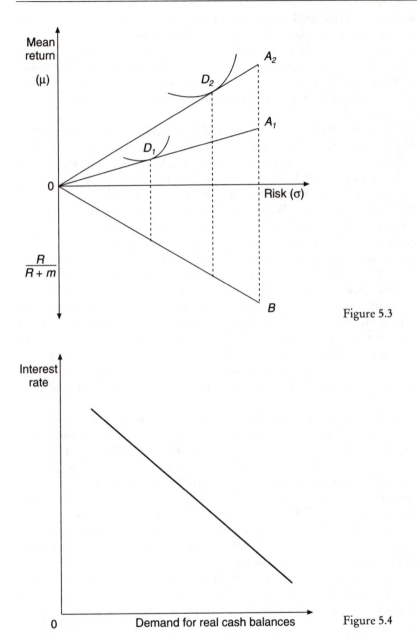

Figure 5.3

Figure 5.4

In Figures 5.2(a) and 5.2(b) we plot the indifference map of a risk averter. More risk will be undertaken only if the mean return goes up. In Figure 5.2(a) we plot the indifference map of a diversifier because at low absolute risk levels a 1 per cent increase in risk requires less than 1 per cent increase in mean return to keep the wealth holder on the same indifference curve;

whereas at high risk levels a 1 per cent increase in risk requires a larger than 1 per cent increase in mean return to keep the individual on the same indifference curve. Thus this wealth holder diversifies. For the opposite reasons, the individual whose preferences are shown in Figure 5.2(b) is a plunger. The individual whose preferences are shown in Figure 5.2(c) is a risk lover since she will trade off return for higher risk to increase the chance of a capital gain.

Let us analyse the choice problem in this situation. Suppose we are dealing with a risk averter who is a diversifier. She can hold her speculative balances in cash, earn zero return and incur zero risk, or she can invest some in the risky asset. Figure 5.3 visualises the possibilities for this individual.

In Figure 5.3(a) we have plotted the risk/return combination afforded by the individual's portfolio. With cash she gets zero risk and zero return. As she increases the proportion of the risky asset in this portfolio she gets higher μ and higher σ. With interest payment on the risky asset at i_1, $0A_1$ shows the investment opportunities available to this individual. As the proportion of assets held in R increases, the mean return increases and so does the risk. Hence $0A_1$ is upward sloping. With a higher interest rate i_2, this opportunity locus twists to $0A_2$. With i_1 the consumer comes to an equilibrium at D_1 and with i_2 the equilibrium is at D_2. The proportion in R can be read off from $0B$ in Figure 5.3(b). An increase in the rate of interest has a substitution effect that should encourage the individual to take greater risks. The income effect would make the person want more security which would mean a reduction in risk. In Figure 5.3 it has been assumed that the substitution effect dominates.

Under this set of conditions, then, the higher the rate of interest the lower the demand for money for speculative purposes. The individual's demand for money for speculative purposes is negatively related to the rate of interest. The economy's speculative demand for money is obtained by adding up the individuals' demand for money. This is portrayed in Figure 5.4.

The theory of the speculative demand for money outlined above was developed by Tobin (1958) and is a vast improvement on the approach taken by Keynes (1936, 1973). This approach is important also because it is a precursor of the modern portfolio approach to the demand for financial assets of which money is just one constituent.

For operational purposes we now have a demand for money function which says that the demand for real cash balances is positively related to real national income and negatively related to the rate of interest,

$$\frac{M}{P} = L(y, i) \atop \scriptstyle + \ -$$

(5.30)

It is not necessary that this function be separable in its two arguments. Equation (5.30) provides the theoretical foundation for the demand for money function used in this book.

Mainstream macroeconomics – the open economy

6

Macroeconomic policy in an open economy

INTRODUCTION

So far we have assumed that the economy we have been studying is closed, i.e. it does not have any interaction with the outside world. It is time to relax this assumption and realise that since most economies are open, we must understand the impact and design of macroeconomic policy in an open economy.

Throughout we shall assume that we are dealing with a small open economy (SOE). This implies that the economy we are considering is too small to affect world prices of goods and services and world interest rates. This is a safe assumption to make for most developing countries. There are some exceptions, however. If India was to buy wheat in international markets the world price of wheat would likely go up. However, these exceptions are rather rare.

In this chapter we first introduce the foreign balance (FB) constraint into the IS–LM framework and then consider the design of optimal policies under fixed and flexible exchange rates. We shall also consider the so-called 'assignment problem'.

THE FOREIGN BALANCE AND IS–LM ANALYSIS

With an open economy the notion of macroeconomic equilibrium has to be reinterpreted. In the IS–LM framework, full macroeconomic equilibrium is established when there is simultaneous equilibrium in the goods and money markets and the rest of the world (ROW). We shall assume that we can condense all trading partners of this country into this convenient phrase ROW. The domestic currency (the currency of the developing country) is the rupee (Rs). The currency of the ROW is the dollar ($).

We write the equation of the IS schedule as

$$I(r) + \bar{G} + X = S(r, y) + Z + T \tag{6.1}$$

where I is investment, S is savings, $\bar{G}$ is exogenous government expenditure, X are exports, Z imports and T are tax collections.

The exchange rate between the domestic currency and the world currency (e) is defined as the price of one dollar in terms of rupees. Let P be the domestic price level and P^* the foreign price level (asterisks refer to foreign magnitudes). Then we can define the real exchange rate as (eP^*/P). Exports are assumed to depend positively on the real exchange rate. When the real exchange rate goes up (the rupee price of a dollar goes up or the foreign price level goes up or the domestic price level falls) the goods of the domestic economy become more attractive abroad as the price of domestic goods to foreigners drops. Thus we write

$$X = X(eP^*_+/P) \tag{6.2}$$

Imports are a function of the real exchange rate and the level of real national income at home,

$$Z = Z(eP^*/P, \underset{+}{\underset{-}{y}}) \tag{6.3}$$

As the real exchange rate rises (the price of a dollar rises, the foreign price level rises or the domestic price level falls) home goods become more attractive to domestic residents as compared with foreign goods as the relative price of home goods falls. As national income rises demand for imports goes up because imports are assumed to be normal goods with positive income elasticities of demand. We also assume that the marginal propensity to import lies between zero and one, $0 < Z_y < 1$.

We write the equation of the IS schedule as

$$I(r) + \bar{G} + X\left(\frac{eP^*}{P}\right) = S(r, y) + Z\left(\frac{eP^*}{P}\right) + T \tag{6.4}$$

We shall write the money market equilibrium as

$$\frac{M}{P} = L(y, r, \Omega) \tag{6.5}$$

L_Ω, $L_y > 0$, $L_r < 0$, where Ω is wealth. This formulation of the money market equilibrium will help us concentrate on the demand for money as an asset. The supply of money is assumed to be controllable by the monetary authorities. In an open economy with fixed exchange rates the money supply will increase whenever there is a surplus in the balance of payments (foreign exchange is part of the monetary base of the central bank), and whenever there is a deficit foreign exchange will flow out and the money supply will decrease. Thus under fixed exchange rates we may write

$$M = D + R = PL(y, r, \Omega) \tag{6.6}$$

where D are nominal domestic assets and R are foreign exchange reserves. A rise in domestic assets unaccompanied by a decline in reserves increases the

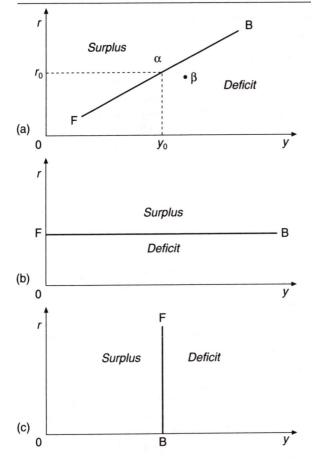

Figure 6.1

money supply. This would happen if the central bank purchased government securities. If the central bank purchased foreign exchange in order to
stabilise the exchange rate, reserves would rise and so would the money
supply. Finally if domestic assets rise and the foreign exchange reserves fall
by an equal amount nothing would happen to the money supply. With flexible exchange rates, e would adjust continuously in response to balance of
payments disequilibrium and equation (6.5) would hold continuously.

Balance of payments equilibrium itself occurs when the net surplus on
the current and capital accounts sum to zero. If this is not zero then there is
a compensating change in official reserves. Ignoring interest income from
abroad we can write the balance of payments surplus as $X - Z + K$, where K
is the net inflow of capital.

The balance of payments is in equilibrium (equivalently there will be foreign balance or external balance) if

$$X - Z + K = 0 \qquad (6.7)$$

We have already discussed the determinants of X and Z. We shall assume that the net inflow of capital can be written as

$$K = K[r - r^* - E(\Delta e/e)] \tag{6.8}$$

In equation (6.8) $E(\Delta e/e)$ is the expected appreciation of the foreign currency. The term inside the square brackets in equation (6.8) is the expected gain to a unit of foreign capital by being invested in the domestic economy. Since the domestic country is an SOE, r^* is treated as a parameter. For the time being we shall further suppose that $E(\Delta e/e) = 0$, so that equation (6.8) can be written as

$$K = K(r) \qquad \text{with } K_r > 0 \tag{6.9}$$

The equation for the FB can be written as

$$X\left(\frac{eP^*}{P}\right) - Z\left(y, \frac{eP^*}{P}\right) + K(r) = 0 \tag{6.10}$$

In the ry plane we can draw (6.10) as the FB schedule as in Figure 6.1. Let us first look at Figure 6.1(a). Suppose at point α the balance of payments is in equilibrium. Suppose, now, that real income is higher than y_0. Since e, P and P^* are fixed, exports remain unchanged. But with a higher income, imports are higher. At the same rate of interest (r_0) net capital imports are unchanged. Hence a point like β is characterised by a balance of payments deficit. If the interest rate was to rise from r_0, *ceteris paribus*, more capital would be attracted into the domestic economy and the balance of payments deficit would be eliminated. Thus the FB schedule which shows the r,y combinations giving balance of payments equilibrium is upward sloping. Above the FB schedule at any level of income the rate of interest is too high to maintain equilibrium in the balance of payments. Hence r,y combinations above FB denote balance of payments surplus. For the opposite reasons below the FB schedule we must have balance of payments deficit.

The slope of the FB schedule reflects the degree of international capital mobility. Figure 6.1(b) shows a situation characterised by perfect capital mobility. The domestic rate of interest cannot be different from the world rate of interest r_0. In Figure 6.1c the FB schedule denotes complete capital immobility.

In Figure 6.2 we have plotted the equilibrium of the economy in the balance of payments and the money and commodity markets. a denotes the point of simultaneous equilibrium. In Figure 6.2 we have drawn the FB schedule flatter than the LM schedule. This denotes a high degree of capital mobility. McKinnon (1984) calls this a financially open economy. If the LM schedule was flatter than the FB schedule then the degree of capital mobility would have been low. McKinnon calls this a financially insular economy.

It turns out that the distinction between a financially open and a financially insular economy is a useful one. The effects of monetary and fiscal

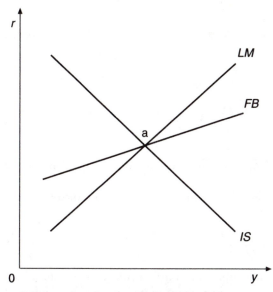

Figure 6.2

policies under fixed and flexible exchange rates depend crucially on the degree of international capital mobility.

The following discussion of macroeconomic policies is classified under two major headings: policies under fixed exchange rates and policies under flexible exchange rates. Within each category we make distinctions on the basis of international capital mobility.

MACRO POLICY WITH FIXED EXCHANGE RATES

Without any loss of generality let us write the IS–LM–FB model as

$$I = I_0 + I_r r \tag{6.11}$$
$$S = S_0 + S_y y \tag{6.12}$$
$$Z = Z_0 + Z_y y \tag{6.13}$$
$$M_s = L_0 + L_y y + L_r r \tag{6.14}$$
$$K = K_0 + K_r r \tag{6.15}$$

where I_0, S_0, Z_0, L_0 and K_0 represent constants. Write the IS–LM–FB schedules (in linear form) as

IS $\quad (S_y + Z_y)y - I_r r = -S_0 - Z_0 + I_0 + G + X = E_1 \tag{6.16}$
LM $\quad L_y y + L_r r = M_s - L_0 \tag{6.17}$
FB $\quad -Z_y y + K_r r = -X + Z_0 - K_0 = E_2 \tag{6.18}$

where E_1 and E_2 are appropriately defined constants. We can now write the system as:

$$\begin{bmatrix} S_y + Z_y & -I_r \\ -Z_y & K_r \end{bmatrix} \begin{bmatrix} y \\ r \end{bmatrix} = \begin{bmatrix} E_1 \\ E_2 \end{bmatrix} \tag{6.19}$$

so that in equilibrium

$$\begin{bmatrix} y^* \\ r^* \end{bmatrix} = \begin{bmatrix} K_r/D & I_r/D \\ Z_y/D & (S_y + Z_y)/D \end{bmatrix} \begin{bmatrix} E_1 \\ E_2 \end{bmatrix} \tag{6.20}$$

where $D = K_r(S_y + Z_y) - I_r Z_y > 0$. These results are independent of the money supply.

Substitute y^* and r^* into the LM equation to get the equilibrium money supply:

$$M_s^* = \frac{L_0 + (L_y K_r + L_r Z_y)E_1 + [L_y I_r + L_r(S_y + Z_y)]E_2}{D} \tag{6.21}$$

The supply of money, in equilibrium, is a constant. Its value is determined solely by the need to maintain a fixed exchange rate between the home and foreign currency. Nothing much can be done with monetary policy except to create disequilibrium and alter the level of foreign exchange reserves. This result is independent of the degree of international capital mobility.

To illustrate this we consider the case of perfect capital mobility in Figure 6.3. The domestic interest rate is fixed at the world level r_0. Domestic income is y_0. The monetary authorities conduct an open market purchase to increase the money supply and the LM schedule shifts outwards to LM'. Point b now characterises 'domestic' equilibrium. However, at b there is a deficit in the balance of payments.

Since exchange rates are fixed, the monetary authorities are obliged to support the legal value of the rupee. Hence the monetary authorities sell dollars at the existing exchange rate. This means that the money supply declines. A monetary survey shows the following changes in the balance sheet of the central bank of the country.

Assets	Liabilities
$+\Delta D =$	$+\Delta M$
$-\Delta R =$	$-\Delta M$

The LM curve must, necessarily, go all the way back and the old equilibrium must be restored. Hence monetary policy is completely ineffective. As remarked earlier this result does not depend on the degree of international capital mobility and so will hold for all cases.

The effects of fiscal policy, however, are very different. We realise that G is exogenous. Totally differentiating equations (6.20) and (6.21) we have the following multipliers:

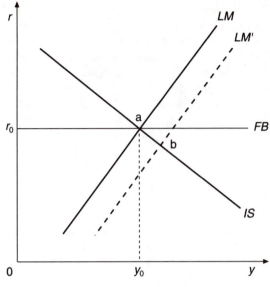

Figure 6.3

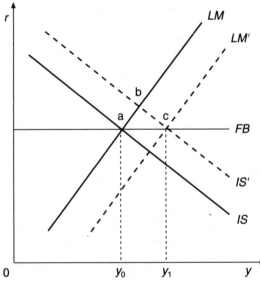

Figure 6.4

$$\frac{\mathrm{d}y^*}{\mathrm{d}G} = \frac{K_r}{K_r(S_y + Z_y) - I_r Z_y} \tag{6.22a}$$

$$\frac{\mathrm{d}r^*}{\mathrm{d}G} = \frac{Z_y}{K_r(S_y + Z_y) - I_r Z_y} \tag{6.22b}$$

$$\frac{\mathrm{d}M_s^*}{\mathrm{d}G} = \frac{L_y K_r + L_r Z_y}{K_r(S_y + Z_y) - I_r Z_y} \gtreqless 0 \tag{6.22c}$$

We examine the effects of increasing government expenditure in a world with perfect capital mobility in Figure 6.4. Initial equilibrium is once again at a. Expansionary fiscal policy shifts the IS schedule to IS'. The new 'domestic' equilibrium is at b where there is a balance of payments *surplus*. This is the crucial difference between the effects of expansionary monetary and fiscal policies. The surplus at b means that there will be a capital inflow. The monetary authorities prevent the local currency from appreciating by buying dollars at the going exchange rate. This, then, induces an increase in domestic money supply. A monetary survey shows the asset–liability position of the central bank as:

Assets	Liabilities
$+\Delta R =$	$+\Delta M$

Following this induced monetary expansion, the LM schedule must shift outwards all the way to LM' so that we once again have r_0 as the domestic interest rate and the balance of payments surplus is eliminated. The expansionary effect on y, however, is very powerful.

The above analysis and equation (6.22) suggest that the degree of capital mobility is very important in determining the magnitude of the effects of expansionary fiscal policy. If capital is perfectly mobile $K_r \rightarrow \infty$ and the multipliers become

$$\frac{dy^*}{dG} = \frac{1}{Z_y + S_y} > 0 \tag{6.23a}$$

$$\frac{dr^*}{dG} = 0 \tag{6.23b}$$

$$\frac{dM_s^*}{dG} = \frac{L_y}{S_y + Z_y} = L_y\left(\frac{dy^*}{dG}\right) > 0 \tag{6.23c}$$

Realise that the rise in income equals the simple multiplier as in the extreme Keynesian case (i.e. when $L_r \rightarrow -\infty$) because the money supply automatically adapts by rising in direct proportion to the change in income with the cash balance ratio L_y being the factor of proportionality.

When capital is completely immobile, $K_r = 0$, and the multipliers become

$$\frac{dy^*}{dG} = 0 \tag{6.24a}$$

$$\frac{dr^*}{dG} = \frac{-1}{I_r} \tag{6.24b}$$

$$\frac{dM_s^*}{dG} = \frac{-L_r}{I_r} \tag{6.24c}$$

The first two multipliers are equivalent to the classical closed economy result with $L_r = 0$. The equilibrium money supply drops because the higher interest rate induces liquidity preference. Foreign exchange reserves drop an equal amount.

When capital mobility is less than perfect the multipliers written in equation (6.22) are relevant. Both the equilibrium level of income and the equilibrium rate of interest rise in response to the fiscal stimulus. However, as can be seen by inspecting equation (6.22c) the equilibrium money stock may rise or fall, depending on whether $L_y K_r + L_r Z_y$ is greater or less than zero. If $L_y K_r + L_r Z_y > 0$ it follows that

$$\frac{-L_y}{L_r} > \frac{Z_y}{K_r}$$

which implies that the slope of the LM schedule is greater than the slope of the FB schedule. In this case capital is relatively mobile and the equilibrium money stock rises as foreign exchange is accumulated by the monetary authority. However, if $L_y K_r + L_r Z_y < 0$, the slope of the LM curve is less than the slope of the FB curve. Capital is, therefore, relatively immobile, the equilibrium money stock declines and the monetary authority loses foreign exchange.

THE FLEXIBLE EXCHANGE RATE MODEL

With flexible exchange rates the IS equation may be written as

$$I(r) = S(y) - G + Z(y,e) - X(e) \tag{6.25a}$$

P and P^* are still fixed.

The LM equation is

$$M_S = L(y,r) \tag{6.25b}$$

The FB function is

$$X(e) - Z(y,e) + K(r) = 0 \tag{6.25c}$$

We have three equations in three endogenous variables: y, r and e.

Total differentiation of (6.25) yields

$$\begin{bmatrix} S_y + Z_y & -I_r & Z_e - X_e \\ L_y & L_r & 0 \\ Z_y & -K_r & Z_e - X_e \end{bmatrix} \begin{bmatrix} dy \\ dr \\ de \end{bmatrix} = \begin{bmatrix} dG \\ dM_s \\ 0 \end{bmatrix} \tag{6.26}$$

Solving, we have

$$
\begin{bmatrix} dy \\ dr \\ de \end{bmatrix} = \begin{bmatrix} L_r(Z_e-X_e)/D & (I_r-K_r)(Z_e-X_e)/D & -L_r(Z_e-X_e)/D \\ -L_y(Z_e-X_e)/D & S_y(Z_e-X_e)/D & L_y(Z_e-X_e)/D \\ -(L_yK_r+L_rZ_y)/D & [K_r(S_y+Z_y)-K_rZ_y]/D & [-L_r(S_y+Z_y)+L_yI_r]/D \end{bmatrix} \begin{bmatrix} dG \\ dM_s \\ 0 \end{bmatrix}
$$

where $D = (Z_e - X_e)(L_rS_y - L_yK_r + I_rL_y) > 0$.

Hence, using Cramer's rule we can calculate the multipliers as

$$
\frac{dy^*}{dM_s} = \frac{I_r}{L_rS_y + I_rL_y} > 0 \tag{6.27a}
$$

$$
\frac{dr^*}{dM_s} = \frac{S_y}{L_rS_y + I_rL_y} < 0 \tag{6.27b}
$$

These are equivalent to the closed economy multipliers. Moreover,

$$
\frac{de}{dM_s} = \frac{-I_rZ_y}{(Z_e - X_e)(L_rS_y + I_rL_y)} > 0 \tag{6.27c}
$$

or, using (6.27a), we have

$$
\frac{de}{dM_s} = \frac{-Z_y}{(Z_e - X_e)} \frac{dy^*}{dM_s} > 0 \tag{6.27d}
$$

so the depreciation of the home currency increases as income change increases.

When capital mobility is perfect $K_r \to \infty$ and the multipliers become:

$$
\frac{dy}{dM_s} = \frac{1}{L_y} > 0 \tag{6.28a}
$$

$$
\frac{dr}{dM_s} = 0 \tag{6.28b}
$$

$$
\frac{de}{dM_s} = \frac{S_y + Z_y}{-(Z_e - X_e)L_y} > 0 \tag{6.28c}
$$

With perfect capital mobility no change in the interest rate is possible. The income multiplier is the same as the classical closed economy multiplier with $L_r = 0$.

For completeness we analyse the effects of monetary policy with perfect capital mobility in Figure 6.5. We start at point a with full equilibrium. Expansionary monetary policy shifts the LM schedule to LM'. 'Domestic' equilibrium occurs at b, where we have an incipient deficit in the balance of payments. This deficit is incipient because in a world of flexible exchange rates actual deficits or surpluses cannot last long. More relevant, however, is the fact that at b the rate of interest is lower than the world interest rate so that there will be an immediate capital outflow. The depreciation of the home currency because of the incipient deficit will increase exports and reduce imports. This will increase aggregate demand in the goods market

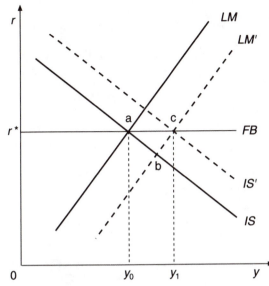

Figure 6.5

and the IS curve will shift outwards so long as the domestic interest rate is below the world interest rate (i.e. to IS'). Final equilibrium occurs at c where y has increased substantially. Monetary policy, which was powerless in a world of fixed exchange rates, suddenly becomes very powerful with flexible exchange rates.

Now let us look at the effects of expansionary fiscal policy. Expansionary fiscal policy shifts the IS curve to IS' in Figure 6.6. Domestic equilibrium moves from a to d. The domestic interest rate rises, so that there is a net inflow of capital into the domestic economy. This causes a capital account surplus and the domestic currency appreciates. Correspondingly, exports fall and imports rise and the IS curve shifts to the left all the way back to its old position. There is no increase in y. Thus fiscal policy which was so powerful in the case of perfect capital mobility and fixed exchange rates is rendered powerless.

An increase in the degree of capital mobility raises the money income multiplier because

$$\frac{\partial(dy/dM_s)}{\partial K_r} = \frac{-L_r S_y}{(L_r S_y - L_y K_r + I_r L_y)^2} > 0 \tag{6.29a}$$

The multipliers with respect to a change in government purchases are:

$$\frac{dy}{dG} = \frac{L_r}{L_r S_y - L_y K_r + I_r L_y} > 0 \tag{6.29b}$$

$$\frac{dr}{dG} = \frac{-L_y}{L_r S_y - L_y K_r + I_r L_y} > 0 \tag{6.29c}$$

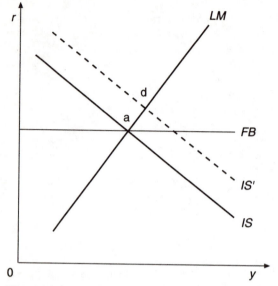

Figure 6.6

Hence, in general, expansionary fiscal policy raises national income and the rate of interest. However,

$$\frac{de}{dG} = \frac{-(L_yK_r + L_rZ_y)}{(Z_e - X_e)(L_rS_y - L_yK_r + I_rL_y)} \gtrless 0 \qquad (6.30)$$

which may be positive or negative because $L_yK_r > 0$ whereas $L_rZ_y < 0$. If $L_yK_r + L_rZ_y > 0$ it follows that

$$\frac{Z_y}{K_r} < \frac{-L_y}{L_r}$$

The term on the left-hand side of the inequality is the slope of the FB schedule, whereas the term on the right is the slope of the LM schedule. In the case above, the slope of the LM is greater than the slope of the FB. This is the case of relatively mobile capital in which case the local currency appreciates because expansionary fiscal policy causes an incipient surplus.

In the absence of capital mobility $K_r = 0$ and equation (6.29) yields

$$\frac{dy}{dG} = \frac{L_r}{L_rS_y + I_rL_y} > 0 \qquad (6.31a)$$

$$\frac{dr}{dG} = \frac{-L_y}{L_rS_y - I_rL_y} > 0 \qquad (6.31b)$$

These equations are identical to the closed economy case. Further, we must have

$$\frac{de}{dG} = \frac{-L_rZ_y}{(Z_e - X_e)(L_rS_y + I_rL_y)} > 0 \qquad (6.32)$$

so the local currency depreciates since fiscal policy affects only the current account.

With perfect capital mobility $K_r \rightarrow \infty$ so that we must have

$$\frac{dy}{dG} = 0 \tag{6.33a}$$

$$\frac{dr}{dG} = 0 \tag{6.33b}$$

$$\frac{de}{dG} = \frac{1}{Z_e - X_e} \leq 0 \tag{6.33c}$$

Hence the local currency cannot depreciate since the capital account effect of the fiscal policy is dominant.

Hence with flexible exchange rates monetary policy becomes very effective whereas fiscal policy loses some of its potential. This result depends upon the degree of international capital mobility. As the degree of international capital mobility increases the expansionary effect of monetary policy improves and that of fiscal policy declines. In the extreme case with perfect capital mobility monetary policy is doubly effective whereas expansionary fiscal policy has no effect on output. We can collect these results in Table 6.1.

Table 6.1 Effects of monetary and fiscal policies on y

Type of policy	Zero mobility	FB steeper than LM	FB flatter than LM	Perfect mobility
Fixed exchange rate regime				
Expansionary monetary policy	0	0	0	0
Expansionary fiscal policy	0	Multiplier increases as degree of capital mobility increases		$\dfrac{1}{S_y + Z_y}$
Flexible exchange rate regime				
Expansionary monetary policy	$\dfrac{I_r}{L_r S_y + I_r L_y}$	Multiplier increases as degree of capital mobility increases		$\dfrac{1}{L_y}$
Expansionary fiscal policy	$\dfrac{L_r}{L_r S_y + I_r L_y}$	Multiplier declines as degree of capital mobility increases		0

THE ASSIGNMENT PROBLEM

The economic policy maker often has several objectives. Sometimes these objectives may be in harmony with each other and at other times they are in conflict with each other. Suppose a country is faced with a balance of payments deficit and unemployment. Suppose the policy maker has only demand management policies at his disposal – fiscal or monetary policy, now labelled aggregate demand policy. If the policy maker attacks the problem of unemployment he would pursue expansionary demand policies. The consequent increase in real income would increase imports and, if expansionary monetary policy lowered the interest rate, the lower interest rate would cause a capital outflow. Hence the balance of payments deficit would become worse, not better. Such situations have traditionally posed a dilemma for policy makers. A general approach to the problem of economic policy making was formulated by Jan Tinbergen. It was popularised by R. Mundell.

The Tinbergen–Mundell approach to economic policy making is as follows. First it is argued that there must be at least as many *independent* policy instruments as policy targets. Second, a policy instrument should be assigned to that policy target on which it has maximal effect. In this section, we examine some aspects of this assignment problem. We shall first examine this under a fixed exchange rates regime and then in a regime of flexible exchange rates.

THE ASSIGNMENT PROBLEM WITH FIXED EXCHANGE RATES

The first part of the Tinbergen–Mundell solution to the assignment problem says that we must have at least as many independent policy instruments as policy targets. Let us try to understand what this means.

Suppose an economy wanted to attain full employment with price stability (internal balance) (we shall make the simplifying assumption that the price level starts rising only when the economy reaches full employment; at all levels of employment below the full employment level, the price level is unchanged) and balance of payments balance (external balance). By the Tinbergen–Mundell rule there must be at least two policy instruments that must be independent of each other and affect internal and external balance differently. Suppose we choose the level of government expenditure (fiscal policy) and the rate of interest (monetary policy). We know that the level of government expenditure and the rate of interest are not very independent of each other. Higher government expenditure, *ceteris paribus*, will lead to a higher interest rate. But we can suppose that they are not so related to each other as to imply that a change in one will necessarily and always imply a change in the other. Hence we shall treat them as independent policy instruments. In the same vein, changes in the stock of money and the interest rate *cannot* be treated as independent policy instruments.

Now the level of government expenditure (G) and the rate of interest (r) affect both internal and external balance. A higher G increases real national income and the increased income will increase imports and cause a deterioration in the balance of payments. Expansionary monetary policy will lead to a lower interest rate which will stimulate investment demand and hence raise national income. However, the lower rate of interest will also lead to a capital outflow and a larger deficit in the capital account of the balance of payments. Moreover, it can be argued that the higher real income will also

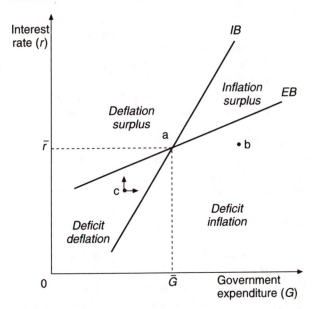

Figure 6.7

lead to higher imports and, therefore, cause a further deterioration in the balance of payments.

The point, however, is the *relative magnitude* of the effects of the two policy instruments on the policy targets. Fiscal policy has a greater effect on internal balance than on external balance and interest rate changes have a greater effect on external balance than on internal balance. This is explained in Figure 6.7.

Figure 6.7 plots government expenditure (G) on the x axis and rate of interest (r) on the y axis. Suppose that at point a in the diagram the economy enjoys internal as well as external balance. Starting from point a, suppose we move to point b where the level of government expenditure is higher than $\bar{G}$ (the level consistent with internal balance) and the interest rate is still $\bar{r}$ (the level consistent with external balance). Because government expenditure is higher at b than the level required to maintain full employment, it must be true that there are inflationary pressures at b. Moreover, since income is higher at b than at a it must be the case that imports are higher at b than at a. Hence there must be a balance of payments deficit at b.

Now let us try to restore internal and external balance starting from b. Suppose the interest rate is raised from $\bar{r}$. As the interest rate rises two consequences follow. First, more capital is attracted into the domestic economy so that there is a surplus in the capital account. Hence the balance of payments starts moving toward equilibrium. Second, the rise in interest lowers investment and hence increases aggregate demand and inflationary pressures. Thus if the interest rate rises from b we move toward internal balance and external balance. However, the rise in the interest rate has, by assumption, a greater effect on external than on internal balance, i.e. external balance is reached before internal balance. In other words, the external balance schedule (EB) is flatter than the internal balance schedule (IB).

To the right of IB the level of government expenditure is too high (given the rate of interest) to maintain full employment. Hence there must be inflationary pressures. To the left of IB the level of government expenditure is too low (given the rate of interest) to maintain full employment. Hence there must be deflationary pressures.

To the right of EB at any rate of interest the level of government expenditure and, hence, national income is too high to maintain balance of payments equilibrium. This means that points to the right of EB are characterised by excessive imports and hence a balance of payments deficit. Conversely, to the left of EB there are too few imports and hence there is a balance of payments surplus. In Figure 6.7 we have plotted the IB and EB schedules and labelled the disequilibrium zones.

Now we consider the second aspect of the Tinbergen–Mundell approach. If the government knew the IB and EB schedules it would follow policies to have interest rate $\bar{r}$ and level of government expenditure $\bar{G}$. The point, however, is that the government does not know the EB and IB schedules. When it is faced with a disequilibrium situation it must know how to react *without prior knowledge* of the exact locations of the IB and EB schedules. The policy advice here is to assign the policy instrument (monetary policy) that has a greater effect on EB the exclusive task of maintaining external balance. Analogously, since fiscal policy has a greater effect on internal balance, the task of maintaining internal balance is assigned exclusively to fiscal policy. This is the solution to the assignment problem.

To consider the significance of this rule consider point C in Figure 6.7. Here we have a balance of payments deficit and deflation. We assign monetary policy to external balance. The money supply is reduced and interest rates raised so that there is a capital inflow and the balance of payments deficit is reduced. We move toward external balance. At the same time, from C we adopt expansionary fiscal policy. G is increased, aggregate demand and national income rise. Hence, proper assignment of instrument to targets moves the economy toward internal balance and external balance.

Suppose, however, that the policy authorities carried out an incorrect assignment of instruments to targets. At C then monetary policy would be assigned the target of achieving internal balance. This would call for a *reduction* in the rate of interest to expand employment. This reduction in the rate of interest causes a capital outflow and exacerbates the problem of external imbalance. Further, fiscal policy is assigned the task of attaining external balance. To reduce imports national income has to be reduced by reducing government expenditure or increasing taxes. This policy, by reducing aggregate demand, further exacerbates the problem of deflation.

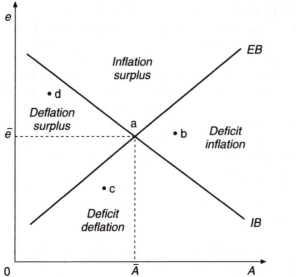

Figure 6.8

Thus by wrong assignment of policy to target we get further and further away from simultaneous internal and external balance.

The student should carry out similar exercises of proper assignment in each of the disequilibrium zones. Proper assignment of instruments to targets is extremely important.

THE ASSIGNMENT PROBLEM WITH FLEXIBLE EXCHANGE RATES

In a world with flexible exchange rates one need not have to adjust the interest rate to get balance of payments equilibrium. As a matter of fact, if world financial markets are highly integrated, a country may have only limited control over its interest rate.

In such a situation we may recast the assignment problem somewhat. The policy targets are the same as before; however, the policy instruments are different. They are now the exchange rate (e) and domestic absorption (A), which is equal to $C + I + G$. The options available to policy makers are shown in Figure 6.8. At point a we have simultaneous internal and external balance. Now suppose the economy finds itself at point b, where, at the same exchange rate $\bar{e}$, domestic absorption is higher – higher domestic absorption than that required to maintain internal balance means that there are inflationary pressures. If foreign currency were to become cheaper (e were to fall) foreign goods would become cheaper in the home currency and home goods would become more expensive in terms of the foreign currency. Hence exports will fall and imports will rise, thus reducing aggregate demand and inflationary pressures. Hence the internal balance schedule in *e, A* space is downward sloping. To the right of IB at any exchange rate domestic absorption is too high so there are inflationary pressures. To the left of IB there are deflationary pressures.

Let us now go back to point *b* and compare it, once again, with point *a*. At *b*, because national income is higher than full employment (at exchange rate $\bar{e}$), imports will be too high and a balance of payments deficit will ensue. If foreign currency is made more expensive (*e* is raised) exports will become cheaper in foreign currency and imports will become more expensive in terms of the home currency. Hence balance of payments equilibrium will be restored. Thus the *EB* schedule – the locus of *e, A* combinations giving external balance – will be upward sloping. To the right of EB at any exchange rate domestic absorption and, hence, imports, are too high so that there must be a balance of payments deficit. To the left of EB there must be a balance of payments surplus. The disequilibrium zones are labelled in Figure 6.8.

To compare the problem in a flexible exchange rate regime with that in a fixed exchange rate regime, let us go to point c in Figure 6.8 where there is a balance of payments deficit and deflation. To cure the deficit the value of *e* can be allowed to rise. This also helps internal balance – with a higher value of *e, ceteris paribus*, exports should rise and imports fall. To attain internal balance *A* should go up. At *d* one could reduce *e* and increase *A*. A proper assignment of policies would, once again, be to alter *e* to attain external balance and to alter *A* to attain internal balance.

DISCRETE ADJUSTMENT

Policy adjustment, as postulated in the solution to the assignment problem, is smooth and continuous. Monetary policy is capable of being continuously adjusted, but a smooth road to equilibrium is not always possible because the effects of monetary policy are not entirely predictable and subject to variable lags. Fiscal policies can be changed only discontinuously.

We may illustrate problems raised by discrete or stepwise adjustment. In Figure 6.9 we consider the case of unstable discrete adjustment and in Figure 6.10 that of discrete stable adjustment.

Let us start from a_1 in Figure 6.9. We have external balance and deflation. To cure the deflation absorption is increased. We reach internal balance at a_2 but we have a deficit in the balance of payments. To cure the deficit *e* is raised and so on. As illustrated in Figure 6.9 these oscillations are unstable. We follow the same sequence of steps in Figure 6.10 but the adjustment is now stable.

From Figures 6.9 and 6.10 it is clear that whether discontinuous adjustment is unstable depends on the magnitude of the (absolute value of the) slopes of the IB and EB schedules. To see this formally let us write the internal balance as

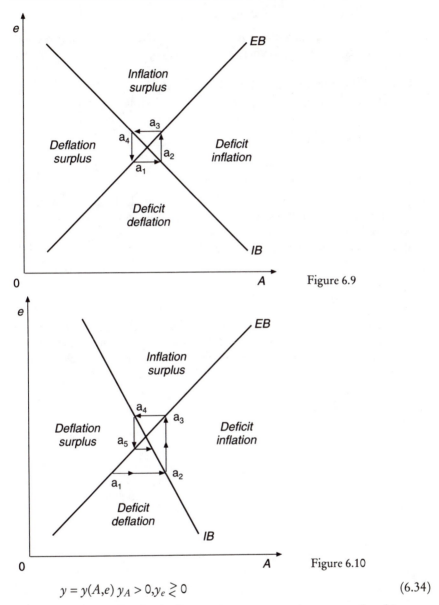

Figure 6.9

Figure 6.10

$$y = y(A,e) \; y_A > 0, y_e \gtrless 0 \tag{6.34}$$

and let y_f be the target level of income. Now $y_A > 0$ because national income rises when absorption rises, but the sign of y_e is uncertain. It could be positive if a rise in the exchange rate raises national income (by raising exports and lowering imports). But the opposite can be true if the demand for imports is inelastic with respect to price.

External balance may be written as

$$B = B(A,e) \qquad B_A < 0, B_e > 0 \qquad (6.35)$$

with B_f as the target current account surplus. A rise in absorption reduces the current account surplus, whereas a rise in the price of foreign exchange increases it.

Totally differentiating equations (6.34) and (6.35) gives the slopes of the IB and EB schedules; $y_A dA + y_e de = 0$ and $B_A dA + B_e de = 0$, so that

$$\left(\frac{de}{dA}\right)_{IB} = \frac{-y_A}{y_e} \gtrless 0 \qquad (6.36)$$

$$\left(\frac{de}{dA}\right)_{EB} = \frac{-B_A}{B_e} > 0 \qquad (6.37)$$

If $y_e > 0$ then IB slopes downwards in the eA plane. In Figures 6.8 and 6.9 we have assumed $y_e > 0$. We shall continue to assume this.

We have been assuming that adjustment in absorption and exchange rate are discontinuous. We may assume that these changes take place in the following manner,

$$\Delta A_t = k_1 (\bar{A} - A_t) \qquad (6.38)$$
$$\Delta e_t = k_2 (\bar{e} - e_t) \qquad (6.39)$$

where $\bar{A}$ and $\bar{e}$ are the levels of absorption and exchange rate consistent with simultaneous internal and external balance. It is assumed that correct assignment requires absorption to target internal balance and exchange rate policy to target external balance. Let us write

$$\bar{A} = a + e_t \qquad (6.40)$$
$$\bar{e} = c + dA_t \qquad (6.41)$$

Now,

$$\frac{1}{b} = \frac{-y_A}{y_e} < 0 \qquad (6.42)$$

$$d = \frac{-B_A}{B_e} > 0 \qquad (6.43)$$

Now

$$\Delta A_t = A_{t+1} - A_t \qquad (6.44)$$

and

$$\Delta e_t = e_{t+1} - e_t \qquad (6.45)$$

Substitute equations (6.44), (6.45), (6.41) and (6.40) into equations (6.38) and (6.39) to get

$$A_{t+1} - A_t = k_1(a + be_t - A_t) \qquad (6.46)$$

$$e_{t+1} - e_t = k_2(c + dA_t - e_t) \qquad (6.47)$$

which is a set of homogeneous, linear, non-homogeneous difference equations. Assume policy attempts to reach its target in one time period so that $k_1 = k_2 = 1$. Substitute (6.47) into (6.46) to eliminate e_t. Similarly substitute equation (6.46) into (6.47) to write

$$A_{t+1} = a + bc + bd\,A_{t-1} \tag{6.48}$$

$$e_{t+1} = c + da + bd\,e_{t-1} \tag{6.49}$$

These equations are linear second-order non-homogeneous difference equations. Notice that the coefficient of A_{t-1} in equation (6.48) is bd and that the coefficient of e_{t-1} in equation (6.49) is also bd.

To eliminate the constant terms and make the equations homogeneous we define

$$A_t = U_t + \tilde{A} \tag{6.50}$$

$$e_t = V_t + \tilde{e} \tag{6.51}$$

Substituting these into equations (6.48) and (6.49) we have

$$U_{t+1} + \tilde{A} = a + bc + bd(U_{t-1} + \tilde{A}) \tag{6.52}$$

$$V_{t+1} + \tilde{e} = c + da + bd(V_{t-1} + \tilde{e}) \tag{6.53}$$

In equilibrium U_t and V_t are zero so that equilibrium values are

$$\tilde{A} = \frac{a + bc}{1 - bd} \tag{6.54}$$

$$\tilde{e} = \frac{c + da}{1 - bd} \tag{6.55}$$

Substituting equations (6.54) and (6.55) into equations (6.52) and (6.53) we have

$$U_{t+1} = bdU_{t-1} \tag{6.56}$$

$$V_{t+1} = bdV_{t-1} \tag{6.57}$$

We try a solution like $U_t = Z_1\lambda^t$ and $V_t = Z_2\lambda^t$ in equations (6.56) and (6.57) to get $Z_1\lambda^{t+1} = bdZ_1\lambda^{t-1}$ and $Z_2\lambda^{t+1} = bdZ_1\lambda^{t-1}$ so that the characteristic equation is $\lambda^2 - bd = 0$ giving us roots $\lambda_1 = (bd)^{1/2}$ and $\lambda_2 = -(bd)^{1/2}$ which are equal but of opposite sign. We may write the complete solution as

$$A_t = \tilde{A} + Z_{11}[(bd)^{1/2}]^t + Z_{12}[-(bd)^{1/2}]^t \tag{6.58}$$

and

$$e_t = \tilde{e} + Z_{21}[(bd)^{1/2}]^t + Z_{22}[-(bd)^{1/2}]^t \tag{6.59}$$

If $y_e > 0$, bd would be positive and $(bd)^{1/2}$ would be real. The sign of $[(bd)^{1/2}]^t$ would be positive and the sign of $[-(bd)^{1/2}]^t$ would alternate between positive and negative values. Since neither root is dominant the system would oscillate.

Stability of equilibrium requires the roots to be between -1 and $+1$. Therefore $|(bd)^{1/2}| < 1$ whence $|bd| < 1$ so that stability requires $|d| < |1/b|$. Now $|d|$ is the absolute value of the slope of the external balance schedule and $|1/b|$ is the absolute value of the slope of IB. Hence stability would require the IB schedule to be steeper than the EB schedule. If not, the assignment of policies to targets is incorrect and destabilising and must be reversed.

When $y_e > 0$ the IB schedule is negatively sloped. Hence $bd < 0$ and $(bd)^{1/2}$ is a complex number. We can write the complex conjugates as

$$\lambda_1 = \alpha + \beta i = 0 + (-bd)^{1/2} (-1)^{1/2} \tag{6.60}$$

$$\lambda_2 = \alpha - \beta i = 0 - (bd)^{1/2} (-1)^{1/2} \tag{6.61}$$

where $i = (-1)^{1/2}$, α is the real part of the complex root and βi is the imaginary part. The solutions are now

$$A_t = \tilde{A} + Z_{11}(\alpha + \beta i)^t + Z_{12}(\alpha - \beta i)^t \tag{6.62}$$

$$e_t = \tilde{e} + Z_{21}(\alpha + \beta i)^t + Z_{22} (\alpha - \beta i)^t \tag{6.63}$$

Define the modulus of the complex roots as $M = (\alpha^2 + \beta^2)^{1/2}$, $\alpha = M \cos \theta$, $\beta = M \sin \theta$, $A_t = \tilde{A} + Z_{11}(M \cos \theta + Mi \sin \theta)^t + Z_{12}(M \cos \theta - Mi \sin \theta)^t$. We may factor M^t from the term in parentheses and use DeMoivre's theorem which states that $(\cos \theta + i \sin \theta)^t = \cos(\theta t) + i \sin(\theta t)$ to get $A_t = \tilde{A} + M^t[S_1 \cos(\theta t) + S_2 \sin(\theta t)]$. The term in parentheses is an oscillating wave with constant amplitude. The growth or diminution of the cycles depends on M^t. But $M^t = (\alpha^2 + \beta^2)^t$ so that stability depends on whether M is greater or less than one. The difference equation would be stable if the modulus of the complex roots are within the unit circle of the complex plane, i.e. $1 > \alpha^2 + \beta^2 = -bd$, or $d < |1/b|$. Hence stability requires that the absolute value of the slope of IB be greater than the slope of EB as in Figure 6.10.

Hence we realise that when policy adjustments are discrete, the attainment of stability depends on the relative slopes of the IB and EB schedules.

THE ASSIGNMENT PROBLEM IN DEVELOPING COUNTRIES

We now attempt to analyse the assignment problem within the context of a 'typical' developing country. Our assumptions will reflect some stylised facts about developing countries. We assume that international capital mobility to and from the developing country is low. We shall also assume that the developing country in question is a small open economy. Our analysis here will follow the work of Salter (1959), Hansen (1973) and Prachowny (1984). A mathematical derivation appears in the appendix.

Since the terms of trade cannot be affected it is possible to collapse exports and imports into one traded good called, simply, 'tradable'. There is another good which is called 'non-tradable'. The supply of tradable and

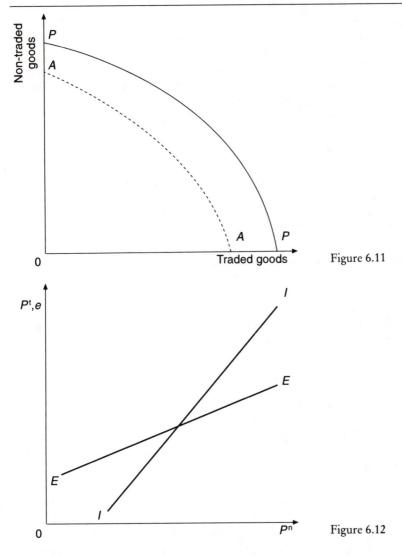

Figure 6.11

Figure 6.12

non-tradable goods depends on their relative prices and, in some instances, upon the supply of real cash balances (Chapter 3).

The domestic economy is highly distorted so that actual production possibilities are less than potential. In Figure 6.11 PP is the potential production possibility frontier between tradables and non-tradables and AA is the actual production possibility frontier.

Domestic demand for each of these two goods depends on relative prices, real income and money balances. The price of non-tradables adjusts quickly to equate the domestic demand and supply of non-tradables. The domestic price of tradables is given by their world price multiplied by the nominal exchange rate. We also assume that net exports always adjust immediately to the excess of domestic production over consumption of the traded good.

We can depict internal and external balance for this economy as follows. In Figure 6.12 we measure the price of tradables (P^t) and the nominal exchange rate (e) on the vertical axis. On the horizontal axis we measure the price of non-tradables (P^n). Internal balance requires equality of supply and demand for the non-tradable good since the assumed infinite elasticity of foreign demand means that imbalances in the market for tradables can easily be resolved. We depict the internal balance as II in Figure 6.12. As P^n rises demand for non-tradables falls and supply rises. This excess supply manifests itself, by Walras' law, as excess demand for tradables. If P^t rises this disequilibrium will be eliminated. Hence II must be upward sloping.

The external balance line EE along which the traded goods sector is in equilibrium is also upward sloping. A rise in the price of tradables leads to an excess supply of tradables or, equivalently, an excess demand for non-tradables. This can be eliminated if P^n rises.

It can be shown that the slope of II is greater than one whereas the slope of EE is less than one. A proportional increase in both prices around a 45° line from the origin would leave relative prices and, hence, supplies unchanged. However, the increase in price would lower the real value of money balances and, therefore, demand. Equilibrium in the market for tradables requires that the price of non-tradables should rise *less* than proportionately in order to maintain equilibrium in the market for non-tradable goods. Similarly the price of tradables should rise *more* than proportionately to maintain equilibrium in the market for tradable goods. Hence the II schedule is steeper than the EE schedule.

Figure 6.12 assumes that exchange rates are flexible. Exchange rates can be pegged if the government allows reserve movements (an outflow in the case of a balance of payments deficit and an inflow in the case of a balance of payments surplus) or borrowing. In such cases the EE schedule no longer determines the external balance. The external balance will be given by a horizontal line whose vertical intercept is equal to the value at which the nominal exchange rate is fixed. Domestic prices of tradables are simply equal to the nominal exchange rate multiplied by the world price of these goods.

INTERNAL AND EXTERNAL BALANCES: RESPONSE TO SHOCKS

First, suppose there is an adverse supply shock at home – say a crop failure. We analyse this situation in Figure 6.13. A crop failure will raise the price of non-tradables for every value of P^t. The II schedule, therefore, shifts to the right. The external balance schedule remains undisturbed because of the SOE assumption. With flexible exchange rates the domestic currency would depreciate from A to B. The price of the non-traded good rises more than

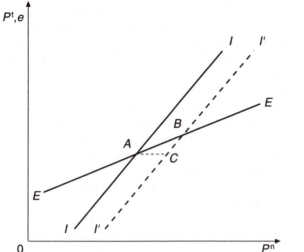

Figure 6.13

the price of the tradables and the consumption of foreign goods rises and more resources are transferred to the production of non-tradables. If the supply shock is expected to be temporary a more appropriate policy would be to hold the exchange rate pegged at its value at A. This would hold down the domestic price of tradables and reduce hardship in the economy. The economy would move from A to C where there is a balance of payments deficit (since C is below the flexible exchange rate EE schedule). This deficit could be covered by temporary borrowings.

Now, let us examine the case where there is a difference between domestic and world rates of inflation. This means that the price of tradables rises for every P^n. This would mean that the EE schedule would shift up and the real exchange rate will drop.

If the exchange rate were kept pegged the rise in domestic prices of traded goods would generate a surplus in the balance of payments, leading to reserve gains and monetary expansion.

We now consider the case of changes in the terms of trade. A change in the terms of trade changes the definition of the traded good. Consider, first, a rise in import prices. The supply of foreign exchange is reduced as supply shifts from exportables to importables. The demand for foreign exchange rises or falls according to whether the demand for imports is inelastic or elastic since the supply of imports is, by assumption, infinitely elastic.

If the demand is inelastic the exchange rate depreciates, further raising the home price of imports and that of exportables. This will lead to a shift of supply toward production of tradables. This will lead to a rise in the price of non-tradables as well. The extent of this rise depends upon the strength of the complementarity/substitutability between the two goods. With pegged exchange rates and an inelastic demand for imports, all prices would rise less, since the depreciation of the currency is avoided (or postponed).

If the import demand is sufficiently elastic to overcome the reduction in export supply, the exchange rate appreciates, reducing the magnitude of the increase in import prices and lowering the domestic price of exports. The price of non-traded goods rises by less than in the inelastic case (if at all). Pegged exchange rates would cause import prices to rise more and prevent export prices from falling.

Now let us consider a fall in export prices. The reduction in foreign exchange earnings will result in a depreciation of the exchange rate, partially offsetting the reduced domestic price of exports and raising the price of importables. The price of non-traded goods may rise or fall, depending upon the strength of the substitution toward exportables and away from imports. Pegged exchange rates would eliminate the depreciation, so that import prices would not rise. In this case, demand would shift toward exportables and supply toward non-tradables, reducing the price of non-tradables.

EXCHANGE RATE POLICIES FOR DEVELOPING COUNTRIES

We have examined the impact of various shocks on the internal and external balance. The economy is subject to various shocks from time to time. The optimal exchange rate policy, from a stabilisation point of view, depends on the type of shock to which the economy is most frequently exposed. For example, if most shocks are generated by changes in the level of world prices relative to domestic prices, the goals of external and internal balance will be served best by a flexible exchange rate policy, as it will tend to insulate domestic prices from the effects of fluctuations in world prices. For example, in Figure 6.14 a country with no net capital imports is faced with random fluctuations in world prices. A flexible exchange rate could allow the EE curve to remain unaffected by world price fluctuations. But a pegged exchange rate policy would cause domestic prices of tradables to fluctuate from, say, GG to G'G' so that prices, including those of non-tradables, would fluctuate from D to J.

If, however, most shocks come from temporary fluctuations in harvests or other domestic production, a pegged exchange-rate policy achieved by use of borrowing from abroad is optimal. In Figure 6.15 we consider fluctuations in domestic production of non-traded goods. Price fluctuations will be substantially reduced by pegging the exchange rate at the level indicated by the line GG since the range is reduced from LL to MM. If most shocks come from fluctuations in the terms of trade the situation is more complex.

APPENDIX: MODEL OF INTERNAL AND EXTERNAL BALANCE

Domestic demand for traded and non-traded goods depend on relative prices, real income and real money balances. Net exports of tradables (X)

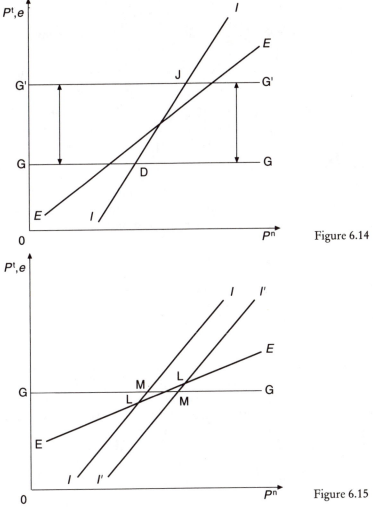

Figure 6.14

Figure 6.15

are equal to the excess of domestic production over consumption. We describe these conditions in equations (A6.1) and (A6.2) respectively.

$$D^n \; (\overset{+}{p^t}, \overset{-}{p^n}, \overset{+}{pY}, \overset{+}{M}) = S^n \; (\overset{-}{p^t}, \overset{+}{p^n}) \tag{A6.1}$$

$$D^t \; (\overset{-}{p^t}, \overset{+}{p^n}, \overset{+}{pY}, \overset{+}{M}) + X = S^n \; (\overset{+}{p^t}, \overset{-}{p^n}) \tag{A6.2}$$

where D^i, S^i represent, respectively, the demand and supply of commodity i, $(i = n, t)$, Y is real income, p is the aggregate price level and M is the nominal stock of money. These functions are assumed to be differentiable and homogeneous of degree zero in the nominal variables (p^t, p^n, pY, M). The signs of the partial derivatives are given below the arguments. Money income (pY) is equal to the factor cost of production plus the excess of government spending $(\bar{G})$ over taxes $(\bar{T})$. Thus

$$pY = p^t S^t + p^n S^n + \bar{G} - \bar{T} \qquad (A6.3)$$

The price level is a weighted average of the prices of tradables and non-tradables,

$$p = \alpha^t p^t + \alpha^n p^n \qquad (A6.4)$$

with α^t, $\alpha^n > 0$ and $\alpha^t + \alpha^n = 1$.

We can write the balance of payments as the domestic value of changes in foreign reserves (ΔF), being equal to the sum of net exports ($p^t X$) and exogenous net capital imports ($\bar{K}$) valued at the current exchange rate (e), i.e.

$$\Delta F = p^t X + e\bar{K} \qquad (A6.5)$$

We assume that all foreign exchange is held by the central bank and that change in the domestic money supply (ΔM) is equal to foreign-exchange accumulation plus the government deficit plus credit granted to domestic business ($\Delta \bar{L}$):

$$\Delta M = \Delta F + \bar{G} - \bar{T} + \Delta \bar{L} \qquad (A6.6)$$

Finally the domestic price of tradable goods is equal to the exogenous world price of tradables p^{ft} times the value of the world currency in terms of the home currency. Thus foreign demand for tradables is infinitely elastic:

$$p^t = p^{ft} e \qquad (A6.7)$$

Under pegged exchange rates the value of e is fixed and these seven equations suffice to determine the seven variables p^t, p^n, p, Y, M, X and F. The solution of this model in the case of flexible rates is also quite similar. Since $\Delta F = 0$, from equation (A6.6), the money stock is an exogenous variable controlled by the central bank. Net exports must equal the value of capital outflow ($X = -K/p^{ft}$). Then equation (A6.3) can be substituted into (A6.1) and (A6.2) for money income, leaving two equations in two unknowns, the price of tradables (or, equivalently, the exchange rate) and non-tradables.

7

Current account and asset demand approaches to balance of payments

INTRODUCTION

We have examined the effects of expansionary monetary and fiscal policies on macroeconomic equilibrium. In other words, we have examined the effects of policies that change aggregate expenditure. In addition to such policies there is another set of policies that is often available to the policy makers. This set is called the set of expenditure switching policies. Such policies include exchange rate adjustment (devaluation or revaluation), import controls, tariffs and the like. We saw in Chapter 6 that, in a flexible exchange rate regime, expansionary monetary and fiscal policies had implications for exchange rate adjustment.

In a fixed exchange rate regime, exchange rate adjustment often becomes necessary to meet policy objectives. To see this, let us suppose we live in a world of fixed exchange rates and the policy authorities wish to maintain full employment (internal balance) and balance of trade equilibrium (external balance). (We specifically abstract from capital account considerations.) Suppose further that the economy is facing unemployment and a balance of trade deficit. Expansionary aggregate demand policies would increase employment and real income. As real income expands, imports rise. However, with a fixed exchange rate and fixed domestic and foreign price levels, exports do not change. Hence the balance of trade worsens. In this kind of situation the goals of internal and external balance are in conflict with each other. Aggregate demand or expenditure changing policies are going to be inadequate. If this economy could devalue its currency and pursue expansionary aggregate demand policies it could simultaneously attain internal and external balance. The devaluation would encourage exports and discourage imports and the expansionary aggregate demand policy would increase real income.

We also saw in Chapter 6 that, in many situations, it is not possible to pursue the objectives of external and internal balance with just expenditure changing as the policy instrument. Expenditure switching is also often necessary. For developing countries expenditure switching often takes the form of devaluation.

In this chapter we examine the extant theories of devaluation as they apply to developed countries. In Chapters 9 and 11 we shall study some integrated models of balance of payments adjustment in developing countries. Criticisms of the standard approach to less developed country (LDC) devaluation will be taken up in Chapter 12.

Even if (occasional) exchange rate adjustment is allowed for, does it necessarily follow that a devaluation will necessarily reduce the balance of payments deficit of a country? A clear answer to this question is terribly important for a country contemplating exchange rate adjustments in a world of fixed exchange rates. The currencies of several developing countries are tied to a major international currency or a basket of such international currencies. Hence the above question remains significant for developing countries even in a flexible exchange rate regime. Two different approaches were developed to answer this query. One of them (the elasticity approach) focuses on the terms of trade effect of a devaluation. The second (the absorption approach) concentrates on the income–expenditure effects of a devaluation. We shall consider each of them in turn. Later we shall examine broader approaches to devaluation – those that combine current and capital account concerns.

THE ELASTICITY APPROACH TO DEVALUATION

The elasticity approach is the oldest modern approach to analysing the effects of a devaluation. We are here interested in finding out whether a devaluation increases earnings of foreign exchange. If it does, then a devaluation would be considered beneficial, otherwise it would not.

Write the net exports in foreign exchange ($ terms) as

$$NX^* = X^* - Z^* \tag{7.1}$$

where NX^* is net exports in dollar terms, X^* and Z^* are, respectively, exports and imports in dollar terms.

Totally differentiating gives

$$dNX^* = dX^* - dZ^* \tag{7.1a}$$

Write $X^* = p_f x$, where p_f is the dollar price of exports and x is the physical quantity of exports, and define p_d as the home price of exports so that $p_d = e p_f$ where e is the exchange rate.

Exports are bought by foreign nationals, so that elasticity of demand for exports (η_x) must be stated in terms of dollar prices, i.e.

$$\eta_x = \frac{-dx/x}{dp_f/p_f} \tag{7.2}$$

Since exports are supplied by the home country so the elasticity of supply of exports must be defined in terms of home (rupee) prices. Therefore, the elasticity of supply of exports with respect to price (S_x) is given by

$$S_x = \frac{dx/x}{dp_d/p_d} \qquad (7.3)$$

From $p_d = ep_f$ we get

$$\frac{dp_d}{p_d} = \frac{de}{e} + \frac{dp_f}{p_f} \qquad (7.4)$$

Substitute this into the expression for S_x to get

$$S_x = \frac{dx/x}{dp_f/p_f + de/e} \qquad (7.5)$$

Equation (7.5) expresses supply elasticities in terms of foreign prices and the exchange rate. From equation (7.2) we can write

$$\frac{dx}{x} = -\eta_x \frac{dp_f}{p_f} \qquad (7.6)$$

Substitute this into equation (7.5) to get

$$\frac{dp_f}{p_f} = \frac{-S_x}{\eta_x + S_x} \frac{de}{e} < 0 \qquad (7.7)$$

if $de/e > 0$, i.e. if there is a devaluation of the home currency. Substitute this into equation (7.2) to calculate the proportionate change in the quantity of exports as

$$\frac{dx}{x} = \frac{\eta_x S_x}{\eta_x + S_x} \frac{de}{e} > 0 \qquad (7.8)$$

if $de/e > 0$, i.e. if there is a devaluation.

Equation (7.7) shows that dp_f/p_f is negative. The foreign price of exports, therefore, falls. Adding the proportionate change in foreign price to the proportionate change in quantity given the proportionate change in the value of exports we get

$$\frac{dx^*}{x^*} = \frac{dp_f}{p_f} + \frac{dx}{x} \qquad (7.9)$$

This will be positive if the proportionate rise in quantity exceeds the proportionate decline in price. Substituting from equation (7.7) and equation (7.8) into equation (7.9) we get

$$\frac{dx^*}{x^*} = \frac{S_x(\eta_x - 1)}{\eta_x + S_x} \frac{de}{e} \qquad (7.10)$$

as the proportionate change in the value of exports. If we divide both sides of equation (7.10) by de/e we shall get the elasticity of supply of foreign exchange with respect to the exchange rate as $S_x(\eta_x - 1)/(\eta_x + S_x)$. This elasticity is positive if the demand for exports is elastic. In Figure 7.1 we plot

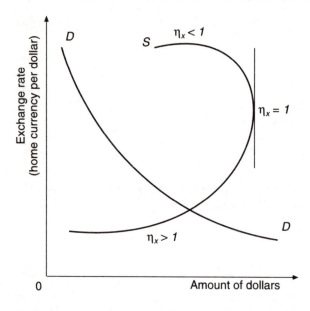

Figure 7.1

the demand and supply of dollars. Equation (7.10) tells us that the supply schedule is upward sloping. If $\eta_x < 1$ the supply curve will be downward sloping.

The supply of foreign exchange would be constant if the elasticity of supply is zero, i.e. $S_x = 0$. In this case, the domestic price of exports rises in direct proportion to devaluation, i.e. there is no decline in the dollar price of exports and, therefore, no increase in the volume of exports.

Further, if η_x is high it would be advantageous to have a high S_x. But if η_x is low, it would be better to have a low S_x so as to minimise the reduction in foreign exchange earnings.

In the ultra Keynesian case, if $S_x = \infty$ the elasticity of supply of foreign exchange with respect to the exchange rate is $\eta_x - 1$. Devaluation increases foreign exchange earnings if $\eta_x > 1$, but decreases foreign exchange earnings if $\eta_x < 1$.

Now let us look at imports. The value of imports in dollar terms is

$$Z^* = p_F z \tag{7.11}$$

where z is the physical volume of imports and p_F is the foreign price of imports. The domestic price of imports is p_D. We define

$$\eta_z = \frac{-dz/z}{dp_D/p_D} \qquad \text{domestic price elasticity of demand for imports}$$

$$S_z = \frac{dz/z}{dp_D/p_D} \qquad \text{foreign price elasticity of supply of imports}$$

$$p_D = e p_F$$

From equation (7.11) it follows that

$$\frac{dZ^*}{Z^*} = \frac{dz}{z} + \frac{dp_F}{p_F} \tag{7.12}$$

From $p_D = e p_F$ we have that

$$\frac{dp_D}{p_D} = \frac{de}{e} + \frac{dp_F}{p_F} \tag{7.13}$$

Using equation (7.13) and the definitions of the elasticities

$$S_z = \frac{dz/z}{dp_F/p_F} \qquad \eta_z = \frac{-dz/z}{dp_F/p_F - de/e}$$

we have that

$$\frac{dz}{z} = \frac{-S_z\eta_z}{\eta_z + S_z} \frac{de}{e} < 0 \tag{7.14a}$$

$$\frac{dp_F}{p_F} = \frac{-\eta_z}{\eta_z + S_z} \frac{de}{e} < 0 \tag{7.14b}$$

From equation (7.14) we have that devaluation reduces both the physical volume of imports and the foreign price of imports so that the value of imports must decline. Substituting the results in equation (7.14) into (7.12) yields

$$\frac{dZ^*}{Z^*} = \frac{-\eta_z (1 + S_z)}{\eta_z + S_z} \frac{de}{e} < 0 \tag{7.15}$$

Hence, devaluation reduces the value of imports and the demand for foreign exchange. The demand curve for foreign exchange, therefore, is, negatively sloped throughout as shown in Figure 7.1. Substituting from equations (7.15) and (7.10) into equation (7.1a) we get the overall balance of trade measured in foreign currency

$$NX^* = \left[X^* \frac{S_x (\eta_x - 1)}{\eta_x + S_x} + Z^* \frac{\eta_z (1 + S_z)}{\eta_z + S_z} \right] \frac{de}{e} \tag{7.16}$$

This is the final expression for the effect of devaluation on net foreign exchange earnings.

A much discussed special case arises when supply elasticities are infinite and trade is initially balanced ($X^* = Z^*$). Then equation (7.16) reduces to

$$dNX^* = X^*(\eta_x + \eta_z - 1) \frac{de}{e} \tag{7.17}$$

For $dNX^* > 0$ it is necessary that $\eta_x + \eta_z > 1$, i.e. the sum of the elasticity of demand for exports and the elasticity of demand for imports should exceed unity. This is the so-called Marshall–Lerner condition.

To summarise then, devaluation is seen by foreign purchasers as an increase in supply. The foreign price drops and the quantity of exports increases. But if the elasticity of supply of exports is infinite there is no increase in the domestic price of exports despite rise in demand. The foreign price of exports must, therefore, drop in proportion to the devaluation. The elasticity of the supply of foreign exchange with respect to the exchange rate, therefore, is exactly the same as the elasticity of demand for exports.

The devaluation is seen by importers as a reduction in supply. The domestic price of imports rises and the volume of imports falls. But if the elasticity of supply of imports is infinite, the additional demand causes no change in the foreign price of imports. Hence the domestic price of imports rises in the same proportion as the proportionate rise in the exchange rate. The elasticity of demand for foreign exchange then equals the elasticity of demand for imports.

Another relevant small country assumption is infinite elasticity of supply of imports. The domestic economy's demand for imports may be too small to affect world demand and price. On the export side it sells in a competitive world market, so the amount it sells has no effect on the world price. So far as the domestic economy is concerned the elasticity of demand for exports, η_x, is infinite. Then $dNX^* = (X^*S_x + Z^*\eta_x)(de/e)$, or, if trade is initially balanced,

$$dNX^* = X^*(S_x + \eta_z)\frac{de}{e} > 0 \tag{7.18}$$

In this case devaluation is bound to increase net foreign exchange earnings. The devaluation expands export sales without reducing the foreign price of exports and reduces imports at a fixed foreign price.

As one can imagine, a great deal of time and effort has been expended by economists to measure the supply and demand elasticities for exports and imports. An important difficulty in assessing the effects of devaluation on net exports is that it takes time for trade flows to adjust to relative price changes. In other words, elasticities are low in the short run and increase as time elapses after the relative price change.

A recent very significant illustration of this fact is the oil crisis of 1972–73. The price of fuel oil quadrupled overnight. Elasticity of demand was very low initially. Many countries spent large amounts on the import of oil and this reduced demand for other goods. The world economy slipped into a recession. Over time, however, the elasticity of demand for oil increased. Industries and households learnt to economise on the use of oil. OPEC certainly is not as powerful today as it was in 1972–73.

The analysis suggests that the time pattern of foreign exchange earnings in response to a devaluation may therefore follow a J curve, first declining and then rising. This is shown in Figure 7.2. At time t_1 the devaluation occurs. Foreign exchange earnings first fall and then rise.

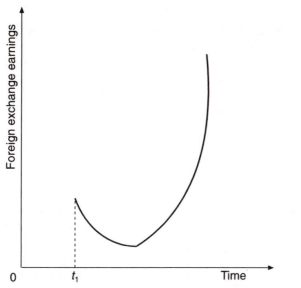

Figure 7.2

The J curve describes the time pattern of the balance of trade following a devaluation. The pattern of the effect of the devaluation on domestic absorption can also be similar. To continue with the example of the quadrupling of oil prices in 1973, initially consumers of imported oil found themselves spending a larger proportion of their incomes on imported oil. Thus the demand for domestic goods (i.e. absorption) falls. As substitutes are developed for oil, the proportion of income spent on imported oil falls and, hence, domestic absorption rises.

An obvious weakness of the elasticities approach is its failure to go beyond the foreign exchange market to the economy as a whole. This weakness leads directly to a discussion of the absorption approach to devaluation.

ABSORPTION APPROACH TO DEVALUATION

The absorption approach to devaluation also concentrates exclusively on the current account. This approach was launched by Sidney Alexander and further elaborated by Harry Johnson. Alexander criticised the elasticities approach for concentrating purely on the relative price effects of devaluation and neglecting the income effect. He defined domestic absorption (A) as consumption expenditure plus government expenditure:

$$A = C + I + G$$
$$Y = A + X - Z$$

so that

$$X - Z = Y - A \tag{7.19}$$

Net exports are then equal to national income minus domestic absorption. A devaluation can increase net exports only if it increased real income (Y) or reduced A. However, policy is complicated by the fact that what increases A often increases Y and a reduction in A often reduces Y.

To see this point more clearly, suppose I and G are fixed. Devaluation increases exports and reduces imports and hence increases aggregate demand. So $\Delta(X - Z) = \Delta Y - \Delta A$ and $\Delta A = c\Delta Y$, where c is the marginal propensity to consume. Hence

$$\Delta Y - \Delta A = (1 - c)\Delta Y = s\Delta Y \tag{7.20}$$

where s is the marginal propensity to save.

Equation (7.20) makes it clear that devaluation will increase net exports only in the event that additional income is saved. It does not help to raise production if the resulting increase in income simply raises consumption by an equal amount. Resources will be released to expand net exports only if the rise in income carries with it a rise in savings. This necessitates a positive marginal propensity to save. If income taxation exists, then it also helps, provided the government does not consume the tax receipts. These conditions are likely to be met in industrial countries but are less likely to be met in less developed nations.

The rise in real income that permitted net exports to expand was termed the *idle resource effect* by Alexander. However, one must subtract from this the loss in real income due to the deterioration in the terms of trade caused by a devaluation.

To understand this let us go back to equations (7.7) and (7.14) to get

$$\frac{dp_f}{dp_f} - \frac{dp_F}{p_F} = \left(\frac{-S_x}{\eta_x + S_x} - \frac{-\eta_z}{\eta_z + S_z} \right) \frac{de}{e} \tag{7.21}$$

as the difference between the change in the foreign price of exports and the foreign price of imports.

We know that equation (7.21) is negative. Hence

$$\frac{-S_x}{\eta_x + S_x} - \frac{-\eta_z}{\eta_z + S_z} < 0$$

or

$$\frac{S_x (\eta_z + S_z) - \eta_z(\eta_x + S_x)}{(\eta_x + S_x)(\eta_z + S_z)} > 0$$

Hence the terms of trade will deteriorate if $S_x S_z > \eta_z \eta_x$. Hence the product of the supply elasticities must exceed the product of the demand elasticities. The lower is η_x, the greater is the reduction in the foreign price of exports.

Similarly, a reduction in the elasticity of demand for imports, η_z, means a smaller fall in the price of imports. A country that is too small to influence the world price of its imports is bound to suffer a deterioration in the terms of trade when it devalues its currency.

The above suggests that there is a need to understand the terms of trade effect of devaluation within the absorption approach. We develop the following analysis. Write the macro equilibrium of the economy as

$$\left.\begin{array}{ll} y = C(y) + I(r) + G + X(e) - eZ(y,e) & \text{IS} \\ M_s = L(y,r) & \text{LM} \\ X(e) - eZ(y,e) + K(r) = 0 & \text{FB} \end{array}\right\} \tag{7.22}$$

We have put $p = p^* = 1$ without any loss of generality. Totally differentiating equation (7.22) we have

$$\left.\begin{array}{l} (S_y + eZ_y)dy - I_r dr - Hde = dG \\ L_y dy + L_r dr = dM_s \\ eZ_y dy - K_r dr - Hde = 0 \end{array}\right\} \tag{7.23}$$

where $S_y = 1 - C_y$ and $H = X_e - Z(y,e) - eZ_e$. Further, without loss of generality, assume $e = 1$. We can solve (7.21) to get

$$\begin{bmatrix} dy \\ dr \\ de \end{bmatrix} = \begin{bmatrix} HL_r/D & -H(I_r - K_r)/D & HL_r/D \\ HL_y/D & -HS_y/D & -HL_y/D \\ -(L_y K_r + L_r Z_y)/D & [K_r(S_y + Z_y) - I_r Z_y]/D & [-L_r(S_y + Z_y) + L_y I_r]/D \end{bmatrix} \begin{bmatrix} dG \\ dM_s \\ 0 \end{bmatrix} \tag{7.24}$$

where $D = -H(L_r S_y - L_y K_r + L_y I_r)$. Now $de/dG = -(L_y K_r + L_r Z_y)/D$ and $de/dM_s = [K_r(S_y + Z_y) - I_r Z_y]/D$. The signs of de/dG and de/dM_s depend on the sign of H. For de/dM_s to be positive H must be positive. Now $X_e = (e/X)(\partial X/\partial e)(X/e) = \eta_x(X/e)$ and $Z_e = (e/Z)(\partial Z/\partial e)(Z/e) = -\eta_z(Z/e)$, whence $H = X(\eta_x + \eta_z - 1)$. Hence for H to be positive the Marshall–Lerner condition must be satisfied. If $H > 0$ the elasticities analysis predicts a rise in net exports following a devaluation. This prediction will still be valid even when the adverse effect of income change on imports is taken into account.

Thus an approach that incorporates both relative price and absorption effects is desirable. Recognising this, Harry Johnson suggested a general theory of the balance of payments which says that, for deficit countries, an *expenditure switching* policy such as devaluation would have to be accompanied by *expenditure reducing* policies such as lowering monetary growth or reducing the budgetary deficit. The above analysis refers to a deficit country that is experiencing inflationary pressures. However, other kinds of disequilibria are also possible. These possibilities have been examined in Chapter 6.

Having said this, however, we must realise that although devaluation could improve the trade balance if the economy is at less than full employment, the prospects for successful devaluation are less favourable when the

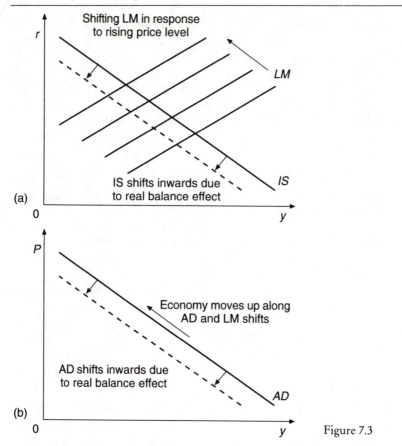

Figure 7.3

economy is already at full employment since total production cannot then be raised. A rise in net exports can then only be achieved by a reduction in absorption. Hence we must inquire whether devaluation can reduce absorption when the economy is already at full employment.

Devaluation tends to raise the home currency prices of both exports and imports. These price increases feed through the economy and are reflected in a rise in the general price level. This rise in the price level may have expenditure changing effects and thus may change absorption. Let us look at some of the expenditure changing effects of the price level increase following a devaluation.

THE KEYNES EFFECT

When the domestic price level rises, the real value of the economy's money supply falls and the LM schedule shifts inwards. In other words, we travel leftward along the aggregate demand schedule in Figure 7.3. This effect, however, keeps the IS schedule fixed.

THE REAL BALANCE EFFECT

If consumption expenditure depends upon the real value of cash balances then an increase in the price level will shift the IS curve (Figure 7.3). This will also result in a shift of the aggregate demand schedule as in Figure 7.3(b).

THE MONEY ILLUSION EFFECT

In countries with progressive income taxes based on personal money income, a rise in money income raises the average rate of income tax even if the rise in money income is caused entirely by inflation and not by a rise in real income. This will then reduce real after-tax disposable income and therefore depress consumption and absorption. This is due to the money illusion in the structure of income taxes, i.e. by the failure of the tax system to distinguish between a rise in real income and a rise in nominal income caused by inflation. The significance of this effect is likely to be less important in some developed countries where some indexation of income taxes to the price level is practiced. In developing countries such indexation is rare.

INFLATIONARY EXPECTATIONS EFFECT

The above three effects tend to reduce aggregate expenditure. However, there are some effects that tend to increase expenditure.

If people expect higher prices in the future they will engage in anticipatory buying, especially of durable goods, in order to beat the expected price increase. If this happens, absorption and import demand will rise. Devaluation is normally seen as a supply restraint on importers. The domestic price of imports rises and the quantity of imports is diminished. In the face of anticipatory buying, however, the demand curve for imports shifts to the right, adding to an increase in the price of imports as well as their prices. Foreign suppliers will see no reduction in demand and the foreign price of imports will not fall. Hence there will be no reduction in the amount of foreign exchange spent on imports.

On the export side, normally devaluation will raise the domestic price of exports, therefore providing an incentive for exporters and their suppliers to increase production. This may neutralise the price incentive supplied by devaluation.

THE EXCISE TAX EFFECT

Consider a developing economy that devalues its currency but discovers that the price elasticity of demand for imports is low. Combine this with the fact that this country is a small open economy so that a reduction in its demand for imports does not alter the world price of imports. Consequently the domestic price of imports rises by the same percentage as the percentage of devaluation. Hence the value of imports in home currency rises. Sometimes this increase can be very sharp.

Suppose now that the elasticity of demand for imports is low. The proportionate rise in the domestic price of imports vastly exceeds the proportionate reduction in the quantity imported. Hence more real income is spent on imports so that less income is available to be spent on other goods. This leads to a fall in output and employment. This effect has been highlighted by the structuralist school and will be considered in Chapter 12.

THE TERMS OF TRADE EFFECT

This works against the excise tax effect. Devaluation usually involves a worsening of the country's terms of trade. This reduces real income. This will increase the fraction of income consumed if the consumption function is of the form $C = a + by$ with $a > 0$. Hence real consumption in terms of domestic prices rise. Hence domestic absorption rises due to the change in the terms of trade.

The sum total of the expenditure changing effects of a devaluation in an economy that is close to full employment (or, more generally, an economy with low supply elasticities) depends on the relative strengths of all these effects.

MONETARY AND ASSET MARKET BALANCE APPROACHES TO BALANCE OF PAYMENTS

The approaches to the balance of payments that we have discussed so far have concentrated exclusively on the current account. To arrive at a more comprehensive understanding we must include the capital account into the analysis. There is also the possibility that some of the conclusions we derived within the context of the current account may not hold when we take the capital account into consideration. Furthermore, it can be argued that in these days of highly integrated capital markets capital account effects can, perhaps, occur faster than any effect that works its way through changes in the real national income. The monetary and asset market approaches, which we shall study now, have consistently denied any artificial segmentation of the balance of payments accounts. They have consistently argued in favour of treating the balance of payments as one analytical entity although distinctions between the current and capital accounts may be useful for some purposes. The principal difference between these two approaches lies in their treatment of the substitution possibilities in investors' portfolios between foreign and domestic assets. Whereas the monetary approach believes that foreign and domestic assets are perfect substitutes, the asset market approach treats domestic money, foreign assets and domestic bonds as imperfect substitutes.

Our analysis is expository in nature. In the next section we explore the monetary approach's analysis of balance of payments under fixed exchange rates. Next, we apply the monetary approach to a flexible exchange rate regime and also attempt to understand the 'overshooting' phenomenon. We then study the asset market balance approach of financial equilibrium under flexible exchange rates and, then, its explanation of the 'overshooting' phenomenon. The chapter ends with some concluding comments.

THE MONETARY APPROACH WITH FIXED EXCHANGE RATES

The monetary approach to the balance of payments rejects separate analysis of the current and capital accounts. It is a theory of the overall balance of payments. Let us write the overall balance of payments surplus as

$$X - Z + i^*I_f + K = \Delta R = \Delta M - \Delta D \tag{7.25}$$

where $X - Z$ is net imports, i^*I_f is investment income from abroad (i^* is the foreign interest rate and I_f is foreign investment by domestic residents) and K is the capital account surplus. The expression on the left-hand side of equation (7.25) is therefore the change in foreign reserves (ΔR). Additions to foreign exchange reserves and additions to domestic assets (ΔD) form the base for monetary expansion by the banking system (ΔM). Thus foreign and domestic assets are assumed to be perfect substitutes.

The monetary approach argues that, under fixed exchange rates, a balance of payments surplus implies an accumulation of foreign reserves which can serve as the basis for monetary expansion. Conversely, a balance of payments deficit implies a loss in foreign exchange reserves which, therefore, leads to monetary contraction. To the proponents of the monetary approach the most important implication of a balance of payments disequilibrium is its impact on the supply and demand for money in the economy. In line with its counterpart (monetarism) for the closed economy, the monetary approach to the balance of payments views the supply and demand for money as *the* most important behavioural relation in the economy. Other behavioural relations, like the consumption function, are relatively unimportant.

We can write from equation (7.25)

$$\Delta R + \Delta D = \Delta M \tag{7.26}$$

This is the fundamental equation of the monetary approach to the balance of payments. Money is created by expansion of domestic credit, ΔD, and by a balance of payments surplus, ΔR, since a surplus requires the monetary authority to purchase foreign exchange, thereby increasing money supply. If $\Delta M > \Delta D$ there must be a balance of payments surplus, because otherwise the supply of money cannot be brought into balance with the demand for money. Equation (7.26) also makes clear the key assumption of the monetary approach that domestic and foreign assets are perfect substitutes in investors' portfolios.

Consider now the nominal money demand function

$$M = L(Y, P, i) \qquad (7.27)$$

with $L_Y > 0$, $L_P > 0$, $L_i < 0$ (where i is the domestic rate of interest and Y is the level of real national income).

From equation (7.27) we can write

$$\Delta M = L_Y \Delta Y + L_P \Delta P + L_i \Delta i \qquad (7.28)$$

Equation (7.28) splits up changes in the demand for money into its various components. Hence we have

$$\Delta R = L_Y \Delta Y + L_P \Delta P + L_i \Delta i - \Delta D \qquad (7.29)$$

Hence a rise in income causes an increase in the demand for money and a surplus. A rise in the price level increases the demand for money and, hence, increases the surplus. A rise in the rate of interest reduces the demand for money and may, therefore, cause a deficit. A rise in domestic assets, *ceteris paribus*, reduces the need for foreign exchange and hence causes a deficit.

Realise that these predictions are exactly the opposite of those made by standard Keynesian theory. Keynesian theory would predict that (i) a rise in Y will increase imports and, therefore, cause a deficit, (ii) a rise in P would increase imports and cause a deficit, and (iii) a rise in i would increase capital inflows and hence cause a surplus. The monetary approach looks upon the balance of payments as a purely monetary phenomenon. Its break with Keynesian theory is fundamental and complete.

It must be said, however, that the monetary approach has an advantage over the Keynesian approach. In *flow* equilibrium, a current account surplus may be offset by a capital account deficit so that the balance of payments is not in equilibrium in the short run. However, this equilibrium cannot be maintained because a current account surplus implies that domestic residents are accumulating foreign IOUs. Hence their portfolios are undergoing continuous change and this will feed back into changes in the balance of payments. The monetary approach recognizes this *stock adjustment* and has, therefore, an advantage over the Keynesian approach.

We now undertake an analysis of the predictions of the monetary approach under fixed exchange rates. The monetary approach's analysis of the fixed exchange rate regime makes three key assumptions. First, it is assumed that there is perfect capital mobility. This is actually a consequence of the assumption that domestic and foreign assets are perfect substitutes. Domestic open market operations which involve the purchase and sale of domestic bonds for money have effects which are identical to purchases and sales of foreign assets. If the central bank buys bonds, D increases and so does M. If it buys foreign exchange, R increases and so does M. Since it is

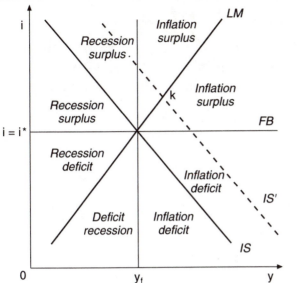

Figure 7.4

only the change in M that matters, open market operations and exchange rate stabilisation transactions are, in effect, identical. Hence $i = i^*$. Second, it is assumed that there is perfect arbitrage in commodity markets so that price levels world-wide are the same so long as we measure price levels in the same currency. In other words, we must have $P = eP^*$ where e is the nominal exchange rate and P^* is the foreign price level measured in foreign currency. This is also called 'the law of one price': the real exchange rate cannot be permanently altered. Third, it is assumed that wages and prices are flexible and will adjust to ensure that the economy equilibrates automatically (and always) at full employment. Competitive markets combined with the law of one price ensure market clearing because any excess supply of goods in the domestic market is absorbed in foreign markets. Thus aggregate expenditure expansion cannot raise the equilibrium level of real national income. Such increases can come about only through the expansion of aggregate supply by factors such as economic growth or productivity increases. Hence actual income $Y = Y_f$, where Y_f is the full employment level of output.

We can now analyse the implications of the monetary approach in the IS–LM–FB framework of Figure 7.4. In this diagram full employment income is labelled Y_f. To the right of Y_f we have inflationary pressures and to the left of Y_f we have recessionary tendencies. The FB schedule is horizontal at $i = i^*$, given the assumption of perfect capital mobility. Above FB we must have a balance of payments surplus, below FB there must be a deficit. In full equilibrium IS and LM intersect at Y_f.

Suppose that the foreign price level rises. Commodity arbitrage causes an immediate export surplus as domestic goods are diverted to foreign

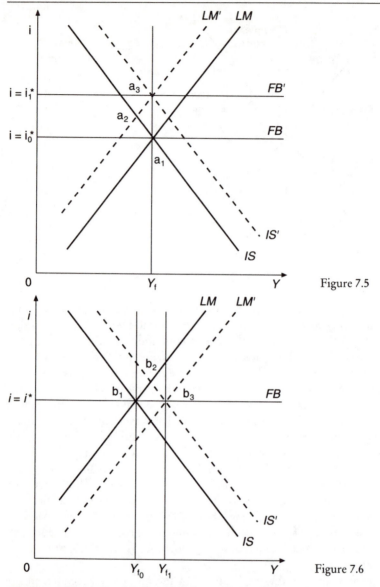

Figure 7.5

Figure 7.6

markets. This shifts the IS schedule to IS' in Figure 7.4. 'Domestic' equilibrium occurs at k. At k the domestic price level starts rising. This would shift the LM schedule leftward. However, at k there is also a balance of payments surplus which implies that reserves are being accumulated. This would shift the LM curve rightward. On balance, suppose that the LM curve stays unchanged. Hence the domestic price level keeps rising and reserves keep getting accumulated. The rising price level starts reducing the export surplus and the IS schedule starts shifting inwards from IS'. Once the price level has

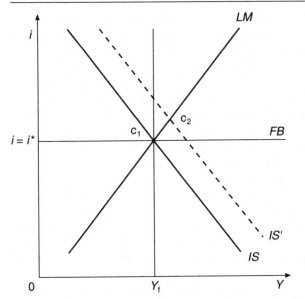

Figure 7.7

risen sufficiently the export surplus is eliminated. Thus suppose P^* has risen by x per cent. In final equilibrium P would also have risen by x per cent and the law of one price will once again hold.

Now suppose that the world interest rate rises. This situation is analysed in Figure 7.5. Initially the world interest rate is i_0^* and full equilibrium occurs at a_1. The world interest rate now climbs up to i_1^*. a_1 is now a position of balance of payments deficit. Hence the economy loses reserves, the money supply shrinks and the LM schedule shifts to LM'. Domestic equilibrium is now at a_2. The deflationary pressure at a_2 causes prices and wages to fall. This increases Y. This also increases net exports by arbitrage so that the IS curve shifts outwards to IS'. This move eliminates the initial deficit. Final full equilibrium is established at a_3.

Let us now analyse a situation in which economic growth increases the full employment income of the domestic economy. This situation is analysed in Figure 7.6. Initially the full employment level of income is Y_{f_0} and full employment occurs at b_1. Economic growth causes the full employment income to rise to Y_{f_1}. At b_1 there is unemployment. Falling prices and wages shift the IS schedule to IS'. 'Domestic' equilibrium occurs at b_2 and now involves a surplus in the balance of payments. The surplus means that reserves will accumulate and there will, hence, be an expansion of domestic money supply. An additional reason for the LM to shift rightward is the fall in the domestic price level. LM shifts outwards to LM'. Final equilibrium occurs at b_3.

Let us now examine the consequences of devaluation in the context of the monetary approach. This analysis is done in Figure 7.7. Initial equilibrium occurs at c_1. A devaluation causes an export surplus as exports expand

and imports shrink. This shifts the IS schedule to IS'. At c_2 there is inflationary pressure in the economy and a balance of payments surplus. The surplus leads to an accumulation of foreign exchange which will increase the money supply and shift the LM rightward. However, the rise in the price level will shift the LM leftward. On balance, let us suppose the LM stays in place. The rise in the price level will also reduce net exports. This will shift the IS' back to IS. In final equilibrium (at c_1) the domestic price level will have risen in proportion to the devaluation so that the law of one price is again established at the new exchange rate. Devaluation produces nothing more than a temporary balance of payments surplus.

How realistic are the pronouncements of the monetary approach? Some predictions are almost uncannily accurate. Consider the following example. Between 1960 and 1980 industrial production grew at an average annual rate of 4.1 per cent in the USA. Over the same twenty-year period industrial production in Japan grew at a rate of 8.6 per cent – more than double the US rate. During the same period the rate of inflation was 7.5 per cent per annum in Japan and 5.2 per cent per annum in the USA. Standard Keynesian theory would argue that the higher Japanese growth as well as the higher Japanese inflation rate would tend to raise imports in Japan. Conversely US imports would be lower. Hence the US dollar would be stronger compared with the Japanese yen. However, the facts fly in the face of Keynesian theory. It was the Japanese yen that was stronger.

The monetary approach has no difficulty in explaining these facts. It would argue that the higher Japanese growth rate would increase the demand for money in Japan as would the higher Japanese inflation rate as compared with the USA. This would, in turn, increase the Japanese surplus and strengthen the Japanese yen.

It is true, however, that the monetary approach's assumptions are hard to defend. For instance, Williamson (1983), writing about the law of one price, says that

> The hypothesis . . . has probably been rejected more decisively by empirical evidence than any other hypothesis in the history of economics.

Similarly for most countries the FB function is probably steeper than the LM thus pointing to limited international capital mobility. The assumption of full employment is also suspect. Moreover, it can be argued that under some special assumptions the Keynes theory would give the same results as those offered by the monetary approach.

An important question then arises. Are there special contributions of the monetary approach or is it to be regarded as a special case of the Keynesian approach? Kouri (1976) has taken up this question in an important recent article. Let us consider his analysis.

From the relation $\Delta R = \Delta M - \Delta D$ subtract the current account surplus (CS) to get

$$\Delta R - CS = \Delta M - \Delta D - CS \tag{7.30}$$

The left-hand side of equation (7.30) is the capital account surplus. So

$$K = \Delta R - CS = (\Delta M - \Delta D) - CS \tag{7.31}$$

From equation (7.31) we can write

$$K = (L_P \Delta P + L_Y \Delta Y + L_i \Delta i - \Delta D) - \left[X\left(\frac{eP^*}{P}\right) - Z\left(Y, \frac{eP^*}{P}\right) + i^* I_f \right] \tag{7.32}$$

where the term inside the square brackets is the current account surplus. Equation (7.32) represents an integration of the flow Keynesian approach and the stock adjustment monetary approach. It tells us that the change in the money supply depends on the change in domestic credit and the levels of P and Y. Hence we have the following conclusions: with fixed exchange rates and fixed P, P^* and Y the current account surplus remains fixed while the interest rate is the only variable available to equate the demand for money with its supply. If there is excess demand for money there will be a capital account surplus until the interest rate rises by enough to eliminate the excess demand.

It follows that in the short run the capital inflow and the interest rate are closely linked. In particular we can write

$$K = K(i - i^*) \tag{7.33}$$

If we lived in a world of flexible exchange rates we would write

$$K = K\left[i - i^*, E\Delta\left(\frac{eP^*}{P}\right)\right] \tag{7.34}$$

where E is the expectations operator.

Hence there seems to be little conflict between the two approaches in terms of short-run analysis. Nevertheless there are two important differences. First from equation (7.33) we see that a given interest rate differential provokes a uniform flow of capital through time. The flow of capital depends on the *level* of the interest rate. According to the monetary approach this capital inflow, by raising the money supply, reduces excess demand for money, thereby rendering the capital inflow temporary. This implies that the capital inflow depends on the change in the rate of interest as seen in equation (7.32).

Second, if we use equation (7.33) to predict the change in the capital flow caused by a change in the rate of interest, we get $dK = K_i di$. But if capital mobility is perfect, K_i is infinite so that this expression would be useless for predicting the magnitude of the change in the capital inflow. Hence an equation like (7.32) is more useful for forecasting capital inflows.

Suppose now that capital is completely immobile so that the inflow of capital is zero. From equation (7.32) we have

$$L_Y\Delta Y + L_P\Delta P + L_i\,\Delta i = \Delta D + X\left(\frac{eP^*}{P}\right) - Z\left(Y, \frac{eP^*}{P}\right) + i^*I_f$$

The terms on the left-hand side of this expression add up to changes in the demand for money. Here the change in reserves is the current account surplus. Hence if capital is immobile and the change in domestic credit is fixed any change in the money supply will require adjustment in the current account of the balance of payments. If P, Y and i are exogenously determined it must be the case that

$$\Delta D = -\left[X\frac{eP^*}{P} - Z\left(Y, \frac{eP^*}{P}\right) + i^*I_f\right] \tag{7.35}$$

Thus the creation of domestic credit implies a current account deficit. This is a particularly important prediction for LDCs. We shall see in a later chapter that the International Monetary Fund (IMF) uses this argument to rationalise its recommendation of a reduction of domestic credit by LDCs which come to the IMF for assistance to tide over balance of payments difficulties.

When the economy is in long-run equilibrium the demand for money equals the supply of money. P, Y and i are at their equilibrium values. If domestic credit does not change the demand for money will equal the supply of money only if the current account is balanced. Thus

$$0 = X\left(\frac{eP^*}{P}\right) - Z\,(Y, eP^*/P) + i^*I_f$$

Hence when income is at full employment level, balance of payments adjustments with fixed exchange rates require price level adjustment. If a country wishes to avoid long-term balance of payments problems it must hold domestic inflation close to the world average.

MONETARY APPROACH WITH FLEXIBLE EXCHANGE RATES

Under fixed exchange rates the balance of payments equation of the monetary approach is used to predict movements in foreign exchange reserves. When the exchange rate is flexible the balance of payments equation is used to predict movements in the exchange rate. The money supply is then free to be determined by conscious monetary policy.

When analysing a regime of flexible exchange rates the monetary approach makes the following critical assumptions. (a) Portfolios adjust instantaneously to disequilibrium. Domestic and foreign financial assets are perfect substitutes so that there is no distinction between domestic and foreign assets (such as bonds). This assumption is sometimes called *uncovered interest parity*, i.e.

$$i - i^* = E\left(\frac{\Delta e}{e}\right) \tag{7.36}$$

which states that the expected rate of depreciation of the local currency must equal the difference between the domestic and foreign rates of interest. (b) The law of one price holds. Domestic and foreign goods are seen as perfect substitutes by consumers and prices are flexible and determined in competitive markets. Thus $P = eP^*$.

To see the implications of flexible exchange rates consider the following example. Let the demand for money function be

$$m = p + \alpha y - \beta i \qquad (7.37)$$

where $m = \ln M$ (log of money demand); $p = \ln P$ (log of price level); α is the income elasticity of demand for money $((dM/M)/(dY/Y))$; β is the interest semi-elasticity of demand for money with respect to the rate of interest $((dM/M)/di)$; and $y = \ln Y$ (log of income).

The foreign economy has an identical demand for money function

$$m^* = p^* + \alpha y^* - \beta i^* \qquad (7.38)$$

The monetary approach assumes that α and β are the same world-wide. Subtracting equation (7.38) from equation (7.37) we have

$$m - m^* = p - p^* + \alpha(y - y^*) - \beta(i - i^*) \qquad (7.39)$$

Rearrange equation (7.39) with $p - p^*$ as the dependent variable to get

$$p - p^* = m - m^* - \alpha(y - y^*) + \beta(i - i^*) \qquad (7.40)$$

Now from the law of one price we have $\ln e = p - p^*$. We use this in equation (7.40) to get

$$\ln e = m - m^* - \alpha(y - y^*) + \beta(i - i^*) \qquad (7.41)$$

Equation (7.41) says that the price of foreign exchange will rise if the domestic money supply rises relative to foreign money supply, the price of foreign exchange will fall if domestic output rises relative to foreign output, the price of foreign exchange will rise if the domestic–foreign interest rate differential widens.

Now substitute the condition for uncovered interest parity $i - i^* = E(\Delta \ln e)$ in equation (7.41) to get

$$\ln e = m - m^* - \alpha(y - y^*) + \beta E(\Delta e) \qquad (7.42)$$

so that a rise in the expected price of foreign exchange will raise the current price of foreign exchange. Equation (7.42) points to a potential source of instability: the higher the expected rate of appreciation of the foreign currency the greater the actual appreciation, and the greater the actual rate of appreciation the greater the expected rate of appreciation.

If the expected rise in the price of foreign exchange equals the difference between the expected domestic and foreign inflation rates, we may write $E(\Delta \ln e) = E(\Delta p) - E(\Delta p^*)$.

Substituting equation (7.42) we have

$$\ln e = m - m^* - \alpha(y - y^*) + \beta[E(\Delta p) - E(\Delta p^*)] \qquad (7.43)$$

This equation states that a relative increase in the domestic money supply raises the price of foreign exchange, and a rise in the relative expected rate of inflation also raises the price of foreign exchange.

It is further assumed that full employment is continuously maintained both at home and abroad. We may now write equation (7.43) as

$$\ln e = m - m^* - \alpha(y - y^*) + \beta[E(\Delta p) - E(\Delta p^*)] \qquad (7.44)$$

which implies that the country with the higher real growth rate will experience appreciation.

If differential interest rates equal expected differences in monetary growth rates we have $E(\Delta p) - E(\Delta p^*) = E(\Delta m - \Delta m^*)$. If we further suppose that the best prediction of future monetary growth rate is today's monetary growth rate, we can write equation (7.44) as

$$\ln e = m - m^* - \alpha(y - y^*) + \beta(\Delta m - \Delta m^*) \qquad (7.45)$$

For a given full employment income differential the exchange rate depends entirely on differential money stocks and their rates of growth. The countries with least rapid monetary growth rates will experience appreciation whereas countries with rapid monetary growth rates will experience depreciation.

The experience with flexible exchange rates, however, has been that exchange rates have been very volatile – much more volatile than any application of equation (7.45) would suggest. To explain this excessive volatility within the framework of the monetary approach is a challenge. This issue was addressed in a pathbreaking paper by Dornbusch (1976).

Dornbusch argues that in the short run prices and wages are sticky. They become fully flexible only in the long run. Dornbusch assumes that equation (7.45) helps determine the long-run exchange rate e_L. Thus we write

$$\ln e_L = m - m^* - \alpha(y - y^*) + \beta(\Delta m - \Delta m^*) \qquad (7.46)$$

The short-run exchange rate is denoted by e. When the short-run exchange rate is different from its long-run equilibrium value e_L the short-run exchange rate is assumed to change at a rate proportional to the difference in the two exchange rates. The part of this exchange rate due to this discrepancy is written as $-\gamma(\ln e - \ln e_L)$ where γ is the factor of proportionality.

Since the long-run, rationally expected, change in the exchange rate is the difference between the monetary growth rates, i.e. $\Delta m - \Delta m^*$, the overall expected change is

$$E(\Delta \ln e) = -\gamma(\ln e - \ln e_L) + (\Delta m - \Delta m^*) \qquad (7.47)$$

Uncovered interest parity holds so that $E(\Delta \ln e) = i - i^*$. Using this in equation (7.46) and rearranging terms we have

$$\ln e - \ln e_{\text{L}} = \frac{-1}{\gamma} \left[(i - \Delta m) - (i^* - \Delta m^*) \right] \qquad (7.48)$$

Now, since the expected inflation rates equal the monetary growth rates, it must be the case that $i - \Delta m = r$ and $i^* - \Delta m^* = r^*$, where r and r^* are, respectively, the home and foreign real rates of interest. Hence, the difference between the log of the short-term exchange rate and the log of the long-term exchange rate depends on the difference between the real interest rates:

$$\ln e - \ln e_{\text{L}} = -\frac{1}{\gamma}(r - r^*) \qquad (7.49)$$

Substituting for e_{L} from equation (7.46) we have

$$\ln e = m - m^* - \alpha(y_{\text{f}} - y_{\text{f}}^*) + \beta(\Delta m - \Delta m^*) - \frac{1}{\gamma}(r - r^*) \qquad (7.50)$$

From equation (7.49) we realise that as the real interest rate gap narrows, the gap between the long-run and short-run exchange rates narrows. Now, suppose there is a monetary shock in the domestic economy and the money supply grows unexpectedly. In the long run, when prices will have risen sufficiently, the old real interest rate will prevail. In the short run, however, prices respond sluggishly. Hence the monetary shock causes the domestic real interest rate to decline temporarily. Expected inflation is still the same as the growth of the money supply. However, the actual inflation is below its long-run equilibrium value because of sluggish prices. Thus the real interest rate falls temporarily. This causes a capital outflow which raises the spot (short-term) exchange rate e. In general, whenever foreign and domestic monetary shocks are different from each other, one might expect differences in real interest rates internationally. This will cause short-run movements in the spot exchange rate unrelated to the forces discussed in equation (7.45). This makes for excessive volatility of the exchange rate as this has to retrace its steps as prices become more flexible in the long run. Dornbusch calls this the *overshooting* phenomenon.

ASSET MARKET ANALYSIS OF FLEXIBLE EXCHANGE RATES

The asset market balance (AMB) approach to the balance of payments tries to rectify (in the specific context of flexible exchange rates) some of the principal weaknesses of the Keynesian and monetary approaches to the balance of payments. The AMB approach recognises the fact that monetary approach represents a significant advance over earlier approaches in so far as it looks at the balance of payments as a whole and emphasises the role of stocks in balance of payments adjustments. But the AMB approach does agree with the view that the monetary approach makes some extreme assumptions.

In particular, the AMB approach drops the assumption that foreign and domestic assets are perfect substitutes. Even if domestic and foreign assets are similar (which is certainly not the case in most LDCs) investors may perceive differences in risk caused by differences in liquidity, tax treatment, exchange risk, political risk and default risk. Another important reason why investors view domestic and foreign bonds as imperfect substitutes at any point in time is that international business cycles and national economic policies are not perfectly synchronised with respect to time.

SHORT-RUN ASSET MARKET EQUILIBRIUM

Among the important variables that affect the balance of payments are real income levels, price levels, interest rates and exchange rates. The AMB approach believes that total financial wealth may be an important factor · affecting the balance of payments.

To simplify the analysis we ignore foreign developments and study the asset market in a single country. There are three assets: money M, domestic bonds B and foreign bonds F. Nominal wealth W is then

$$W = M + B + eF \tag{7.51}$$

where F is in foreign currency and, eF in home currency. Since M, B and F are imperfect substitutes it follows that the rational asset holder's portfolio will contain all three assets. We further assume that the level of national income is fixed so that the demand for assets depends on the nominal interest rate i and total nominal wealth W. We write the demand for money as

$$M = L(i, W) \qquad L_i < 0, L_W > 0 \tag{7.52}$$

A rise in the interest rate lowers the demand for money and a rise in wealth increases it.

The demand for bonds is

$$B = B(i, W) \qquad B_i > 0, B_W > 0 \tag{7.53}$$

A rise in the interest rate lowers the price of bonds and, therefore, raises the demand for bonds. A rise in wealth will increase the demand for bonds. Finally we write the demand for foreign assets as

$$eF = F(i, W) \qquad F_i < 0, F_W > 0 \tag{7.54}$$

Realise from equations (7.52), (7.53) and (7.54) that a rise in the interest rate raises the demand for B and lowers that of M and eF. By Walras' law, then, the fall in the demand for money and foreign bonds must exactly equal the rise in the demand for domestic bonds, i.e.

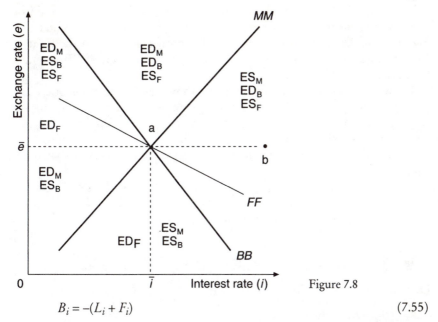

Figure 7.8

$$B_i = -(L_i + F_i) \tag{7.55}$$

A change in the exchange rate affects asset demands by altering W. We may understand that a change in the exchange rate does not provide a relative price effect that leads to portfolio substitution. There is only the effect on wealth.

The model consists of four equations in three unknowns: e, W and i. Hence one equation can be eliminated. For example, once the demands for money and foreign assets are known, the demand for domestic bonds would just be the residual $B = W - M(i,W) - F(i,W)$. The exogenous variables are nominal money supply M, the nominal value of the stock of domestic bonds B and the foreign currency value of the stock of domestically held foreign assets.

For any value of W we can depict equilibrium in e,i space as in Figure 7.8. Suppose that at point a there is simultaneous equilibrium in all three financial markets. Suppose that at the same exchange rate $\bar{e}$ the interest rate was higher. This would lower the demand for money so that at point b there must be excess supply of money. Now, starting from b, if the exchange rate were to rise this would raise eF and hence W and, hence, the demand for money. So the MM schedule, which shows combinations of e and i giving money market equilibrium, must be upward sloping. To the right of MM we must have excess supply of money. To the left of MM there must be excess demand for money.

Let us go back to point b and realise that at this point the price of domestic bonds is too low to give domestic bond market equilibrium. Hence, there is an excess demand for bonds at b. Now if the exchange rate were to fall the value of W would fall and the excess demand for bonds would be eliminated. Thus the BB schedule, which shows combinations of i and e giving bond market equilibrium, must be downward sloping. To the right of BB we must have excess demand for bonds and to the left of BB we must have excess supply of bonds.

By Walras' law, then, the FF schedule showing combinations of e and i giving equilibrium in the market for foreign bonds, must be downward sloping and flatter than the FF schedule. The excess supply and excess demand conditions are as noted in Figure 7.8.

We can demonstrate all this mathematically as follows. Our behavioural equations are

$$M = L(i,W) \qquad \text{MM function}$$

$$B = B(i,W) \qquad \text{BB function}$$

$$eF = F(i,W) \qquad \text{FF function}$$

$$W = M + B + eF = L(i,W) + B(i,W) + F(i,W) \qquad \text{wealth constraint}$$

Differentiating the wealth constraint with respect to W we have

$$(1 - L_W - B_W - F_W)dW = 0$$

Since L_W, B_W and F_W are all positive it follows that $L_W + B_W + F_W = 1$. Now to obtain the slopes of the three schedules we totally differentiate each one of them with respect to e, i and W to get

$$L_i di + L_W dW = 0 \tag{7.56}$$

$$B_i di + B_W dW = 0 \tag{7.57}$$

$$F_i di + F_W dW = Fde \tag{7.58}$$

Now $dW = Fde$ so that

$$L_i di + L_W Fde = 0 \tag{7.59}$$

$$B_i di + B_W Fde = 0 \tag{7.60}$$

$$F_i di + F_W Fde = Fde \tag{7.61}$$

From equation (7.59) the slope of the MM schedule is

$$\left(\frac{de}{di}\right)_{MM} = \frac{-L_i}{FL_W} > 0$$

From equation (7.60) the slope of the BB schedule is

$$\left(\frac{de}{di}\right)_{BB} = \frac{-B_i}{FB_W} < 0$$

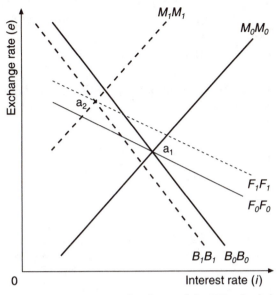

Figure 7.9

From equation (7.61) the slope of the FF schedule is

$$\left(\frac{de}{di}\right)_{FF} = \frac{F_i}{F(1 - F_W)} < 0$$

Walras' law requires that BB be steeper than FF. In fact it is easy to demonstrate that this condition must be satisfied to ensure stability.

We are now in a position to analyse the comparative static properties of the model. Suppose the government runs a deficit and finances it by creating more money. So far as the private sector is concerned $\Delta M = \Delta W$. The effects are traced in Figure 7.9. Initially there is simultaneous equilibrium in all three markets at a_1. The original financial market equilibrium relations are labelled $M_0 M_0$, $B_0 B_0$ and $F_0 F_0$. Now the money supply and, hence, nominal wealth expands. Hence now at a_1 there will be an excess demand for foreign and domestic bonds and a corresponding excess supply of money. (The rise in W increases the demand for money as well. Walras' law, however, requires that there be excess supply of money at a_1 to match the excess demand for domestic and foreign bonds.) To restore equilibrium in the money market at any exchange rate the interest rate must be lower. Hence the MM schedule shifts leftward to $M_1 M_1$. The excess demand for bonds at a_1 can be eliminated by raising the price of bonds, i.e. lowering the interest rate. Hence the BB schedule shifts down to $B_1 B_1$. To eliminate the excess demand for foreign bonds the rate of interest must rise. Thus the FF schedule shifts right to $F_1 F_1$. Final equilibrium occurs at a_2 with a lower interest rate and higher exchange rate.

We can illustrate the same results mathematically. Totally differentiate the BB, FF and MM schedules to get

$$\begin{bmatrix} B_i & B_W & 0 \\ F_i & F_W & -F \\ L_i & L_W & 0 \end{bmatrix} \begin{bmatrix} di \\ dM \\ de \end{bmatrix} = \begin{bmatrix} dB \\ edF \\ dM \end{bmatrix} \qquad (7.62)$$

The determinant of the matrix on the left-hand side is $\delta = F(B_i L_W - B_W L_i) > 0$. Now, from equation (7.62) we have

$$\begin{bmatrix} di \\ dW \\ de \end{bmatrix} = \frac{1}{\Delta} \begin{bmatrix} FL_W & 0 & -FB_W \\ -FL_i & 0 & FB_i \\ F_i L_W - F_W L_i & B_W L_i - B_i L_W & B_i F_W - B_W F_i \end{bmatrix} \begin{bmatrix} dB \\ edF \\ dM \end{bmatrix}$$

$$(7.63)$$

When the government finances its deficits by selling bonds to the central bank, the central bank will expand money supply to the same extent. On the right-hand side of equation (7.63) the column vector terms become

$$dB = 0$$
$$edF = 0$$
$$dM = dB$$

whence

$$\frac{di}{dB} = \frac{-B_W}{B_i L_W - B_W L_i} < 0 \qquad (7.64)$$

$$\frac{dW}{dB} = \frac{B_i}{B_i L_W - B_W L_i} > 0 \qquad (7.65)$$

$$\frac{de}{dB} = \frac{B_i F_W - B_W F_i}{\delta} > 0 \qquad (7.66)$$

Money-financed budget deficits, therefore, lower the interest rate and raise the exchange rate. Recall that in the case of the monetary approach the domestic interest rate was determined completely by the world interest rate.

Now suppose that the government deficit is financed by selling bonds to the public instead of the central bank. Thus $\Delta B = \Delta W$. This increase in wealth raises the demand for foreign bonds. Thus higher F prices would be needed to eliminate excess demand. In Figure 7.10 we show this change with a shift of the FF schedule from $F_0 F_0$ to $F_1 F_1$. At a_1 there is an excess demand for foreign bonds and an excess supply of domestic bonds. To eliminate the latter there must be a fall in the price of bonds (a rise of the interest rate). Hence the BB schedule shifts to $B_1 B_1$. Further, at a_1 there is an excess demand for money which can be eliminated by shifting the MM schedule from $M_0 M_0$ to $M_1 M_1$. Final equilibrium occurs at a_2. The rate of interest is definitely higher at a_2 than at a_1; however, the change in the

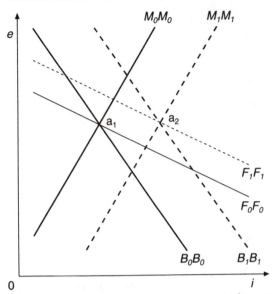

Figure 7.10

exchange rate depends on the relative shifts of the BB and FF (and MM) schedules. In Figure 7.11 we have shown a rise in the exchange rate. Clearly the exchange rate could easily have fallen.

Mathematically, the terms in the right-hand side of equation (7.62) would become

$$dB = dB$$
$$edF = 0$$
$$dM = 0$$

Hence

$$\frac{di}{dB} = \frac{L_W}{B_i L_W - B_W L_i} \quad > 0 \tag{7.67}$$

$$\frac{dW}{dB} = \frac{-L_i}{B_i L_W - B_W L_i} \quad > 0 \tag{7.68}$$

$$\frac{de}{dB} = \frac{F_i L_W - F_W L_i}{\delta} \quad \gtrless 0 \tag{7.69}$$

One can see that the home currency will appreciate if $F_i L_W - F_W L_i < 0$, i.e. if $F_i/F_W < L_i/L_W$. This condition may be satisfied if the rise in the interest rate leads to a larger substitution of domestic bonds in favour of foreign bonds combined with a low degree of substitution from money to domestic bonds.

Now let us look at the effects of monetary policy. Suppose the central bank conducts an open market purchase of domestic bonds. Wealth does

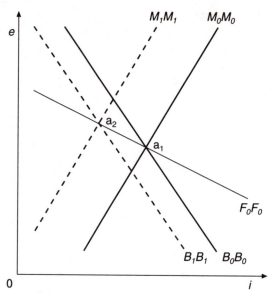

Figure 7.11

not change. Let us now refer to Figure 7.11. Initially equilibrium is at a_1. The increased supply of money creates an excess supply of money. To restore equilibrium in the money market the interest rate must fall, i.e. the MM schedule shifts from M_0M_0 to M_1M_1. The reduction in the supply of bonds creates an excess demand for bonds. To restore equilibrium bond prices must rise, i.e. interest rates must fall. The BB schedule then shifts from B_0B_0 to B_1B_1. The equilibrium interest rate is lower and the exchange rate is higher.

Mathematically, the terms in the right-hand side of equation (7.62) become

$$dB = -dM$$
$$edF = 0$$
$$dM = dM$$

whence we have

$$\frac{di}{dM} = \frac{-(L_W + B_W)}{B_i L_W - B_W L_i} > 0 \qquad (7.70)$$

$$\frac{dW}{dM} = \frac{L_i + B_i}{B_i L_W - B_W L_i} > 0 \qquad (7.71)$$

$$\frac{de}{dM} = \frac{-F_i}{\delta} > 0 \qquad (7.72)$$

The monetary authorities can conduct open market operations by buying and selling foreign assets. Suppose, for instance, the monetary authorities

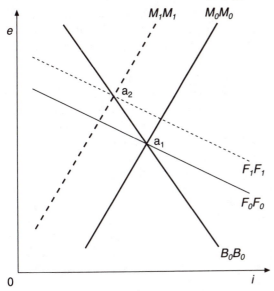

Figure 7.12

buy foreign assets. We analyse this situation in Figure 7.12. Initially the equilibrium is at a_1. The government buys foreign assets. This creates an excess supply of money and an excess demand for foreign assets at a_1. To remove the excess supply of money the interest rate must fall. Hence the MM schedule shifts from M_0M_0 to M_1M_1. The excess demand for foreign assets can be eliminated by raising the interest rate at every exchange rate, i.e. by a shift of the FF schedule from F_0F_0 to F_1F_1. Final equilibrium is at a_2. Mathematically, the terms in the right-hand side of equation (7.62) become

$$dB = 0$$
$$edF = -dM$$
$$dM = dM$$

from which we will get

$$\frac{di}{dM} = \frac{-B_i}{B_iL_W - B_WL_i} < 0 \tag{7.73}$$

$$\frac{dW}{dM} = \frac{B_i}{B_iL_W - B_WL_i} > 0 \tag{7.74}$$

$$\frac{de}{dM} = \frac{-B_i}{\delta} > 0 \tag{7.75}$$

The AMB approach provides the additional insight that the balance of payments *cannot* be balanced unless the current account is balanced. It will not do to simply have an overall equilibrium in the balance of payments.

This is because a current account surplus or deficit has implications for the accumulation of foreign assets. A current account surplus means that foreign assets are being accumulated whereas a current account deficit means the opposite.

Suppose that the domestic economy has a current account surplus. This would mean that foreign assets will be accumulated and wealth would increase. Moreover, the balance between the three assets in the portfolios of investors is disturbed. Investors would like to convert the additional foreign assets into domestic bonds and money. This will tend to appreciate the domestic currency and thus lower the value of the increase in W. Since wealth holders increase their demand for money the rate of interest would tend to rise. However, since the demand for domestic bonds also rises, this would tend to raise the price of bonds, i.e. lower the interest rate. On balance, suppose the interest rate stays unchanged. Then the appreciation of the local currency will wipe out the increase in wealth. In the long run, then, a current account surplus will lead to a proportionate appreciation of the domestic currency whereas a current account surplus will cause an equiproportionate depreciation of the local currency.

ASSET MARKET BALANCE'S EXPLANATION OF OVERSHOOTING

If exchange rates are fully flexible then the overall balance of payments must be in equilibrium with any current account surplus (deficit) being matched by a capital account deficit (surplus). However, as we have realised, asset markets (and hence the exchange rate) will not be in equilibrium. Therefore, in the medium run, the balance of payments cannot be in balance unless the current account is also balanced.

Suppose that current income is at full employment level, then the net inflow of foreign assets consequent upon a current account surplus can be written as

$$\Delta F = X\left(\frac{eP^*}{P}\right) - Z\left(Y_f, \frac{eP^*}{P}\right) + i^*F$$

With $\Delta F > 0$, i^*F will keep rising and so, *ceteris paribus*, will the current account surplus. As domestic residents try to convert foreign assets into domestic bonds and money the value of the local currency rises. Over time, then,

$$\Delta F = 0 = X\left(\frac{eP^*}{P}\right) - Z\left(Y_f, \frac{eP^*}{P}\right) + i^*F$$

In the short run suppose that a country such as the USA has large investment income from abroad. Then it can maintain a current account surplus even though its exports are less than imports, i.e.

$$i^*F > Z - X > 0$$

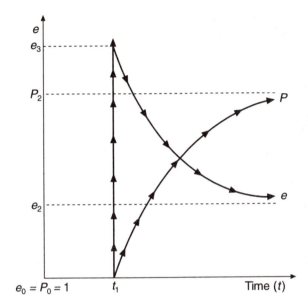

Figure 7.13

The AMB approach predicts, quite correctly, that such a country can continue to export less than it imports *and yet experience an appreciation of its currency.* This is precisely what seems to have happened in the USA in recent times. It continues to enjoy more imports than exports. However, it had such a large investment income from abroad that it had a current account surplus and the dollar continued to rise.

Let us now try to understand the overshooting phenomenon within the context of the AMB approach. It is easy to see that if the domestic price level adjusts slowly it is possible for the exchange rate to overshoot its equilibrium value.

Consider an economy with income fixed at the full employment level Y_f and, to simplify the analysis, with net exports and foreign investment equal to zero. i^* and P^* are treated parametrically. Further, suppose without loss of generality that initially the exchange rate and the domestic price level are each equal to 1, i.e. $e_0 = P_0 = 1$.

Now, suppose there is a monetary shock. The money supply increases suddenly to a higher level. As a consequence the exchange rate and the price level begin to rise. We analyse the situation in Figure 7.13.

Initially $e_0 = P_0 = 1$ and the supply of money rises. The economy is in a flexible exchange rate regime with flexible price level. The exchange rate immediately jumps up to e_3 and then starts falling. The critical jump in the exchange rate creates an export surplus and investment income rises.

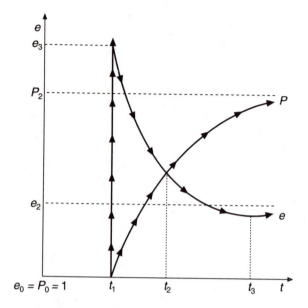

Figure 7.14

Domestic residents start converting foreign assets into domestic assets and so e starts falling.

The jump in the money supply also causes the price level to rise. At time t_2 the exchange rate and the price level are again equal to each other and net exports should again equal zero. However, because of the initial rise in e and the consequent accumulation of foreign assets, there would be a current account surplus at t_2. Hence, after t_2, the exchange rate must continue to fall and the price level continue to rise to balance the current account. The new equilibrium value of e is e_2, that of the price level P_2. Unlike the monetary approach, the real exchange rate is permanently altered.

Let us now suppose that the price level adjusts only slowly. We analyse this situation in Figure 7.14. We have the same initial conditions as in Figure 7.13. At time t_1 there is a monetary shock and the exchange rate jumps to e_3 and this causes an export surplus. The price level also starts rising but its rise is slow. The exchange rate drops and, at t_2 once again, e and P are the same. Net exports are again zero at t_2, but because of the accumulation of foreign assets there is a current account surplus at t_2. Hence e keeps falling and P keeps rising. Now, since the rise in the price level is slow, the exchange rate may drop to a level below e_2 before current account balance is attained. Let us suppose that this occurs at t_3. However, the price level is still rising at t_3 so that we now develop a current account deficit. As a consequence, the exchange rate now starts rising. We once again reach exchange rate e_2 and price level P_2; however, the exchange rate reaches its equilibrium value from *below* rather than from above. The real exchange rate is again permanently altered.

CONCLUSIONS

In this chapter we have examined various approaches to balance of payments adjustments. Both current account and integrated approaches have been examined. The immediate applicability of these approaches to developing countries is somewhat limited. Nevertheless, they serve as an important backdrop for the analysis conducted in Parts III and IV of this book.

8

A generalised version of the open economy model

INTRODUCTION

We have studied the open economy fairly extensively in Chapters 6 and 7. In this chapter we want to consider a generalisation to consider the case where the rate of inflation is variable. In essence, this implies a reinterpretation of the IS–LM–AS apparatus in the case of a small open economy (SOE). We shall retain the same assumptions as in Chapter 7. To repeat, these assumptions are as follows. (i) The home economy produces one good but consumes two goods – the home good and imports. These two goods are imperfect substitutes for each other. (ii) The home economy has a bond which is perfectly substitutable for the foreign bond when expected yields are equalised. (iii) Domestic currency is not accepted abroad. (iv) In international transactions the SOE takes world prices and interest rates as given.

THE OPEN ECONOMY IS SCHEDULE

Let S represent the natural log of savings, taxes and imports and I the natural log of investment, government expenditures and exports. We write S as a function of the natural log of output Y and τ, the log of the reciprocal of the real exchange rate ($\tau = p - p^* - \hat{e}$) where p is the log of the domestic price level, p^* is the log of the world price level and $\hat{e}$ is the log of the nominal exchange rate). We shall also refer to τ as the terms of trade.

$$S = \beta_0 + \beta_1 Y + \beta_{11}\tau \tag{8.1}$$

where $\beta_{11} > 0$ denotes the price elasticity of imports.

The relative price effect also operates on exports. Hence we write

$$I = \beta_2 + \beta_3 Y - \beta_4(i - \pi^e) - \beta_{12}\tau \tag{8.2}$$

An increase in τ rising from a higher p causes consumers to move away from domestic goods to foreign goods and, therefore, reduces exports. This explains the sign on β_{12}.

Equating S and I we obtain the IS schedule as

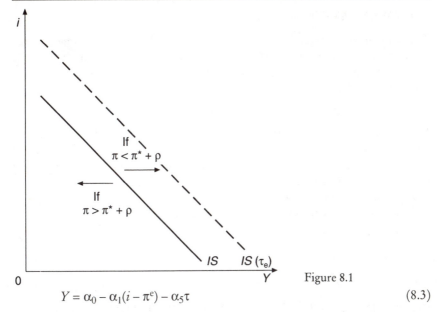

Figure 8.1

$$Y = \alpha_0 - \alpha_1(i - \pi^e) - \alpha_5 \tau \qquad (8.3)$$

where $\alpha_0 = (\beta_2 - \beta_0)/(\beta_1 - \beta_3)$, $\alpha_1 = \beta_4/(\beta_1 - \beta_3)$ and $\alpha_5 = (\beta_{11} + \beta_{12})/(\beta_1 - \beta_3)$. In Chapter 5 we had argued that $\beta_1 > \beta_3$, a condition that is not changed by the inclusion of imports and exports. Hence the denominators of all the αs are positive. We further assume that $\beta_2 > \beta_0$ and thus ensure that $\alpha_0 > 0$.

We know that an increase in τ will reduce exports and increase imports thus reducing the trade balance. At a particular level of τ, say τ^e, the trade balance is zero. In other words $\alpha_5 \tau^e = 0$.

To allow for continuing inflation in the home country and the rest of the world and its effects on the terms of trade we can write

$$\tau - \tau_{-1} = \pi - \pi^* - \rho \qquad (8.4)$$

where $\rho = E(\Delta e/e)$. Thus τ increases over time if $\pi > \pi^* + \rho$. Substituting (8.4) into (8.3) we have

$$Y = \alpha_0 - \alpha_1(i - \pi^e) - \alpha_5(\pi - \pi^* - \rho + \tau_{-1}) \qquad (8.5)$$

The new IS schedule is drawn in Figure 8.1. We should realise that unless τ is constant the IS curve (even in the non-stochastic case) does not stay stationary. For τ to stay constant π should equal $\pi^* + \rho$.

If $\pi > \pi^* + \rho$ the demand for home goods will keep falling and, therefore, the IS curve will shift to the left. Conversely if $\pi < \pi^* + \rho$ demand for home goods will rise both at home and abroad and the IS schedule will shift to the right. Moreover there is only one τ (τ_e) such that the current account is balanced. Such an IS schedule is shown in Figure 8.1 as IS(τ_e). We have, for reference, also drawn an IS schedule with a deficit at the current τ.

THE OPEN ECONOMY LM SCHEDULE

The demand for money is still determined by real national income and the nominal rate of interest. However, the domestic interest rate is tied to the world interest rate and the expected depreciation of the home currency through the relation

$$i = i^* + \rho^e \tag{8.6}$$

However, the money supply is not exogenously determined by the central bank. We know from Chapter 7 that if we were operating in a fixed exchange rate system a deficit in the balance of payments would involve a fall in the money supply and a surplus would involve an increase in the growth rate of money supply.

The LM curve in an open economy is written as

$$m - p = \alpha_2 Y - \alpha_3 i \tag{8.7}$$

and, in terms of growth rates, as

$$\mu - \pi = \alpha_2 Y - \alpha_3 i - (m - p)_{-1} \tag{8.8}$$

In summary, then, the LM curve looks very much like its closed economy counterpart except for the important fact that the growth rate of the money supply is endogenously determined when the country operates under a fixed exchange rate system.

THE OPEN ECONOMY AGGREGATE SUPPLY CURVE

In the open economy aggregate supply responds to two price indices: p, which is of interest to producers, and p_c which is of interest to consumers/workers. We retain the assumption that employment is constrained by demand for labour. Hence $w - p$ remains the relevant wage for determining actual employment. In terms of growth rates employment and output rise if the rate of producer price inflation exceeds the rate of growth of nominal wages, i.e. $\pi > \omega$. However, the supply of labour will be determined by $w - p_c$ and we may expect that workers will negotiate nominal wages to maintain their command over consumption goods, i.e. they will set $\omega = \pi_c^e$ where π_c^e is the rate of inflation of consumer prices (part of which is the price of importables). It follows that the terms of trade will play an important role in determining labour and, hence, output supply. Since these terms of trade are subject to changes the supply of labour and, hence, that of output cannot be taken to be fixed as was the case in the closed economy model.

We present labour market equilibrium in Figure 8.2. The demand for labour depends only upon $w - p$ which is measured on the vertical axis, but the supply of labour is related to $w - p_c$. We can write the supply of labour as

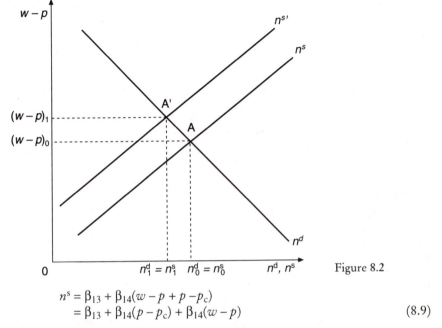

Figure 8.2

$$n^s = \beta_{13} + \beta_{14}(w - p + p - p_c)$$
$$= \beta_{13} + \beta_{14}(p - p_c) + \beta_{14}(w - p) \tag{8.9}$$

Thus the horizontal intercept in Figure 8.2 depends on β_{13}, which incorporates key factors in the work–leisure choice, as well as $\beta_{14}(p - p_c)$, which is determined by the terms of trade. In this setting it is possible for a nominal change to affect employment and output. To see this define the consumer price index as

$$p_c = \theta p + (1 - \theta)(p^* + \hat{e}) \tag{8.10}$$

where $\theta \; (0 < \theta < 1)$ is the fraction of consumption coming from home goods. Now suppose p^* rises (price of imports goes up), i.e. there is a deterioration in the terms of trade. The labour demand schedule stays in place whereas labour supply shifts to the left. A new equilibrium is established at A' where, from the firms' point of view, real wages are higher and employment lower. Naturally equilibrium output Y^e also drops. Hence we can write the AS schedule as

$$Y = Y^e_{-1} - \alpha_4(\pi^e_c - \pi) \tag{8.11}$$

Since Y^e is no longer unique it has to be dated and equation (8.11) incorporates the assumption that the economy starts with an equilibrium position but may not return there. Substituting for τ we have

$$Y = Y^e_{-1} + \alpha_4(1 - \theta)(\tau - \tau_{-1}) \tag{8.12}$$

An increase in import price causes τ to fall and forces the AS curve to shift to the left. Unless there is a subsequent reversal in the terms of trade, the AS curve will stay in its new location and become the new Y^e. We must be clear, however, that although output is determined by the terms of trade, equilibrium in the labour market is preserved at any terms of trade without policy intervention.

DIAGRAMMATIC REPRESENTATION – THE CASE OF FIXED EXCHANGE RATES

The first thing we realise is that, since domestic interest rate is pegged to the world interest rate, the IS–LM apparatus does not determine the interest rate. Moreover, in addition to the inflation rate and real output the model must determine either the exchange rate or the balance of payments.

From the interest parity condition (8.6), the IS equation (8.5), the LM equation (8.8) and the AS schedule (8.12) we can solve for Y, π, i and μ.

The LM curve is no longer relevant for determining aggregate demand since the domestic interest rate is pegged to world levels. The IS schedule determines a relation between π and Y with real interest rates held constant. The AD and AS schedules are drawn in Figure 8.3. In both schedules expectational variables are treated as exogenous for the time being. Further i^* and π^* are assumed to be determined in the rest of the world and impervious to home country actions. Finally, past values of τ and Y^e are predetermined and α_0 is controlled by fiscal policy. Thus π and Y remain the only endogenous variables and they are determined by the intersection of the AD and AS schedules in Figure 8.3. Once we know all this we can use the equation for the LM curve to solve for μ, given $(m - p)_{-1}$. If μ is larger than previously there is a balance of payments surplus and the money supply expands. π_c can be calculated from π^* and π given θ.

FLEXIBLE EXCHANGE RATES

With flexible exchange rates we substitute the interest parity condition $i = i^* + \rho^e$ into the LM equation which, then, becomes the AD schedule. The IS schedule becomes superfluous. The negative relation between π and Y comes from the money market alone. Suppose Y goes up. This will create an excess demand for money but with i^* and ρ^e given, i cannot change. The only adjusting variable will be π. We have drawn the AD and AS schedules in Figure 8.4. Together they determine Y and π. We can then write the IS schedule as

$$\rho = \alpha_5[Y - \alpha_0 + \alpha_1(i^* + \rho^e - \pi^c)] + \pi - \pi^* + \tau_{-1} \tag{8.13}$$

which has, on the right-hand side, all the information needed to calculate ρ. All the other variables can then be calculated. The causal link, therefore, is exogenous i^* and ρ determine i; then the LM and AS schedules solve for Y and π; finally the IS schedule determines ρ.

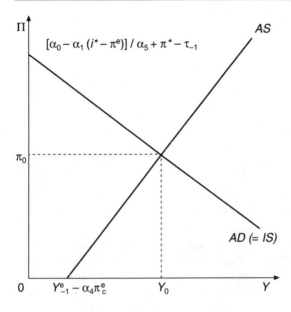

Figure 8.3

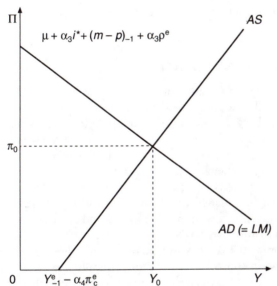

Figure 8.4

POLICY ANALYSIS IN THE PRESENCE OF FOREIGN AND DOMESTIC SHOCKS

The model we have considered so far has not dealt with stochastic disturbances. It is now time to change this. We can write down the stochastic version of the IS–LM–AS model as

$$Y = \alpha_0 - \alpha_1(i - \pi^e) - \alpha_5\tau + \varepsilon_g \qquad\qquad \text{IS schedule} \qquad (8.14)$$

$$\mu - \pi + \varepsilon_m = \alpha_2 Y - \alpha_3 i - (m - p)_{-1} \qquad\qquad \text{LM schedule} \qquad (8.15)$$

$$Y = Y^e_{-1} - \alpha_4[\phi\,\pi^e + (1 - \phi)(\pi^{*e} + \rho^e) - \pi - \varepsilon_s] + \varepsilon_s \qquad \text{AS schedule} \qquad (8.16)$$

$$i = i^* + \rho^e + \varepsilon_{i^*} \qquad\qquad \text{FB condition} \qquad (8.17)$$

$$\tau = \pi - \pi^* - \varepsilon_{\pi*} - \rho + \tau_{-1} \qquad\qquad \text{Terms of trade} \qquad (8.18)$$

All previously introduced variables have the same meaning. In addition to the shocks originating in the goods, labour and money markets at home there are foreign shocks as well. $\varepsilon_{\pi*}$ is a shock due to random variations in foreign inflation and ε_{i^*} is a shock due to random variations in the foreign interest rate. A positive value of $\varepsilon_{\pi*}$ is tantamount to an unanticipated increase in the foreign inflation rate. It causes the IS curve to shift outwards as, *ceteris paribus*, home goods become more attractive both to domestic residents as well as foreigners. ε_{i^*} represents unanticipated changes in the foreign interest rate and affects the interest parity condition. Initially foreign shocks are represented by non-zero values for $\varepsilon_{\pi*}$ and ε_{i^*}. If the foreign event is a one-time shock to a particular market the trend values of π^* and i^* will be unaffected and the foreign shocks should then be treated as temporary; but if the event is permanent, it should be translated into changes in π^* and i^*.

INSTRUMENTS OF MONETARY POLICY

In a closed economy the central bank can control the money supply or the nominal interest rate. It should be understood that there can be only one control variable – the central bank cannot control both the interest rate *and* the money supply. If the shocks originate in the money market, interest rate adjustment is the optimal policy response. If the shocks originate in the goods market then money supply change is the optimal response.

In the open economy the choice is not quite so simple since the foreign balance condition (FB) must be satisfied at all times if capital mobility is perfect. In equation (8.17), given i^*, assuming that $\varepsilon_{i^*} = 0$ and since ρ^e cannot change in the wake of a disturbance to the system, there can be only one value of i that is consistent with FB. It is not possible, therefore, for the central bank to choose between control over the money supply and interest rate adjustments but it can choose between the money supply and exchange rate adjustments. In other words, in an open economy with perfect capital mobility, the monetary authorities can allow a shock to be absorbed by exchange rate adjustments (if exchange rates are flexible) with no changes in the money supply or through changes in the money supply (if exchange rates are fixed) while the exchange rate is maintained at a pre-designated level.

We depict these choices in Figure 8.5 which illustrates the FB condition.

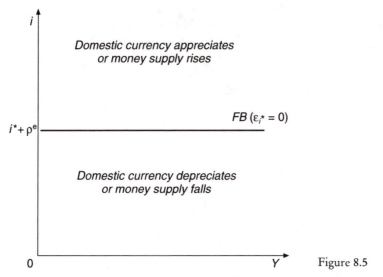

Figure 8.5

The FB line is horizontal in i, Y space. There is only one domestic interest rate that is consistent with equality of expected yields between domestic and foreign bonds regardless of the value of Y. If the domestic interest rate was higher than that denoted by the FB line there will be a flood of capital into the country which would, in turn, put pressures on the home currency to appreciate (if exchange rates are flexible) or the money supply to rise (if exchange rates are fixed). Conversely, if the domestic interest rate is below the FB line there will be an outflow of capital from the home country leading to a drop in the value of the home currency (if exchange rates are flexible) or a reduction in the monetary base and, hence, money supply (if exchange rates are fixed). It thus follows that the interest rate cannot be different from that given by the FB condition.

Once the interest rate is determined by the FB condition the equilibrium level of output is derived from the intersection of FB with either the IS or LM curves. If the monetary authorities control the rate of monetary growth then the LM curve becomes relevant. If, however, the exchange rate is controlled, then the IS schedule becomes relevant and the LM schedule loses its relevance. Thus the FB and LM equations constitute the AD schedule in the flexible exchange rate case and the IS and FB schedules in the fixed exchange rate case. In either case, the AD and AS equations help us solve for Y and π.

Suppose we are interested in finding out which exchange rate regime is better. How do we articulate this question? A fair way would be to find out the exchange rate regime that keeps Y closest to Y^e in the presence of random shocks. We realise, of course, that in an open economy there are many values of Y^e because of terms of trade changes. However, any movement in Y because of random shocks can be distinguished from changes that occur

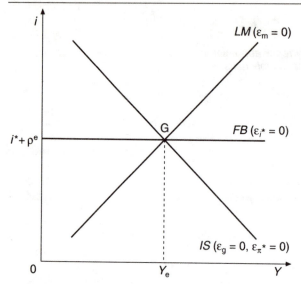

Figure 8.6

because of terms of trade effects. Any movement from any Y^e causes a disequilibrium in the labour market. We measure the efficacy of any exchange rate mechanism by looking at its capability to insulate the economy against various shocks.

The initial IS, LM and FB schedules are drawn in Figure 8.6. In all three schedules we assume that εs are zero. The three schedules intersect at G: there is only one combination of i and Y that satisfies the long-run equilibrium. Here there is no distinction between controlling the money supply or the exchange rate. In the long run there is only one combination of i and Y that satisfies the long-run equilibrium condition. We must have $\mu = \pi$ and $\rho = \pi - \pi^*$. We now analyse the effects of (a) a domestic monetary shock, (b) a domestic goods market shock, (c) a foreign monetary shock and (d) a supply shock. These stochastic events can be imposed on this long-run equilibrium and the effect on output or employment compared for the two exchange-rate systems. The system that leads to the smallest deviation of output from its equilibrium level is the best under these circumstances.

Our *modus operandi* is as follows. We hold the rate of growth of money supply constant along with the change in the exchange rate. In other words, if the superscript 1 refers to the situation after the shock, and the superscript 0 to the situation before the shock, we ensure first that $\mu^1 = \mu^0$ and then that $\rho^1 = \rho^0$. We want to find out how Y^1 deviates from Y^0 when there is a random shock of a particular kind. Let us first deal with the case when the rate of growth of money is constant and the LM schedule becomes the AD schedule. With money market equilibrium we must have $m - p + \varepsilon_m = \alpha_2 Y - \alpha_3 i$. Subtract $(m - p)_{-1}$ from both sides of this equation to get

$$\mu - \pi + \varepsilon_m = \alpha_2 Y - \alpha_3 i - (m - p)_{-1} \tag{8.15'}$$

because $m - m_{-1} = \mu$ and $p - p_{-1} = \pi$. Now first difference both sides of (8.15') and set $\mu^1 = \mu^0$ to get

$$Y^1 - Y^0 = \frac{1}{\alpha_2} [\alpha_3(i^1 - i^0) - (\pi^1 - \pi^0) + \varepsilon_m] \qquad (8.19)$$

The last two terms provide us with the sources of a horizontal shift of the LM schedule. We know that $i^1 - i^0 = \varepsilon_{i*}$ from the FB condition. Substituting this into equation (8.19) we have

$$Y^1 - Y^0 = \frac{1}{\alpha_2} [\alpha_3\varepsilon_{i*} - (\pi^1 - \pi^0) + \varepsilon_m] \qquad (8.20)$$

The vertical shift in the AS schedule is given by

$$(\pi^1 - \pi^0) = \frac{1}{\alpha_4} [(Y^1 - Y^0) - (1 + \alpha_4)\varepsilon_s] \qquad (8.21)$$

We substitute this for $\pi^1 - \pi^0$ in equation (8.20) and solve for $Y^1 - Y^0$ to get

$$Y^1 - Y^0 = \frac{\alpha_4}{1 + \alpha_2\alpha_4} \left(\varepsilon_m + \alpha_3\varepsilon_{i*} + \frac{1 + \alpha_4}{\alpha_4} \right) \varepsilon_s \qquad (8.22)$$

This relates changes in Y to the εs via the parameters of the system.

Turning now to the regime of exchange control, we have after first differencing the IS schedule

$$Y^1 - Y^0 = -\alpha_1(i^1 - i^0) - (\tau^1 - \tau^0) + \varepsilon_g \qquad (8.23)$$

which gives $\tau^1 - \tau^0$ and ε_g as the source of the horizontal shift of that curve. We know that

$$\tau^1 - \tau^0 = \pi^1 - \pi^0 - \varepsilon_{\pi*} \qquad (8.24)$$

Substituting into (8.23) we have the horizontal shift of the AD schedule as

$$Y^1 - Y^0 = -\alpha_1\varepsilon_{i*} - \alpha_5(\pi^1 - \pi^0 - \varepsilon_{\pi*}) + \varepsilon_g \qquad (8.25)$$

Now substitute for $\pi^1 - \pi^0$ from the supply side, equation (8.21), and write the final change in output as

$$Y^1 - Y^0 = \frac{\alpha_4}{\alpha_4 + \alpha_5} \left[\varepsilon_g - \alpha_1\varepsilon_{i*} + \alpha_5\varepsilon_{\pi*} + \frac{\alpha_5(1 + \alpha_4)}{\alpha_4} \varepsilon_s \right] \qquad (8.26)$$

We are now in a position to analyse the effects of various shocks. This requires an examination of equation (8.22) for the flexible exchange rate case and equation (8.26) for the fixed exchange rate case.

DOMESTIC MONETARY SHOCK

Consider first the case where $\varepsilon_m > 0$, i.e. there is a monetary shock. We shall assume that all expectational variables are kept at their previous levels.

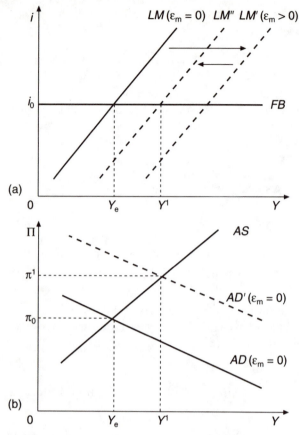

(a)

(b)

Figure 8.7

We realise immediately that in the fixed exchange rate case a domestic monetary shock shifts the LM curve outwards and it immediately shifts back inwards since it is the IS, FB and AS equations that determine output. The LM schedule is irrelevant to the determination of equilibrium output with fixed exchange rates.

To examine the impact under flexible exchange rates let us set all other shocks except ε_m equal to zero in equation (8.22). The LM shifts outwards in response to $\varepsilon_m > 0$ in Figure 8.7(a). So does the AD schedule in Figure 8.7(b). If the central bank does not alter μ, ρ will rise above its previous value to absorb the incipient deficit in the balance of payments. π and Y rise. The rise in π implies a shift back of the LM schedule to LM". Its location is dictated by the need for the new Y (Y^1) to be the same in the IS–LM–FB panel as in the AS–AD panel. The extra output is sold to foreigners because the depreciation of the home currency is not completely offset by the rise in the home rate of inflation. Further, τ also falls so that home goods become more attractive in the world market. From the point of view of workers this outcome is not desirable since all expectational variables remained at their previous levels whereas domestic inflation rose and the home currency depreciated. This leads to a reduction in their real incomes.

It would therefore appear that if the home economy was very prone to money market shocks, it would be better to have fixed rather than flexible exchange rates. This conclusion holds irrespective of whether the shocks are transitory or persistent so long as they are monetary in nature.

DOMESTIC GOODS–MARKET SHOCK

Let us suppose that there is a goods market shock ($\varepsilon_g > 0$) and all other shocks are zero. An examination of equation (8.22) indicates that with flexible exchange rates there is no effect on output (ε_g does not appear in equation (8.22)). The IS curve shifts outwards because of the shock but this does not affect output since the IS curve plays no role in output determination. The home currency appreciates and this completely compensates for the goods market shock. The IS curve shifts back inwards.

We examine the situation with fixed exchange rates in Figure 8.8. A

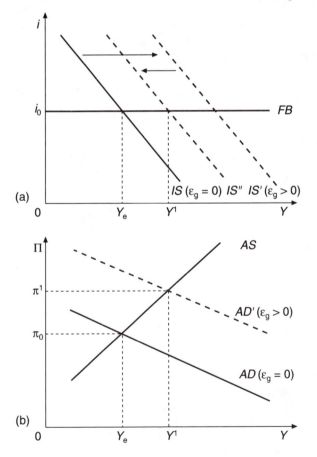

Figure 8.8

goods market shock shifts the IS schedule outwards in part (a) and the AD schedule outwards in part (b). Both π and Y rise. As π rises, the terms of trade rise and demand shifts to foreign goods. This shifts the IS curve back inwards somewhat. Its exact position is dictated by the change in Y in the AS–AD part of the diagram. Thus with a goods market shock there is a rationale for allowing exchange rates to fluctuate.

An examination of these two cases points to the desirability of not committing policy to one or the other type of exchange rate regime and preferring, instead, to have a managed exchange rate system. When monetary shocks are more important the economy would stick to a value of π and allow the money supply to fluctuate; and if goods markets shocks are more important a value of μ should be adhered to.

FOREIGN MONETARY SHOCK

Now assume that the rest of the world suffers a temporary positive monetary shock. In the domestic economy this will show up as $\varepsilon_{\pi*} > 0$ and $\varepsilon_{i*} < 0$ since an unanticipated increase in the growth of the world money supply will reduce world interest rates and raise world inflation. The fact that $\varepsilon_{i*} < 0$ implies that there is a shifting down of the FB schedule by the amount of this fall. There will be a capital inflow as domestic bonds become more attractive – temporarily.

. With fixed rate of monetary growth the LM schedule does not initially move as in Figure 8.9. But because of the shift of the FB line the AD schedule shifts to the left. Both π and Y fall. As π falls the LM schedule shifts to the right. The new equilibrium occurs at (π^1, Y^1).

Let us move now to a situation of exchange rate control. With $\varepsilon_{\pi*} > 0$ the IS curve shifts to the right as home goods become more attractive. The AD curve also shifts to the right by $\alpha_5\varepsilon_{\pi*} - \alpha_1\varepsilon_{i*}$. Both π and Y rise and the rise in the home inflation reduces demand for home goods and shifts the IS schedule to the left beyond its original position. However, Y must rise. This situation is analysed in Figure 8.10. Initial equilibrium in parts (a) and (b) occurs at E. A foreign monetary shock shifts FB downwards and IS outwards. AD also shifts outwards. IS then shifts back. Final equilibrium occurs at point s.

DOMESTIC SUPPLY SHOCK

Let us analyse, now, the consequences of an adverse supply shock. Let us suppose that $\varepsilon_s < 0$ and analyse the consequences with monetary control in Figure 8.11 and with exchange rate control in Figure 8.12.

With control over the rate of growth of money supply an adverse supply shock has the following effects. The AS schedule shifts to the left, raising π

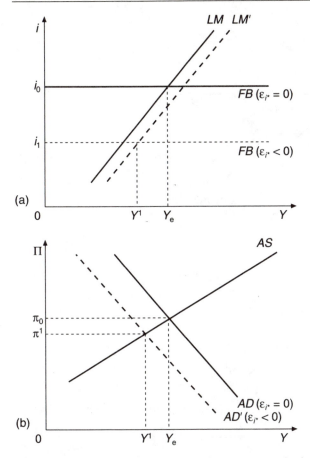

Figure 8.9

and lowering Y. The higher π shifts the LM schedule to the left. In final equilibrium π is higher and Y is lower.

When the central bank controls the exchange rate an adverse supply shock shifts the AS schedule to the left and π rises. This leads to a change in the terms of trade and home goods become less attractive. This shifts the IS schedule to the left. Hence, once again, π is higher and Y lower.

We conclude, therefore, that neither fixed nor flexible exchange rates provide a defence against a change in the world interest rate. Further, neither provide any protection against domestic supply shocks.

RANDOM SHOCKS AND THE EXCHANGE RATES

Let us finally try to understand the exchange rate effects of various random shocks. Let us take first differences in the IS equation of (8.14) and use the terms of trade definition of equation (8.18) to write

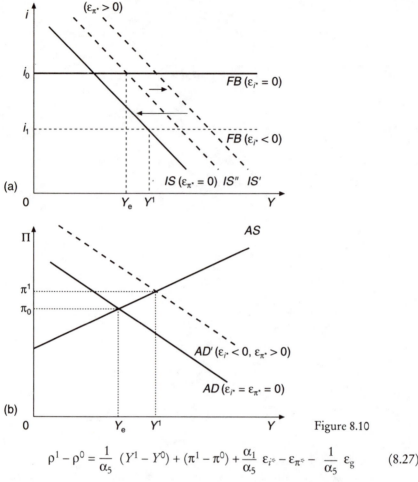

Figure 8.10

$$\rho^1 - \rho^0 = \frac{1}{\alpha_5} (Y^1 - Y^0) + (\pi^1 - \pi^0) + \frac{\alpha_1}{\alpha_5} \varepsilon_{i^*} - \varepsilon_{\pi^*} - \frac{1}{\alpha_5} \varepsilon_g \qquad (8.27)$$

Substituting the AS curve for $\pi^1 - \pi^0$ and then substituting equation (8.22) into (8.27) yields

$$\rho^1 - \rho^0 = \frac{\alpha_4 + \alpha_5}{\alpha_5 + \alpha_2\alpha_4\alpha_5} \varepsilon_m - \varepsilon_{\pi^*} - \frac{1}{\alpha_5} \varepsilon_g +$$

$$\frac{\alpha_1 + \alpha_1\alpha_2\alpha_4 + \alpha_3\alpha_4 + \alpha_3\alpha_5}{\alpha_5 + \alpha_2\alpha_4\alpha_5} \varepsilon_{i^*} + \frac{(1 + \alpha_4)(1 - \alpha_2\alpha_5)}{\alpha_5 + \alpha_2\alpha_4\alpha_5} \varepsilon_s \qquad (8.28)$$

This equation links changes in the exchange rate directly to the shocks.

The first thing to notice about this expression is that all three domestic shocks as well as both foreign shocks affect the exchange rate. Second, some shocks, e.g. the domestic monetary shock ε_m, have a determinate effect on the exchange rate whereas others do not. For example, only if the sign of ε_{i^*}

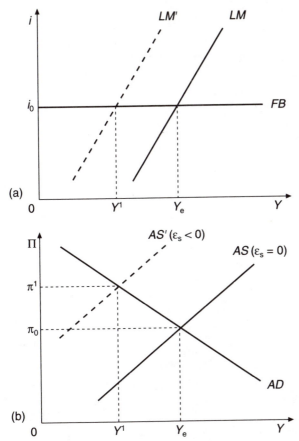

Figure 8.11

is opposite to that of $\varepsilon_{\pi*}$ can the effects of foreign shocks be determinate. Further, the term attached to ε_s cannot be unambiguously signed. This is because of two conflicting effects. On the one hand, the AS curve shifts downwards and reduces domestic inflation which lowers the terms of trade and makes home goods more attractive and the resulting trade surplus puts pressure on ρ to fall. On the other hand the higher income raises domestic demand for goods, leaving less available to foreigners and putting upward pressure on ρ.

CONCLUDING COMMENTS

In this chapter we have discussed a generalisation of the IS–LM–FB model. It has often been argued that this representation is inadequate for a developing economy. We consider this argument and some alternative models in Part III.

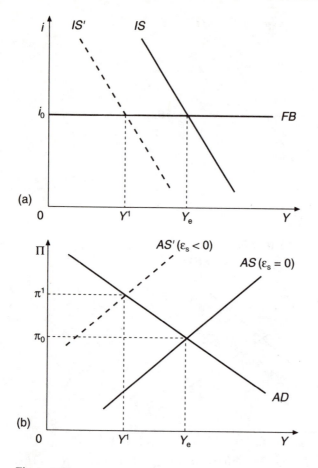

(a)

(b)

Figure 8.12

Part III

Alternative approaches to less developed country macroeconomics

9

A macro model with distinguishing features of developing countries

INTRODUCTION

The macro models we have studied thus far have two distinguishing characteristics so far as developing countries are concerned. First, they focus almost exclusively on the short run, and second, they could well have been macro models of developed countries. Indeed, students who have gone through standard macro courses will recognise most of these models. Hence from this vantage point there is not much difference between the theoretical approaches needed to study the macro problems of developed and developing countries.

Many eminent macroeconomists would disagree with this assessment. In this chapter we shall study an important alternative to this standard macro model. Indeed one reason why the standard model has been used so frequently to study the short-run macro problems of developing countries is the fact that alternatives to the neoclassical paradigm were mainly articulated to study problems of long-run growth (Chapter 15). This was only proper, for some time, because the concerns of developing countries mainly concentrated on their long-run growth prospects.

However, ever since the collapse of the Bretton Woods Agreement in 1971 and the subsequent oil price shocks, many developing countries faced severe balance of payments problems and had to seek the assistance of the International Monetary Fund (IMF). The IMF imposed some conditionalities on its loans (discussed within the context of the IMF's monetary approach to the balance of payments in Chapter 11) which took the form of *short-term* stabilisation measures. The IMF conditions were viewed and continue to be viewed as too harsh, but a cogent intellectual response could be fashioned only if an alternative view of the short-run macro performance of developing countries was available and agreed upon. These IMF conditions had the beneficial effect of giving rise to a whole new school of macroeconomic thinking about the problems of developing countries. Some of this alternative approach drew its inspiration, if not its technique of analysis, from an older and somewhat unorthodox view of the economic problems of developing countries that went under the general rubric of *structuralism*. In this chapter we shall study a model of structuralism. Our discussion here is cast in terms of aggregate supply and demand.

AGGREGATE SUPPLY

Aggregate supply in the economy depends, in general, upon product and labour market demand and supply functions and the behaviour of entrepreneurs and workers. In each of these instances developing countries are perceived to be different from developed countries.

In the aggregate supply schedule studied in Chapter 3 we had assumed that product markets are competitive. In less developed countries (LDCs) product markets are generally characterised by oligopoly with markup pricing. This is because the size of demand for industrial non-tradable goods is rather small. For firms producing tradable goods the government usually provides tariff protection and other incentives, typically subsidised credit and other forms of protection from foreign competition.

In addition wages in the labour markets are too high and do not reflect the true scarcity of labour. A variety of explanations can be offered for this. First, labour unions often emerge in protected manufacturing sectors at a relatively early date as labour unions follow Western patterns. The ruling *elite* in many developing countries finds it profitable to co-opt a section of the labour force to counterbalance the favour shown to domestic capitalists and for political gains. Correspondingly, the growth of labour unions is tolerated – even encouraged. Furthermore, salaries for civil servants also tend to get inflated. Multinational corporations in developing countries mimic wage structures in their home countries. All this leads to a situation of persistent excess supply of labour. In the short run, anyway, a considerable part of the labour force is unemployed, underemployed or employed at very low wages in the 'informal' sector. In the face of all this the money wage for regular employment is fixed.

Another important distinguishing characteristic of production in developing countries is that imported intermediate inputs are extremely important in industrial production. They, along with labour, are the major constituents of variable costs. It is often assumed that labour's marginal product is diminishing. However, it is not uncommon to find unused capacity in the industrial sector. Moreover, working capital is financed largely by borrowing cash. With capital markets that are not well developed, equity investment is relatively unimportant. Correspondingly, the rate of interest is an important determinant of the cost of working capital and, hence, of aggregate supply. Since imported intermediate inputs are an important element of cost, so is the exchange rate. As the price of foreign exchange goes up, *ceteris paribus*, we would expect the price of imported inputs to go up and hence supply to fall. We can then write the aggregate supply function as

$$Y^s = Y^s(\underset{+}{P}, \underset{-}{i}, \underset{-}{w}, \underset{-}{e}) \tag{9.1}$$

where Y is real output, P is the price level, i is the interest rate, w is the nominal wage rate and e is the exchange rate. In the PY plane an increase in i, w or e would shift the aggregate supply schedule leftward. Furthermore, since excess supply exists in industry we would expect the AS schedule to be relatively flat, not steep.

To be precise we must specify which good's supply we are talking about. There are several goods in the model. First, there are intermediate inputs which are not produced domestically and need to be considered. Second, there is the domestic good which is consumed as well as invested. Third, there are exports. We shall club the last two goods into one category and study demand and supply for it. Our analysis follows, in the main, the work of Taylor (1987) and Porter and Ranney (1982).

AGGREGATE DEMAND

Aggregate demand in developing countries is also affected by their institutional characteristics. In the first instance, financial intermediation and, sometimes, even the use of money is not very widespread in developing countries. There are many indicators of financial underdevelopment in developing countries. The ratio of financial assets to national income is low. The number of banks is low and unduly concentrated in urban areas. Furthermore bank interest rates are controlled by the government – a policy which has been called 'financial repression' by McKinnon (1973). A large part of investment is self-financed.

This has two significant implications for monetary policy. First, large parts of the economy are outside the purview of the central bank. Second, open market operations are not very important. The central and commercial banks hold government debt at artificially low interest rates and, therefore, are not traded in the bond market. In Table 9.1 we detail the prototype of accounts for four major economic agents in a typical developing country.

In this table we distinguish between four different types of economic agents: the central bank, the commercial banks, firms and households. We neglect currency holdings since no great insight is obtained by including it. We make the realistic assumption that domestic residents do not hold foreign exchange. This assumption may not always be satisfied. From the table we have

$$\Sigma\Delta + \Sigma\beta = R \tag{9.2}$$

$$R + L_b = D_f + D_h \tag{9.3}$$

$$D_f + PK = L_b + L_h + N_f \tag{9.4}$$

$$D_h + L_h + N_f = N_h \tag{9.5}$$

Table 9.1 Balance sheets of four agents of a typical developing country

Assets	Liabilities
The central bank	
$\Sigma\Delta$	R
$\Sigma\beta$	
Commercial banks	
R	D_f
L_b	D_h
Firms	
D_f	L_b
PK	L_h
$-N_f$	N_f
Households	
D_h	
L_h	N_h
N_f	

Notes: $\Sigma\Delta$, sum of past government budget deficits; $\Sigma\beta$, sum of past balance of payments surpluses; R, commercial bank reserves; L_b, short-term working capital loans to firms; D_f, deposits of firms; D_h, deposits of households; PK, nominal value of current capital stock; L_h, loans from households; N_f, net worth of firms; N_h, net worth of households.

The monetary base is determined completely by the sum of past government budget deficits and the sum of the past balance of payments surpluses. In any time period

$$\Delta = wN_g + PI_g - T \tag{9.6}$$

$$\beta = e(X - M) \tag{9.7}$$

where N_g is the size of the labour force employed by the government, I_g is the amount of investment undertaken by the government, T is tax revenue, X are exports and M are imports. We have normalised world price to equal one.

Thus any change that increases the government budget deficit or the balance of payments surplus will cause a direct and cumulating increase in the monetary base.

The central bank imposes a reserve requirement ratio θ on the commercial banks:

$$R = \theta(D_f + D_h) \tag{9.8}$$

Using (9.2), (9.3) and (9.8) the supply of bank loans is determined as

$$L_b = (\Sigma\Delta + \Sigma\beta) \frac{1 - \theta}{\theta} \tag{9.9}$$

Any increase in the monetary base or decrease in the reserve requirement ratio increases L_b.

The demand for real balances is modelled as a function of real income Y and the interest rate i. For simplicity we ignore the rates of return on capital and firms' equity as possible determinants of the households' demand for money. The demand for real balances by households is written as D_h/P where

$$\frac{D_h}{P} = \phi_h\,(Y,i) \tag{9.10}$$

Firms demand money in order to finance their variable costs during the period of production. These costs consist primarily of labour and imported raw materials, and hence

$$\frac{D_f}{P} = \phi_f\left[\frac{wN + emY}{P}, i\right] \tag{9.11}$$

where w is the nominal wage rate, N is the level of employment, and m is the marginal propensity to import. Empirically, in LDCs, the elasticity of money demand by firms with respect to cost is near unity whereas the elasticity with respect to the interest rate is near zero.

Substituting appropriately and eliminating the financial variables we derive a single equation that defines the financial equilibrium of the economy:

$$P\phi_f\left(\frac{wN + emY}{P}, i\right) + P\phi_h(Y,i) - \frac{\Sigma\Delta + \Sigma B}{\theta} = 0 \tag{9.12}$$

This is the LM equation for this economy. It says that money demand by firms and households must equal money supply $((\Sigma\Delta + \Sigma\beta)/\theta)$. It has three endogenous variables: the price level P, national output Y and the interest rate i. This interest rate is to be distinguished from the fixed bank lending rate i_b. The past values of the budget deficit and balance of payments deficit are unalterable; however, the current values of these variables can be influenced. The two obvious policy variables in this equation are the exchange rate e and the reserve requirement ratio θ. Holding all other ingredients constant, the slope of the LM schedule is

$$\left(\frac{di}{dy}\right)_{LM} = -\frac{[(\partial\phi_f/\partial(wN + emY))\,em + (\partial\phi_h/\partial Y)]}{1 + (\partial\phi_h/\partial i)} > 0$$

Hence the LM curve is upward sloping. This is the same as in developed countries but in LDCs the LM schedule is definitely steeper, *ceteris paribus*. Several reasons can be advanced for this. The ratio of money to gross national product (GNP) is smaller in LDCs and this may mean that it is largely held for transactions purposes: $\partial\phi_h/\partial i \approx 0$. An increase in the price level will lower the real supply of money and shift the LM curve upward and to the left. An increase in e, θ or w will have the same effect. An increase in Δ or β will imply an increase in the monetary base and the LM curve will shift to the right.

GOODS MARKET EQUILIBRIUM

As before, goods market equilibrium occurs when aggregate goods demand equals aggregate supply. Aggregate demand has the usual components. Real consumption expenditure depends upon real disposable income. Moreover the functional distribution of income is important in LDCs. It is often argued that the marginal propensity to consume out of wage income is lower than that out of capital income. We further introduce an aggregate (proportional) income tax rate into the consumption function and write it as

$$C = C(\underset{+}{Y}, \underset{-}{S_l}, \underset{-}{\tau_y}) \tag{9.13}$$

where S_l is the share of labour in total income. τ_y is the proportional income tax rate. Consumption rises when real income rises and drops when the share of labour in total income or the income tax rate rises.

Let us now look at investment demand. Investment is assumed to depend positively on the desired capital stock which, in turn, depends on output. Investment funds are borrowed from official sources (commercial banks and the like) at the fixed interest rate i_b. However, because this interest rate is below the equilibrium interest rate, there will be an excess demand for investment which spills over to the curb market where the interest rate i is flexible. In a functional form for investment it will be convenient to express investment as a function of the average of these interest rates. We know that this average interest rate will also be a function of the availability of loans (L_b) at the official rate. From equation (9.9) we know that L_b increases as total reserves ($\Sigma\Delta + \Sigma\beta$) increase. Hence we can write the private investment function as

$$I = I(\underset{+}{Y}, \underset{-}{i}, \underset{-}{i_b}, \underset{+}{\Delta}, \underset{+}{\beta}, \underset{-}{\theta}, \underset{-}{w/P}, \underset{-}{e/P}) \tag{9.14}$$

As output goes up, so does the optimal capital stock and investment; as i or i_b rise investment drops for the standard reasons; as total reserves rise the amount of loans available from official sources rises and hence investment rises. When the reserve requirement rises, the amount of funds available for investment drops. When the real wage or the real exchange rate rise the cost of financing inputs goes up and investment drops. It is to be noted that changes in the official bank rate, i_b, affect the commodity market equilibrium and, hence, the IS schedule but not the LM schedule.

Government spending in developing countries is composed largely of wage payments and the wage paid to government employees is kept in line with those in the private sector – or vice versa. Any decrease in the real wage bill would decrease government expenditure. Another major component of government expenditure is public investment. We shall assume that this is fixed in the short run in real terms. We may, therefore, write real government expenditure G as

$$G = G(\underset{+}{wN_g/P}, \underset{+}{I_g}) \tag{9.15}$$

The signs of the partial derivatives are as noted above.

We may now investigate the determinants of net exports. For most developing countries the assumption of a small open economy is appropriate. Hence the domestic price of tradables depends on world prices, subsidies, tariffs and the exchange rate. Because of capacity and other constraints the price elasticity of supply of exports is likely to be small in the short run.

In most developing countries imports and domestic goods are very poor substitutes. For LDCs that have embarked on a course of import substitution and have completed most of it, imports consist largely of non-competitive imported inputs. We suppose that imports are a fixed proportion of domestic output.

It should also be pointed out that many LDC governments derive substantial revenues from *ad valorem* taxes on imports (τ_m). We shall also model a tax on exports (τ_x) – which may actually be a subsidy $\tau_x < 0$. Further, the trade sector is a very important part of national accounts and many significant macroeconomic problems of developing countries have their genesis in a large deficit in their current accounts.

We write net exports (NX) as

$$NX = \frac{e}{P}\left[(1 - \tau_x)X\frac{e(1 - \tau_x)}{P} - (1 + \tau_m)mY\right] \tag{9.16}$$

where X is the value of exports in foreign currency. We can write the goods market equilibrium condition as

$$Y = C(Y, S_1, \tau_y) + I\left(Y, i, i_b, \Sigma\Delta, \Delta\beta, \theta, \frac{w}{P}, \frac{e}{P}\right) + G\left(\frac{wN_g}{P,}, I_g\right)$$

$$+ \frac{e}{P}\left[(1 - \tau_x)X\frac{e(1 - \tau_x)}{P} - (1 + \tau_m)mY\right] \tag{9.17}$$

The equilibrium relation between i and Y from the above equation will be the IS schedule. This schedule will have a negative slope in the iY plane for fixed values of other variables. This IS schedule is likely to be quite steep. A major reason for this is the low interest elasticity of investment demand. However, as Leff and Sato (1980) argue, the IS curve may not be too steep on two counts: first, the large value of the marginal propensity to consume in developing countries and, second, the high income elasticity of investment demand.

An increase in government expenditure will shift the IS curve outwards. An increase in τ_x or τ_m will reduce the value of net exports in domestic currency for a given foreign currency balance, thus shifting the IS curve inwards. This is counteracted to some extent if export supply or import demand are price elastic.

When there is a devaluation of the real exchange rate (e/P) the terms of trade are adversely affected and investment declines because the cost of intermediate inputs rises. From our study of the Marshall–Lerner condition in Chapter 7 we know that if B is the initial trade balance in domestic currency, η_{XS} is the export supply elasticity, ε_{MD} is the (absolute value of the) import demand elasticity and M is imports in foreign currency, the balance of trade will worsen (ignoring taxes) if

$$\frac{B}{e} + X\eta_{XS} + M\varepsilon_{MD} < 0 \tag{9.18}$$

For developing countries it would seem that both η_{XS} and ε_{MD} are small. Furthermore, in times of severe balance of payments problems, B may be a very large negative number. Hence, under these conditions, it would seem that devaluation will reduce aggregate demand and shift the IS curve inwards (see Krugman and Taylor 1978).

Finally a reduction in the real wage rate (w/P) will shift the IS curve down and to the left through its effect on the wage share S_1, but up and to the right through the effect on retained earnings and hence fixed private investment. In most LDCs we would expect the former effect to dominate.

The price level is the third endogenous variable in the goods market equilibrium equation. An increase in the price level implies both a revaluation of the real exchange rate (a decrease in e/P) and a fall in the real wage (a decrease in w/P). The net effect would, therefore, be ambiguous. We shall assume that this effect is zero.

THE AGGREGATE DEMAND SCHEDULE

The LM schedule and the IS schedule can be combined in the usual way to remove one of the three endogenous variables. We choose to remove the curb market interest rate i. Since i_b is a parameter we are left with a relation between P and Y which can be written as (with Y^d denoting output demanded)

$$Y^d = Y^d \left(\underset{-}{P}, \underset{-}{\theta}, \underset{-}{i_b}, \underset{+}{N_g}, \underset{+}{I_g}, \underset{-}{\tau_y}, \underset{-}{\tau_x}, \underset{-}{\tau_m}, \underset{?}{e}, \underset{?}{w}, \underset{+}{\Sigma\Delta}, \underset{+}{\Sigma\beta} \right) \tag{9.19}$$

With all other factors held constant, this AD schedule is downward sloping in the YP plane. However, this AD schedule is likely to be much steeper than the AD schedule derived in Chapter 3. There are two reasons for this. First, following a price rise, the IS schedule shifts to the left in the standard model but does not do so in developing countries. Furthermore, the IS curve is relatively steep due to a high marginal propensity to import and a low interest elasticity of investment demand.

It is also noteworthy that devaluation reduces aggregate demand in the case of developing countries whereas, students will recall, devaluation increases aggregate demand in developed countries. Further, the nominal wage enters aggregate demand with an uncertain sign.

AGGREGATE SUPPLY

We now move on to consider aggregate supply. In general it is possible to write down the aggregate supply function as

$$Y^s = Y^s \underset{+ \ - \ - \ -}{(P, i, e, w)} \tag{9.20}$$

Furthermore, removing variables that are inessential for the time being, we can write the aggregate demand function as

$$Y^d = Y^d \underset{- \ - \ +^g \ + \ + \ + \ +}{(P, \theta, I_g, e, w, \Sigma\Delta, \Sigma\beta)} \tag{9.21}$$

The signs of the partial derivatives below the Y^d equation have already been discussed. So far as aggregate supply is concerned a rise in the price level will evoke the normal supply response, an increase in the interest rate will make production more costly and reduce supply, an increase in the value of foreign exchange will make production more costly and, hence, reduce supply, and so will an increase in the nominal wage which, in turn, will have the same effect on the supply of output.

It ought to be pointed out that, as before, any change in the IS–LM equilibrium and, therefore, the curb market interest rate will be a function of the price level (changes in which induce shifts of the LM schedule) and exogenous variables of the model. Hence, it is possible to write down the curb market interest rate as a function of the price level and the exogenous variables:

$$i = i \underset{+ \ + \ +^g \ ? \ + \ - \ -}{(P, \theta, I_g, e, w, \Sigma\Delta, \Sigma\beta)} \tag{9.22}$$

The signs of the partial derivatives of equation (9.22) are those appropriate to the LDC model discussed above. Since the IS curve does not shift there is an unambiguously positive sign below P. As P rises the supply of money falls and the interest rate rises. This effect is not altered by any goods market effects. Similarly as θ rises the money supply drops and the interest rate rises. The rationale for the other effects is also straightforward.

Using equation (9.22) we eliminate the interest rate from the aggregate supply, aggregate demand framework and write them as functions of two endogenous variables P and Y. Substituting for i in the aggregate supply equation (9.20) we have

$$Y^s = Y^s \underset{-+ \ + \ +^g \ ? \ + \ - \ - \ -+ \ - \ -}{[i(P, \theta, I_g, e, w, \Sigma\Delta, \Sigma\beta), P, e, w]} \tag{9.23}$$

The slope of the aggregate supply function represented by equation (9.23) in YP space will be steeper than that in equation (9.20). This is because the effect of the price level through interest rate changes is captured in equation (9.23) but ignored in equation (9.20).

Moreover, changes in exogenous or endogenous variables may affect the monetary base, called the *cumulative effect*. An increase in P increases both nominal government spending (to the extent that real government

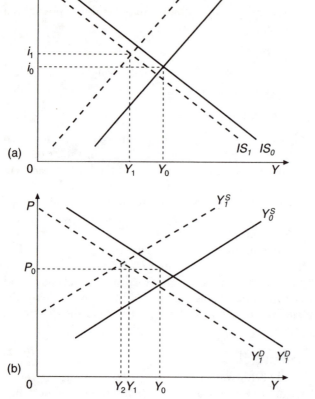

Figure 9.1

expenditures are fixed) and tax revenues (to the extent that there are direct income-related taxes). We assume that the net effect is negligible. An increase in Y increases imports, reducing the balance of payments surplus and increasing import duty revenues, which, in turn, decreases the budget deficit. Hence the monetary base decreases. This decrease shifts both the aggregate demand and the aggregate supply to the left so that output falls. We now examine the effects of various policy shocks.

MONETARY CONTRACTION

The impact of monetary contraction in the standard model is shown in Figure 9.1. The initial position of various schedules is denoted by the subscript 0 and the final position by the subscript 1. An increase in the reserve requirement ratio θ, for example, will reduce the money supply and will shift the LM curve up to the left and the IS curve to the left and down. Because of the low interest elasticity of money demand the shift in the LM schedule is greater and the interest rate rises to i_1 and output falls to Y_1. We draw the old and new Y^d schedules in Figure 9.1(b). Aggregate supply and aggregate demand will shift inwards. Because of underutilisation of capacity the output supply function is relatively flat and the price level registers a small rise. Had the output supply function not shifted, output would have fallen to Y_1. Because of the rise of the price level there is a second round fall in Y. In part (a) the LM schedule shifts leftwards again with the IS schedule staying stationary – remember that it has been assumed that the IS schedule does not respond to changes in the price level. Output falls to Y_2. In the case of developed economies the price level falls in response to a monetary contraction. In the case of LDCs, however, the price level may increase.

It ought to be stressed, however, that the cumulative effects of the increase in reserve ratio requirement will reverse the drop in the money supply and output will tend to revert back to Y_0.

RESTRICTIVE FISCAL POLICY

Let us now look at the effects of a restrictive fiscal policy. We analyse this in Figure 9.2. A decrease in government spending shifts down the IS schedule in Figure 9.2(a) from IS_0 to IS_1. This results in output falling to Y_1 and, in part (b), the AD schedule shifting down from Y_0^d to Y_1^d. Output would have fallen to Y_1 had the aggregate supply schedule been horizontal. However, a fall in government expenditure means that the curb market interest rate also falls. This stimulates aggregate supply and the aggregate supply schedule shifts out from Y_0^s to Y_1^s. Output starts to rise and the price level starts to fall. We may come to an equilibrium income like Y_2 with the LM schedule shifting outwards because of the price fall. (Remember the price fall does not affect the IS schedule.) The contractionary fiscal policy can turn out to be expansionary. Hence fiscal policy becomes a very important policy tool in LDCs, at least in the short run.

The reduction in government spending increases the government surplus and leaves the balance of trade essentially unchanged. The cumulative effect is a reduction in the monetary base. Thus, over time, recession appears or worsens.

DEVALUATION

The difference between developed and developing countries is most evident when we consider the effects of a devaluation. We have already considered the effects of a devaluation in the case of developed countries. As a matter of fact we analysed several different approaches to devaluation. The general result from this was that, except in some extreme cases, a devaluation can help improve the balance of payments position of developed countries running a deficit.

For the case of developing countries we know that the IMF has almost

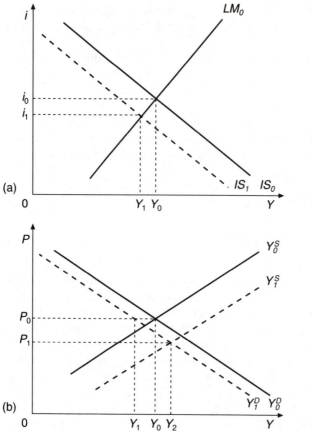

Figure 9.2

always insisted on a devaluation as a condition for extending loans to deficit developing countries. In Chapter 12 we discuss, in greater detail, the effects of the IMF stabilisation package. In this section we want to analyse the effects of devaluation within the context of the model studied in this chapter.

Let us examine these effects in Figure 9.3. For a given price level, devaluation shifts both the IS and LM curves to the left (from IS_0 and LM_0 to IS_1 and LM_1, respectively). Aggregate demand falls to Y_1^d. But the effect on i is ambiguous (in Figure 9.3(a) we show no change). Even when the interest rate is constant the increase in the price of foreign goods following a devaluation shifts the aggregate supply schedule to Y_1^s. Output falls to Y_2 ultimately with the price level going up or, perhaps, staying constant.

Although the fall in output suggests an expansionary cumulative effect, devaluation has the direct impact of reducing the monetary base. Tax revenues from trade increase in terms of home currency, while balance of payments deficit increases. The net effect is ambiguous.

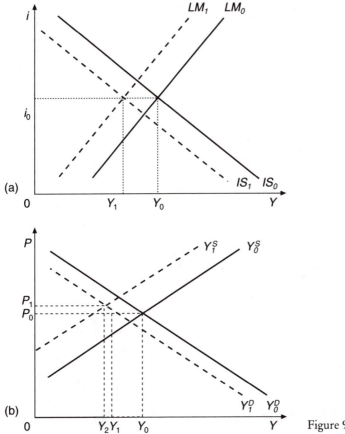

Figure 9.3

WAGE RESTRAINT

An incomes policy that calls for cuts in workers' nominal wages affects the model in a variety of ways. First, if we assume that the decrease in government spending and the redistribution of income away from workers have a large impact relative to the increased investment resulting from increased retained earnings, the IS schedule will shift inwards to the left. Second, since there is less demand for financing working capital, the demand for money falls and the LM schedule shifts to the right. Because wage and interest costs fall, supply conditions improve and the aggregate supply schedule shifts to the right.

The analysis of these effects is carried out in Figure 9.4. In part (a) the leftward shift of the IS schedule from IS_0 to IS_1 dominates the rightward shift of the LM schedule (from LM_0 to LM_1). In part (b) aggregate demand falls from Y_0^d to Y_1^d. Had the supply curve been horizontal, output would

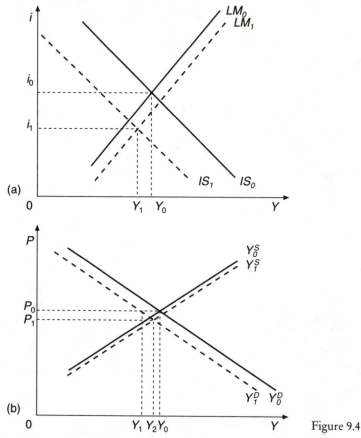

Figure 9.4

have fallen to Y_1 and the price level would have stayed at P_0. However, not only is the supply curve upward sloping but it also shifts during the process of adjustment. Output rises, somewhat, to Y_2 and the price falls so that the LM schedule shifts again to intersect IS at Y_2. Thus a wage restraint reduces the price level but may cause a drop in output.

CONCLUDING COMMENTS

From the analysis in this chapter it is clear that traditional stabilisation policies have very different, and generally less desirable, effects in LDCs than in advanced countries, at least within the structuralist framework. Most importantly, contractionary policy may fuel rather than dampen inflationary tendencies. It seems to be difficult to get rid of balance of payments difficulties except through severe output contraction to reduce import demand. Devaluation is not able to help very much. Second, all macro policies have effects on the government budget and balance of payments deficits. This severely restricts the government's ability to conduct stabilisation programmes. Third, most restrictive policies are likely to adversely affect the distribution of income. The standard IMF recipe for the balance of payments problems of developing countries is, according to this point of view, counterproductive. According to this school of thought, then, developing countries face a formidable task in stabilising output and the price level.

10

Dualistic models of output and inflation in less developed countries

INTRODUCTION

In Chapter 9 we studied a macro model with some salient features of developing countries. We concentrated on the role of imported intermediate inputs and imperfect capital markets in the determination of aggregate supply. In that chapter and earlier chapters particular emphasis was placed on the role of the foreign sector in determining output and inflation. In this chapter we wish to introduce some other complications peculiar to LDCs.

In particular we wish to concentrate on the dualistic nature of many LDC economies – a characteristic that makes an aggregative model like that of Chapter 9 somewhat untenable. It is possible to argue that there is a fundamental schism between the traditional agricultural sector and the relatively modern industrial sector. There are several differences between the two sectors. For instance, the agricultural sector is operated by peasant-owners, relies mainly on family labour and operates relatively outdated technology. On the other hand, in the industrial sector production is carried out in capitalist profit-seeking enterprises using relatively modern technology and hiring labour and other inputs in impersonal factor markets. There are two important links between the two sectors: food is the most important item of consumption of industrial workers and industrial goods are needed for investment in the agricultural sector. It must be admitted, however, that the differences between the two sectors do tend to narrow down with the development of the economy. In order to focus on the problems associated with dualism we assume that the economy we are studying is closed. The models studied in this chapter are those of closed dual economies rather than the aggregative open economy version studied in Chapter 9.

The dualistic view of LDC economies has a long and distinguished history. For a recent survey of this vast literature see Ranis (1989). This literature has, for the most part, concentrated on real (non-monetary) issues and on long-run growth. Only very recently has this model been adapted to address macroeconomic questions (see, for instance, van Wijnbergen (1983), Edwards and van Wijnbergen (1989) and Taylor (1987, 1988)).

In this chapter we wish to study two simplified versions of these models. First, we emphasise the role of differences in adjustment mechanisms between the two sectors. Output of the agricultural sector is fixed and the market for agricultural goods clears through price adjustment. The industrial sector is modelled as being of recent origin. In the context of LDCs this has two implications (Taylor 1987). First, in the labour market, labour presses for certain wage demands and, second, the market for industrial goods is characterised by markup pricing. In other words, both labour and output markets are characterised by imperfect competition. Money and other financial assets enter the model through wealth effects. This model is being discussed as a prototype of a low saving–low growth LDC. Hence we focus attention on short-run equilibrium rather than long-run growth.

The second version of the dual economy macro model is based primarily on the work of Taylor (1983) and Rattso (1989). We consider questions of adjustment within a broader perspective with Keynesian and neoclassical adjustment mechanisms considered *seriatim*. We also examine the implications of differences in the propensities to save of different income classes. We explicitly model savings and investment in this section although monetary issues are eschewed. It would be only slightly oversimplifying matters if the matter of Chapter 9 is termed 'structuralist and applicable to Latin American countries'; the first model in this chapter can then be said to be representative of the relatively less developed economies of Africa where agriculture has been stagnant, though important, and where the nascent manufacturing sector is characterised by high degrees of imperfection in both factor and product markets. The second model in this chapter is applicable to countries where the industrial sector has taken firm roots although the economy is still essentially dual. Rattso and others have estimated variants of this last model for India – but clearly the model has wider applicability. Both models in this chapter assume that the factor of production constraining output is capital, not labour.

A SHORT-RUN DUALISTIC MACRO MODEL WITH DIFFERENCES IN ADJUSTMENT

Consider an economy with two sectors: agriculture (A) and manufacturing (M). Agricultural output (sometimes called food) is determined by supply conditions in sector A which, as we have discussed above, have several non-market characteristics. We make the simplifying assumption that agricultural output is exogenously determined. We denote this level as $\bar{X}_A$. The price of food is determined in competitive markets. We assume that this price is flexible.

We denote by X_M, P_A, P_M and P_R the output of the manufacturing sector, the price of food, the price of manufactured goods and the relative price of sector A to sector M goods, respectively: $P_R = P_A/P_M$. $P_R\bar{X}_A + X_M$ is total income in terms of sector M goods. α is the fraction of income spent on sector M goods and $1 - \alpha$ is the fraction spent on sector A goods ($1 \geq \alpha \geq 0$). Since the share of income spent on either good is fixed it follows that we are assuming unitary price elasticity of demand for both goods. Let γ be the marginal propensity to consume.

The market for agricultural goods clears when supply equals demand, i.e. when

$$P_R\bar{X}_A = (1 - \alpha)\gamma(P_R\bar{X}_A + X_M) \tag{10.1}$$

The left-hand side of equation (10.1) is the value of agricultural supply, and the right-hand side is the value of agricultural demand, both in terms of sector M output. From equation (10.1) we can calculate the equilibrium value of P_R as

$$P_R = \frac{(1 - \alpha)\gamma X_M}{[1 - (1 - \alpha)\gamma]\bar{X}_A} \tag{10.2}$$

Clearly this has a meaningful solution only when $1 - (1 - \alpha)\gamma > 0$. In Figure 10.1 we depict equation (10.2) as the line AA.

If agricultural price moves sluggishly the economy may not be on the line AA. In Figure 10.1 MM denotes the equilibrium relation between P_R and X_M in the market for manufactured goods. We shall assume that this market clears through quantity rather than price adjustments. The market clearing level of sector M output is

$$X_M = \alpha\gamma(P_R\bar{X}_A + X_M) + \bar{G} \tag{10.3}$$

where $\bar{G}$ is exogenous government expenditure in terms of sector M output and the first term on the right-hand side represents private consumption.

From equation (10.3) we can write

$$X_M = \frac{\alpha\gamma\bar{X}_A P_R}{1 - \alpha\gamma} + \frac{\bar{G}}{1 - \alpha\gamma} \tag{10.4}$$

Equation (10.4) is plotted in Figure 10.1 as the MM schedule. If $1 - (1 - \alpha)\gamma < 1 - \gamma\alpha$, it follows that the MM schedule is steeper than the AA schedule. $1/(1 - \alpha\gamma)$ is a Keynesian multiplier type relation. We shall assume that this multiplier relation is always satisfied so that the economy is always on the line MM.

The market for industrial goods is characterised by imperfect competition so that P_M is a markup (assumed fixed) over unit labour cost:

$$P_M = (1 + \varphi)\beta W \tag{10.5}$$

where φ is the markup factor, β is the amount of labour required to produce one unit of industrial output and W is the nominal wage rate in sector M. Capital is not used for production in the M sector.

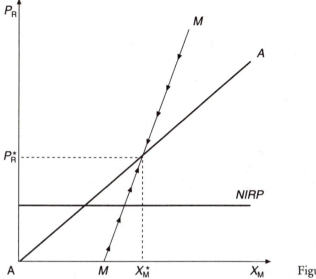

Figure 10.1

The labour market is also characterised by imperfect competition. Workers are assumed to have a target real wage ω (denoted in units of both goods). Let us define the consumer price index, P_C, as

$$P_C = P_A{}^{1-\alpha}P_M^{\alpha} \tag{10.6}$$

so that the target nominal wage W_τ can be defined as

$$W_\tau = \omega P_C \tag{10.7}$$

We admit a degree of money illusion in the model by postulating that the actual wage adjusts slowly to the gap between the actual wage W and the target wage W_τ. When $W = W_\tau$ there is no inflation of wages or prices. We can solve for non-inflationary relative price $\bar{P}_R$ by substituting from equation (10.6) into equation (10.5):

$$\bar{P}_R = [(1 + \varphi)\beta\omega]^{-1/(1-\alpha)} \tag{10.8}$$

$\bar{P}_R$ is positively related to the markup factor, the labour–output ratio and the desired real wage. This is denoted as the horizontal line NIRP (Non-Inflationary Relative Price) in Figure 10.1.

Our assumption about the movement of nominal wages implies that

$$\frac{\dot{W}}{W} = \eta\left[\left(\frac{P_R}{\bar{P}_R}\right) - 1\right] \tag{10.9}$$

where $1 \geq \eta \geq 0$ and a dot above a variable denotes a time derivative. Further, since the markup factor is constant it must be the case that the rate of inflation of P_M is the same as that of W. In other words,

$$\frac{\dot{P}_M}{P_M} = \frac{\dot{W}}{W} \tag{10.10}$$

Finally we postulate that the relative price P_R, adjusts as per excess demand for food:

$$\frac{\dot{P}_R}{P_R} = \iota \left[(1 - \alpha) \left(\frac{X_M}{P_R} + \bar{X}_A \right) - \bar{X}_A \right] \tag{10.11}$$

where $1 \geq \iota \geq 0$ and the expression inside the square brackets is the excess demand for food.

From equation (10.2) it can be seen that, if there is no excess demand for food, i.e. if we are on the line AA, then $\dot{P}_R = 0$. If P_R is above AA, P_R must be falling. Equations (10.9), (10.10) and (10.11) fully describe the dynamics of inflation in this economy.

STABILITY

By assumption the market for industrial goods always clears. We substitute for X_M from equation (10.4) into equation (10.11) and rearrange to get a first-order linear differential equation in P_R:

$$\dot{P}_R = \frac{\bar{G}\iota(1 - \alpha)\gamma}{1 - \alpha\gamma} - \frac{\iota(1 - \gamma)}{1 - \alpha\gamma} \bar{X}_A P_R \tag{10.12}$$

Stability requires that

$$(1 - \alpha) \frac{\gamma}{1 - \alpha\gamma} < 1 \tag{10.13}$$

in other words that the MM schedule be steeper than the AA line.

EQUILIBRIUM AND COMPARATIVE STATICS

Equilibrium in this model obtains when both the manufacturing and agricultural markets clear. The equilibrium relative price (P_R^*) can be obtained by setting $\dot{P}_R = 0$ in equation (10.12) and solving for equilibrium P_R^*:

$$P_R^* = \frac{(1 - \alpha)\gamma\bar{G}}{(1 - \gamma)\bar{X}_A} \tag{10.14}$$

With P_R at its equilibrium value and agricultural output predetermined, the market for X_M clears. To find the equilibrium value of manufacturing sector output, substitute the value of P_R^* into equation (10.4) and solve for X_M to get

$$X_M = \frac{[1 - (1 - \alpha)\gamma]\bar{G}}{1 - \gamma} \tag{10.15}$$

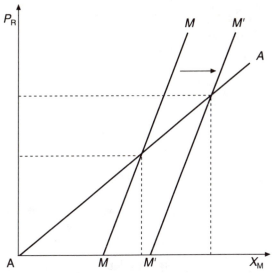

Figure 10.2

When relative prices have stopped changing P_A, P_M, W and the overall price level are all changing at the same rate. Using equations (10.10) and (10.9) we can write the following expression for π, the overall rate of inflation,

$$\pi^* = \eta\left[\frac{(1-\alpha)\gamma\bar{G}}{(1-\gamma)\bar{X}_A P_R^*} - 1\right] \qquad (10.16)$$

We now turn to comparative statics. An increase in government expenditure raises aggregate demand and the MM line shifts to the right. This is depicted in Figure 10.2. The increase in government expenditure increases X_M via a Keynesian type relation. Given agricultural output, then, P_R will rise.

An increase in agricultural output implies a downward rotation of the AA schedule and the MM schedule shifts to the right. Since demand for food has unitary price elasticity, the incomes of farmers does not change, i.e. the percentage increase in X_A is exactly equal to the percentage drop in P_R. This is depicted in Figure 10.3.

ASSET EFFECTS

Much of the financial wealth in many developing countries is held in the form of government debt and money. In this section we alter the model we have been studying to incorporate asset effects in consumption because of the accumulation of cash balances. No other forms of wealth will be admitted. We shall simplify the analysis still further and assume that the government does not issue debt because the market for such debt is underdeveloped. Hence, nominal wealth is simply money, M. We define real wealth m as nominal wealth divided by industrial prices:

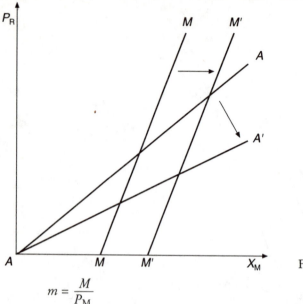

Figure 10.3

$$m = \frac{M}{P_M} \tag{10.17}$$

Real asset accumulation must be

$$\dot{m} = \frac{\dot{M}}{P_M} - \frac{M}{P_M}\frac{\dot{P}_M}{P_M} \tag{10.18}$$

The government earns revenue by issuing new money and by taxing incomes in both sectors (at the common proportional rate v). Hence we can write the government's budget constraint as

$$\dot{M} = P_M\bar{G} - v(P_M X_M + P_A\bar{X}_A) \tag{10.19}$$

Substituting equation (10.19) into equation (10.18) we get an expression for the rate of change of real wealth

$$\dot{m} = \bar{G} - v(X_M + \bar{X}_A P_R) - m\delta \tag{10.20}$$

where δ is the rate of inflation of the industrial price. Using a linear Taylor approximation we write

$$m\delta \approx m_0\delta_0 + m_0\delta + \delta_0 m \tag{10.21}$$

where the subscript 0 denotes initial values. Hence we can write

$$\dot{m} = \bar{G} - v(X_M + P_R X_A) - m_0\delta \tag{10.22}$$

assuming, for simplicity, that initial inflation is zero. From this equation government expenditure must equal the sum of tax revenue, the revenue from the inflation tax and the change in real assets. Consumers consider the change in real assets at par with income and, therefore, consume a fraction γ of it.

Now, the agricultural market clears when

$$\bar{X}_A P_R = (1 - \alpha)\gamma(1 - v)(\bar{X}_A P_R + X_M) + (1 - \alpha)\gamma m \qquad (10.23)$$

Hence, equilibrium relative price $\bar{P}_R$ occurs when

$$\bar{P}_R = \frac{[1 - \alpha)\gamma(1 - v)X_M + (1 - \alpha)\gamma m]}{\bar{X}_A[1 - (1 - \alpha)\gamma(1 - v)]} \qquad (10.24)$$

For a reasonable solution we must have $1 > (1 - \alpha)\gamma(1 - v)$.

The market for manufactured goods clears when

$$X_M = \alpha\gamma(1 - v)(\bar{X}_A P_R + X_M) + \alpha\gamma m + \bar{G} \qquad (10.25)$$

which can be solved for X_M to yield

$$X_M = \frac{\bar{X}_A P_R \, \alpha\gamma(1 - v) + \alpha\gamma m + \bar{G}}{1 - \alpha\gamma(1 - v)} \qquad (10.26)$$

For a meaningful solution $1 > \alpha\gamma(1 - v)$. The value of the government expenditure multiplier is now altered. It is now $1/[1 - \alpha\gamma(1 - v)]$. It is higher because there is another source of consumption demand, namely real assets. We now discuss short-run equilibrium and comparative static analyses just as in the non-monetary version of the model. The derivation of the condition for local stability is algebraically tedious and unilluminating. It is mentioned below and the formal derivation is left as an exercise for the reader.

SHORT-RUN EQUILIBRIUM

To simplify the analysis we discuss short-run equilibrium under the assumption that both the food and manufacturing sector markets clear immediately. Substitute (10.24) into (10.26) and simplify to get

$$X_M = \frac{\alpha\gamma m + \bar{G}}{1 - \alpha\gamma(1 - v)} + \frac{\alpha\gamma(1 - v)(1 - \alpha)\gamma m}{[1 - \alpha\gamma(1 - v)][1 - (1 - \alpha)\gamma(1 - v)]} \qquad (10.27)$$

which is a reduced form equation for the manufacturing sector output. All we need to get now is a reduced form equation for P_R. We obtain this by substituting equation (10.26) into equation (10.24):

$$\bar{P}_R = \frac{\alpha\gamma m + \bar{G}}{H\bar{X}_A} + \frac{[1 - \alpha\gamma(1 - v)][(1 - \alpha)\gamma m]}{H\bar{X}_A} \qquad (10.28)$$

where $H = [1 - \alpha\gamma(1 - v)][1 - (1 - \alpha)\gamma(1 - v) - (1-\alpha)\gamma(1 - v)\alpha\gamma(1 - v)]$ is assumed positive. Indeed it must be under plausible assumptions about the values of parameters and if the model is to be locally stable.

COMPARATIVE STATIC ANALYSIS

Suppose that government spending $\bar{G}$ goes up. Suppose, further, that before this increase the government budget was balanced. The increase in government expenditure, then, creates a budgetary deficit. From equation (10.27) the increase in government expenditure causes X_M to go up. The budgetary deficit is covered by additional money creation which, in turn, is considered to be wealth by the consumers. As consumption expenditure goes up, so does P_R. Thus the increase in the government expenditure has the effect of stimulating industrial output, increasing inflation and increasing the relative price of food. In this model, then, much like the model of Chapter 9, restraining government expenditure is inimical to output growth.

When agricultural output rises, industrial output remains unaffected as an examination of equation (10.27) would reveal. From equation (10.28) though, P_R would drop and so would, therefore, overall inflation. An increase in agricultural output would, then, leave manufacturing output unchanged, and lead to a drop in the overall rate of inflation and the relative price of food.

A MEDIUM-TERM DUALISTIC MODEL WITH AN IMPORTANT MANUFACTURING SECTOR

In the model studied above, agricultural output was constant and there was no serious discussion of savings and investment. The model to be studied in this section is complementary to the previous model. Production conditions in both agriculture and industry are considered important and there is much more serious modelling of savings and investment. However, although the relative price of food plays an important role in the analysis, dynamics of inflation are not studied. In other words, we concentrate on the real sector to the exclusion of monetary issues. Agricultural output is determined by the stock of capital in agriculture whereas industrial output is initially modelled as being demand determined, in a different version of the model, on the capital stock. The analysis here is based on the work of Taylor (1983) and Rattso (1989). Two versions of the model are considered. In both versions there is a well-defined production relation for agricultural output. However, in the first version (called Keynesian), manufacturing sector output is determined purely by demand whereas in the second version (called neoclassical) there exists a well-defined production relation for manufacturing sector output.

There is a good reason for considering these different adjustment mechanisms. The Keynesian version corresponds to the case where effective demand constrains industrial output; supply is passive. In the neoclassical version the role of supply is extremely important. This becomes particularly obvious when we consider the comparative static properties of the two models.

THE KEYNESIAN VERSION

Output of food (X_A) is equal to its consumption (C_A). Food cannot be invested:

$$X_A = C_A \tag{10.29}$$

Output of the manufacturing sector (X_M) can be consumed (C_M) or invested (I),

$$X_M = C_M + I \tag{10.30}$$

The economy being considered here has a surplus of labour. (Remember our initial motivation that this is a 'South Asian' variant of the 'alternative' model.) Hence labour is plentiful, capital is scarce. To keep the analysis simple we assume that the output of the agricultural sector depends solely on the amount of capital in agriculture (K_A):

$$X_A = \lambda K_A \tag{10.31}$$

where λ is a fixed output–capital ratio.

Total demand can be written as the sum of the demand for food and the demand for manufactured goods, both measured in terms of P_M. We distinguish between three income classes according to propensities to save: agriculturists with propensity to save (s_a), workers in the manufacturing sector with propensity to save (s_w), and profit recipients with propensity to save (s_z). Now, given the labour output ratio (β) in the manufacturing sector and the real wage (θ) in terms of P_M, we can write total agricultural and industrial demand in terms of the manufactured good (D) as

$$D = (1 - s_a)P_R X_A + [(1 - s_z) + (s_z - s_w)\beta\theta]X_M \tag{10.32}$$

The demand relationships for the two sectors are formulated as linear expenditure systems. Let the parameter ε allocate consumption demand between the two sectors and the parameter ρ represent the Engel effect. Thus we can write demand for the outputs of the two sectors as

$$P_R C_A = \varepsilon D + \rho P_R \tag{10.33}$$

$$C_M = (1 - \varepsilon)D - \rho P_R \tag{10.34}$$

with $1 > \varepsilon > 0$.

We now move to a discussion of investment in agriculture (I_A) and the manufacturing sector (I_M). Total investment is the sum of the investment in the two sectors:

$$I = I_A + I_M \tag{10.35}$$

There is a simple behavioural hypothesis for investment in agriculture. There is a target capital stock K_A^d which is related in a linear fashion to the relative price of agricultural goods.

$$K_A^d = k_1 + k_2 P_R \tag{10.36}$$

with $k_1, k_2 > 0$. It is hypothesised that the higher the relative price of agricultural goods the higher, *ceteris paribus*, is the profitability of agricultual operations and the higher, therefore, is the desired capital stock in agriculture. Current investment in agriculture is postulated to be a constant fraction of the gap between the desired and current capital stock:

$$I_A = k(k_1 + k_2 P_R - K_A) \tag{10.37}$$

with $1 \geq k > 0$.

Investment in sector M is the residual amount of manufacturing sector output left over after current consumption and investment in agriculture:

$$I = I_A + I_M \tag{10.38}$$

Equations (10.30)–(10.35), (10.37) and (10.38) provide eight equations in eight unknowns: X_A, X_M, C_A, C_M, I_A, I, D and P_R. The parameters s_a, s_z, s_w, β, ε, ρ, k, k_1 and k_2 are fixed. There are two predetermined variables K_A and θ.

Substituting from equations (10.29), (10.31), (10.33), (10.35), (10.36) and (10.37) into (10.32) we can derive the excess demand equation for sector A goods as

$$[(1 - \varepsilon)\lambda(1 - s_a)K_A - \rho + k_1 k_2]P_R + [(1 - \varepsilon)(1 - s_z)$$
$$+ (s_z - s_w)\beta\theta - 1]X_M + k(k_1 - K_A) + I_A = 0 \tag{10.39}$$

We can, similarly, write the excess demand equation for sector M output as

$$[(\varepsilon\lambda(1 - s_a) - \lambda)K_A + \rho]P_R + \varepsilon[(1 - s_z) + (s_z - s_w)\beta\theta]X_M = 0 \tag{10.40}$$

THE STATIONARY EQUILIBRIUM OF THE KEYNESIAN VERSION

The stationary equilibrium depends on the values of the predetermined variables K_A and θ. As these values change so will the stationary equilibrium. We must, first, discover when K_A and θ are constant. From equation (10.37) we have

$$\frac{dK_A}{dt} = I_A = k(k_1 + k_2 P_R - K_A) \tag{10.41}$$

This allows for a negative growth of the capital stock which may be interpreted as depreciation or scrapping. Capital stock in agriculture will be constant when $dK_A/dt = 0$, i.e. when $P_R = (K_A - k_1)/k_2$.

Turning to $d\theta/dt = 0$ now, we assume a target real wage. The real wage in terms of agricultural goods is θ/P_R and the target real wage is θ_τ. It is assumed that the real wage adjusts according to the relation

$$\frac{d\theta}{dt} = \phi \left(\theta\tau \ \frac{-\theta}{P_R} \right) \qquad \phi > 0 \tag{10.42}$$

Hence the real wage will be constant if $d\theta/dt = 0$ or $P_R = \theta/\theta_\tau$.

We can use this model to study the medium-term dynamics of the economy. The strong rigidities of the production structure reflect the supposition that this economy has surplus labour. The domestic terms of trade, P_R, has a central role since it affects both the capital accumulation and the wage formation through equations (10.37) and (10.42). It is natural, therefore, to seek to understand the dependence of P_R on θ and K_A – the two predetermined variables of the system.

When θ goes up, real consumption expenditure goes up if $s_z > s_w$, which we assume. Hence, following an increase in θ, there develops an excess demand for food and the terms of trade move in favour of agriculture.

When K_A goes up, so does agricultural output and an excess supply of agricultural goods develops. This should lead to a drop in P_R. Hence we write

$$P_R = P_R \ (\underset{-}{K_A}, \ \underset{+}{\theta}) \tag{10.43}$$

where a sign below a variable denotes the sign of the corresponding partial derivative.

Let us now examine the impact of changes in K_A and θ on the supply of manufactured goods X_M. When θ rises there will be an expansionary effect on X_M given that the labour–output ratio is fixed. However, a strong Engel effect may disturb the picture through a negative real income effect related to changes in P_R. We assume that the Engel effect does not dominate.

Using these results in the dynamical equations for K_A and θ we have

$$\frac{dK_A}{dt} = k[k_1 + k_2 P_R(K_A, \theta) - K_A] = G_1(\underset{-}{K_A}, \underset{+}{\theta}) \tag{10.44}$$

and

$$\frac{d\theta}{dt} = \phi \left[\theta_\tau - \frac{\theta}{P_R(K_A,\theta)} \right] = G_2(\underline{K}_A, \underline{\theta}) \tag{10.45}$$

Let us study these two dynamic equations in the θK_A plane.

Totally differentiating $G_1(K_A,\theta) = dK_A/dt = 0$ gives

$$\frac{\partial G_1}{\partial K_A} \, dK_A + \frac{\partial G_1}{\partial \theta} \, d\theta = 0$$

or

$$\left(\frac{d\theta}{dK_A} \right)_{dKA/dt \, = \, 0} = \frac{-\partial G_1/\partial K_A}{\partial G_1/\partial \theta} > 0 \tag{10.46}$$

Thus this schedule is upward sloping in the θK_A plane.

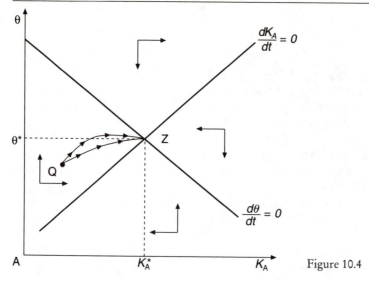

Figure 10.4

Totally differentiating $d\theta/dt = G_2(K_A,\theta) = 0$ we have

$$\frac{\partial G_2}{\partial K_A}\,dK_A + \frac{\partial G_2}{\partial \theta}\,d\theta = 0$$

or

$$\left(\frac{d\theta}{dK_A}\right)_{d\theta/dt\,=\,0} = \frac{-\partial G_2/\partial K_A}{\partial G_2/\partial \theta} < 0 \qquad (10.47)$$

Hence this schedule is downward sloping in the θK_A plane.

The two loci $dK_A/dt = 0$ and $d\theta/dt = 0$ are plotted in Figure 10.4. The equilibrium occurs at point Z with the equilibrium real wage rate being θ^* and the equilibrium capital stock being K_A^*. It is straightforward to check that Z is locally stable.

Let us, for instance, look at the path of adjustment from point Q. At Q both the real wage and the agricultural capital stock are below levels consistent with stationary equilibrium. Two alternative paths of adjustment are depicted in Figure 10.4 and are labelled 1 and 2. Along path 1 both the real wage and the agricultural capital stock grow steadily. X_M will also increase since growth of θ and K_A stimulate X_M growth.

Along path 2, on the other hand, the real wage grows too fast compared with K_A. As K_A and X_A grow in zone II terms of trade move against agriculture so that θ starts to drop until we reach equilibrium at point Z.

COMPARATIVE STATIC PROPERTIES OF THE KEYNESIAN VERSION

Suppose that investment demand goes up. This implies that the K_A necessary to have $dK_A/dt = 0$ will be higher for every θ. In other words, the

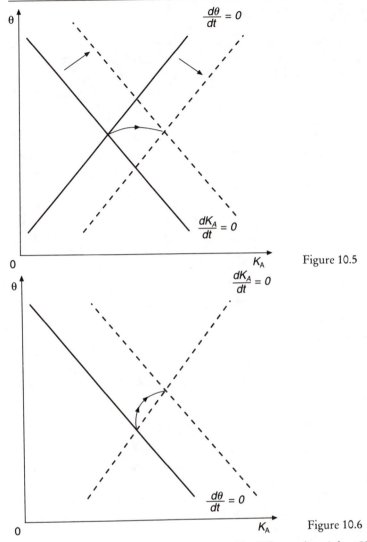

Figure 10.5

Figure 10.6

$dK_A/dt = 0$ schedule in Figure 10.5 will shift to the right. Similarly the increase in investment will imply that the $d\theta/dt = 0$ schedule will shift to the right. As is evident from Figure 10.5, K_A will certainly rise. We have placed θ as having remained unchanged.

Consider now the case when the real wage target goes up. This stimulates demand for food and, therefore, the terms of trade move in favour of agriculture. This, in turn, increases agricultural investment, capital stock and output. In Figure 10.6 an increase in the wage target shifts the $d\theta/dt = 0$ line to the right but leaves the $dK_A/dt = 0$ line unchanged.

This version of the model, then, is entirely demand driven: the greater the demand, the greater will be output and investment.

A NEOCLASSICAL VERSION

The preceding version of the model does not consider capital or capacity to be a constraining factor. This is particularly at odds with the facts in most developing countries which have traditionally been capital-poor. We now assume that production of X_M depends on capital stock in the manufacturing sector.

$$X_M = \beta_M K_M \tag{10.48}$$

where β_M is the fixed output–capital ratio in the manufacturing sector. We also assume that there is a paucity of savings in the economy, hence investment is determined by available savings.

We now have three state variables, θ, K_A and K_M, instead of the previous two, θ and K_A. This may complicate the dynamics – hence we make the simplifying assumption that the real wage is rigid,

$$\theta = \theta_\tau P_R \tag{10.49}$$

It is being assumed that the real wage in terms of the agricultural good stays the same, i.e. the adjustment of the real wage is instantaneous. This is the reason that this version of the model is being called neoclassical. Now we are left with two state variables K_A and K_M.

An immediate task now is to construct the investment function for the manufacturing sector. In line with our hypothesis for the agricultural sector we postulate that the desired capital stock in sector M depends on the terms of trade between agriculture and industry:

$$K_M^d = \mu_1 - \mu_2 P_R \tag{10.50}$$

where K_M^d is the desired stock of capital and μ_1 and μ_2 are positive parameters. The higher the P_R, the lower is profitability in sector M and the lower the desired stock of capital.

Investment in the manufacturing sector is a partial adjustment to the gap between the actual and desired capital stock:

$$I_M = \mu(\mu_1 - \mu_2 P_R - K_M) \tag{10.51}$$

$\mu(1 \geq \mu \geq 0)$ is a positive parameter.

The new temporary equilibrium determines values of X_A, X_M, C_A, C_M, I_A, I_M, I, D, θ and P_R from equations (10.29)–(10.34), (10.48), (10.49) and (10.51).

The excess demand equations can now be written as

$$\{[\varepsilon(1 - s_a) - 1]\lambda K_A + \rho + \varepsilon(s_z - s_w)\beta\beta_M K_M \theta_\tau\}P_R$$
$$+ \varepsilon(1 - s_z)\beta_M K_M = 0 \tag{10.52}$$

and

$$[(1 - \varepsilon)(1 - s_a)\lambda K_A - \rho + (1 - \varepsilon)(s_z - s_w)\beta\beta_M K_M \theta_\tau - \mu_2] P_R$$
$$+ \{[(1 - \varepsilon)(1 - s_z) - 1]\beta_M - \mu\}K_M + \mu\mu_1 + I_A = 0 \tag{10.53}$$

In these two equations K_A and K_M are treated as predetermined (state) variables, given values of P_R and I_A as functions of K_A and K_M. The rest are parameters. We will assume the following functional relation between K_A, K_M and P_R and I_A.

$$P_R = P_R (\underset{-}{K_A}, \underset{+}{K_M}) \tag{10.54}$$

$$I_A = I_A (\underset{-}{K_A}, \underset{+}{K_M}) \tag{10.55}$$

A justification for the above sign patterns runs as follows. When K_A goes up, so does agricultural output. Hence the relative price P_R falls. When K_M goes up, so does X_M and, therefore, so does income in the M sector. This will tend to increase demand for food and, therefore, P_R. Further, we assume that an increase in K_M and, therefore, X_M will mean higher supply of investment goods to agriculture so that investment in agriculture, I_A, goes up. With an increase in the capital stock in agriculture the gap between the actual and desired capital stock in agriculture goes down and so, therefore, does I_A.

We now write

$$\frac{dK_A}{dt} = I_A = I_A(\underset{-}{K_A}, \underset{+}{K_M}) \tag{10.56}$$

$$\frac{dK_M}{dt} = I_M = \mu[\mu_1 - \mu_2 P_R(K_A, K_M)] = I_M(\underset{+}{K_A}, \underset{-}{K_M}) \tag{10.57}$$

We can depict the equilibrium $dK_A/dt = 0$ and $dK_M/dt = 0$ schedules as in Figure 10.7. Totally differentiating equation (10.56) gives

$$\frac{\partial I_A}{\partial K_A} dK_A + \frac{\partial I_A}{\partial K_M} dK_M = 0 \tag{10.58}$$

Similarly, upon totally differentiating (10.57) we have

$$\frac{\partial I_M}{\partial K_A} dK_A + \frac{\partial I_M}{\partial K_M} dK_M = 0 \tag{10.59}$$

From equation (10.58) we have

$$\left(\frac{dK_M}{dK_A}\right)_{dK_A/dt = 0} = \frac{-\partial I_A/\partial K_A}{\partial I_A/\partial K_M} \quad > 0$$

Thus in the $K_M K_A$ plane this schedule is upward sloping. From equation (10.59) we have

$$\left(\frac{dK_M}{dK_A}\right)_{dK_M/dt = 0} = \frac{\partial I_M/\partial K_A}{\partial I_M/\partial K_M} \quad > 0$$

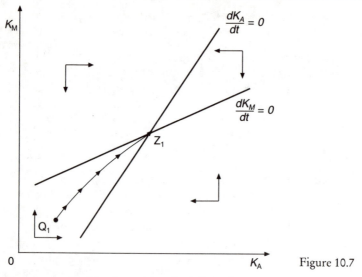

Figure 10.7

Thus in the $K_M K_A$ plane this schedule is also upward sloping.
If

$$\left(\frac{dK_M}{dK_A}\right)_{dKA/dt = 0} > \left(\frac{dK_M}{dK_A}\right)_{dKM/dt = 0}$$

then the model will be stable. In Figure 10.7 we have assumed this to be the case. Starting from Q_1 where we have less than optimal capital stock we can have balanced growth to Z_1. The equilibrium capital stocks are labelled K_A^* and K_M^*. Now, since the wage rate is rigid it is not possible for the wage rate to overshoot its target, unlike the case in Figure 10.4.

COMPARATIVE STATICS WITH THE NEOCLASSICAL MODEL

With the neoclassical model we conduct the same comparative static exercises that we have attempted with the Keynesian version. Consider, first, an increase in investment. In the present case investment in both sector A and sector M are important. We shall here interpret an increase in investment demand as an increase in investment in the manufacturing sector. Increased investment in the M sector means that capital stock and output in this sector rise. Shifts in output in favour of the manufacturing sector mean that terms of trade move in favour of agriculture. The real wage in terms of M goods also goes up. Both these factors put the brakes on increased investment in the M sector. Hence, in the short run, the two sectors are in competition with each other. The effect of the increase in non-agricultral investment is shown as an upward shift of the $dK_M/dt = 0$ schedule as in Figure 10.8.

This conclusion need not hold when we move to the medium term. Suppose that the increased investment is financed by additional savings so

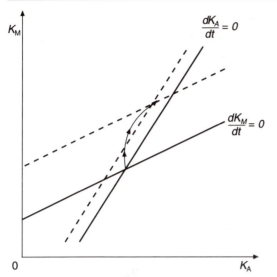

Figure 10.8

that there is an equal drop in private consumption. This will tend to reduce demand for food and, therefore, relative price, will start to move against agriculture. In response to the fall in relative price, investment in agriculture starts to drop. In Figure 10.8 this means that the $dK_A/dt = 0$ schedule shifts to the left. The dynamics are as plotted in the diagram.

The dynamics studied in Figure 10.8 constitute the philosophy behind some planning models for developing countries – particularly the Mahalanobis model applied to Indian five-year plans. An increase in investment in the manufacturing sector allows us to both increase manufacturing sector capital stock and transfer agricultural surplus to the manufacturing sector through a change in the terms of trade. Since the agricultural sector is supposed to be (ultimately) subject to diminishing returns to scale while the manufacturing sector is productive, an obvious policy prescription would be to direct more and more investment away from agriculture into industry.

This line of reasoning has its limitations, of course. Some of these may be mentioned here. First, as non-agricultural incomes rise, the demand for food may go up. This will ultimately start to exert upward pressure on the relative price of food. Moreover, it is wrong to presume that the productivity of the manufacturing sector will keep rising. A cursory glance at the Indian experience with the Mahalanobis model should convince us about this. Year after year the capital–output ratio in Indian manufacturing has kept rising – pointing to severe inefficiencies. This is particularly true because an important assumption of the Mahalanobis model is that the economy has very limited trade possiblities and that production in the manufacturing sector is best organised in the public sector. The shielding of the manufacturing sector from both internal as well as international

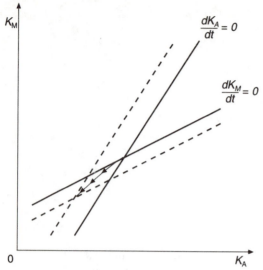

Figure 10.9

competition has had the effect of severely affecting the efficiency of operation of this sector. See, for instance, Jha and Sahni (1993) for details.

Let us now consider the effect of a change in the wage target. In the Keynesian version of the model an increase in the real wage target was seen to be expansionary. In the present version, however, a higher real wage shifts the distribution of income in favour of workers. Since workers have a lower propensity to save than profit earners, savings and therefore investment decline. In Figure 10.9 the $dK_A/dt = 0$ schedule shifts to the left and the $dK_M/dt = 0$ schedule shifts downwards. The economy moves to a lower value of both capital stocks and, therefore, outputs. In stark contrast to the Keynesian version, an increase in real wage no longer stimulates output and growth. One can indeed make the more general statement that demand factors do not play a significant role in the growth process. This, the careful reader will recognise, is an essential message of the neoclassical theory of economic growth beginning with Solow (1956).

The analysis in this chapter underlines the differences between demand- and supply-side effects in determining output in a dualistic set-up. In the low growth 'African' model demand factors were paramount. In the 'semi-industrialised dual economy South Asian' model both demand and supply factors could be important. It is probably the case that demand factors are important in the short run but over the longer run supply considerations become more significant.[1]

Dualistic models of output determination are potentially relevant in countries where the rural sector is fairly traditional and where a conscious attempt has been made (principally by the state) to embark on a path of rapid industrialisation. A significant difference between such industrialisation and that in the present industrialised countries is that whereas the latter enjoyed the benefits of relatively free competition, the former are beset by a number of imperfections in commodity and factor markets. Politically aligned trade unions can exert considerable pressure on wages and indeed affect the choice of technology in the industrial sector.[2] Given the limited size of the market in most LDCs and the complexity of modern technology, producing units are very large and product markets are oligopolistic.

It should be appreciated that this experience is not characteristic of some LDCs, in particular of some Latin American countries. Compared with such countries most African and Asian LDCs attained independence relatively recently. This meant that the urge to industrialise quickly was more pronounced in them and, given the state of the world economy in the immediate post-Second World War period, the appeal of centralised planning was also more significant. In some important sense, then, the degree of dualism is more severe in African and Asian countries than in Latin American countries. It is in this sense that the macro model of Chapter 9 is presented as a prototype of a macro model for Latin American countries, and we make the claim that the macro models of this chapter are more relevant 'alternative' macro models for the developing countries of Asia and Africa.

NOTES

1 This point is discussed in Chapters 12 and 14.
2 For instance, Jha and Sahni (1993) show in the case of India, that bad factor pricing policy has led to the adoption of labour saving and capital and energy using technology in this labour abundant country.

11

The causes and consequences of inflation in developing countries

INTRODUCTION

Inflation is a process of continuously rising prices, or equivalently of a continuously falling value of money. This common definition of inflation underscores the symptoms of inflation but says little about its underlying causes. It implies that a rise in the prices of individual commodities is not inflationary if offset by a fall in the prices of other commodities. Moreover, a once and for all rise in the price level is not inflationary: this may be the result simply of the price level finding its equilibrium value. A rise in the price level has to be *sustained* in order for it to constitute inflation. A sustained rise in the price level clearly implies that a given quantity of money will buy a smaller basket of goods and services – hence the alternative definition of inflation as a fall in the value of money.

Inflation is an economic phenomenon but it has profound political and social consequences in developing countries. So much so that any meaningful analysis of inflation in developing countries cannot be divorced from the more general and pervasive problem of underdevelopment. Any attempt to obfuscate this link will reduce a complex social and economic phenomenon to a 'straightforward' technical one. Hirschman (1981: 177) has argued that

> It has long been obvious that the roots of inflation ... lie deep in the social and political structure in general, and in social and political conflict management in particular ... it would be difficult to find an economist who would not agree that 'underlying' social and political forces play a decisive role in causing both inflation and the success and failure of anti-inflationary policies.

This chapter is organised as follows. In the next section we consider the record of inflation in LDCs. We then attempt an explanation of inflation in terms of the standard aggregate supply demand framework that has been developed in Chapter 3. Following this we examine the monetarist–structuralist controversy in the theory of inflation. The implications of inflation for the balance of payments difficulties of developing countries are discussed next. The chapter closes with some concluding comments.

THE RECORD OF INFLATION IN DEVELOPING COUNTRIES

In Table 11.1 we describe the recent experience of inflation in developing countries. The first point that emerges from this table is that developing countries are far more prone to inflation than developed countries. Over the period 1967–76 the weighted average rate of inflation in developing countries was approximately three times greater than that of developed countries. In the 1980s this gap widened still further. The second point that emerges from this table is that even within the developing countries the experience with inflation is quite varied. Typically Latin American developing countries appear to have higher rates of inflation than Asian countries.

A further point that emerges from Table 11.1 is that there is greater variability of inflation around trend in developing countries than in developed

Table 11.1 Behaviour of world wholesale prices, 1962–91, index numbers 1985 = 100

	World	Industrial countries	Developing countries	Africa	Asia	Europe	Middle East	Western hemisphere
1962	15.6	28.1	0.9	9.9	–	–	7.6	–
1963	16.1	28.3	1.0	10.0	–	–	7.6	–
1964	16.6	28.6	1.2	10.4	–	–	7.9	–
1965	17.3	29.2	1.4	11.0	–	–	8.2	0.1
1966	18.0	30.1	1.6	11.3	–	–	8.6	0.1
1967	18.3	30.2	1.7	11.7	–	–	8.8	0.1
1968	18.8	30.8	1.8	11.8	–	7.7	8.8	0.1
1969	19.5	31.8	1.9	12.2	–	8.0	8.9	0.1
1970	20.4	33.1	2.1	12.7	–	8.6	9.4	0.1
1971	21.3	34.2	2.3	13.1	23.3	9.5	9.9	0.1
1972	22.4	35.6	2.7	14.1	25.5	10.2	10.3	0.1
1973	25.6	40.0	3.4	16.1	30.0	11.3	11.7	0.2
1974	31.2	48.4	4.3	19.3	40.3	13.8	14.0	0.3
1975	34.5	52.4	5.3	22.0	43.3	16.3	15.6	0.4
1977	41.8	60.2	8.6	29.4	49.3	18.5	20.3	0.8
1978	45.0	63.6	10.3	32.9	51.3	19.8	23.2	1.1
1979	51.5	70.5	13.4	39.0	61.7	21.2	27.4	1.7
1980	60.5	80.2	17.9	45.8	72.3	24.7	36.9	2.7
1981	68.4	87.4	23.6	53.8	79.7	30.5	46.9	4.3
1982	75.8	92.1	32.4	62.5	82.4	46.0	56.2	7.9
1983	84.3	95.1	49.1	75.1	88.1	55.8	68.8	18.6
1984	92.7	98.5	70.5	85.2	94.7	73.6	84.4	43.4
1985	100.0	100.0	100.0	100.0	100.0	100.0	100.0	100.0
1986	102.0	96.7	129.2	119.3	103.2	129.4	116.9	181.4
1987	109.4	97.6	182.8	134.9	112.3	179.3	143.0	400.7
1988	122.8	100.5	301.9	151.5	125.5	322.2	172.4	1324.5
1989	143.2	105.0	578.6	173.9	137.9	1078.6	199.5	6102.1
1990	165.8	107.9	1146.0	197.8	143.1	3838.4	229.2	32665.1
1991	178.6	108.5	1677.3	219.0	156.2	6214.0	273.0	74829.9

Source: IMF Financial Stastics Yearbook, 1992

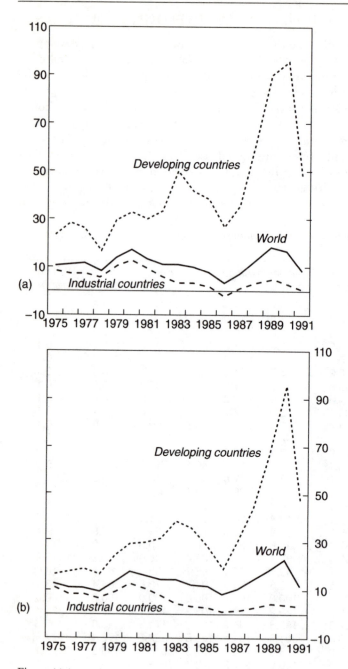

Figure 11.1

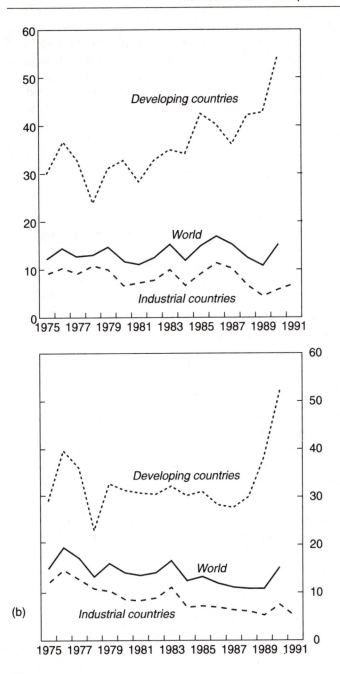

Figure 11.2

countries. Very few developing countries experience steady rates of inflation. It is also to be noted that there is positive association between the level
and variability of inflation of different countries: the higher the rate of inflation, the greater its variability. Moreover, the high level and extreme variability of inflation in Latin American countries has been truly astounding.
In Figure 11.1 we present evidence, similar to Table 11.1, on the characteristics of inflation in developing countries. Inflation has indeed been higher
and more volatile in developing countries than in developed countries.
Consistent with this is the information provided in Figure 11.2 which
shows that growth of money has been higher and more volatile in developing as opposed to developed countries. In sum, although most developing
countries have not experienced hyperinflation, most have, since the mid-
1960s, had higher and more volatile inflation than industrialised countries.
An important theoretical problem, therefore, is an explanation of these phe-
nomena.

Traditionally, two schools of thought, *monetarism* and *structuralism*,
have attempted to explain inflation in developing countries. The two
schools disagree with each other on fundamental points.

EXPLANATIONS OF INFLATION

We shall now consider the monetarist and structuralist explanations of
inflation in developing countries. In Chapters 9 and 10 we have encountered
the sharp differences between the two schools.

> At the heart of the controversy are two different ways of looking at eco-
> nomic development, in fact two completely different attitudes toward the
> nature of social change, two different sets of value judgements about the
> purpose of economic activity and the ends of economic policy, and two
> incompatible views on what is politically possible.
>
> (Seers 1964: 89)

In an appendix to this chapter we discuss a hybrid model of inflation in
developing countries that seeks to combine structuralist and monetarist elements.

THE STRUCTURALIST VIEW

The structuralist view argues that inflation is inevitable in an economy that
was attempting to grow rapidly in the presence of structural bottlenecks.
There are three key bottlenecks. (i) The first is the inelastic supply of foodstuffs. With primitive technology in agriculture there is very little scope for
rapid expansion of output of food in the short run. The process of economic
growth generates additional employment in industry. Food is the most
important consumption item for workers in developing countries. The

demand for food goes up. Given the inelastic supply of food there is bound to be an excess demand for food. Food prices rise and, given their importance in the aggregate consumption basket, so does the general price level. (ii) The second important constraint is the paucity of foreign exchange. Foreign exchange is very scarce in developing countries. Furthermore, it is argued, since developing countries primarily produce agricultural goods, prices of which do not rise very much in international markets, their ability to earn foreign exchange is also rather limited. When developing countries begin a phase of industrialisation their demand for industrial inputs and technology also goes up. They make the initial investment in plant and equipment but, given the scarcity of foreign exchange, find it very difficult to import industrial inputs and technology on schedule. This exacerbates the already tight supply situation as the excess demand for investment (in terms of home currency) remains unfilled. Prices are, therefore, bound to rise. (iii) The third major constraint facing developing countries is the government budget constraint. As the economy expands, the role of the government becomes even more important: in several important cases the government is the driving force behind industrialisation as much of the new industrial investment is in the public sector; in others the government's role as regulator and guarantor of investment becomes very important. Hence the revenue requirements of the government go up. However, tax revenues are very inelastic. Direct taxes (taxes on incomes, wealth, property etc.) do not fetch much revenue. Incomes are very low in most developing countries and it is very difficult to tax the most significant form of wealth – agricultural land. Indirect taxes (taxes on commodities) cannot be raised very much for fear of causing large-scale evasion. Import duties cannot be raised very much as this will lead to a rise in costs for the nascent domestic industry. Tax collecting bureaucracies are antiquated, inefficient and corrupt. Hence the government has to resort to inflationary methods of financing its expenditure. The most significant form of this is deficit financing: the budgetary deficit is covered by additional money creation. With lagging supplies this dose of additional government demand leads to higher inflation. The government deficit which leads to additional money creation is a permissive factor which allows the inflationary spiral to manifest itself and become cumulative – it is a symptom of the structural rigidities which give rise to inflationary pressures, rather than the cause of inflation itself.

The structuralist school of thought, therefore, believes that the very process of economic growth creates additional consumption, investment and government. However, supply is unresponsive and, therefore, prices rise. As prices rise, workers ask for and receive wage increases which tighten supply still further. This process of demand led (or demand pull) inflation can be sustained for a considerable time. This is illustrated in Figure 11.3.

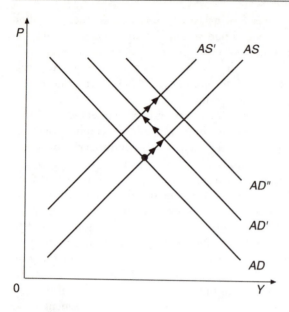

Figure 11.3

THE MONETARIST VIEW

Monetarists see inflation as a purely monetary phenomenon, originating in and sustained by expansionary monetary and fiscal policies (government deficit spending, expansionary credit policies and expansionary operations of central banks). The control of inflation requires controls on the supply of money such that it grows at a rate consistent with the growth of the demand for money at stable prices.

The monetarist explanation therefore visualises a stable demand for money along the lines suggested in Chapter 5: money is demanded for pre-cautionary, speculative and transactions purposes. Money demand is a func-tion of the level of income and the opportunity cost of holding money – the return (summarised by the rate of interest) on other assets – is assumed to be exogenous and controllable by the government. (We saw in Chapter 5 that this is only partially true.) Inflation is the result of money supply out-stripping money demand. The excess supply of money is equivalent to an excess demand for goods and the consequent rise in the price level is an equilibrating tendency.

Monetarists do not deny the importance of structural bottlenecks in developing countries. However, it is argued, these structural bottlenecks are the results of wrong policies being followed by the government. For exam-ple the inelastic supply of foodgrains is the result of the government follow-ing a policy of administered prices for agricultural products. The scarcity of foreign exchange comes from an artificially overvalued exchange rate. With devaluation, it is argued, exports would pick up and foreign exchange receipts would go up. Bottlenecks to development do exist but they are, for the most part, the monetarists argue, the result of bad policies on the part of the government. Monetarists agree that economic growth is important but they emphasise their view that meaningful economic growth can occur only in an atmosphere of stable or gently rising prices. Structuralists argue that if monetary controls are imposed, the impetus behind growth (remember that growth is assumed to be demand led) is stifled. Growth is slow but because structural bottlenecks exist, prices continue to rise. We enter a period of *stagflation* – low growth and high inflation. The role of policy, in the structuralist view, is not to overemphasise controls on monetary expansion but to encourage supply-side measures that will lead to a relaxation of the structural bottlenecks.

EMPIRICAL EVIDENCE

Several authors have tried to empirically verify the structuralist and monetarist positions. The evidence seems to be mixed. Edel (1969) found, in the case of Latin American countries, that the direction of relationship between food supply and inflation is that indicated by the structuralist theory. However, the degree of price controls on foodstuffs did not appear to be related systematically to agricultural performance whereas there was evidence that land tenure and low productivity were related to one another. In an important study of Brazil, Kahil (1973) discovered that structural weaknesses did not play any significant role in the evolution of the price level over the period studied by him (1946–64). Price rises were caused by large increases in the budget deficit, a too rapid expansion of bank credit in the early part of the period and unnecessarily large increases in the minimum wage. Argy (1970) attempted to assess the contribution of structural elements to inflation using data points for twenty-two countries for the period 1958–65. Argy concluded that there was little support for the structuralist hypothesis. However, he also pointed out that it is inherently difficult to test the structuralist hypothesis. For example, to test the foreign exchange bottleneck Argy used (a) the average annual percentage change in terms of trade, and (b) the ratio of imports to gross domestic production. But neither of these measures indicates the capacity to import. Therefore neither is a satisfactory test for the *ex ante* balance of payments constraint.

In a significant analysis Harberger (1963) tested the monetarist interpretation of inflation for Chile for the period 1939–58. He came to the conclusion that the annual rate of inflation was well explained by the rate of growth of the money supply for that and the previous period. His analysis, therefore, corroborates the monetarist hypothesis. Vogel (1974) extended Harberger's analysis to twenty-two countries and found broad support for the monetarist hypothesis. Such analyses, however, can be faulted for confusing high correlation between rate of money supply growth and inflation with a causal relation and not offering a cogent analysis of the links between high monetary growth and high inflation.

In recent years there has been considerable dissatisfaction with the extreme positions taken by the structuralist and monetarist schools. Some efforts are underway to develop hybrid models that combine elements of both schools. (A prototype of such a model is discussed in the appendix to this chapter.) The importance of such hybrid models can be understood from the work of Bhalla (1981) who, after amending the Harberger model to incorporate structural elements, found that these elements are important as explanations of inflation.

EFFECTS OF INFLATION ON THE BALANCE OF PAYMENTS

High rates of inflation, particularly in some Latin American countries, led to severe balance of payments deficits for these countries. In such situations the International Monetary Fund (IMF) was called upon to help redress these difficulties. The frequency and severity of these difficulties necessitated the IMF's developing a theoretical stance toward them. The pioneering intellectual work in this area was done by Robert Polak (1957). His model was the forerunner of the monetary approach to the balance of payments developed by Harry Johnson, Jacob Frenkel, Robert Mundell and others in the University of Chicago and elaborated in Chapter 7.

Polak begins with the assumption that cash balances are a constant fraction of nominal national income:

$$Y_t = \frac{1}{k} M_t \tag{11.1}$$

where Y_t and M_t are, respectively, nominal national income and nominal money stock at time t. k is a constant of proportionality. The second major assumption is that imports, Z_t, are directly proportional to the preceding period's nominal national income. Hence

$$Z_t = \delta Y_{t-1} \tag{11.2}$$

where δ is the marginal propensity to import with respect to money income. To these Polak added the assumptions of fixed exchange rates (quite rightly since he was writing in 1957), zero capital mobility and exogenously determined exports. Imports can be changed only by changing the stock of money. Combining equations (11.1) and (11.2) we have

$$Z_t = \frac{\delta}{k} M_{t-1} \tag{11.3}$$

If X_t is (exogenously given) exports, net exports (NX_t) can be written as

$$\text{NX}_t = X_t - Z_t = X_t - \frac{\delta}{k} M_{t-1} \tag{11.4}$$

From this it follows that a balance of payments deficit implies that the money stock is too large whereas a surplus implies the opposite. Now under fixed exchange rates any increase in the money supply can be decomposed into an increase in domestic credit (D) and an increase in international reserves (R). If Δ is the difference operator then $\Delta M = \Delta D + \Delta R$. The change in foreign exchange reserves depends on net exports, i.e.

$$\Delta R_t = \text{NX}_t = X_t - Z_t = X_t - \frac{\delta}{k} M_{t-1}$$

so that

$$\Delta M_t = \Delta D_t + \Delta R_t = \Delta D_t + X_t - \frac{\delta}{k} M_{t-1} \tag{11.5}$$

So the change in the money stock depends on autonomous exports, the growth of domestic credit and the preceding period's money stock. Further, since $\Delta M_t = M_t - M_{t-1}$, equation (11.5) can be written as

$$M_t = \left(1 - \frac{\delta}{k}\right) M_{t-1} + X_t + \Delta D_t \tag{11.6}$$

Hence this period's money stock is determined by money stock last period, autonomous exports and changes in domestic credit. If money stock was to remain constant, i.e. $M_t = M_{t-1} = \bar{M}$, we would have from equation (11.6)

$$\bar{M} = \frac{X_t}{\delta/k} + \frac{\Delta D_t}{\delta/k}$$

But if money supply is constant $\Delta M_t = \Delta D_t + \Delta R_t = 0$, so that $-\Delta D_t = \Delta R_t$.

Hence under these conditions, a balance of payments deficit can exist only if there is positive domestic credit creation. The solution to a deficit in the balance of payments lies in reducing domestic credit creation. If ΔD is reduced to zero, any ongoing balance of payments deficit will require the monetary authority to sell foreign exchange. Since that reduces the money stock, the demand for imports declines and the balance of payments is brought back into equilibrium. Hence, after a disturbance, a balance of payments imbalance will be temporary unless accompanied by credit changes.

The IMF's approach to the balance of payments is simple but extremely important since it forms the intellectual background to IMF's stabilisation packages for developing countries. In the 1960s an alternative version of the monetary approach to the balance of payments was developed. A distinction is drawn between internationally traded and non-traded goods. With the initial monetary equilibrium disturbed by an increase in domestic credit creation, part of the increase in demand is for domestically produced goods. The economy is producing near to full capacity and the increased demand leads to an increase in the prices of these goods. This diverts productive resources from the traded to the non-traded goods sector, reducing the supply of exports and worsening the trade account. The increase in the prices of non-traded goods may lead to demands for wage increases which puts further upward pressure on the price level. The policy prescription is the same as in the Polak model. Unless domestic credit is curbed it would not be possible to reduce inflation and the trade deficit. A third variant of the monetary approach was the so-called global monetarism approach. (For a review see Whitman 1975.) Its policy prescriptions are also similar to those of the Polak model.

THE STRUCTURALIST APPROACH TO BALANCE OF PAYMENTS

As would be expected, structuralists disagree with both the monetarists' analysis of balance of payments problems and their policy prescriptions. The structuralists argue that the growth in export earnings is insufficient to meet the rapidly increasing import requirements of developing countries. Shortfalls in essential imports have a deleterious effect on domestic economic activity and output. This point has come to be increasingly appreciated in the aftermath of the several fold increase in petroleum prices since 1973 and the global inflation that followed the initial shock in 1973 and the second one in 1979.

In the structuralist view the principal channels through which 'external shocks' manifest themselves in developing countries are as follows:

1 the rise in the price of imported commodities, especially key inputs such as capital goods and petroleum products,
2 the rise in the price of imported services such as the interest rate on borrowings,
3 additional international borrowing which leads to a rise in the base for monetary expansion,
4 forced reduction in imports which cause prices to go up nationally because of supply restrictions,
5 forced import substitution or export promotion resulting from a deteriorating current account which cannot be externally financed.

Inflationary pressures can also increase as a result of the policies adopted by a country in response to exogenous adverse movements in the balance of payments. If import controls and quotas are used to restrict the level of imports, the result will be excess demand and domestic shortages with an increase in the domestic prices of imported items. This increase in prices may lead to demands for wage increases – hence inflationary tendencies get well entrenched.

A persistent balance of payments deficit may lead to a devaluation of the domestic currency. This will immediately lead to an increase in the domestic prices of imports. As imported inputs become more expensive so will the costs of non-traded goods. As their prices rise, labour will press for and obtain wage increases. This rise in prices will lead to a fall in the real volume of bank credit. As firms search for alternate sources of credit they might explore sources of credit which carry higher rates of interest. Higher interest costs mean higher costs of production and, hence, higher prices.

As domestic prices rise, home exports become less competitive in international markets and, at home, foreign goods become more attractive. Hence unless these inflationary tendencies are checked, the beneficial effects of devaluation will not be realised. Consequently it is extremely important that, following a devaluation of the home currency, aggregate demand at home be curtailed.

THE CONSEQUENCES OF INFLATION

Inflation and economic growth

The early structuralist literature argued that there is a positive association between inflation and growth and that inflation was unavoidable if economic growth was to occur. Another branch of the literature argued that inflation by transferring income from wage earners (with low marginal propensities to save) to profit earners (with higher propensities to save) increased savings and, therefore, investment. Further it has been argued that inflation acts as a tax on money balances.

To see this let us recast the demand for money function encountered in Chapter 5 in an inflationary environment. Suppose, purely for the sake of simplicity, that expectations of inflation are always realised. Actual inflation π equals expected inflation π^*. Demand for real cash balances can then be written as

$$m = \frac{M}{P} = L(\underset{+}{y}, \underset{-}{i}, \underset{-}{\pi}) \tag{11.7}$$

where y is real income and i is the nominal interest rate. The signs of the partial derivatives are written below the arguments. An increase in the rate of inflation will lead to a drop in the real value of cash balances with the public. In Figure 11.4 we draw the demand for money as a function of the rate of inflation.

How is inflation a tax on cash balances? For the government cash is (almost) costless to print. As first user of the new money the government is able to purchase resources it could not otherwise. This makes prices and nominal incomes rise for the public. If everyone's expenditures increased at the same rate as their nominal incomes (which would be necessary in order to purchase the same quantity of real goods at the higher prices), no one's cash balances would rise proportionately with their income. In order to add

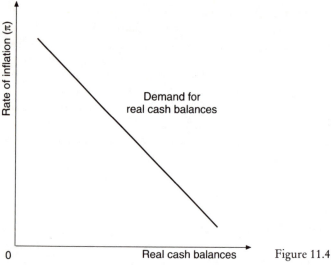

Figure 11.4

enough to their nominal balances to maintain the desired level of real balances relative to income at the higher prices, people must spend less than their income for some time. Doing so releases real resources equivalent in value to those acquired by the government. Inflation is therefore a literal tax on cash balances held by the public.

As long as the public is willing to hold a particular positive quantity of real money balances at any given inflation rate, it is subject to the tax, even if real balances demanded decline as inflation rises. The tax rate is the rate of inflation (i.e. the rate at which money held loses value) and the tax base is the quantity of real balances held. The total revenue obtained by the government from any tax (T) is the product of the tax rate and the tax base. For the inflation tax the revenue T_π can be written as

$$T_\pi = \pi\, m \tag{11.8}$$

Against all this it can be argued that inflation often leads to a drop in the real interest rate (McKinnon 1973) which would therefore cause drops in savings and investment. Private investment will be depressed if resources are transferred to the government. If private investment is more productive this would not portend well for the developing country. Furthermore, if both investment and foreign exchange are binding constraints on economic development and inflation is associated with balance of payments difficulties, additional savings and investment, even if they are forthcoming, may not be of much use. Compound this with the fact that high rates of inflation cause considerable uncertainties about the health of the economy and we cannot escape the conclusion that, although low rates of inflation might stimulate better resource allocation in developing countries and might encourage savings, high rates of inflation are definitely counterproductive.

In a recent paper De Gregorio (1993) presents compelling evidence of the deleterious effects of high inflation on the rate of economic growth. In an endogenous growth model along the lines of Romer (1986) and Lucas (1988), De Gregorio models the effects of inflation on the rate of investment and on the productivity of investment. He considers an empirical model for twelve Latin American countries for the period 1950–85 and comes to the conclusion that high inflation is to be considered as an inefficiency of the tax system. This then leads to a lowering of the rate of investment (along the lines argued above) and to a drop in the efficiency of investment since, in periods of high inflation, speculative investment (such as in real estate) is more attractive than productive investment in manufacturing industries. The final outcome of this is a lowering of the rate of physical as well as human capital accumulation and, hence, a drop in the rate of growth.

The effects of inflation on distribution and poverty

What are the likely effects of inflation on other aspects of the development process? The effects of inflation on different sectors will depend on how the individual prices of these sectors move. Relative prices do change during inflation and those sectors whose prices are more flexible are likely to benefit. This is particularly true because inflation is rarely fully anticipated and it is hard for individual agents to fully insure themselves against the effects of inflation. The effects of inflation on real income standards depends on the source of income receipts and the ability of the income group concerned to offset the price increase. In the case of wages, many observers have argued that the resistance of organised labour to a reduction in real income standards creates a distributional conflict. Clearly organised labour would have to be very important politically to ensure that it does not suffer a loss in real wages. The effect of inflation on the unorganised labour force is harder to analyse. If the prices of goods sold by self-employed people in the unorganised sector go up at the same rate as the general price level then they are protected against the effects of inflation. Rural workers are going to suffer from inflation as the prices of foodgrains and other important items of consumption go up.

Inflation may also favour one group of property owners or capitalists at the expense of others. If inflation occurs during a period of fixed exchange rates and import controls, exporters experience a decline in real incomes, whereas those who hold import licenses at the overvalued exchange rates enjoy an equivalent gain. If inflation occurs in a period of fixed nominal interest rates those neocapitalists who have access to institutional credit benefit.

So far as poverty is concerned, the effects of inflation are quite complex. Consider, for instance, the case of increasing food prices. For the urban poor who purchase food, poverty is likely to increase. For landless workers in the rural sector the same is likely to hold. For small and marginal farmers, however, there are likely to be some real income gains. Hence the net effect on the poor depends on these complex sets of forces. In general, lower income groups tend to have the least access to assets whose values rise proportionately with inflation and most likely hold their savings in monetary form – whose real value declines with inflation. Furthermore, the fact that these same groups are often the weakest in their ability to secure effective indexation of their wages, strongly suggests that reducing inflation is an egalitarian move.

APPENDIX

In this appendix we detail a model with structuralist as well as monetarist features to explain inflation in developing countries. The model has considerable similarity with the Polak model discussed in this chapter. The major difference is that, in deference to structuralist considerations, we allow national income to be influenced by supply considerations with labour as well as credit influencing aggregate supply. The model is written as follows.

1 There is a pure transactions demand for money:

$$\frac{M}{P} = L(Y) \qquad L_Y > 0 \tag{A11.1}$$

where Y is real national income.

2 The nominal money supply is the sum of nominal domestic credit (D) and nominal bank reserves (R):

$$M = D + R \tag{A11.2}$$

3 The foreign price level is fixed at one (for convenience). Exports depend on the real exchange rate (e/P) and imports depend on the real exchange rate and the level of income. Change in reserves is the sum of exports and net capital inflow less imports – all measured in units of the home currency. Thus

$$\Delta R = PX\left(\frac{e}{P}\right) - eZ\left(Y, \frac{e}{P}\right) + F \tag{A11.3}$$

$$X_e > 0 \qquad Z_Y > 0 \qquad Z_e < 0$$

4 National income depends on an aggregate production function which has labour (N) and the supply of real credit as arguments:

$$Y = \varphi\left(N, \frac{D}{P}\right) \tag{A11.4}$$

$$\varphi_N > 0 \qquad \varphi_D > 0$$

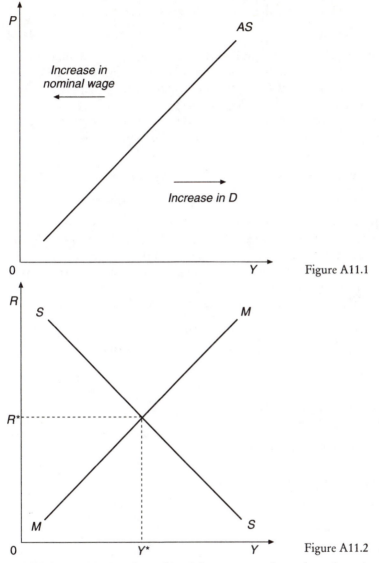

Figure A11.1

Figure A11.2

5 Profit maximising firms hire labour up to the point where its marginal product equals the real wage rate:

$$\frac{W}{P} = \varphi_N \left(N, \frac{D}{P} \right)$$ (A11.5)

All the standard assumptions apply,

$$\varphi_{NN} < 0 \qquad \varphi_{ND} > 0$$

We can illustrate the model in a simple diagram. Combine equations

(A11.4) and (A11.5) to give the following aggregate supply equation:

$$P = P(Y, W, D) \tag{A11.6}$$

We depict equation (A11.6) in Figure A11.1 as an upward sloping supply schedule in the PY plane. With an increase in the nominal wage rate the supply schedule shifts upwards. With an increase in D the supply schedule shifts downwards. Thus $P_Y > 0$, $P_W > 0$ and $P_D < 0$.

By combining equations (A11.1) and (A11.2) and substituting equation (A11.6) for P the model can be expressed as a system of two equations in two unknowns R and Y:

$$R = \mu_1 Y + \mu_2 W - \mu_3 D \qquad\qquad \text{MM schedule} \tag{A11.7}$$

$$\Delta R = -\kappa_1 Y - \kappa_2 W + \kappa_3 D + \kappa_4 e + \kappa_5 F \qquad \text{SS schedule} \tag{A11.8}$$

where all the coefficients are positive. MM stands for 'monetarist' and SS stands for 'structuralist'. From equation (A11.7) $dR/dY > 0$ so that in the RY plane the MM schedule is upward sloping. From equation (A11.8) the SS schedule is downward sloping since, along it, $dR/dY < 0$. We have drawn these two schedules in Figure A11.2.

Totally differentiating equations (A11.7) and (A11.8) we can write

$$\begin{bmatrix} 1 & -\mu_1 \\ 1 & \kappa_1 \end{bmatrix} \begin{bmatrix} dR \\ dY \end{bmatrix} = \begin{bmatrix} \mu_2 dW - \mu_3 dD \\ \kappa_2 dW + \kappa_3 dD + \kappa_4 de + \kappa_5 dF \end{bmatrix} \tag{A11.9}$$

Using Cramer's rule we can solve for

$$\frac{dR}{dW} = \frac{-\kappa_1 \mu_2 + \mu_1 \kappa_2}{\kappa_1 + \mu_1} \gtrless 0$$

$$\frac{dR}{dD} = \frac{\kappa_1 \mu_3 + \kappa_3 \mu_2}{\mu_1 + \kappa_1} \gtrless 0$$

$$\frac{dR}{de} = \frac{\mu_1 \kappa_4}{\mu_1 + \kappa_1} > 0$$

$$\frac{dR}{dF} = \frac{\mu_1 \kappa_5}{\mu_1 + \kappa_1} > 0$$

$$\frac{dY}{dW} = \frac{-(\kappa_2 + \mu_2)}{\mu_1 + \kappa_1} < 0$$

$$\frac{dY}{dD} = \frac{\kappa_3 + \mu_3}{\mu_1 + \kappa_1} > 0$$

$$\frac{dY}{de} = \frac{\kappa_4}{\mu_1 + \kappa_1} > 0$$

$$\frac{dY}{dF} = \frac{\kappa_5}{\mu_1 + \kappa_1} > 0$$

Table A11.1 Comparative static properties of the hybrid model

Endogenous variables		Exogenous variables			
		D	W	e	˙F
	Y	+	−	+	+
	R	?	?	+	+
	M	+	?	+	+
	P	?	?	+	+

From this it is straightforward to intuit the effects of changes in the exogenous variables on money supply and the price level. We collect all our results in Table A11.1.

From a policy point of view the D and e columns are most relevant. There is some support for both the structuralist and the monetarist points of view. Credit restraint lowers output as the structuralists would predict and a devaluation expands output as the monetarists would predict. An increase in the nominal wage rate would lower output as the monetarists would predict. But this is exactly the opposite of what the structuralists would predict. (See Chapters 9 and 10 for further details.) A devaluation improves the balance of payments as the monetarists would argue.

However, the effect of credit control on the balance of payments is uncertain as the structuralists would argue. A devaluation exerts upward pressure on the price level as do capital inflows, as both monetarists and structuralists would argue. However, although monetarists would argue that expanding credit or increasing the nominal wage would increase the price level, the corresponding signs in Table A11.1 are uncertain in deference to structuralist arguments.

The model in this appendix is particularly simple but it combines the essential elements of monetarism and structuralism. Moreover it is strictly a short-term model. A variant of this model has been used by Gylfason (1987) to study the effectiveness of IMF stabilisation packages. We shall study his results in Chapter 12.

12

Structuralist critiques of International Monetary Fund stabilisation packages

INTRODUCTION

In recent years several developing countries have undertaken macroeconomic stabilisation measures recommended by the International Monetary Fund (IMF). The IMF has, in turn, made the undertaking of specific stabilisation measures a condition for granting of loans to most less developed countries (LDCs). We have had occasion to remark that these 'IMF conditionalities', as they have come to be called, have led to an outpouring of research. This research has had two major purposes. At a general level it has tried to propound a macroeconomic theory for developing countries. At a more specific level, it has tried to analyse the macroeconomic consequences of IMF loans and conditions. The reformulation of the structuralist approach is an important aspect of this research. We have already studied the structuralist model in some detail in Chapter 9. In this chapter we want to study the structuralist critique of IMF conditionalities.

The plan of this chapter is as follows. In the next section we present a brief summary of the growing number of IMF interventions in LDCs in recent years. We then outline a general model along structuralist lines, elements of which have already appeared in earlier chapters, within the context of which stabilisation policy and the structuralist critique can be discussed. We then examine IMF's defence of its position and offer some concluding remarks.

A SUMMARY OF INTERNATIONAL MONETARY FUND INTERVENTION IN LESS DEVELOPED COUNTRIES

In its original *Articles of Agreement*, as drafted in the Bretton Woods Conference in 1944, the IMF was entrusted with the task of promoting international monetary cooperation. The underlying philosophy behind the role of the IMF was that greater monetary cooperation among the nations of the world would lead to greater exchange rate stability. This stability would, in turn, lead to reductions in exchange and trade restrictions. This

Table 12.1 International Monetary Fund funding arrangements as of financial years ending 30 April 1953–90

	Numbers				Amounts in millions of SDRs				
Year	SBA	EFF	SAF	ESAF	Total	SBA	EFF	SAF	ESAF	Total
1953	2				2	55				55
1954	3				3	112.5				112.5
1955	3				3	112.5				112.5
1956	3				3	97.5				97.5
1957	9				9	1194.78				1194.78
1958	9				9	967.53				967.53
1959	11				11	1013.13				1013.13
1960	12				12	351.38				351.38
1961	12				12	416.13				416.13
1962	21				21	2128.6				2128.6
1963	17				17	1520.0				1520.0
1964	19				19	2159.8				2159.8
1965	23				23	2154.3				2154.3
1966	24				24	575.35				575.35
1967	25				25	591.15				591.15
1968	31				31	2227.3				2227.3
1969	25				25	538.15				538.15
1970	23				23	2381.2				2381.2
1971	18				18	501.7				501.7
1972	13				13	313.75				313.75
1973	12				12	281.85				281.85
1974	15				15	1394.00				1394.00
1975	12				12	337.25				337.25
1976	17	2			19	1158.96	284.2			1443.16
1977	17	3			20	4672.9	802.2			5475.12
1978	19	3			22	5075.09	802.2			5877.29
1979	15	5			20	1032.8	1610.5			2643.35
1980	22	7			29	2340.3	1462.8			3803.1
1981	22	15			37	5331.0	5464.1			10795.1
1982	23	12			35	6296.2	9910.1			16206.3
1983	30	9			39	9464.4	15561.0			25025.4
1984	30	5			35	5448.1	13121.2			18569.3
1985	27	3			30	3925.3	7750.0			11675.3
1986	24	2			26	4075.7	831.0			4906.7
1987	23	1	10		34	4313.1	750.0	327.4		5390.5
1988	18	2	25		45	2187.2	995.4	1357.4		4540.0
1989	14	2	23	7	46	3054.0	1032.3	1566.2	955.0	6607.5
1990	19	4	17	11	51	3597.0	7834.4	1109.6	1370.2	13911.2

Source: IMF annual reports
Notes: SBY, stand-by arrangements; EFF, extended fund facility; SAF, structural adjustment facility; ESAF, extended structural adjustment facility.

would lead to larger international trade and growth and, hence, greater prosperity for the nations of the world.

It ought to be emphasised that the IMF was *not* created to finance long-term economic development. This latter task was entrusted to the World

Bank, which was also created at the Bretton Woods Conference. The principal role of the IMF was to assist countries with short-term balance of payments difficulties. The Bretton Woods Agreement further stipulated that the IMF's assistance would be made available to countries *only* if they followed a well-specified stabilisation package which itself was more in keeping with the broader objectives of the IMF as discussed above.

In Table 12.1 we provide a summary of the number of IMF interventions during the period 1953–90. The numbers of stand-by arrangements, extended facility arrangements, structural adjustment facilities and extended structural fund facilities are provided. We also provide the amounts loaned out against each category of fund facility. Stand-by arrangements are generally drawn over a period of one year and are usually repayable over five years. The extended fund facility was established in 1974 to provide medium-term assistance to member countries to overcome serious imbalances in production, trade and prices. Extended fund facility credits are normally drawn over a period of two to three years and are repayable over a maximum of ten years. Under the structural adjustment facility resources are made available on concessional terms 'to support medium term macroeconomic and structural adjustments in LDCs facing protracted balance of payments difficulties'. Under the enhanced structural adjustment facility the conditions for eligibility and programme features are similar to those under the structural adjustment facility. However, the scope and strength of structural policies as well as access levels, monitoring procedures and sources of funding are different in the two programmes.

As Table 12.1 indicates, both the numbers of and the special drawing rights (SDR) amounts of assistance under the various programmes have changed considerably over the years. It would not be an exaggeration to suggest that IMF assistance plays a very significant role in the stabilisation programmes of many LDCs – even very large LDCs such as India. Needless to say, the recent unsatisfactory performance of many LDCs with regard to the rate of growth of real output, inflation and especially external payments, has contributed to the rapid growth of IMF assistance to these countries. This is evident from Table 12.2 where we compare the macroeconomic indicators of programme and non-programme countries for the periods 1973–79 and 1980–83. It appears, on average, that the countries which accepted an IMF adjustment package had higher rates of inflation, lower real growth rates and larger current account deficits in proportion to GDP than non-programme countries for both time periods. To be sure, a fair comparison would compare the performance of programme countries with the package with their performance had they not accepted IMF aid. Clearly, this is not possible and the above comparison, with all its faults, can at best be taken as being indicative.

Table 12.2 Macroeconomic indicators in International Monetary Fund programme and non-programme countries in year prior to programme period, 1973–83

	Average annual real growth rate (%)		Average inflation rate (%)		Average ratio of current account to GDP (%)	
	1973–79	*1980–83*	*1973–79*	*1980–83*	*1973–79*	*1980–83*
Programme countries	2.4	1.8	96.7	37.1	−5.3	6.3
Non-programme countries	6.2	3.9	20.9	31.4	−2.5	3.9

Source: Goldstein and Montiel 1986.
Note: Non-programme countries are all non-oil LDCs that do not have IMF programmes in the specified year.

As a condition for its balance of payments support by credits in the upper tranches, the IMF requires that a stabilisation programme be implemented to eliminate 'disequilibrium between demand and supply in the economy, which typically manifests itself in balance of payments deficits and rising prices'. The objectives of a stabilisation programme are twofold: to restore basic equilibrium in the balance of payments and to reduce the rate of inflation.

Typically, the IMF advocates the use of one or more of the following four policy instruments: (a) domestic credit ceilings, (b) restraint of public expenditure, (c) restrictions on new external debt and (d) exchange rate depreciation. In LDCs (b) and (c) are connected with (a) for the following reasons. With financial markets poorly developed there is hardly any market for government bonds. Hence the central bank becomes the principal source of credit for the government. Consequently the distinction between monetary and fiscal policy breaks down. A change in fiscal policy directly affects government borrowing from the central bank and, hence, the supply of money and credit in the economy. Restrictions on new external debt are also in accordance with this. Many LDC governments often use external credit to finance their expenditure programmes and, therefore, a policy of external credit restraint becomes an essential ingredient of any policy of credit restraint. This policy, however, may be independently needed to control serious external payment problems of LDC governments. Hence, instruments (b) and (c) are related to instrument (a).

Policy measure (d) (exchange depreciation) is less commonly insisted upon by the IMF. It is more common for the IMF to ask for an exchange depreciation *before* any loans are disbursed for correcting balance of payments imbalances.

CRITICISMS OF THE INTERNATIONAL MONETARY FUND STABILISATION PACKAGE

The role of the IMF in LDCs has been the subject of great controversy. This literature is vast, diversified and growing rapidly. It is not our purpose here to discuss the perceived general defects of the IMF as an institution, nor will we discuss the legal character of its conditionality programme.[1] Instead, we shall confine ourselves to the economic criticisms of the IMF stabilisation package.

As we have seen, the standard IMF stabilisation prescription for short-term economic management of balance of payments and inflation problems consists of demand restraint through credit restrictions on the private sector as well as the government (with its implications for fiscal policy) and devaluation. The emphasis on credit policies has been explained as being the result of the Polak model and the academic monetary approach to the balance of payments. The basic lesson from this analysis is that credit policies are directly linked to the balance of payments situation. A devaluation may shorten the adjustment period by absorbing excess money balances. This package is assumed to be necessary to restore equilibrium between aggregate supply and aggregate demand in the economy.

Some critics complain that such programmes lead to unnecessary losses in output, growth and employment. This debate goes back to the structuralist–monetarist debate of the 1950s and 1960s in Latin America. The monetarists believed in a vertical aggregate supply curve in the price level–real output plane with the position of the aggregate demand curve being determined by the quantity of nominal money in the economy. Thus, they argued, credit restraint which arrests the upward flight of the aggregate demand schedule would ease inflationary pressures and have other associated beneficial effects while leaving real output largely untouched.

On the other hand, as we have seen in Chapter 11, structuralists argue that inflation is largely the result of various supply bottlenecks such as rigid agricultural supply (primarily due to the archaic agrarian structures), persistent inadequacy of savings (due to vicious circle of poverty), weakness of the tax system and the like. In their view, economic policy should aim to remove these bottlenecks following which inflationary pressures will abate. The controversy between the structuralists and monetarists remains unresolved with each side not convinced about the other's argument.

The *new structuralists* have sharpened the criticisms of the monetarist position and have used sophisticated modelling techniques to drive their point home. The monetarists, in general, and the IMF, in particular, have also devised more sophisticated and elaborate defences of their position.

An essential component of the neo-structuralist criticisms of the IMF position is the argument that particular characteristics of the economies of most LDCs make the IMF stabilisation package counterproductive. These characteristics are, broadly, as follows.

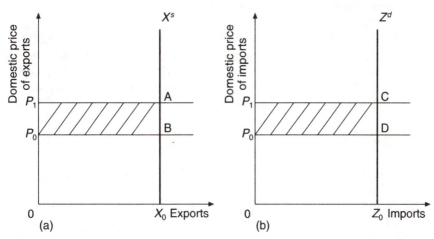

Figure 12.1

1 Because most LDCs are primarily exporters of primary products and importers of 'advanced' industrial products, there tends to be a low substitutability between export goods, import goods and non-traded goods. It therefore follows that a restraint of domestic demand is less likely to release exportable output than in advanced industrialised countries where export goods are more akin to the domestically absorbed products. Hence it is difficult for LDCs to redirect existing output toward exports and they have to withdraw factors of production from the non-traded goods sector to the traded goods sector. This transfer will, therefore, take time to improve the balance of payments.

2 Prices of exports and imports are often fixed in foreign currency. Hence a devaluation can only increase export earnings in foreign currency through induced increases in supply. These supply elasticities are usually small in the short run, particularly in the primary goods sector. Further, considerable time may elapse before these supply increases can take place.

   This problem can be understood with the help of Figure 12.1. This diagram represents the extreme situation where export supply and import demand are perfectly price-inelastic. Because of the fact that the LDCs are price takers in the international markets (in terms of foreign currency) the price elasticities of export demand and import supply are assumed to be infinite in Figure 12.1.

   From the vantage point of the absorption approach to the balance of payments adjustment, these low price elasticities can be related directly to the level of domestic output. In Figure 12.1(a) devaluation increases the domestic currency price of exports from P_0 to P_1 so that domestic currency receipts of exports rise by ABP_0P_1. In the market for imports, however, there is an increase in the domestic currency outlay on imports. Thus aggregate expenditure falls (by the area CDP_0P_1 in Figure 12.1(b)) and expenditure may fall in net terms if CDP_0P_1 is greater than ABP_0P_1. This is the *expenditure reducing* effect of devaluation and, the new structuralists argue, will lead to a drop in equilibrium real output and growth. It should be pointed out, however, that devaluation may not *necessarily* be contractionary in a situation less extreme than that depicted in Figure 12.1.

3 Capital markets in LDCs are often underdeveloped and the banking system is the only viable source of financial intermediation. There is hardly any market for government bonds and firms are highly dependent on retained earnings and on the banking system for savings. Hence some of the standard instruments of monetary policy have very different effects in LDCs. This fact must be taken into account when designing stabilisation packages for LDCs.

With this in mind, the structuralist school argues that devaluation has expenditure reducing as well as expenditure switching effects. This inflationary effect has been pointed out in other contexts as well. Dornbusch (1973) examines a monetarist model with a small open economy facing fixed world prices and where the domestic price level is determined entirely by the world price level. A devaluation would raise the domestic price level by the same rate as the depreciation of the home currency. This would lower the real value of cash balances and, assuming a Pigou-type real balance effect, lower aggregate demand.[2]

While Dornbusch's argument is well taken by most analysts, the neo-structuralist school would argue that the particular circumstances of the LDCs *necessarily* make the expenditure reducing effects more important than the expenditure switching effects. This argument is based on the extent of the initial trade deficit, on the presence of a substantial foreign debt and on redistributive and fiscal considerations.

First, Cooper (1971a) has argued that if the initial trade deficit is very large (as is likely to be the case with LDCs) a devaluation which succeeds in improving the trade balance in terms of foreign currency may, nevertheless, have contractionary aggregate demand effects by making the trade balance in terms of home currency much worse. This argument can be illustrated in Figure 12.1. Suppose $M_0 > X_0$ so that $CDP_0P_1 > ABP_0P_1$. In this situation devaluation will necessarily have contractionary effects notwithstanding the satisfaction of the conventional Marshall–Lerner condition.

Second, as Diaz-Alejandro (1963) and others have pointed out, a devaluation may have significant redistributive effects. A devaluation may increase the incomes of capitalists (by increasing the proportion of tradables) and decrease the real incomes of workers (if nominal wages are sluggish). If workers have a larger marginal propensity to consume than capitalists then there will be a drop in aggregate demand.

Third, most LDCs have substantial foreign debt. A devaluation will increase the home currency cost of servicing foreign debt which is denominated in foreign currency. If domestic prices do not rise by the same proportion as the depreciation of the home currency (i.e. purchasing power parity does not hold), then the real value of external liabilities will rise. Hence, there is a contractionary effect on aggregate demand (Ahmad 1986; and Cooper 1971b).

A fourth argument is advanced by Krugman and Taylor (1978). They consider a macroeconomic model of a LDC as a small open economy. In the short run export production is limited by available capacity and any amount of exports can be sold in international markets at given world prices. A fixed amount of imports is required per unit of domestic production. However, imports are not consumed. The production of exports and the volume of imports are not responsive to price changes in the short run. The nominal wage and interest rate are assumed fixed. Suppose that the government imposes *ad valorem* taxes on exports and imports. In this case, then, a devaluation by redistributing funds from the government sector would lower aggregate demand if the government had a higher marginal propensity to save in the short run. (Krugman and Taylor assume it to be one.) Another important conclusion that emerges from their analysis is that starting from an initial position of high trade deficit, a devaluation will necessarily increase home currency spending on imports by more than the increase in earnings from the fixed quantity of exports. Therefore, in the short run, aggregate demand, home goods production and, hence, real output will fall. We depict this situation in Figure 12.2(a).

This conclusion becomes even sharper if we introduce aggregate supply into the picture. Krugman and Taylor consider a mark up cost function to determine home goods prices. P_H, the price of home goods, is determined as follows:

$$P_H = (\alpha_{LH}w + \alpha_{MH}P_M)(1 + z) \tag{12.1}$$

where α_{LH} and α_{MH} are, respectively, input coefficients of labour and imports in production of home goods, w is the nominal wage rate, P_M the domestic price of imports and z is a markup factor. P_M, in turn, is determined by the nominal exchange rate (e), the world price in foreign currency (P_M^*) and an *ad valorem* import tax (t_M). In other words

$$P_M = e(1 + t_M) P_M^* \tag{12.2}$$

It is implicit in equation (12.2) that a devaluation will increase the domestic currency price of imports and, to a lesser degree, the price of home goods. Hence the aggregate supply schedule in Figure 12.2(b) will shift left-

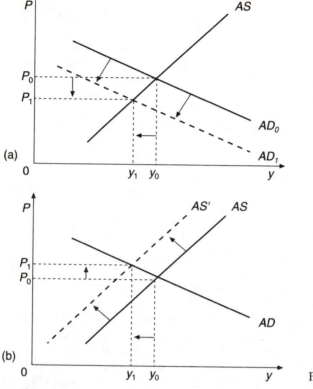

(a)

(b)

Figure 12.2

wards in response to a devaluation. This will lead to an increase in the price level and a reduction of output (stagflation). This result is more likely the greater the possibility that the AS schedule may shift leftwards in response to a devaluation.

Along the same lines van Wijnbergen (1986) has argued that devaluation will lead to a drop in aggregate supply. There are three channels through which this can happen.

First, when imported goods play a significant role in the production process, a devaluation by raising import prices will push home country costs and prices up. The ensuing increase in variable costs produces a drop in the amount of output that firms are willing to produce. This effect may be partly offset to the extent that there are substitution possibilities between home and imported inputs.

Second, if home wages are indexed to the consumer price index that accounts for both home and foreign goods, real product wages in terms of the home goods will rise. This will lead to a drop in supply.

Third, the rise in the home price level following a devaluation will lead to a drop in the real supply of money and, therefore, an increase in the interest rate. This pushes up production costs.

CONTRACTIONARY EFFECTS OF MONETARY RESTRAINT

As is well known a key ingredient of the IMF's stabilisation packages is credit restraint. This was seen to be beneficial for both domestic output as well as the balance of payments as espoused by Polak. In the long run in a small open economy with a fixed exchange rate, a reduction in domestic credit will be completely offset by international reserve inflows, thereby improving the balance of payments. Domestic monetary equilibrium would be restored and there would be no long-run effect on the rate of growth of output. Hence it was safe to assume fixed long-run supply and, therefore, real income. The real demand for money was assumed to be a stable function of real income and was, hence, predetermined. Consequently, monetary authorities could only determine the composition (domestic or foreign) of monetary assets and *not* their absolute size. A reduction in the domestic component of credit would, in the long run, lead to an increase in foreign assets. It is acknowledged, however, that this process may take some time and it might well be the case that the short-run impact of credit control may be deflationary.

The new structuralists further argue that credit restraint will have a deleterious effect on aggregate supply as well. It is argued that the financial system of LDCs is rather underdeveloped. In particular, securities markets are underdeveloped and cannot be relied upon for financing of firms' investment activities. In such a situation the principal source of finance for investment is the firms' retained earnings. Correspondingly banks play a very important role in financing both short-term working capital as well as long-term fixed investment. Moreover, credit is usually supplied at below equilibrium rates of interest so that there is a perpetual excess demand for credit. When credit becomes tight, excess demand conditions in the credit market are exacerbated. Hence investment, rather than consumption, is the principal component of expenditure that suffers the most when credit conditions are tightened. This argument was put forward by van Wijnbergen (1983). Moreover, credit restraint by increasing the opportunity cost of capital (either directly through higher interest rates or indirectly through greater difficulty in obtaining credit) will adversely affect aggregate supply conditions. This argument was put forward by Bruno (1979). A typical aggregate supply equation that explicitly models cost of credit could be written along the lines of the discussion in Chapter 9:

$$P = f[(1 + i)w, (1 + i)eP_0, rP] \tag{12.3}$$

where P is output price (the price level), i is the nominal interest rate, P_0 is the price of imports in foreign currency and r is the profit rate. An increase in i will shift the AS schedule to the left as in Figure 12.3 and could lead to severe stagflation. It is not being argued that the cure to sluggish growth in output in many LDCs is high rates of monetary growth – only that

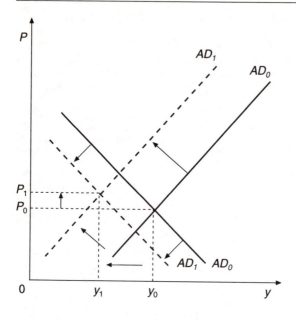

Figure 12.3

excessive credit restraint may only exacerbate an already dismal output growth picture.

GLOBAL RAMIFICATIONS OF CREDIT RESTRAINT

The new structuralists argue that the IMF places too much reliance on domestic demand management. In particular, irrespective of the source of disequilibrium (whether endogenous to the concerned LDC or external, i.e. emanating in world events entirely outside the control of the concerned LDC) emphasis is always placed on demand management within the LDC. Williamson (1983) has argued that excessive credit restraint in several countries simultaneously may lead to world-wide recessionary conditions with harmful effects for all countries. In such a situation it might be better to work for a coordinated expansion in world demand rather than advocating the use of deflationary credit restraint in individual countries – particularly LDCs.

SUMMARY OF THE NEW STRUCTURALIST ARGUMENTS

The new structuralists have argued that IMF stabilisation programmes – with devaluation and credit restraint as central instruments of policy – may have contractionary effects in the short run. Normally devaluation is regarded as an expenditure switching instrument, and is assumed to have a stimulative effect on the traded goods sector. The new structuralists argue that devaluation is also an expenditure reducing mechanism with stagflationary consequences for LDCs in the short run. Furthermore, developing countries have characteristics that reinforce the negative aspects of devaluation on the demand side. On the supply side, a devaluation by raising the prices of essential imports may raise costs and, hence, shift the aggregate supply curve inwards.

With respect to monetary restraint, the new structuralists argue that because financial markets are relatively underdeveloped in LDCs credit restraint has aggregate supply as well as aggregate demand effects. In LDCs banks provide most of the credit for investment both in inventories as well as in fixed capital. Credit restraint, by raising the cost of investment, has a deleterious effect on output in both the short run and the long run. It is further argued that IMF prescriptions are too sweeping and general: irrespective of the source of disequilibrium, credit restraint and devaluation are regarded as useful policy instruments and the burden of adjustment is often forced onto LDCs which are least able to afford such adjustment. It is argued that if the source of disequilibrium lies outside the control of LDCs – say a general slowdown of world output – then it would be better to pursue alternative policies.

The new structuralists put forward a number of policy suggestions. Devaluation and credit restraint are, in their view, no answers to balance of payments disequilibria that are fundamental or structural in character. In such situations it would be much more advantageous to pursue policies that expand the size of the traded sector. This would largely avoid the contractionary effects of devaluation. A carefully thought-out tax/subsidy scheme that would leave imported inputs intact is proposed by Islam (1984). He suggests a policy that imposes additional *ad valorem* taxes on consumer imports and that provides additional subsidies to exports in such a way that the relative price between exports and consumer imports measured in domestic currency remains unchanged. Hence, imported inputs are left untouched. So this policy is equivalent to a devaluation so far as exports and consumer imports are concerned. But imported inputs are spared. Hence the home price of imported inputs does not rise and, therefore, the aggregate supply schedule does not shift leftwards. (It is implicitly assumed that nominal wages are held constant.) The negative effects on aggregate demand also decrease because the rise of the export income is higher now as the adverse input price shock is eliminated.

Along similar lines Taylor (1981) has argued that a policy of modernising the agricultural and non-trade goods sector may be useful. This will help improve inter-industry linkages and, if such a policy necessitates land reforms and other social changes, would have a positive effect on equity as well. Other policy measures include the development of appropriate financial institutions and instruments that may increase the savings rate and the availability of working capital. This will help ameliorate the impact of interest rate changes on production costs.

THE INTERNATIONAL MONETARY FUND'S DEFENCE OF ITS STABILISATION PACKAGE

When trying to understand the IMF's defence of its position it is important to keep in mind the fact that there are two levels of criticisms. The first states that current international monetary arrangements are unsatisfactory and need to be improved. The second criticism suggests that, within the existing international monetary arrangements, the IMF's role can be improved. The first criticism is beyond the scope of this book and, indeed, beyond the scope of the IMF as well. The second criticism needs to be considered carefully, however.

The IMF's position is that in any given situation it has to act within the mandate afforded to it by its charter. If a LDC is running up against balance of payments disequilibria that are not merely transient, corrective action must be taken so that more painful medicine may be avoided later. It is not enough to argue, the IMF maintains, that, since a disequilibrium exists because of factors beyond the control of the LDC, it is the world economy that should do the adjustment. Taking the international situation as a parameter, corrective action must be taken by the concerned LDC and the IMF recommendations are, according to the IMF, the best antidote to the balance of payments disequilibrium. See, for instance, Nowzad (1981).

The IMF denies that it is a dogmatically monetarist institution. Although the balance of payments can be analysed in terms of current account and capital account it is more practical, the IMF argues, to use monetary accounts since monetary aggregates are more easily available and are more reliable in many LDCs. Although it appears to be monetarist in its general approach, the IMF often does set specific targets for the current account and the basic deficit in its stabilisation packages (see, for instance, Killick 1984). Moreover, although domestic credit control is indeed the most important instrument, the use of devaluation, interest rate policies and tax measures reveal that the IMF is a flexible, open-minded and eclectic institution.

It is harder, however, to reject the criticism that the IMF stabilisation package concentrates almost exclusively on the demand side with a virtual neglect of the supply-side factors. No doubt this demand-oriented approach is a product of the view that the IMF was supposed to help redress balance of payments difficulties in the short run and not to be an agency for providing long-term development assistance. In the short run it is not uncommon to view aggregate supply to be fixed; hence attention may be devoted exclusively to aggregate demand. This line of reasoning suggests that though increases in aggregate supply are an important objective of economic policy, this may not be possible in the short run or through policies which affect short-term behaviour.

More recently, the IMF has started espousing the view that its stabilisation package contains many measures that would encourage a rise in aggregate supply (see, for instance, Khan and Knight 1985). These policies include those designed to improve the efficiency of factor utilisation such as reductions of price distortions and trade liberalisation which lead countries to focus on activities in which they have international comparative advantage. Further, there are measures to raise the long-term growth of capacity output such as interest rate policies and policies designed to increase the inflow of foreign capital. It is further argued that devaluation with appropriate wage restraint is primarily an expenditure switching policy.

Another part of the IMF's response to its structuralist critics is that many of the policy measures advocated by them are part of the IMF stabilisation package. As an example we have interest rate policies designed to increase savings and other policy measures that would increase the incomes of farmers. In one area, however, there is a fundamental disagreement between the IMF and its structuralist critics. Whereas the latter advocate the use of controls to achieve policy objectives, the IMF's view is that, although a theoretical case can be made for the use of controls under certain conditions, the experience with controls in most LDCs has been rather disappointing. Controls are rarely operated efficiently and lead to serious distortions in the economy if applied on a large scale. In the long run, the IMF argues, controls are counterproductive and inimical to the growth prospects of LDCs. As Nowzad (1981) has argued, the supply-side measures of the IMF clearly favour market solutions. There is a clear assumption in the IMF's thinking that market forces, liberalised trade payments and the general freedom in economic matters are usually more efficient than a system characterised by controls and restrictions. This point of view is, surely, influenced by the circumstance in which the IMF was established and by the views of those member countries which provide the bulk of the funding for the IMF.

Finally, recently the IMF has tried to examine the view that simultaneous credit controls by a number of member countries may have a significant deflationary effect on the world economy. In a study that examines the impact of simultaneous credit restraint by thirty-five member countries, Goldstein and Montiel (1986) concludes that the size of the impact on world trade and economic activity is likely to be small. The principal reason for this is that countries which have undertaken the IMF stabilisation package (programme countries) still account for only a small portion of world trade and economic activity. Further, there is little trade among the programme countries themselves and the impact of the IMF stabilisation package on the level of imports in major programme countries has been rather small. Expenditure changes in the non-programme countries (most notably the advanced industrialised countries) have the greater influence on world trade and economic activity. However, the IMF does not deny that the risk of a world economic slowdown following the adoption of IMF stabilisation packages by several programme countries may not rise over time.

EMPIRICAL EVIDENCE ON EFFECTS OF INTERNATIONAL MONETARY FUND STABILISATION PACKAGES

The debate between the IMF and the structuralist school on the effects of the IMF stabilisation package is continuing. The preceding analysis should suggest that this debate is unlikely to be resolved on a theoretical basis alone. Whether the IMF stabilisation package has had a deleterious effect on the growth prospects of developing countries is, essentially, an empirical question and must be resolved empirically.

The evidence on the effects of IMF intervention presented in Table 12.2 is not convincing proof of the effects of the IMF interventions for several reasons. Two of the most significant reasons are: (i) it does not compare programme countries with what their own performance would have been had they not agreed to undertake the IMF stabilisation package, and (ii) it does not formally test for the difference between programme and non-programme countries.

As would be expected, several authors have tried to address these questions. An excellent summary statement on the results can be found in Khan and Knight (1985).

They estimate that the short-run impact of credit restraint (advocated by the IMF) is to reduce the rate of economic growth: every 10 per cent reduction in the rate of expansion of monetary credit is associated, on the average, with a reduction in economic growth by 0.5 per cent. The Khan and Knight study, however, does not carry out a formal statistical test to check for the deleterious effect of credit restraint on economic growth. Nor does it separate the effects of credit restraint from other factors that may adversely affect the rate of economic growth.

An important advance in this direction was made by the work of Gylfason (1987). He considered IMF stabilisation programmes of 1977, 1978 and 1979 for thirty-two developing countries. These stabilisation programmes were particularly relevant because they were undertaken soon after the first major oil price shock (1973). Gylfason compares the performance of these thirty-two developing countries with that of ten other developing countries that had severe balance of payments difficulties at about the same time but did not opt for IMF assistance. Furthermore, Gylfason formally tests for differences in the experience of these thirty-two countries and ten reference countries. Hence there is a serious attempt here to address the two limitations of extant analysis mentioned above and, therefore, his results merit serious study.

A complete characterisation of the effectiveness of credit policy in these countries would ideally be based on a fully specified econometric model for each country. However, paucity of reliable data does not permit this. Gylfason opts for comparing the values of each of five key macroeconomic variables in the year before and after the IMF sponsored stabilisation programme. These macroeconmic variables are (i) the rate of domestic credit expansion; (ii) the rate of growth of the money supply, broadly defined; (iii) the ratio of overall balance of payments to gross domestic product (GDP); (iv) the rate of growth of real GDP; and (v) the rate of inflation of the consumer price index. The developing countries and the years in which the stabilisation programme was instituted are as follows: 1977 (Argentina, Burma, Egypt, Jamaica, Pakistan, Peru, Romania, Sri Lanka and Zaire); 1978 (Burma, Gabon, Guyana, Panama, Peru, Portugal, Turkey and Zambia); and 1979 (Bangladesh, Congo, Ghana, Kenya, Malawi, Mauritius, Panama, Philippines, Sierra Leone, Togo, Western Samoa and Zaire). The performance of these countries is compared with that of ten other developing countries that were having macroeconomic difficulties and did not opt for IMF assistance. These countries are Bolivia, Dominican Republic, Liberia, Morocco, Senegal, Syria, Tanzania, Thailand and Yugoslavia.

Table 12.3 provides a categorisation of the programme countries by the type of IMF packet agreed to. Gylfason divided his sample of developing countries with IMF stabilisation packages into three groups: (i) countries that devalued, (ii) countries that went through structural adjustments (changes in tax/subsidy and import tariff policy and the like) and (iii) catalytic countries – those whose stabilisation programmes were accompanied by substantial inflow of foreign capital.

Table 12.3 Classification of programmes

Programmes	1977	1978	1979
Devaluation	Burma Peru Sri Lanka	Portugal Turkey Zambia	Mauritius Western Samoa Zaire
Structural adjustment	Burma Egypt Jamaica Peru Sri Lanka	Panama Peru Portugal Zambia	Bangladesh Ghana Turkey Western Samoa
Catalytic	Burma Pakistan Sri Lanka	Burma Peru Portugal	Bangladesh Kenya Philippines Sierra Leone Turkey

Source: Gylfason 1987

We compare the performance of the programme countries in the year prior to the IMF programme being instituted, the year of the programme and the year after the programme in Table 12.4. The comparison is made with respect to the performance of these countries with regard to credit and monetary expansion, balance of payments, rate of economic growth and the rate of inflation. Thus, for instance, the first column indicates that the countries that devalued their currencies saw their rate of credit expansion drop from 33 per cent in the year prior to the devaluation to 27 per cent in the year of devaluation and then jump back up to 32 per cent in the year after the devaluation.

Table 12.4 Average measures of performance under stabilisation programmes by subgroup, 1977–79 (percentages)

	Credit expansion	Monetary expansion	BOP/GDP	Output growth	Inflation rate
Devaluation					
Year before	33	28	−3.4	3.0	24
Programme year	27	20	−1.8	2.1	33
Year after	32	41	−0.4	2.9	33
Non-devaluation					
Year before	30	24	−1.8	3.0	22
Programme year	24	25	−0.3	3.1	23
Year after	28	29	−1.1	3.2	27
Structural adjustment					
Year before	32	28	−3.2	3.1	27
Programme year	29	30	−0.8	2.3	27
Year after	37	40	−1.1	3.7	37
Demand management					
Year before	29	23	−1.6	2.9	19
Programme year	22	18	−0.7	3.1	25
Year after	23	27	−0.7	2.7	22

Source: Gylfason 1987

Table 12.5 Comparison of performance under International Monetary Fund stabilisation programmes and in reference countries

Programmes	Hypotheses				
	Credit expansion fell	Monetary expansion fell	Balance of payments improved	Output growth fell	Inflation rate fell
1977	Yes**	Uncertain	Yes**	Uncertain	Uncertain
1978	Uncertain	Uncertain	Yes**	Uncertain	Uncertain
1979	Uncertain	Uncertain	Yes*	Uncertain	Uncertain
All years combined	Yes**	Uncertain	Yes**	Uncertain	No*
Devaluation	Yes**	Uncertain	Yes**	Uncertain	Uncertain
Non-devaluation	Yes*	Uncertain	Yes**	Uncertain	Uncertain
Structural adjustment	Uncertain	Uncertain	Yes**	Uncertain	Uncertain
Demand management	Yes**	Uncertain	Yes**	Uncertain	No*

Source: Gylfason 1987
Notes: Testing is for differences between programme and reference group countries using Mann–Whitney U statistic: * significant at 5% in a one-tailed test; ** significant at 1% in a one-tailed test.

Gylfason carried out significance tests for differences between the experiences of programme and non-programme countries. The test used for this was the Mann–Whitney (1947) test for stochastic differences between random variables. In Table 12.5 we report Gylfason's results. From this table we learn that, on average, the rate of credit expansion was reduced significantly during the programme years (the first column). The reduction in the growth of money, however, was insignificant. We also see a strong improvement in the balance of payments and an insignificant reduction in the rate of growth of output. The performance of inflation was unclear, however.

Gylfason then turned his attention to the effects of devaluation. As has been noted above, devaluation of the home currency is often, but not always, a precondition for the granting of assistance by the IMF. Gylfason discovered that the overall balance of payments deficit was considerably larger in the devaluation programme countries than in the non-devaluation programme countries in the year before the programme, but the two groups registered a similar strengthening of their external position in the programme year. This improvement continued in the devaluation group, however, and overall balance of payments equilibrium was reached, on average, in the year after the programme; but the initial improvement for the non-devaluation group was reversed immediately after the programme period.

We know from our analysis of devaluation that a devaluation is likely to be inflationary. Consistent with this, Gylfason discovered that the inflation rate increased substantially in the devaluation group but remained virtually unchanged in the countries not going through a devaluation. The difference between the rate of economic growth in the programme year between the devaluating and the non-devaluating countries was rather small and insignificant.

Gylfason's conclusions strongly support the IMF stabilisation packages. It therefore appears to be the case that this stabilisation package has had beneficial effects in all time frames except, perhaps, the very short run.

CONCLUDING OBSERVATIONS

The central conclusion of the new structuralist critique of the IMF stabilisation package is that the combination of devaluation and credit restraint may have stagflationary consequences. Their policy prescriptions include a combination of tariffs and subsidies that would leave the price of domestic inputs unaffected. This would, it is argued, have the same effects as devaluation on the balance of payments but would leave the level of real output intact. With respect to monetary policy their proposal is to stimulate the development of the financial system to make working capital easier to obtain.

Although the new structuralists make a valid theoretical point when they argue in favour of a mix of tariffs and controls, the experience of many

LDCs with import substitution has clearly indicated that controls are hard to manage efficiently and that they result in a maze of distortions in the economy. These distortions may lead to an inefficient use of resources in the long run and thus harm the growth prospects of the LDCs. Moreover, if devaluation does not work as an expenditure switching device because of low price elasticities, other policy instruments may run up against the same difficulty. The structuralist argument that the financial system needs to be further developed is well taken, but it is not clear how this would be possible without raising the interest rates (which, according to the structuralists, would lead to stagflationary conditions).

The structuralists are right when they argue that policies designed to reduce demand may end up reducing supply by even more than they lower demand. This would be especially true in the case of those countries where domestic production is significantly dependent on the availability of bank credit and imports. In case this is true then a basic assumption (namely that there is a positive correlation between devaluation and output growth) of the IMF position is violated and the IMF stabilisation package may indeed be stagflationary in the short run. It therefore follows that there is no simple theoretical resolution to the debate between the structuralists and the IMF. Whether the IMF stabilisation package has had a favourable impact on LDC economies is a question that can only be answered empirically. In this connection, Gylfason's results suggest that the IMF package has indeed had favourable impacts on LDC economies in all time frames except, perhaps, the very short run.

When an LDC (usually with high inflation and large balance of payments deficit) approaches the IMF for assistance, the principal options are the reduction of demand and an increase in supply. The former is much easier and quicker to put in place. The latter involves microeconomic issues and may take a long time to take effect. As long as aggregate supply has not caught up with aggregate demand, the balance of payments will show a deficit which will have to be financed from external sources. But given the already precarious foreign debt positions of several LDCs, further inflows of foreign capital may not be possible.

In this situation the role of the IMF needs reiteration. It is not there to provide long-term development assistance. Nor is it in a position to oversee the long-term growth plans of LDCs. In many situations the IMF is called upon to provide assistance in an emergent situation. It therefore leaves the supply side largely untouched and focuses attention on the demand side. It tries to reduce the payments gap by lowering the growth of aggregate demand so that it is in better balance with a sluggishly growing aggregate supply so that the balance of payments is within manageable limits.

Therefore it follows that many of the criticisms of the IMF, while they may be theoretically valid, are besides the point. What is perhaps needed is better coordination between the World Bank, which is interested in medium- and long-term growth problems of LDCs. Now there is better realisation that the LDC debt problem is not a short-term one of one to three years. It would, hence, be inappropriate for the international community to leave the task of overseeing its management to the IMF alone. The World Bank and other multilateral agencies must play a more significant role and there needs to be greater coordination between these agencies. (We consider LDC debt problems in Chapter 13.)

Recent programmes such as structural adjustment facility and extended structural adjustment facility announced by the IMF are clear indications of the growing recognition that the debt crisis is not a short-term problem. Similarly, the structural adjustment loans which the World Bank created in 1980 may be complementary to these newly announced IMF facilities. (Loans disbursed under these schemes have already been given in Table 12.1.)

It is hoped that a judicious mix of IMF and World Bank loans and policies for the medium and long terms and Fund assistance for the short term may help ameliorate the considerable payments difficulties that the LDCs are currently facing. In this chapter we have tried to underscore the point that, notwithstanding theoretical criticisms of its role, the IMF has an important role to play in the redressal of payments difficulties of the LDCs. This task will be better performed and the pains associated with it will be the less the more clearly the dimensions of the debt problem are understood and the greater the effort made to provide a portfolio of policy help and loans to meet short-term, medium-term and long-term needs of the LDCs. After all, the most important reason why IMF stabilisation packages are painful is because most LDCs do not have and cannot afford a social security programme that would reduce the hardship associated with large-scale structural adjustment.

NOTES

1   It has, for instance, been argued that IMF conditionalities have superseded the legislative sovereignty of developing countries. Along the same lines, there is some discussion in the literature of the fact that the IMF can impose fiscal discipline on developing countries but not on developed countries.

2   See the discussion in Chapters 3 and 4.

Part IV

Special policy problems of developing countries

13

Developing country debt

INTRODUCTION AND DIMENSIONS OF THE PROBLEM

Several developing countries are facing severe problems of public and international debt. In Tables 13.1 and 13.2 we summarise some relevant information about the domestic and international debt of selected developing countries. It is worth noting that, save for some small fluctuations, there has been, in general, a continuing upward trend in the public and international debt positions of the developing countries since about the beginning of the first oil price shock (1973).

It is important to realise that (internal) public debt and external debt, although related, are somewhat different constructs. The internal public debt is the accumulated debt (denominated in home currency) of the government to citizens of the country. External debt is the accumulated debt of the government to foreign agencies (foreign banks, government agencies, international organisations like the IMF and the like). External debt is usually denominated and repaid in foreign currency. Both these debts are *stocks* at any point in time. Changes in these stocks – *flows* – are related through the government budget constraint. The burden of the debt for selected developing countries is depicted in Tables 13.1 and 13.2. In Table 13.1 we give information on internal and external debt in selected developing countries. Table 13.2 gives information on the burden of the external debt by groups of countries. The picture, although improving mildly, does not look very promising.

Although interest payments on foreign debt as a percentage of exports have declined in most severely indebted countries, for low income countries this burden has grown. Moreover, total debt service has gone up sharply for the low income countries although there has been some respite for the most severely indebted countries. Over the recent past, domestic debt has been rising sharply for many developing countries. The debt crisis of developing countries is far from over. What has been achieved, however, is that the risk of default on international debt has been reduced to some extent.

In this chapter we examine some issues relating to debt in developing

Table 13.1 Developing country central government domestic and external debt

	Domestic debt as a percentage of total expenditure and lending minus repayments					Foreign debt as a percentage of total expenditure and lending minus repayments				
	1985	1987	1989	1990	1991	1985	1987	1989	1990	1991
Mauritius	137	114	103	107	116	120	91	70	64	58
Nigeria	254	117				20	11			
Tunisia	28	33	37	41	49	91	110	110	108	110
Zimbabwe	86	90	99	99		60	63	59	63	
India	184	201	206	·222		31	30˙	27	28	
Indonesia	2	7	11	9		144	245	230	222	
Phillipines	100	187	165	135	134	135	129	102	119	117
Sri Lanka	114	125	143	134	127	123	145	191	177	180
Thailand	112	136	113	99	64	42	51	48	31	27
Cyprus	70	72	75	91	98	72	86	79	64	67
Malta	12	24	34	38		20	13	10	11	
Israel	215	196	237	226		116	76	81	75	
Jordan	50	72	107	106		101	113	220	263	
Urugay	62	37	37	31		100	81	94	103	

Source: IMF Financial Statistics Yearbook, 1992
Notes: Figures rounded off to nearest integer. Data for Latin American countries is rather scarce.

Table 13.2 Characteristics of external debt of developing countries

	Total external debt as a percentage of				Total debt service as a percentage of goods and services, GNP		Interest as a percentage of export earnings	
	Exports		GNP					
	1980	1990	1980	1990	1980	1990	1980	1990
Low income countries	105.1	218.5	16.4	41.0	10.3	20.1	5.1	9.3
China and India	69.0	132.3	5.3	19.0	6.4	15.3	2.6	7.6
Other low income countries	120.4	306.5	33.2	82.6	11.9	24.9	6.1	11.0
Middle income countries	135.2	155.6	31.9	39.9	24.3	19.1	12.5	8.3
Lower middle income countries	115.2	179.0	31.7	53.3	18.8	20.3	9.1	8.4
Upper middle income countries	159.6	132.1	32.0	29.8	31.0	17.9	16.6	8.2
Lower and middle income countries	127.0	171.3	26.2	40.2	20.5	19.4	10.5	8.5
Severely indebted countries	180.7	273.8	34.4	46.4	35.1	25.3	17.7	11.8

Source: IMF Financial Statistics Yearbook, 1992

countries. We begin by examining the budget constraint of the government. Next, we consider the question of sustainability of domestic debt. Finally we consider the issue of international debt and examine some proposed solutions to the present crisis.

THE GOVERNMENT'S BUDGET CONSTRAINT

Let us suppose, for simplicity, that the government can issue two kinds of bonds: very short-term bonds with fixed nominal price (set equal to one for simplicity) and a variable interest rate r^s and long-term bonds (perpetuities) with payments of x per period and a variable market price $p_t^1 = x/r_t^1$ where r_t^1 is the long-term interest rate at time t. At time t, the amounts of short-term and long-term bonds outstanding are, respectively, B_t^s and B_t^1. We can then write the government's budget constraint at an instant of time as

$$\frac{1}{P}(\dot{M} + \dot{B}^s + p^1\dot{B}^1 + e\dot{F}^b - e\dot{F}) = G - T + \frac{r^sB^s + xB^1}{P} + \frac{er^*F^b}{P} \quad (13.1)$$

where $\dot{F}^b$ is borrowing abroad, F is official foreign exchange reserves, G is government expenditure, T is tax revenue, e is the exchange rate, P is the domestic price level, r^* is the world interest rate and F^b is accumulated foreign debt. A dot above a variable denotes its time derivative.

The left-hand side of equation (13.1) says that the government revenue comes from issuing money, short- and long-term domestic bonds, borrowing abroad and running down foreign exchange reserves. This revenue is spent on net government purchases $(G - T)$, payment for accumulated internal debt $((r^sB^s + xB^1)/P)$ and interest payment on accumulated foreign debt.

It is important to realise that equation (13.1) is actually a budget identity imposed on the government partly by the government itself and partly by the institutional–political structure of the economy. Thus we may have constraints on the government's ability to borrow at home (upper limits on B^1 or B^s or both) or borrow abroad (upper limit on F^b); or the government may feel that a certain minimum of foreign exchange reserve is necessary (setting a limit on $-\dot{F}$) or that there might be political limits on the government's ability to collect seignorage $(\dot{M}/P)$ through money creation. We are assuming in equation (13.1) that it is only the government that can borrow from abroad. So far as domestic wealth holders are concerned, it must be the case that the rate of return on the short-term bond must equal the expected rate of return on the long-term asset. The latter includes the instantaneous return (x/p_t^1) plus the expected capital gain $E(\dot{p}_t^1/p_t^1)$, where E is the expectations operator. Thus

$$r_t^s = \frac{x}{p_t^1} + \frac{E(\dot{p}_t^1)}{p_t^1} \quad (13.2)$$

When is debt – internal or external – excessive? For a developing country external debt is almost always a problem. It has to be paid for in foreign currency which requires running up a trade surplus. Transfer of resources from poor economies to rich ones is, in principle, not very desirable. Moreover, large external debt may reduce the worth of the home currency increasing the resource cost (in terms of home currency) of paying the debt.

This does not mean that developing countries should not borrow externally. If the domestic productivity of such loans exceeds the cost of paying the debt, clearly the borrowing is desirable. In recent times, however, developing countries have had to borrow from abroad under duress. Following the oil price shock of the 1970s many developing countries found themselves in very great difficulties. The scarcity of fuel oil could not be allowed to shut down whole industries and increase unemployment and poverty uncontrollably. Developing countries borrowed externally to finance oil imports. The bills for these soon reached dizzy heights and the ability of developing countries to repay fell drastically, particularly since the prolonged recession in developed countries meant sluggish growth of developing country exports. Some developing countries found themselves in the 'debt trap' – a situation in which they had to borrow externally merely to pay the interest (not principal) on the accumulated debt. This situation acquired dramatic overtones when, in one weekend in 1982, the Mexican president informed his US counterpart that Mexico was not going to be able to meet its scheduled payment to some US banks the following Monday.

The possibility of default by the developing countries came as a great shock to financial circles. The Mexican crisis was averted somehow but third world indebtedness was, and still is, so huge that the threat of default by individual nations or even groups of nations remains alive. This risk is lower now than it was some years ago. We will consider policy responses to this problem later in this chapter.

Although it may not have as conspicuous *international* overtones as external debt, 'excessive' internal debt has serious consequences for a developing country. What are the economic consequences of large-scale internal borrowing by the government? First, we know from Chapter 12 that the government in a developing country often has to resort to deficit financing to raise resources. We also know that part of the deficit is covered by forcing government bonds on the banking system which then leads to increases in the monetary base and, hence, money supply. Only a part of the deficit is covered by borrowing from the public. (This is largely because bond markets are not well developed.)

If current government borrowing from the public is high it means that the government deficit must be higher still. Excessive government borrowing competes for the same savings as private sector investment. An increase in government borrowing will, therefore, raise interest rates and increase the cost of borrowing for the private sector. In an economy in which interest rates are controlled (so-called financial repression) this would imply that more and more of the available savings would be taken up by the government rather than by private investors. With financial repression interest rates have an upper ceiling and investment is restricted to available savings at the currently set interest rate (see Chapter 15).

Private investment, therefore, declines. Presumably private sector borrowing is for more productive purposes than government borrowing. The growth rate of the economy falls. This is called 'crowding out'. In its most extreme form the decline in private sector borrowing is exactly equal to the increase in government borrowing.

A developing country government can get into an 'internal debt trap' if it has to borrow to pay interest (not principal) on its accumulated internal debt. Moreover, high government debt reduces the ability of the government to borrow from financial markets. If government expenditure cannot be reduced significantly immediately then the government may have to rely on financing its deficit by money creation and, indeed, monetising part of its accumulated debt. This can become critical. If the increase in the monetary base is equal to the government deficit, the money supply becomes endogenous, the distinction between monetary and fiscal policy breaks down and high inflation results.

SUSTAINABILITY OF INTERNAL DEBT

When can we say that the government's solvency is seriously in doubt? In a steady-state situation the answer to this question is relatively straightforward. If all tax rates are constant and the economy is growing at a constant rate along the steady-state growth path then, if the rate of growth is higher than the interest rate, it would seem that the debt will not grow indefinitely. Tax revenues will grow at a faster rate than debt servicing obligations. Conversely, if the rate of growth is less than the rate of interest then it is possible that the debt will grow without limit and the government's solvency can be questioned.

A priori, however, it is difficult to forecast the long-term rate of growth and the rate of interest. Moreover, we might be interested in the behaviour of debt outside steady state. In view of this, it is better to work directly with the government budget constraint. Let us take a simplified version of this constraint in order to understand the basic point involved.

Consider an economy in which there is only one type of government bond, B, the nominal interest on which is r_t at time t. Let the primary surplus (budgetary surplus bereft of all interest obligations) be defined as X_t. In a discrete time framework we may write the intertemporal budget constraint of the government as (assuming that there is no external debt)

$$B_{t+1} = (B_t - X_t)(1 + r_t) \qquad (13.3)$$

Hence it must be the case that

$$B_t = X_t + \frac{1}{1 + r_t} B_{t+1} \tag{13.4}$$

Starting from time zero and solving recursively forward in time gives

$$B_0 = X_0 + \frac{1}{1 + r_0} X_1 + \cdots \tag{13.5}$$

In this framework we can impose the constraint that the nominal debt does not grow faster than the nominal interest rate forever, i.e. that

$$\lim_{t \to \infty} [(1 + r_0)\ (1 + r_t)]^{-1} B_{t+1} = 0 \tag{13.6}$$

It should be clearly understood that equation (13.6) does *not* imply that the debt remains constant or that it is ultimately all paid off. If we let $R_t = [(1 + r_0)\ (1 + r_t)]^{-1}$ we must have

$$B_0 = \sum_{t=0}^{\infty} R_t X_t \tag{13.7}$$

Equation (13.6) is one form of expressing the intertemporal solvency constraint. Sometimes the solvency constraint is expressed in terms of the *debt to gross national product (GNP)* ratio. We proceed to derive this now.

Let Y_t be nominal GNP, γ_t be the rate of growth of real output and π_t be the rate of inflation at time t. By definition of nominal output we must have

$$Y_{t+1} = (1 + \gamma_t)(1 + \pi_t)Y_t \tag{13.8}$$

Divide both sides of equation (13.4) by Y_t as expressed in equation (13.8) to get

$$b_t = x_t + \frac{(1 + \gamma_t)(1 + \pi_t)}{1 + r_t} b_{t+1} \tag{13.9}$$

where b_t is the debt/GNP ratio and x_t is the primary surplus/GNP ratio at time t. Solving this first-order difference equation we have

$$b_0 = \sum_{t=0}^{\infty} \delta_t^t\, x_t \tag{13.10}$$

where

$$\delta_t^t = \left[\frac{(1 + \gamma_0)(1 + \pi_0)}{1 + r_0} \ \cdots\ \frac{(1 + \gamma_{t-1})(1 + \pi_{t-1})}{1 + r_{t-1}} \right]$$

If the government is to remain solvent δ_t^t should not explode. For other examples of the solvency constraint see Boskin *et al.* (1987).

We have discussed briefly the problems associated with high internal debt. What measures can be taken to control it? An obvious answer is the control of government expenditure. However, this may not be as simple as it looks at first glance. Reducing government expenditure may lower real national income and hence tax revenues and *exacerbate* the debt situation. In most developing countries the control of government expenditure has been combined with a sudden and unanticipated burst of temporary inflation. This is achieved through a sudden devaluation or a sudden monetisation of the debt. The inflation has the effect of reducing the real value of the debt and, some others argue, reducing the cost of debt servicing because the real interest rate falls through the so-called Fisher–Mundell–Tobin effect. However, as Jha *et al.* (1990) demonstrate, this effect may *increase or decrease* the real interest rate. Moreover, in such a policy measure the element of surprise is terribly important. If the inflation is anticipated, borrowers will discount government bonds, prices of government bonds will go down or nominal interest rates will go up. In an economy where interest rates are administered the competition for stagnant savings will go up.

A major difficulty in controlling domestic debt in developing countries is that, in the absence of well-developed bond markets, domestic debt often gets monetised and, therefore, may lead to inflation which further pushes up costs and prices. In Chapter 12 we encountered the structuralist point of view that reducing government expenditure may have deflationary effects on output and employment with very little reduction in the rate of inflation. The monetary view is, however, quite different as we discovered in Chapter 12. There does not seem to be widespread agreement on the need to curb debt. However, the harmful effects of large debt – crowding out and, in extreme cases, the debt trap – are recognised and there is almost general agreement on the need to reduce debt in such situations.

It must be recognised, however, that in the 1990s the credibility of all governments – of developing as well as developed countries – is suspect. A LDC government that has a high debt/GNP ratio risks having its creditworthiness reduced. Consequently it may be extremely difficult for this country to borrow internationally except on very disadvantageous terms. An unwillingness to reduce internal debt implies an ever increasing monetisation of the government deficit. The government can, in principle, unload its debt onto the banking sector but the increase in the money supply is controlled by the budgetary requirements of the government. The money supply becomes endogenous to the budgetary process, the distinction between fiscal and monetary policy breaks down and the ensuing high inflation threatens the financial stability of the economy.

PROBLEMS WITH INTERNATIONAL DEBT AND POSSIBLE SOLUTIONS

As Tables 13.1 and 13.2 and the ensuing brief discussion indicate, the problem of external debt is fairly serious for most developing countries. Since this debt is owed to foreigners it is not very meaningful to write down long-term solvency conditions as in the case of internal debt. In most cases the terms of the external debt including the repayment schedule are negotiated between the lending agency and the government of the concerned developing country before the loan is advanced and *any* departure from the agreed-upon repayment schedule arouses suspicion and worse.

It does seem at present that developing countries are in severe repayment difficulties. Under extreme economic pressure some repayment schedules have been renegotiated. There is some relief that the fears of large-scale third world insolvency following the 1982 problems of Mexico have turned out to be unfounded. However, there is realisation among even the most conservative banking circles that much more needs to be done to alleviate third world debt burden. Many developing countries continue to stagnate, frustrated and resentful, under the burden of their outstanding debt obligations.

Among advocates of external debt reform two main schools of thought have appeared over time. On the one hand we have the 'evolutionists' who argue that no major structural changes are necessary to effect debt reform, in particular that no *general* approach to debt reform can be taken. Each case of payment difficulty should be judged on its own merit. Any alteration to the previously negotiated debt agreement should be voluntary for both parties (debtor and creditor) and should rely on the market mechanism rather than state intervention. This line of thinking has its philosophical roots in the adjustment packet offered to Mexico when it declared its inability to meet debt repayment schedules. Two later examples of this are the Baker Plan of 1985 and the so-called 'menu approach' introduced in 1987. These schemes may or may not include elements of outright debt relief but they do encompass direct or indirect conversions of various kinds. Examples of this are converting debt into equity in firms of developing countries, rescheduling debt repayments, even using debt reduction as a lever to induce the concerned developing country to undertake nature preserving steps in areas which the developing country was interested in developing for industrial or agricultural purposes. A celebrated example of the latter was the agreement about restraint in cutting down rain forests in Brazil in 1988. As would be expected, support for the evolutionist approach comes mainly from banks and public officials in developed countries. Economists such as Cline (1987) and Williamson (1988) have also endorsed it. It also formed the basis for the debt reduction programme of the Bush administration in the USA and was first outlined by then Treasury Secretary Nicholas Brady (see Kilborn 1989).

The second school of thought has been called the 'creationists'. They plead for more comprehensive and even mandatory solutions usually involving the creation of some public institution to oversee the implementation of these changes. This approach also places much greater emphasis on debt relief and debt reduction than the 'evolutionists'. Prominent advocates of this approach include Kenen (1983), Rohatyn (1983), Sachs and Huizinga (1987), Islam (1988), Sengupta (1988), Rotberg (1988), some members of the USA Congress (LaFalce 1987; and Pease 1988), Robinson (1988), Snowden (1989) and even the Finance Ministry of Japan (1988).

It is possible, however, to think of a third way – a middle ground that underscores the creationists' emphasis on collective action while not abandoning the evolutionists' preference for voluntary and market-oriented actions. The underlying philosophy of this middle way is that in developed and developing countries everyone stands to gain: they are involved in a positive sum game – a strategic interaction among many players with an unexploited opportunity for joint gain. This approach has been advocated by Krugman (1988a) and Cohen (1989).

Under the prevailing arrangements debtors rather than creditors have borne the burden of adjustment from creditor–debtor bargaining. Developing countries have had to give up expansionary policies and, therefore, sacrifice growth, and develop trade account surpluses in order to transfer resources to developed countries. While, in principle, all parties are supposed to share the burden of adjustment, in practice most, in fact almost all, interest has been paid to IMF sponsored or monitored 'stabilisation' programmes for developing countries. The creditor nations, make no mistake about it, have done little to alleviate the payments difficulties of developing countries. The current arrangement is definitely inequitable since it passes on the burden of adjustment to those least able to afford it. Krugman (1988b) has called this 'a low growth–high debt trap' situation for developing countries. The real drawback of the present arrangement is that, given that developing countries are viewed as being illiquid, further international investment in their economies is discouraged. This robs them of the very means with which debt repayment can be facilitated. As a consequence, investment in LDCs has dropped from 25 per cent of GDP in 1982 to 15 per cent in recent years.

Under such conditions a strong case can be made that, at least in some situations, both debtors and creditors will benefit with a cooperative strategy of debt relief. Krugman (1988a) has summarised this argument in what has come to be called the 'debt relief Laffer curve'.[1] We depict this in Figure 13.1. It is argued that at relatively low levels of debt claim, nominal claims of a relatively high order can be expected to be paid off. (We are to the left of the point D* in Figure 13.1.) But as liabilities accumulate, the ability of the LDC government to make large payments is reduced as investment drops off and growth is stifled. (We move to the right of D* in Figure 13.1.) Many authors have argued that several developing countries find themselves on the wrong side of this Laffer curve (to the right of D*).

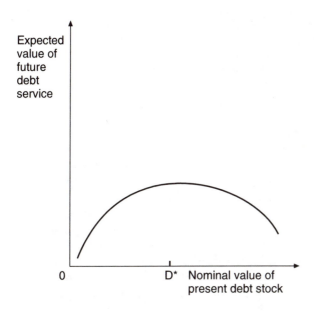

Figure 13.1

WHY ARE DEVELOPING COUNTRIES ON THE WRONG SIDE OF THE LAFFER CURVE?

An important aim of international debt cooperation must be to ensure that developing countries get back to the right side of the Laffer curve. Before we examine policy initiatives that will make this possible we should understand how the developing countries found themselves on the wrong side of the Laffer curve. It has to be clearly understood that most developing countries have been careful, no matter how hard pressed, to abide by the terms of creditor–debtor agreements. Despite the strong incentives to refuse acknowledging the outstanding debt obligations, developing countries have fully cooperated with the developed countries' banks and governments. So much so that the influential magazine *The Economist* described the debt problem among all international economic policy issues 'as the best example of successful cooperation [but] ... at the expense of the developing countries'.

The practice, noted above, is sharply at variance with the words of developing countries' officials and governments. Virtually from the moment Mexico's crisis broke in 1982, developing country leaders have made a point of proclaiming their opposition to the prevailing rules of the game. Debtor governments denounce market norms as unfair with such vigour and persistence that it is hard to believe that these utterances represent mere posturing for domestic or international advantage.

However, even though debtor governments protest the rules as a matter of principle they uphold the norms of sanctity of contract and non-politicisation of exchanges. They seek more rights, but do not deny the fact of obligation.

Many political scientists (see, for example, Kaufman 1986, or Haggard and Kaufman 1989) believe that the elites of developing countries sometimes use the norms that they have to stick by in order to honour international debt as an excuse to postpone radical economic steps at home. So while the rhetoric of resentment against market forces is used for domestic political consumption, the necessity of adhering to the terms of international stabilisation programmes is advanced as an argument to postpone, say, a social security programme for the unemployed at home or, more generally, any redistributive programme. Be that as it may, it is clear that there is a strong argument for reducing the debt burden of the developing countries. With less-pinching external constraints the developing countries' growth prospects would improve. Developed countries would gain because prospects for repayment of debt would improve. Expanding economies of developing countries would provide additional markets for developed countries' exports and avenues for profitable investment. There is much to be said for debt reduction and reform.

PROBLEMS OF DEVELOPING COUNTRY DEBT REDUCTION

In principle three techniques for debt reduction in the international context have been distinguished (see Husain and Diwan 1989). These are

1 a cash repurchase of some of the outstanding debt,
2 the exchange of discounted debt for an alternative foreign claim,
3 the exchange of debt claims for titles to domestic assets.

Let us discuss each in turn.

Cash repurchase of outstanding debt involves operating in a secondary market for outstanding debt. The original creditor sells off claims on LDC foreign exchange earnings. The price of this debt will reflect not the planned stream of earnings when the debt was first issued (this is determined in the primary market for debt when it is first issued) but what the LDC may 'reasonably be expected to pay' over the remaining life of the debt. There is some confusion as to whether this means what the developing country can pay or what it can be coerced into paying. Bulow and Rogoff (1988) consider this valuation problem as follows. Let γ be the probability that some fraction of the present value of the debt will not be repaid so that the probability of full payment is $1 - \gamma$. Following a small purchase X of the outstanding debt B for a discounted unit price $p < 1$, the market valuation will be based on the following expected returns:

$$E(R) = \gamma E(T) + (1 - \gamma)\left(B\frac{-X}{p}\right) \tag{13.11}$$

where $E(T)$ represents the expected value of transfers when full repayment does not occur and $B - X/p$ is the nominal value of the debt remaining after the purchase valued at \$1 per unit. The market price per unit of the debt will be the present value of this sum (discounted by the market discount rate r) divided by the units of debt remaining:

$$p = \frac{E(R)}{r(B - X/p)} \tag{13.12}$$

Substitute $E(R)$ from equation (13.11) into equation (13.12) to get

$$p = \frac{\gamma E(T)}{r(B - X/p)} + \frac{1 - \gamma}{r} \tag{13.13}$$

The first term on the right-hand side is the discounted present value of the eventual transfers per unit of the nominal debt when there is partial default. The second term represents the expected value of the marginal repayment reduction achieved by the buy-back. Since the first term is positive it must be the case that $p > (1 - \gamma)/r$, i.e. the market price exceeds the present value of the actual repayment reduction that the repurchase will achieve.

From equation (13.13) we can calculate

$$\left.\frac{Bdp}{dX}\right|_{x=0} = 1 - \frac{1 - \gamma}{rP} \tag{13.14}$$

Thus when the possibility of repayment is remote $1 - \gamma \to 0$, the rise in the value of the outstanding debt (represented by Bdp evaluated at $X = 0$) approaches the nominal value of the retired debt (dX). Only when there is some prospect of full repayment does the debtor stand to gain by the reduction in the contractual payments which will need to be honoured under these conditions. This is the full extent of the effective debt relief achieved by the debtor in these transactions.

The improbability of full repayment means that the debt becomes a floating (quasi-equity) charge on the developing country's potential foreign exchange earnings. By being able to sell off claims to LDC foreign exchange earnings the creditors are the primary beneficiaries since they get a certain return as against the uncertain possibility of being paid back by the LDC for the original debt. With this approach it is difficult to establish the true price of the secondary debt.

The second method of debt reduction of developing countries involves an exchange of existing debt for a new type of bond which incorporates a prior (or senior) claim over a proportion of future cash flows. The developing country has to earmark a certain fraction of its foreign exchange earnings period after period for paying off the new debt. It is implicitly assumed that the terms of repayment of the new debt will not be renegotiated. The exchange of one kind of foreign claim for another will therefore generate some potential debt relief as the total contractual value of debt repayments will be reduced. Unlike the straightforward market buy-back of the previous arrangement, the exchange offers must be preannounced.

The essential mechanism may be illustrated with reference to the basic valuation framework introduced above. Before the exchange, the market price (V_0) will represent the discounted present value of future cash flows ((ECF_0)/r):

$$V_0 = \frac{ECF_0}{r} \tag{13.15}$$

After the exchange, the expected annual return on the old and new debt will have the following relationship:

$$ERD = ECF_1 - ERB \tag{13.16}$$

where ECF_1 is the expected cash flow after the exchange, ERB is the annual return on the new bonds and ERD is the annual return on the old debt. It must be the case that $ECF_0 > ECF_1$. This is the implicit debt reduction that is achieved through this method.

As Bulow and Rogoff (1988) show, this arrangement is compatible with both participating and non-participating creditors breaking even. While this is a more satisfactory result for the debtor country than the attempt to buy back debt with cash, the potential debt reduction reaches a limit when all old debt has been exchanged. Well before this point, the idea of seniority would have lost meaning and the only merit in the exchange would be the cash enhancement; the position would be similar to a straightforward cash purchase. In this connection it should be noted that the 1988 Mexican debt swap failed to generate the relief expected largely because of doubts over the effective seniority of the bond issue. Whether by cash buy-back or bond issue, therefore, there are limits to the extent of debt reduction which can be achieved through debtor initiative even if creditors are willing to let new issues proceed. The third technique, that of swapping debt with equity or even claims to natural resources, has similar problems.

TOWARD GENUINE DEBT REFORM

The methods of debt relief discussed above carried the perception that there could well be losers in the process of debt reduction. They also subscribe to the point of view of the evolutionists who believe in market-oriented solutions. But the basic point of the Laffer curve analysis carried out above was that debt reduction was to everyone's benefit.

Creationists believe that the market for international debt does not work to the benefit of the developing countries because the distribution of power between their creditors and them is highly biased in favour of the former. However, to say that markets may fail does not mean that they may be replaced. It might be enough simply to provide a third party to facilitate mutually beneficial agreements that will help participants avoid the cost of their own imperfections.

Who should that third party be and how would its role be defined? Is it possible to find a middle ground to debt reform that retains the creationists' stress on collective action and yet retains the evolutionists' preference for voluntary market-oriented action? Krugman (1988a) and Cohen (1989) consider this question.

If large banks and other creditors have to be persuaded to opt for reduction in developing country debt they will have to be given sufficient incentives. Creditors' objections to debt relief encompass the following categories.

First, the creditors argue, even one major breakdown of LDC debt payment schedule might cause a ripple effect adversely affecting major intermediaries and, in the extreme, a full blown financial crisis may occur. How might one reduce such fears of banks? Two suggestions have been offered. First, debt relief might be made *selective* rather than *general*. Debt relief might be given only in those cases where it is urgently needed. Second, creditor banks are afraid that debt write-off might lead to reduction in net worth. Such fears might be reduced by enabling banks to incorporate the effects of debt reduction over a number of years rather than at one time.

The second argument that has been put forward against debt reduction is that if debts of developing countries are written off, their credit worthiness and ability to borrow in the future might be adversely affected. A persuasive rebuttal to this argument is that credit worthiness of developing countries is at stake now when they find themselves on the wrong side of the Laffer curve. If they can be helped on to the right side of this Laffer curve their credit worthiness would be improved. A number of international institutions recognise this.

Another argument that has been used against debt reduction is that such reduction would weaken discipline in international financial markets. This argument can be stood on its head by recognising the perverse relationship that exists between debtor performance and credit availability. The deterrent to successful adjustment actually discourages rather than encourages a continued commitment to current arrangements.

Another argument that has been advanced against debt reduction is that if developing countries are aware that their debts may be reduced they might pursue policies that might make such debt reduction likely. This is the so-called *moral hazard* argument. A rebuttal to this argument is that it is always possible to make debt reduction and restructuring contingent on following certain domestic policies.

A final argument that has been put forward is that any scheme for debt relief would inject politics into the creditor–debtor relationships. But this need not necessarily be the case. One could argue that the debt issue is already highly politicised and could actually be defused by an orderly procedure that promises to reduce the cash-flow constraint on developing countries.

The Krugman–Cohen debt reduction plan is supposed to operate in the following manner. First, there would be an international agency consisting of representatives of debtors and creditors. Developing countries would have the option of applying to this agency for debt relief. But in so doing the developing countries would commit themselves *irrevocably* to a process of conciliated negotiation with their creditors and some surveillance of their domestic policies by the agency and creditors. Presumably even with this arrangement an agreement may not be possible. The agency may suggest its own formulae for adjustment and play a role in breaking deadlocks.

However, what we are guaranteed is that creditors will have a strong and transparent role in debt reduction negotiations. Moreover, to the extent that any debt reduction does occur creditors are satisfied that these reductions have been agreed contingent upon developing countries following policies which they have had a role in designing. Moreover they would have a role in monitoring the successful conduct of these policies.

Such an approach to debt reduction combines the stress on market oriented and voluntary action of the evolutionists and the emphasis on debt reduction through collective action of the creationists. Such an approach has much to commend itself. Given the urgency of debt reform from the point of both developing countries and international financial institutions, it is imperative that such measures be contemplated or undertaken. It is true that all the important details of the programme have not been worked out. But it does seem like a worthwhile middle route to take.

CONCLUSIONS

In this chapter we have presented a broad survey of the internal and external debt problems of developing countries. We have pointed out that severe internal debt compromises monetary policy and considered some plans for international debt reduction.

NOTE

1 After Arthur Laffer (1981) who argued that increases in personal taxes would lower tax revenue because work effort would drop substantially.

14

Economic repression and liberalisation in developing countries

INTRODUCTION

Economists have long been aware of the widespread prevalence of economic repression in developing countries. In 1978 two influential economists, Jagdish Bhagwati and Anne Krueger, published separate monographs detailing the maze of physical and quantitative controls prevalent in many developing countries and examining the economic consequences of such controls. With the reduction in the appeal of quantitative control techniques in light of the disastrous experience with centralised planning in most of the former socialist countries, it has become very fashionable to advocate the removal of these quantitative controls and to see consequent economic liberalisation as the shortest route to economic prosperity in developing countries.

Be that as it may, it has to be understood that although economic repression has had significant economic costs, there was a rationale for them. An influential economic planning model developed independently by the Soviet economist Feldman and the Indian economist Mahalanobis posed the development problem in the following manner. A typical less developed country (LDC) faces adverse trading conditions in international markets because it exports mainly primary goods – the demand for which is inelastic. Thus the home economy faces a serious foreign exchange constraint. Coupled with this constraint is the poor availability of savings in the home economy – primarily because of low incomes. The LDC is, hence, faced with the problem of allocating scarce foreign exchange and domestic savings in order to maximise consumption over the long run. Should these scarce resources be used to produce consumer goods or producer goods? If the future was severely discounted the answer would be straightforward: the economy should produce consumer goods. As the discount rate becomes smaller the attractiveness of producing producer goods increases. Emphasis should then be placed on transferring surplus from agriculture to industry. Since the private sector would be unable to gather the resources for manufacturing producer goods and its ability to undertake the risks associated with initiating a programme of industrialisation almost from scratch would be severely limited, much of the production of the manufactured goods would have to take place in the public sector. The logic of the model states that in LDCs a programme of industrialisation would involve considerable investment *across a broad range of sectors.* The transport sector cannot be established unless the steel sector is simultaneously established and so on. If matters were left to the private sector the steel producer, even if willing to establish a steel plant, would not have any way of communicating this decision to the producer of transport services. This has been called 'secondary uncertainty', as distinct from 'primary uncertainty' associated with random acts of nature, by authors such as Dobb (1937).

The paucity of resources makes it necessary for the public sector to invest in these industries. The presence of secondary uncertainty makes it necessary for all these production decisions to be planned and coordinated. The public sector must be at the 'commanding heights' of the economy. The fact that markets for these goods do not exist in the home economy implies that price signals are of little use and quantitative control would have to be exercised. The basic philosophy that industrialisation was most important led to an implicit neglect of agriculture. The need to transfer resources from agriculture to industry was emphasised.

The LDC experience with development is ample proof of the failure of the Feldman–Mahalanobis model. The countries that were more 'outward looking' and learnt the lessons of international comparative advantage are precisely those that have developed fast. Countries that initially followed the logic of the Feldman–Mahalanobis model are now racing each other to dismantle the legacy of centralised planning. Theoretical reasons for the failure of centralised planning are well discussed in Krueger (1978), Bhagwati (1978) and Chenery and Srinivasan (1989).

A cynic might argue that these quantitative restrictions were used as policy instruments in order to placate powerful political and economic interests. Industrial labour stands to gain because food prices are controlled. Industrialists gain becuase they get cheap inputs and enjoy the benefits of protected markets. Bureaucrats stand to gain because they get to make key economic decisions and may profit from such decisions. Above all, a whole generation of politicians has profited from making key economic decisions. This bunching of interest groups presents a formidable opposition to genuine economic reforms in many LDCs. Moreover during a process of economic reforms there are likely to be high costs of adjustment. There is to be considerable industrial restructuring with increasing unemployment, for instance. Economic reforms, then, have significant political, social and economic costs and it may not be feasible for the developing country in question to liberalise very quickly. These costs constitute the principal reason why genuine reforms are often made only under the pressure of a severe economic crisis. There are a number of examples of this – the most recent being that of India which started genuine economic reforms in July 1991. At that time India was about to default on foreign loans, its domestic debt had reached very high proportions, inflation was persistently high after being in the single digits for decades, industry was stagnating and exports were sluggish.

FACETS OF ECONOMIC REPRESSION

In developing countries economic repression takes several forms. On the trade front, in order to placate powerful urban groups, governments restrict the export of foodstuffs and raw materials. Urban labour needs cheap food and urban industry needs cheap agricultural inputs. The domestic terms of trade are often turned against agriculture.

More broadly, foreign trade is repressed by quantitative restrictions and/or high tariffs. The prices of these goods, then, are usually determined by domestic demand and supply considerations and have little to do with global prices. The domestic financial system is usually insulated by exchange controls of various kinds. Obtaining foreign exchange for purposes of foreign trade is very difficult. Given the wide variety of controls on the foreign trade sector, multiple exchange rates exist. The 'official' exchange rate typically undervalues the true scarcity of foreign exchange and there is a thriving black market for foreign exchange.

Moreover, in many countries, investment is subject to controls. Government licenses have to be obtained for investing in certain sectors. In several other 'priority' sectors only public sector investment is permitted. To be sure, the prevalence of this licence-quota *raj* encourages corruption among the government bureaucracy which must make key economic decisions without reference to any market values.

In Chapter 15 we shall examine the implications of financial repression for the growth prospects of developing countries. Official interventions in the allocation of credit may be as pervasive, detailed and bewildering as the proliferation of quantitative restrictions on foreign trade.

In most developing countries stock markets and markets for bonds are rather underdeveloped. Thus the monetary system has to perform the role of intermediating between savers and investors. Most of private savings take the form of bank deposits and highly liquid post-office savings, or claims against commercial banks. Control over a broad monetary aggregate such as M_3 is, therefore, important not just for adjusting the money supply but also for affecting savings.

The backwardness of financial markets means that avenues for government borrowing are rather limited. Governments typically indulge in forced sales of government bonds to the banking system. This is done through an elaborate system of reserve requirements. It is not uncommon for the government to unload its bonds onto the central bank. The central bank uses some of these as base for monetary expansion and, quite often, commercial

banks are required to hold part of their reserves in terms of government
bonds. These reserve requirements are, in turn, often quite high. The fact
that the central bank uses government bonds as base for monetary expansion means that the government debt tends to get monetised. The ensuing
inflation interacts with the reserve requirements to harness even more revenue for the government (the inflation tax). The process of revenue extrac-
tion by the government is much too complicated to be captured in a single
diagram but one can imagine this process taking the form depicted in Figure
14.1. Primary savers – the public – save in the form of currency and cash,
which are liabilities of the central bank. They are also liabilities of the commercial banks. Part of these are effectively transferred to the central bank
through reserve requirements and purchase of government debt, leaving
only a fraction for free lending. The public also saves with savings banks
and post-offices. These savings are channeled in a similar manner. The central bank has to transfer resources to the government (ministry of finance)
through purchase of government bonds. It also has to lend directly to certain 'priority' sectors labelled I, II etc. in Figure 14.1. These priority borrowers may be industrial development banks, agricultural development
banks, public sector undertakings, private sector undertakings in the 'core'
sector and the like.

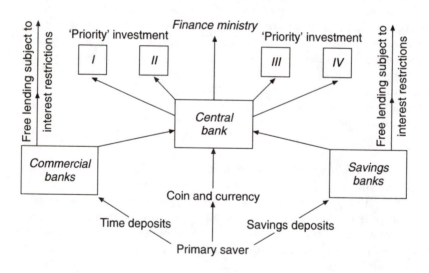

Figure 14.1

COSTS OF ECONOMIC REPRESSION

One of the principal problems with economic repression is the inflationary bias that sets into the economy as a consequence of the repression. This inflationary bias is the result of both demand-pull and cost-push factors. The fact that market prices are highly distorted pushes up costs of production. Moreover, the government adds very significantly to demand-pull pressures on inflation. On the one hand, the government has large and growing expenditures, particularly on an unproductive and unprofitable public sector. Their losses have to be absorbed and the government has to spend vast sums on subsidies of various types – principally those on food, fertilisers and industrial inputs. At the same time, government revenues are rather limited. Since incomes are low, income taxes are unimportant. A significant portion of commodity taxes is avoided because of irrational tax structures and corrupt tax officials. Government deficits are then financed by the government issuing bonds which it forces on to the banking system by making it mandatory for them to buy government bonds (private investors would not purchase these bonds readily). The banking system then uses these bonds as reserves for monetary expansion. Hence, the government deficits get monetised and inflationary tendencies are exacerbated.

It has sometimes been argued that perfectly anticipated inflation has relatively small costs because markets have a chance to adjust completely and the values of real variables such as the real interest rate or the real wage rate remain unaltered. In most developing countries, however, inflation is the result, as argued above, of the government spending beyond tax collections and monetising the deficit by forcing its bonds onto a captive banking system. Hence, inflation is largely unanticipated. Further, key economic variables such as the interest rate and the exchange rate are not free to adjust so that inflation, even if fully anticipated, involves significant economic costs. Government policy is inflationary: sometimes the attempt is to get additional revenues in order to provide additional resources for investment, and at other times it is a direct consequence of the system of controls, e.g. a food subsidy or a fertiliser subsidy.

Once inflation begins, governments have a tendency to exacerbate its ill effects by imposing additional controls. One of the most important of such controls is the pegging or slow adjustment of the nominal exchange rate. Other significant distortions are the fixing of prices of key intermediate and infrastructural sectors such as coal, steel and transport in order to 'control inflation'. As a consequence relative prices get distorted further. These are all very important markets and controlling them imposes significant costs on the economy. Even when there is an attempt to liberalise the economy there is still an attempt to 'control inflation' by controlling administered prices rather than freeing these prices.[1] It is difficult to direct controls and it is not possible to eliminate them without taking into account the underlying macroeconomic structure.

The same political and economic forces that lead to inflationary tendencies lead to balance of payments difficulties as well. The nominal exchange rate is adjusted much too slowly. This leads to an excess demand for foreign goods. The government either rations this excess demand or allows it to be satisfied by running down reserves or borrowing from abroad.

The piling up of debt permits continued expansionary fiscal policies and excessive government expenditure. Once the accumulation of the debt becomes a crisis its payment imposes additional strains on the home economy as budgetary and trade surpluses have to be accumulated in order to pay off the debt.

The urgency of paying off the debt has the undesirable consequence of focusing attention on the external sector to the neglect of the excessive distortions in the home economy. Indeed the ill effects of high internal debt, the blurring of the distinction between fiscal and monetary policies and the endogenising of the money supply to reflect budgetary policies tend to get understated. External debt tends to get emphasised for the simple reason that it is more visible.

Liberalisation of the external sector would require that the domestic price of import competing home goods fall relative to the domestic price of exportables. This can be achieved by sharp devaluations combined with a freeing of imports. This devaluation will itself lead to a large jump in the price level and some contractionary effect on domestic employment and output. This could well turn out to be counterproductive as we have learnt earlier in Chapter 12.

Some argue that, because of such difficulties, it is more appropriate to opt for a floating exchange rate. However, freeing the external sector with other financial markets repressed may not be the best policy measure. Moreover, the simultaneous freeing up of all financial markets – the so-called cold shower effect – is too extreme a policy measure and its short-term social costs in terms of the unemployment of workers in failing, previously protected, industries may be too much to bear for countries with very little social insurance and safety nets for the unemployed and the poor. However, more liberalisation programmes have faltered on their inability to control inflation than any other single factor. In practice liberalisation can be combined, albeit imperfectly, with an anti-inflation programme. Three significant components of such a policy initiative would be (i) a crawling peg rather than sharp devaluations which dampen inflationary tendencies and expectations before freeing up the exchange rate completely, (ii) safeguards to ensure that the government does not resort to price controls to 'control inflation' and does not resort to excessive spending, and (iii) simultaneous efforts being made to loosen controls in other financial and key sectors of the economy.

CONSEQUENCES FOR ECONOMIC GROWTH

It is now fairly well established that countries that have sustained high real rates of interest and more stable price levels have had more robust financial growth. In Table 14.1 we present evidence of this from various issues of *The International Financial Yearbook* published by the International Monetary Fund (IMF). Ratios of M_3 (currency, savings deposits and shorter-term deposits in banks and other quasi-financial institutions such as post-offices) to gross national product (GNP) are typically higher in the high growth Asian economies than the highly inflationary Latin American economies. As a matter of fact even the slower growing Asian economies tend to be more financially developed than Latin American countries. However, all slowly growing economies tend to have low financial development – low levels of M_3/GNP ratio.

Table 14.1 Bank loanable funds in typical less developed countries (ratio of M_3 to GNP)

	1960	1965	1970	1975	1980	1985	Mean (1960–85)
Latin America							
Argentina	0.245	0.209	0.267	0.168	0.234	0.152	0.213
Brazil	0.148	0.156	0.205	0.164	0.175	0.179	0.171
Chile	0.123	0.130	0.183	0.099	0.208	0.263	0.168
Colombia	0.191	0.204	0.235	–	0.222	0.290	0.228
Asia							
India	0.283	0.262	0.264	0.295	0.382	0.412	0.316
Philippines	0.186	0.214	0.235	0.186	0.219	0.204	0.207
Sri Lanka	0.284	0.330	0.275	0.255	0.317	0.371	0.305
Turkey	0.202	0.223	0.237	0.222	0.136	0.228	0.208

Source: IMF, *International Financial Statistics*, various issues.
Notes: Mean ratio of M_3 to GNP for the four Latin American countries is 0.195; mean ratio of M_3 to GNP for the four Asian countries is 0.259.

In Table 14.2 we show that high real interest rates tend to be associated with high growth rates of real gross domestic product (GDP) as well. The evidence is definitely suggestive, if not compelling, evidence of the deleterious effects of financial repression on economic growth. Such conclusions are supported by the recent work of Gelb (1989) who analysed the experience of thirty-four LDCs over the period 1965–85. Gelb further discovered that in a cross-section of LDCs varying investment efficiency was strongly and positively correlated with the average real deposit rate. It might be argued that apart from the investment efficiency effect, changes in the deposit rates will have effects on the volume of savings and investment. It might be argued that higher deposit rates gained by increasing other real interest rates might lead to a drop in the volume of investment. Gelb quantified the strengths of the two effects and discovered that any negative effect on the volume of investment was more than outweighed by the efficiency of investment effect.

Table 14.2 Interest rates on bank deposits, growth of real financial assets and growth of real gross domestic product in selected developing countries, 1971–80 (compound growth rates, percentage per year)

	Financial assets	GDP
Countries with positive real interest rates		
Malaysia	13.8	8.0
South Korea	11.1	8.6
Sri Lanka	10.1	4.7
Nepal	9.6	2.0
Singapore	7.6	9.1
Philippines	5.6	6.2
Countries with moderately negative real interest rates		
Pakistan	9.9	5.4
Thailand	8.5	6.9
Morocco	8.2	5.5
Colombia	5.5	5.8
Greece	5.4	4.7
South Africa	4.3	3.7
Kenya	3.6	5.7
Burma	3.5	4.3
Portugal	1.8	4.7
Zambia	−1.1	0.8
Countries with strongly negative real interest rates		
Peru	3.2	3.4
Turkey	2.2	5.1
Jamaica	−1.9	−0.7
Zaire	−6.8	0.1
Ghana	−7.6	−0.1

Source: IMF, *International Financial Yearbook*

PROBLEMS OF LIBERALISING INDIVIDUAL MARKETS

The general theory of second best tells us that when there are several distortions in an economy it may or may not be second best optimal to remove the distortions in individual markets. We consider here, somewhat tentatively, the welfare gains and losses from liberalising individual markets/sectors in developing countries.

Consider, first, the most important sector in most developing countries: agriculture. Farmers may safely be assumed to base their supply decisions on the relative prices for their produce which they face. Usually producer prices for agricultural goods are fixed in developing countries in order to provide food at relatively low prices to urban workers. Freeing up producer prices will, invariably, increase agricultural output, *ceteris paribus*. In the very short run urban workers may have to pay higher prices for food. But the combination of higher agricultural supplies and a higher demand for industrial goods in agriculture as rural incomes increase, will mean that their welfare will also increase. Hence it must be welfare improving to free agricultural prices even when the home currency is overvalued.

This argument does not carry over very easily to the case of a country with comparative advantage in cash crops. If resources were allocated efficiently these countries would import food. Freeing up producer prices would then lead to higher demand for food and, if food is bought under licenses in a regime of fixed nominal exchange rate, higher food prices. This could lead to a drop in welfare.

In Chapter 14 we shall understand that the growth rate of the economy and welfare can always be improved by freeing up financial markets and reducing financial repression. As interest rates rise and, in particular, when the real interest rate becomes positive, savers are willing to save more. Overvaluation of the home currency and ceilings on domestic interest rates work in the same direction – they tend to reduce the incentive to save and increase the capital intensity of projects. Hence, irrespective of whether the home currency is overvalued, it will be welfare improving to reduce or eliminate financial repression.

We can make similar comments about the labour market. In most developing countries urban wages are well above market clearing levels, mainly because of unions who exercise considerable political clout. Freeing up the labour market would improve welfare. Particularly, if there are exchange rate overvaluation and/or interest rate controls, a reduction in the real wage would lead to the adoption of more labour intensive techniques of production and higher employment.[2]

Similar remarks can be made about changing the value of the exchange rate to more realistic levels even if there are other distortions in the economy. Apart from bringing domestic prices more in line with true international prices, such a measure will reduce the import substitution bias of domestic industrial strategy. Foreign industrial goods become relatively attractive and the world demand for exports improves.

It may safely be concluded that liberalising capital outflows and inflows may not always be welfare improving. If domestic interest rates are controlled, liberalising capital outflows will mean a flight of capital from the home country as savers shift savings to foreign markets where rates of return are higher. Even if domestic financial markets are completely liberalised there might be considerable exchange rate risk in holding one's savings in the form of home currency. It would, therefore, appear that except for capital flows and the agricultural sectors of countries with comparative advantage in cash crops, liberalisation of individual markets/sectors is likely to be welfare improving.

THE SEQUENCING OF ECONOMIC REFORMS

It has often been argued that simultaneous and large-scale reform on a wide front is the best way to proceed. New signals will be set up which will not involve the resource misallocation in response to altered signals before the transition is complete. This conclusion gets further strengthened by empirical evidence that suggests that uncertainty about the directions of future reforms during a process of slow change, delays response to altered signals.

There are some who argue that the complete and total dismantling of all restrictions may not be a good idea. It is often argued that the costs of large-scale reforms are very high in LDCs. With large-scale reforms many inefficient industries may have to shut down with consequent unemployment. Typically there will be a significant time lag before new, more efficient, industries can come up. Moreover, these new industries may have considerably different skill requirements as compared to the industries that had closed down. Workers may have to suffer protracted unemployment. With very little social programmes to support these workers, the short-run welfare costs of quick and widespread reform may be very high. A government that has time on its hands can afford to go slow. Typically this will involve reasonably good economic performance at home and a comfortable foreign exchange position. Unfortunately, most developing countries do not have such luxury. When the domestic economic performance is satisfactory and the foreign exchange position comfortable, governments hardly ever think of deep economic reform. If they did, the social costs of such reform would be much lower and the path of transition to a more efficient economy much smoother. Usually reform is initiated in the face of deep economic crisis – a sluggish domestic economy combined with the possibility of not being able to meet external payments obligations. The more severe the situation the greater the possibility that reforms will have to be widespread and quick. The consequent costs to the poor are then high. It is indeed deplorable that many LDC governments have, in the past, delayed reforms when they were easy to carry out and been forced to effect much deeper adjustments later when the social costs of adjustment have gone up considerably.

Suppose now that large-scale and complete reforms cannot take place all at once. Is it possible to provide some direction for governments on the sequencing of reforms? This is the issue of optimal sequencing of economic reforms which we consider now.

To be sure, the nature of economic crisis that precedes serious economic reforms is different for different countries. Hence the optimal sequence of reforms will be different for different countries. However, some remarks of a general nature can be made.

Before the government embarks upon a programme of economic liberalisation it must get its own finances under control. In most developing countries this involves the government controlling its expenditures and increasing its tax revenues.

Control of government expenditure is extremely important for controlling inflation. As we have remarked earlier, the ability to control inflation is perhaps the most important measure of the success of a programme of economic reforms. Government budgetary deficits in developing countries are highly inflationary because governments tend to dump their debt on captive central and commercial banks so that the debt gets monetised. This, in turn, exacerbates inflationary tendencies. Control of government expenditure involves reducing or eliminating subsidies. Typically, these are subsidies for food, fertilisers and for inputs used in the manufacturing sector. Reducing these subsidies has the dual advantage of reducing the government deficit *and* reducing price distortions. In addition, the government may contemplate selling off unproductive and unprofitable state undertakings.

At the same time as the government attempts to reduce its expenditure it must also attempt to increase its tax revenues. In most developing countries the most important forms of taxes are indirect taxes on domestically produced goods and foreign produced imports. Because personal incomes are so low, direct taxes are relatively unimportant. Governments must try to broaden the tax base by bringing a larger number of goods, services and incomes under the tax net. Further, governments must attempt to reduce tax evasion by lowering marginal tax rates and streamlining the tax collection mechanism.

In the 1990s the credibility of most governments, particularly LDC governments, is low. Hence strict fiscal discipline at home is essential to send the right signals to domestic and foreign investors. Governments must demonstrate their ability to finance their expenditures in a non-inflationary manner, i.e. without printing additional money. In addition governments must reduce accumulated foreign and domestic debt.

The next step in the process of economic reforms is the freeing up of domestic credit markets so that depositors receive, and borrowers pay, substantial real interest rates. But unrestricted borrowing and lending in free capital markets can take place only when the price level is relatively stable and government finances are under control. Without price level stability, real and nominal interests are going to be unstable. This will increase the risk associated with and adversely affect the volume of borrowing and lending. This implies that until such time as the price level has stabilised, bank credit must be strictly *controlled* by the authorities.

Once domestic financial markets have been liberalised the government is well advised to decontrol foreign transactions. The prevailing wisdom is that the current account is best liberalised before the capital account. The capital account should not be liberalised too soon because this might lead to substantial capital flight from the domestic economy. A liberalised current account means that home exports become more competitive in foreign markets.

Before such liberalisation of the trade account is undertaken domestic prices must be rationalised and decontrolled, government finances must be in order and the system of multiple exchange rates with several different exchange rates (depending on tariff and other restrictions) must be abandoned. In their separate works on trade liberalisation Krueger (1978) and Bhagwati (1978) defined liberalisation as consisting of the replacement of quantitative restrictions which are not visible with tariffs that are. The next step in this arrangement is the reduction of the mean and the variance of the tariffs.

As remarked earlier, the rationalisation of foreign trade policy does not imply that full convertibility of the home currency be extended to the capital account. Before allowing enterprises and individuals to borrow and lend freely from abroad domestic financial markets must be fully liberalised and exchange rate risk associated with the home currency reduced so that liberalisation of the capital account does not involve large-scale capital flight from the home economy. This depends crucially on the restoration of fiscal discipline on the part of the government and the attainment of price stability.

THE INTERNATIONAL CONTEXT OF ECONOMIC REFORMS

An implicit assumption behind the analysis of economic reforms contained in this chapter is that the international economy is responsive to the reforms being undertaken by the developing countries. In concrete terms this assumption means several things. For instance, it could mean that when the developing country gets its finances in order and starts producing efficiently it is able to sell more abroad and earn additional foreign exchange. It could also mean that the international community is willing to transfer funds on easy terms to the concerned LDC in order to reduce the pains of deep-rooted structural reforms. Clearly both these conditions are likely to be satisfied only when the world economy – particularly the developed countries – are growing rapidly.

It is ironic that when the world economy was growing most rapidly – in the decades of the 1950s and 1960s – most developing countries were inclined towards economic repression. The Feldman–Mahalanobis model was at the peak of its popularity because it provided an economic rationale for the suspicions of the newly independent countries towards trade with the Western world, important members of which were their former colonisers. The newly industrialised countries (NICs) (Hong Kong, Singapore, Taiwan, South Korea and the like) were among the very few exceptions to this rule. It is not surprising that these NICs attained very high rates of economic growth whereas much of the rest of the developing world lagged behind. It should further be remembered that the rapid expansion of the world economy during this period was itself, at least partly, a result of far reaching tariff and other trade barriers reductions in most developed countries in Europe, the USA and Japan.

The NICs went in for deep economic reforms, indeed integrated themselves into an expanding world economy. Their products found ready markets in the post-war economic boom. The costs of economic reforms in these small economies were low. These economies prospered.

A second major wave of economic reforms in developing countries was initiated during the 1980s – a consequence primarily of IMF pressures in the wake of LDCs seeking loans in the aftermath of the oil price shocks of 1973 and 1979. The early 1980s were a period of economic expansion for the world economy but the oil price shocks had created a tentative atmosphere for continued trade liberalisation. Protectionist pressures were strong in most developed countries as they tried to minimise the harmful effects of the oil price shocks on their own economies.

The last few years of the 1980s were characterised by deep world recession. Protectionist pressures were again strong. In this atmosphere there can be no presumption that developing countries will readily find markets for their products in the markets of developed countries. Moreover, the atmosphere for easy credit availability to tide over the pains of structural adjustment, has certainly not improved.

How bad is the protectionist environment? A World Bank study in 1987 showed that about 21 per cent of developed countries' imports from developing countries in 1986 were subject to formal non-trade barriers (NTBs): about 17 per cent in the USA, to 22 per cent in Japan and 23 per cent in the European Common Market. Eighty per cent of clothing, 61 per cent of textile yarn and fabrics, 55 per cent of steel products, 27 per cent of footwear and 13 per cent of chemicals imported by developed countries from developing countries in 1986 were subject to NTBs. NTBs in developed countries as a whole increased by about 16 per cent between 1981 and 1986. The protectionist movement has been most conspicuous in the USA. But other countries including Japan have been quite protectionist in more subtle ways.

One of the principal ways in which NTBs are applied to developed country imports from developing countries is punitive restrictions following a determination that the LDC has been 'dumping' its products in the markets of the developed country. In the USA there is a special law to deal with this – Article 301.

Article IV of the General Agreement on Tariffs and Trade (GATT) defines dumping as an act in which a product is sold in another country at less than the 'normal' value of the product which is defined as (i) the home market price, (ii) a 'constructed value' based on an estimated cost of production plus 'reasonable sales expenses and normal profits'. This last value is a very abused concept. In estimating 'constructed value' developed countries often add an amount for administrative expenses for its export sales because such expenses are paid by the importer, the importing country may add all of the expenses associated with advertising in the domestic market. The US anti-dumping law even sets a minimum level of selling costs at 10 per cent and a statutory minimum profit margin at 8 per cent, effectively raising the normal value to meet the dumping charges. The European Community (EC) takes the selling costs actually incurred and the profit margin actually realised by the firm in question. In recent proceedings the latter varied between 1 and 33 per cent.

Moreover, it is easy in developed countries to initiate an anti-dumping or countervailing duty charge. Since processing procedures are inordinately long, and since very harsh 'provisional' measures based on information supplied by the petitioners are applied, the anti-dumping and countervailing duty cases have produced monstrous 'procedural protectionism'. Unfortunately, these arrangements have allowed vested interest groups in developed countries to undermine the efforts of exporters in developing countries.

Anti-dumping provisions have been widely used in the EC as well. As a matter of fact this has been the most important instrument of EC protectionist policy. Beseler and Williams (1986) report that between 1980 and 1985 there were 254 investigations and punitive action was taken in 209 cases.

The prevalence of NTBs and other protectionist measures in developed countries introduces a measure of uncertainty in trade planning in developed countries. To be sure, GATT does recognise that developing countries may have to impose tariffs to protect 'infant' industries. But it is required that these tariffs be removed soon after the industry gets going. For various reasons (see Corden 1974, for example) developed countries may find it necessary to subsidise some industries. Some of these industries may, for example, create external economies for other industries. Typically, in such situations, it is advisable to subsidise the costs of this industry since its expansion has beneficial effects on the rest of the economy which are not completely captured by market prices. In practical situations there might be disagreement between developed and developing countries as to which industries deserve protection and this may lead to the imposition of NTBs against LDC exports. Nam (1986), for instance, notes that

> the burden of proof as to whether factors other than subsidies may have been a major cause of injury, or whether initial findings on the amount of subsidies were appropriately estimated, normally falls on the exporters. Such a proof requires not only a large amount of information, but also expensive legal costs which may be too burdensome for many developing countries to bear.
>
> (Nam 1986: 19–20)

Table 14.3 Post-Tokyo most favoured nation tariff averages for major sectors and share of imports from developing countries in EEC, Japan and USA, 1984

Sector	EEC		Japan		USA	
	Tariff averages[a, b]	Share of LDCs in total imports[c]	Tariff averages[a, b]	Share of LDCs in total imports[c]	Tariff averages[a, b]	Share of LDCs in total imports[c]
Food	13.8 (0.89)	55.4	19.5 (2.08)	36.2	7.1 (1.53)	55.6
Agricultural raw materials	3.3 (1.55)	30.5	2.3 (1.97)	39.4	1.7 (1.62)	21.0
Mineral fuels	3.4 (0.88)	65.1	3.0 (0.80)	88.9	1.0 (1.90)	68.8
Ores and metals	4.0 (0.67)	31.2	3.9 (0.76)	46.1	3.8 (0.89)	23.8
Manufactures,	7.0 (0.61)	20.3	6.7 (0.70)	27.9	6.7 (0.94)	28.0
of which:						
chemicals	4.2 (0.60)	14.1	6.0 (0.95)	16.6	5.9 (1.00)	15.6
textiles and clothing	10.5 (0.39)	60.6	10.5 (0.41)	75.6	10.3 (0.61)	70.0
machinery, transport equipment	4.7 (0.69)	10.2	4.6 (0.25)	15.3	3.5 (0.83)	19.1
other manufacturers	5.2 (0.56)	19.0	6.1 (0.68)	31.0	6.2 (1.04)	41.1
All sectors	7.8 (0.92)	40.0	8.0 (2.09)	58.3	6.2 (1.06)	36.9

Source: Erzan and Karsenty 1987
Notes: [a] Arithmetic averages of post-Tokyo MFN tariffs.
   [b] A figure in parenthesis below a tariff value denotes the coefficient of variation (standard deviation of tariff rates divided by their arithmetic average).
   [c] Import shares are in terms of percentages.

Apart from the punitive measures associated with dumping, developing countries also face the problem of tight tariffs being placed, based on their exports in developed countries. In Table 14.3 we report average figures on tariffs in developed countries after the Tokyo Round of GATT negotiations (1984). It is clear from this table that protectionist forces in developed countries are still quite strong. The ongoing recession in industrialised countries has probably made them stronger.

The degree of success that can be achieved by the reforms of developing countries, then, depends partly on the outcome of the tussle between protectionist and liberal forces in developed countries. Past experience suggests that if multilateral trade institutions function effectively it would be possible to contain the protectionist forces. At the transnational level, then, an important element of the strategy of developing countries should be to work toward the success of the GATT and other multilateral institutions such as UNCTAD. This is their best bet for helping the forces favouring free trade in developed countries.

Several basic principles should guide LDC efforts at multilateral organisations and bilateral negotiations. First and foremost, policy makers in developing countries must take these negotiations very seriously. A history of import-subsitution type strategy has led many developing countries to adopt a rather lackadaisacal attitude toward such negotiations. It is amply clear now that *reciprocity* is important. If developing countries seek reductions in tariffs and other barriers in developed countries they should be prepared to grant similar concessions on their own parts.

Moreover, it should be realised by all concerned that the establishment of a truly international liberal trading order is in the best interests of all trading countries. The current tendency towards forming regional free trade blocks has to be eschewed.

Attitudes toward the GATT have to be improved. At the present time the future of the current round of negotiations for tariff reductions known as the Uruguay Round is uncertain. There is considerable ill-will and suspicion among the major developed countries over agricultural policy and intellectual property rights. The fact that most of these countries are currently going through a prolonged recession is not helping matters either. Developing and developed countries should realise that the scope of GATT should be expanded to cover all aspects of trade. The present recession is fanning protectionist pressures in most countries. But at the same time some of the most productive areas of international trade cannot easily be controlled through national tariffs and NTBs. These include items like information systems transfers which can be traded via satellite. Such trade and the progressive liberalisation of many previously highly repressed economies (developing countries and former socialist economies) provides strength to the forces that want international trade to be free. It is hard to predict how matters will ultimately be resolved. Suffice it to say here that a more liberal world trading arrangement will be to the benefit of all. The success of the current phase of reforms in developing countries depends critically on the liberalisation of trade in developed countries. To the extent that they may influence developed countries' policies, multilateral institutions such as the IMF and the World Bank should attempt to make developed countries' markets more open for developing countries' exports. Such efforts would supplement and enhance the effectiveness of the multilateral institutions' insistence that developing countries open up their markets and reduce economic repression.

NOTES

1 Administered prices contribute significantly to allocative inefficiency in industry. See Jha and Sahni (1993).
2 There is some evidence to suggest that biases of technical progress have been induced by the structure of factor prices. See Jha and Sahni (1993).

15

Economic growth in developing countries
Theoretical considerations

INTRODUCTION

In this chapter we shall study theoretical approaches to economic growth in developing countries. There are several factors that distinguish theoretical models of economic growth in developed countries from those thought to be applicable to developing countries.

Some of these factors can be mentioned here. First, as we have noticed in our analysis of structuralism, money can play an important part in the production process. So a growth model that is 'real' (in that it concentrates on non-monetary aspects of growth) is likely to have limited applicability to developing countries. Second, capital markets in developing countries are characterised by various controls. Typically, interest rates are kept low 'in order to encourage investment'. This phenomenon often goes by the name of *financial repression*. Third, the external sector impinges on the growth path of developing countries in somewhat different ways from that in developed countries.

In this chapter we analyse these issues in a simple framework. We begin with a description of 'the standard' real and monetary growth models applicable to developed countries. Then we introduce some complications that arise if money is a producer good. Later we introduce financial repression. Finally we study the implications of an open economy.

THE REAL NEOCLASSICAL MODEL OF ECONOMIC GROWTH

Students have, no doubt, encountered the standard neoclassical model of economic growth. This model was first put forward by Robert Solow (1956) and it has been, for quite some time, *the* model of economic growth around which additional complications have been built and to which other questions have been addressed.

The principal elements of Solow's analysis are as follows.

1 Savings can be considered a fixed fraction of national income. However, it is possible to change this fraction through, say, changes in tax rates.

2 We concentrate on long-run problems so that short-run issues like unemployment can be discarded. In other words, it is assumed that full employment is continuously maintained. The demand side is no longer important and all our efforts can be concentrated on the supply side.

3 Production is defined by an aggregate constant returns to scale production function in which capital can be smoothly substituted for labour and *vice versa*. Perfect competition prevails in all markets so that factors of production are paid their marginal products and, by Euler's theorem, payments to factors of production exhaust total output.

4 Labour grows at an exogenously determined rate n.

We can now specify the Solow model in a little more detail. The production function can be written as

$$y = F(K,L) \tag{15.1}$$

where y is real output, K is the capital stock, L is the labour input and F is a constant returns to scale production function.

Divide through by L to write the production function in its intensive form

$$\frac{y}{L} = F\left(\frac{K}{L},1\right)$$

or

$$q = f(k) \tag{15.2}$$

where $q = y/L$ and $k = K/L$.

The marginal product of capital, $(\partial f/\partial k)$ or f' is the rental payment to capital. The wage rate is the marginal product of labour. This is equal to $f - kf'$. For every unit of labour total factor payments are $f - kf' + kf' = f$. This validates Euler's product exhaustion theorem.

Total savings, S, are a fixed fraction, s, of output, i.e.

$$S = sY \tag{15.3}$$

In per labour terms, savings are $sf(k)$. Savings are always equal to investment which is addition to capital stock,

$$\dot{K} = S = sy \tag{15.4}$$

Now suppose labour grows at the exogenous rate n. Now the rate of growth of k is

$$\frac{\dot{k}}{k} = \left(\frac{\dot{K}}{K}\right) - \left(\frac{\dot{L}}{L}\right) = \left(\frac{sy}{K}\right) - n = s\frac{y}{L}\frac{L}{K} - n$$

$$= \left(\frac{sf(k)}{k}\right) - n,$$

whence

$$\dot{k} = sf(k) - nk \tag{15.5}$$

Equation (15.5) is the fundamental dynamic equation of the Solow model. To see this, realise that once k is known, the model is fully specified given the values of parameters s and n. Once k is known, output, factor payments, savings and investment are all known. Equation (15.5) describes the intertemporal movement of k and is, hence, of fundamental importance.

In Figure 15.1(a) we have drawn the $f(k)$ function. $F(K,L)$ is a constant returns to scale production function. Further it is assumed that $f' > 0$ and $f'' < 0$ – hence the shape of $f(k)$.

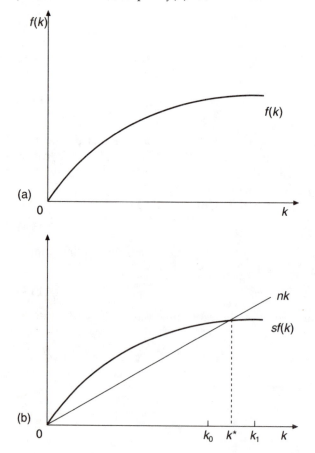

Figure 15.1

In Figure 15.1(b) we have drawn the $sf(k)$ schedule. This is a displacement of the $f(k)$ schedule by the factor s. We have also drawn the straight line nk. At capital–labour ratio k^*, $sf(k) = nk$ and hence $\dot{k}$ would be zero. Hence, if the economy has capital labour ratio k^*, this capital–labour ratio would be indefinitely maintained. Output, capital and labour would all grow at the same rate. Solow defines such a situation as a *steady state*. Clearly with steady-state growth going on in the Solow model, factor rewards would also remain unchanged.

Moreover, the steady-state growth path is stable. At k_0 in Figure 15.1, $sf(k) > nk$ so that by equation (15.5) $\dot{k} > 0$. Similarly at k_1, we have $sf(k) < nk$, so that $\dot{k} < 0$. We draw a phase diagram in Figure 15.2. In Figure 15.2(b) we describe the behaviour of $\dot{k}$ as a function of k. To the left of k^*, $\dot{k}$ is positive. To the right of k^*, $\dot{k}$ is negative. At the steady-state capital labour ratio, $\dot{k} = 0$.

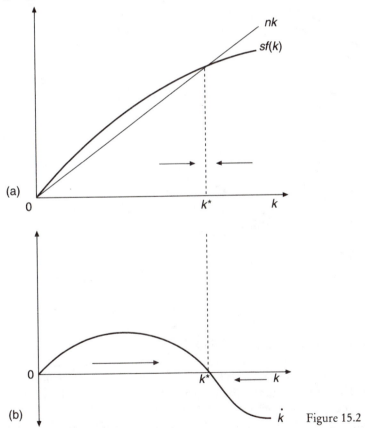

Figure 15.2

We have now seen how the equilibrium capital–labour ratio responds to changes in the values of some parameters. An increase in the savings rate will automatically lead to an increase in investment. With a fixed rate of growth of labour, the equilibrium capital–labour ratio will rise. The return to capital will fall and the wage rate will rise. In steady state, the rate of growth will be the same as before, i.e. n.

This change is analysed diagrammatically in Figure 15.3(a). An increase in the savings rate from s_0 to s_1 twists the $sf(k)$ schedule anti-clockwise while leaving the nk line intact. This raises the equilibrium capital–labour ratio from k^* to k^{**}. Since, in steady state, the capital–labour ratio is constant, the rates of growth of output, capital and labour are again equal to n.

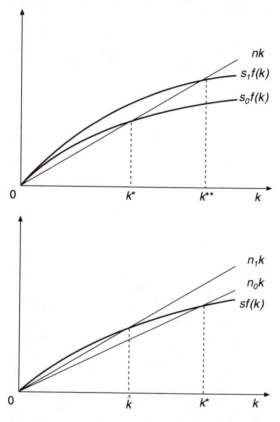

Figure 15.3

In Figure 15.3(b) we analyse the impact of an increase in the rate of growth of population. As n rises from n_0 to n_1 the $sf(k)$ schedule is unaffected. The nk line, however, will twist anti-clockwise to n_1k. The equilibrium capital–labour ratio falls – the wage rate falls and the rate of return to capital rises. The growth of output is now higher at n_1 instead of n_0.

A final query in this section. Suppose the government wanted to choose the savings rate of the economy in order to maximise per capita consumption in steady state. Since savings per capita are $sf(k)$, consumption per capita, c, must be $c = (1 - s)f(k)$. In steady state $\dot{k} = sf(k) - nk = 0$, so that $s = nk/f(k)$ and, hence, $c = (1 - s)f(k) = f(k) - nk$. Maximising this with respect to s we have $dc/ds = (f' - n)(dk^*/ds) = 0$ where k^* is now the optimum steady-state capital–labour ratio. Now since $dk^*/ds > 0$ we must have at optimum $f' - n = 0$ or $f' = n$, i.e. the optimum rate of interest equals the rate of growth of population. This is Phelps' famous *golden rule of economic growth* (see Phelps 1961).

MONETARY GROWTH IN THE SOLOW MODEL

The neoclassical monetary growth model was first presented by Tobin (1965). He assumes that investment is always equal to planned savings and all markets are always in equilibrium.

In this model, money supply changes affect consumption even in the steady state.[1] Tobin assumes that consumption per worker is a constant fraction of disposable income. The latter is the sum of output per worker $f(k)$ and the increment of real balances per worker: $(d/dt)(M/PL)$. Here M is the nominal stock of money and P is the price level. Suppose the money stock grows exponentially at rate μ and π is the rate of inflation. Tobin's postulated consumption function is, then,

$$Z = \frac{C}{L} = \alpha[f(k) + (\mu - \pi)m] \tag{15.6}$$

with $0 < \alpha < 1$ and $m = M/PL$.

Monetary policy will be able to shift the consumption function if it can vary real balances per worker (m), given the capital–labour ratio. It is assumed in all neoclassical monetary growth models that the supply and demand for real balances per worker are always equal, regardless of the rate of price change.[2]

The demand for real balances per worker is a function of (a) transactions demand reflected by $f(k)$, (b) the stock of the other asset per worker, i.e. k, and (c) the opportunity cost of holding real balances. Capital yields an expected return equal to its expected marginal product and real balances yield an expected return equal to the negative of the expected rate of inflation π^e. It is generally assumed that the expected marginal product of labour is equal to the current level – which, of course, is a function of k. Hence the demand for real cash balances per worker can be written as

$$m = L(k, \pi^e) \tag{15.7}$$

Now $L_1 > 0$ because an increase in k will raise output and, therefore, increase the demand for labour. An increase in π^e increases the opportunity cost of holding money. Hence $L_2 < 0$.

A critical determinant of stability is the specification of the determination of π^e. In the steady state, real balances per worker must be constant. Hence the price level ultimately grows at the rate μ. Hence if n is the rate of growth of labour then the steady-state rate of inflation must be $\mu - n$. A simple price expectations formulation is to suggest that the expected rate of inflation is equal to $\mu - n$.

Some authors have experimented with an adaptive expectations formulation

$$\frac{d\pi^e}{dt} = \beta(\pi - \pi^e) \qquad 0 < \beta < 1$$

However, this can often lead to unstable growth. If we stick to the assumption that $\pi^e = \mu - n$, then we can write the per capita consumption function as

$$Z = \frac{C}{L} = Z[k + L(k, \mu - n)] \tag{15.8}$$

Now

$$\begin{aligned} \dot{k} &= sf(k) - nk = f(k) - nk - C/L \\ &= f(k) - nk - Z[k + L(k, \mu - n)] \end{aligned} \tag{15.9}$$

The Solow dynamic equation can be written as (15.9). The behaviour of this equation is described by Figure 15.4.

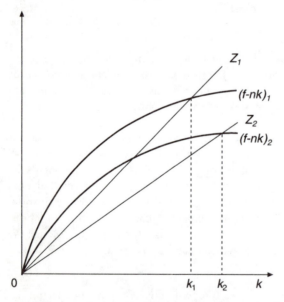

Figure 15.4

In Figure 15.4 we have drawn the $f(k) - nk$ schedule. For a fixed value of μ and the assumption that $\pi^e = \mu - n$ we have drawn the consumption per worker schedule as the straight line Z_1. The equilibrium capital–labour ratio is k_1.

Now suppose that the rate of growth of money supply rises. Expected inflation rises as well. Since $L_2 < 0$ there is a decline in real cash balances per capita at every capital–labour ratio. Since wealth per capita is $k + m$, the decline in $L(k, \pi^e) = m$ reduces real wealth per worker. Consumption per worker is positively related to wealth per worker. Hence the rise in μ shifts us from Z_1 to Z_2. Hence the equilibrium capital–labour ratio rises. Monetary policy is able to affect the time profile of $k(t)$. $f(k) - nk$ is maximised at k^* – the capital–labour ratio associated with the golden rule.

REAL BALANCES AS A PRODUCER'S GOOD

Two conclusions from the preceding sections have been criticised. First, it would appear that inflation is conducive to economic development. We know from Chapter 11 that, if anything, the contrary is the case. Second, monetary policy was able to affect the time profile of the capital–labour ratio because of the real balance effect in the consumption function. Would this disappear if all money was inside money (liabilities of the commercial banking system)?

To the extent that money is inside money, the importance of the real balance effect will be reduced. However, whether or not money is inside money, real balances may be viewed as generating a productive service, complementary with capital and labour. If there was no medium of exchange we would have the inefficiencies of a barter economy. What makes such a situation inefficient is that firms use labour and capital to distribute goods and services which would otherwise be available for production. An explicit medium of exchange which is costless to produce, increases the productivity of the economy by permitting a more efficient means of distribution, and hence a greater rate of production of goods and services with given inputs of capital and labour. If real balances fall below a certain level there will be a real loss to society. There might be more frequent payments, involving additional book-keeping and other administrative expenses or some wages might be paid in kind, entailing the use of some barter. Hence, we may suppose that aggregate output may be a monotonic non-decreasing function of real balances.

If this is the case we can write the intensive production function of the Solow model as

$$q = f(k, m) \qquad f_1 > 0 \qquad f_2 \geq 0 \tag{15.10}$$

With fully developed financial institutions an increase of real balances does not liberate any perceptible amount of resources and $f_2 = 0$.

We can now reframe Tobin's model as follows. The private sector is assumed to allocate its wealth between the two assets, capital and real balances, so that in equilibrium the rates of return on the two assets are equal. The anticipated return on capital is still its marginal product today, i.e. $f_1(k, m)$. The anticipated return on real balances now has three components. First, there is the anticipated marginal product of real balances. We assume that this is the same as the current level $f_2(k,m)$. Second, there is the anticipated appreciation $-\pi^e$ in terms of its command over goods and services. Finally we may consider the liquidity yield of money $\phi(k,m)$ which reflects the feeling that householders usually regard real balances as safer to hold than real capital. Real balances here are not treated as consumer goods which yield utility directly. The liquidity yield reflects the price that asset holders are willing to pay, in terms of yield sacrificed, to hold an asset which may fluctuate less in real value. We assume that this liquidity yield is positively related to k and negatively to m, i.e. $\phi_1 > 0$ and $\phi_2 < 0$. In equilibrium

$$f_1(k,m) = f_2(k,m) - \pi^e + \phi(k,m) \qquad (15.11)$$

Differentiate equation (15.11) and solve for dm to get

$$\mathrm{d}m = \frac{f_{21} - f_{11} + \phi_1}{f_{12} - f_{22} - \phi_2}\, \mathrm{d}k - \frac{\mathrm{d}\pi^e}{f_{12} - f_{21} - \phi_2} \qquad (15.12)$$

If there are diminishing returns to substitution, i.e. sign f_{11} = sign $f_{22} < 0$, and if the two inputs are complementary or independent, $f_{12} \geq 0$, then the denominator of equation (15.12) is positive. Solving explicitly for the desired quantity of real balances per unit of labour we have

$$m = L(k,\pi^e) \qquad L_1 > 0 \qquad L_2 < 0 \qquad (15.13)$$

Equation (15.13) can be derived regardless of whether money is a liability of the public sector or the private sector. The significant features of money so far as equation (15.13) is concerned are that it is a medium of exchange and a store of value.

MONETARY GROWTH MODELS OF DEVELOPING COUNTRIES

The role of money in neoclassical growth models is tangential. In the models of Tobin, studied above, it is less so. A reduction in the amount of money held is beneficial. The role of money as a producer good, studied in the immediately preceding section, is also limited. We know from our study of short-term models of developing countries that money plays a very important role because it finances working capital.

A separate theory of economic growth of developing countries started being developed with the work of McKinnon (1973) and Shaw (1973). In separate contributions they argued that a principal reason why the standard neoclassical model of economic growth is not applicable to developing countries is that the financial sectors of most developing countries are characterised by *financial repression*. Financial repression, as we have seen, refers to a state of affairs in which key financial variables such as the interest rate and the exchange rate are controlled (specifically set below their equilibrium values) by the government. This distortion, it is argued, misallocates resources and keeps the rate of growth of the economy below potential. It is

ironic to note that financial repression is resorted to encourage investment
and growth but it turns out to have the opposite effect.

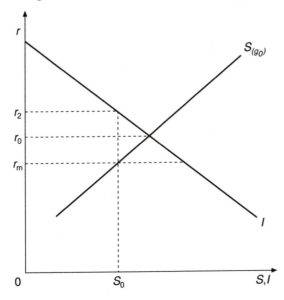

Figure 15.5

The basic analytics of financial repression as they apply to the interest
rate are presented in Figure 15.5. Savings, $S_{(g_0)}$ at the rate of growth g_0, is a
rising function of the real interest rate. The investment function is a downward sloping function of the real interest rate. Had financial markets been
allowed to function freely, the interest rate r_0 would have been established.
However, the government in order to provide cheap credit for industrial
growth mandates that the interest rate shall be r_m. At this interest rate there
exists an excess demand for investment. Actual investment is what is available, namely S_0. This amount can either be rationed among investors at the
effective interest rate of r_2 or it can be allocated by politicians and bureaucrats among their chosen investors. With the effective rate being so high the
rate of economic growth is slowed. Had the economy permitted the equilibrium rate of interest to be established savings and investment and, hence, the
rate of economic growth would have been higher and there would have
been less corruption to boot. As the economy expanded, the savings schedule with higher and higher growth rates would keep shifting to the right.
The interest rate r_m can be attained, albeit at a higher rate of growth.

It is possible, then, to write a demand for money function of the form

$$\frac{M}{P} = \phi\left(Y, \frac{I}{Y}, d - \pi\right) \tag{15.14}$$

where M/P is M_2, Y is real national income, I is investment, d is the nominal
interest rate on deposits and π is the rate of inflation. $d - \pi$ is then the real

rate of interest. McKinnon and Shaw argue that the investment function can actually be written as

$$\frac{I}{Y} = f(\rho, d - \pi) \tag{15.15}$$

where ρ is the real return on investment. It is argued that $\partial(M/P)/\partial(I/Y) > 0$ and that $\partial(I/Y)/\partial(d - \pi) > 0$. An increase in the deposit rate would raise savings and increase the funds available for investment. An increase in investment would effectively increase the money supply.

With investment and money demand functions like equations (15.14) and (15.15) the underlying growth model is going to be very different from that which we have studied in the Solow–Tobin case.

GROWTH MODELS OF FINANCIALLY REPRESSED ECONOMIES

Formal modelling of economic growth with financial repression was initiated in the works of Kapur (1974, 1976a, 1983, 1986) and Mathieson (1977, 1979, 1980, 1982, 1983). This model applies to a labour surplus developing economy with its aggregate supply function given by

$$Y = \sigma K \tag{15.16}$$

where Y is real income, K is the physical capital stock and σ is the capital–output ratio. It is assumed that σ is fixed. Thus it is implicitly assumed that financial repression primarily affects the physical stock of capital and not the capital–output ratio. This assumption is somewhat at variance with reality. It is not necessary to account separately for the labour input, since this is treated as a part of working capital.

The nominal stock of money, M, is divided into two components:

$$M = H + L \tag{15.17}$$

H is defined as 'high powered' money and L is total loans made by the banking system. It is assumed that the public's desired and actual currency deposit ratio and the banks' desired and actual reserve deposit ratio are unchanged through time. Let $L/M = q$, so that $H/M = 1 - q$. Let the rate of expansion of the monetary base be $\dot{H}/H = \mu$. Since q is assumed constant it must be the case that $\dot{L}/L = \dot{M}/M = \mu$.

Let the ratio of working capital to total capital be $1 - \alpha$. It is assumed that because of technical requirements of production α is fixed. Total working capital is thus $(1 - \alpha)K$. At the end of any time period this working capital has to be replenished. It is assumed that a fixed fraction θ is replaced through bank finance and the remaining $1 - \theta$ through internal finance. The amount paid back to the banking system can be made available to other borrowers. Hence the extra amount that the banks have to lend in order to maintain the stock of working capital intact is, in nominal terms, $\dot{P}\theta(1 - \alpha)K$, which represents the increased cost of replacement as a result of a rise in the price level P. Thus the change in the capital stock, $\dot{K}$, can be written as

$$\dot{K} = \frac{1}{1-\alpha} \; \frac{\dot{L} - \dot{P}\theta(1-\alpha)K}{P} \tag{15.18}$$

Equation (15.18) tells us that capital is accumulated through increased lending less the amount that must be paid to replenish working capital. This is multiplied by $1/(1 - \alpha)$ to obtain the net increase in the utilised flow of capital services, both fixed and working. We can rewrite equation (15.18) as

$$\dot{K} = \frac{1}{1-\alpha} \; \left[\frac{\dot{L}}{P} - \pi\theta(1-\alpha)K\right]$$

$$= \frac{1}{1-\alpha} \; \left[\mu q \frac{M}{P} - \pi\theta(1-\alpha)K\right] \tag{15.18'}$$

In this model money is the only asset for wealth holders. We write the desired holding of money balances (M^d/P) as

$$\frac{M^d}{P} = Ye^{-a(\pi*-d)} \tag{15.19}$$

where a is a positive parameter, d is the nominal interest rate paid on money holdings and π^* is the expected rate of inflation. M/P is, then, actual money balances.

Define γ as the rate of growth of the economy $(\dot{Y}/Y)$. Now, since the capital output ratio is constant, it must be the case that $\dot{Y}/Y = \dot{K}/K = \sigma$. Upon substitution from equation (15.18') we have

$$\gamma = \mu \; \frac{\sigma q}{1-\alpha} \; \frac{M}{PY} - \pi\theta \tag{15.20}$$

Let us now work with the quantity theory of money relation $MV = PY$ where V is the velocity of circulation of money. Logarithmically differentiating the relation we have

$$\mu + \frac{\dot{V}}{V} = \pi + \gamma \tag{15.21}$$

THE STEADY STATE

In steady state the velocity of circulation is constant so that $\mu = \pi + \gamma$. Further it must be the case that actual and desired holdings of money are the same, and the expected and actual rates of inflation are the same. From this last condition we have $\pi = \pi^* = \mu - \gamma$. This is a classical property true of monetary growth models of the Tobin variety as well. Using the expression for π in equation (15.19) and then substituting equation (15.19) into equation (15.20) we shall have, in steady state,

$$\gamma = \mu \, \frac{\sigma q}{1 - \alpha} e^{-a(\mu - \gamma - d)} - \mu\theta + \gamma\theta \tag{15.22}$$

We shall restrict attention to the stable solutions of the above equation.

SHORT-RUN DYNAMICS

When we work with short-run dynamics we recognise two differences from the steady-state case. First, actual and expected rates of inflation need not be the same. Second, the velocity of circulation of money need not be constant.

Changes in expected inflation when the actual and expected inflation are not equal to each other are assumed to be given by an adaptive expectations process:

$$\frac{d\pi^*}{dt} = \beta(\pi - \pi^*) \tag{15.23}$$

with $0 < \beta < 1$ and assumed constant.

Let us write velocity of circulation as M/PY. We shall assume that whenever desired money balances are not equal to actual real balances there will be a tendency for π to change. We write

$$\pi = h \left(\frac{M}{PY} - \frac{\hat{M}}{PY} \right) + \pi^* \tag{15.24}$$

where $\hat{M}/PY$ can be interpreted as desired velocity of circulation. We assume that h is a constant. This completes the specification of the model.

Let us define ω as the log of velocity and $\hat{\omega}$ as the log of desired velocity. We can then write equation (15.20) as

$$\mu + \dot{\omega} = \pi + \gamma \tag{15.20a}$$

Furthermore since $M/PY = 1/V = e^{-\omega}$ we can write (15.19) as

$$\gamma = \mu \, \frac{\sigma q}{1 - \alpha} \, e^{-\omega} - \pi\theta \tag{15.19a}$$

Similarly in equation (15.24) we use the fact that $\hat{\omega} = \ln (PY/\hat{M}) = a(\pi^* - d)$ to write

$$\pi = h(e^{-\omega} - e^{-\hat{\omega}}) + \pi^*$$

$$= h(e^{-\omega} - e^{-a(\pi^* - d)}) + \pi^* \tag{15.24a}$$

Substituting from (15.24a) into the adaptive expectations equation (15.22) we can express $d\pi^*/dt$ as a function of these same variables and substituting equations (15.24a) and (15.19a) into equation (15.20a) we can write the following two equations:

$$\dot{\omega} = -\mu \left(1 - \frac{\sigma q}{1 - \alpha} \, e^{-\omega}\right) + (1 - \theta)\pi^*$$

$$+ (1 - \theta)h(e^{-\omega} - e^{-a(\pi^* - d)}) \tag{15.25}$$

$$\frac{d\pi^*}{dt} = \beta h(e^{-\omega} - e^{-a(\pi^* - d)}) \tag{15.26}$$

These two are the fundamental dynamic equations of Kapur's model. In steady state $\dot{\omega} = d\pi^*/dt = 0$. This implies that $\pi = \pi^*$ and that $\omega = \hat{\omega} = a(\pi^* - d)$

We can depict equations (15.25) and (15.26) in a phase diagram in $\omega\pi^*$ space. This is done in Figure 15.6. To derive the $\dot{\omega} = 0$ schedule set $\dot{\omega} = 0$ in equation (15.25) and solve for $d\omega/d\pi^*$. This is positive. To derive the $d\pi^*/dt = 0$ schedule set $d\pi^*/dt = 0$ in equation (15.26) and solve for $d\omega/d\pi^*$. This is also positive. For stability we must have the $\dot{\omega} = 0$ schedule steeper than the $d\pi^*/dt = 0$ schedule. It can be checked that this condition is also sufficient to guarantee stability of steady state. Steady state occurs at (ω_1, π_1^*).

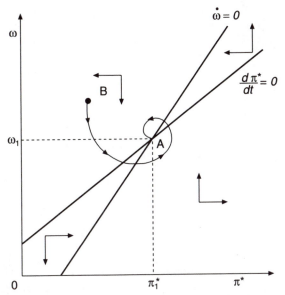

Figure 15.6

In Figure 15.6 we have also labelled the disequilibrium zones. To the left of the $\dot{\omega} = 0$ schedule given the rate of expected inflation the velocity is too high. From equation (15.25) ω will drop. For the opposite reason, to the right of $\dot{\omega} = 0$ ω will rise. To the right of $d\pi^*/dt = 0$, given ω, the rate of expected inflation is too high. From equation (15.26) we discover that π^* will rise – a higher expected inflation leads to higher actual inflation which leads to a further rise in expected inflation. For the opposite reason to the right of $d\pi^*/dt = 0$ the rate of expected inflation will drop. The equilibrium point A is only cyclically stable. Starting from a disequilibrium position such as B the economy reaches A cyclically *not* monotonically.

EFFECTS OF VARIOUS STABILISATION POLICIES

Suppose the government reduces the rate of monetary expansion μ. An examination of equations (15.25) and (15.26) reveals that this change will affect the $\dot{\omega} = 0$ schedule but not the $d\pi^*/dt = 0$ schedule. The $\dot{\omega} = 0$ schedule will shift down and to the left. The economy, in Figure 15.7 will adjust from point A to point C. As can be seen from the path of adjustment ω will rise and then start to fall. The initial rise in ω and fall in π^* imply an excess demand for money which can be eliminated only by a decrease in π and, hence, π^*. We soon reach zone III where the movements in π^* and ω begin to change.

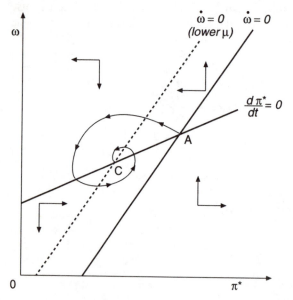

Figure 15.7

From equation (15.19a) we can discover the effects on the rate of growth of the economy. Initially the drop in μ implies a drop in working capital and hence in γ. But working capital is being replenished. As π begins to drop γ starts to recover. On the other hand as ω rises the availability of credit for investment will drop and so will γ. Hence the effect on γ at this stage is, qualitatively, indeterminate. When ω starts to fall γ will recover. It will overshoot its old equilibrium value and then converge to it.

Let us now examine the effect of financial liberalisation. In the present context financial liberalisation takes the form of permitting the deposit rate d to rise. Let l denote the interest rate charged by banks on bank loans and let the costs of the monetary system be a constant fraction z of the money supply M/P. If banks do not make any profits or losses the amount paid out by them for deposits plus the cost of running banks must just cover their earnings from loans, i.e. $d = ql - z$. Hence a change in d requires a concomitant change in l. We analyse the consequences in Figure 15.8.

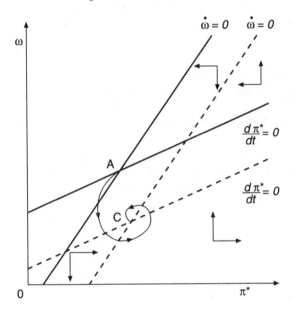

Figure 15.8

An examination of equations (15.25) and (15.26) reveals that an increase in l shifts the $\dot{\omega} = 0$ and the $d\pi^*/dt$ schedules to the right. The equilibrium moves from A to H. The path of adjustment to the new equilibrium is as depicted in the diagram. The initial fall in π^* implies that there is an instantaneous rise in the growth rate of the economy. But the reduction in π reduces the rate of increase in the replacement of worn-out capital. It is safe to assume that the former effect dominates. It is easy to establish that the growth rate of the economy is higher at H than at A.

THE OPEN ECONOMY MODEL

In later contributions Kapur (1983, 1986) has sought to extend the above model to an open economy where the exchange rate is also a policy instrument. He adds to his closed economy model a production function for working capital K_w of the Cobb–Douglas variety:

$$K_w = K_{wd}^{\lambda} K_{wf}^{1-\lambda} \tag{15.27}$$

where K_{wd} is working capital produced domestically and K_{wf} is working capital imported from abroad. K_{wd} and K_{wf} are combined in their cost–minimising ratio:

$$\frac{K_{wf}}{K_{wd}} = \frac{1-\lambda}{\lambda} \frac{P}{e_N} = \frac{1-\lambda}{\lambda} \frac{1}{e_R} \tag{15.28}$$

where e_N is the nominal exchange rate and e_R is the real exchange rate. The competitive price of K_w at the cost-minimising combination must be

$$P_w = \lambda^{-\lambda}(1-\lambda)^{\lambda-1} P^{\lambda} e_N^{1-\lambda} \tag{15.29}$$

Assuming perfect foresight, i.e. $\pi = \pi^*$ and $\dot{e}_N/e_N = (\dot{e}_N/e_N)^*$, we shall have the following expression for the growth rate of the economy,

$$\gamma = \frac{\mu \, \sigma q}{1-\alpha} \lambda^{\lambda}(1-\lambda)^{1-\lambda} e^{-\omega} e_R^{\lambda-1} - \theta \left[\pi + (1-\lambda) \frac{\dot{e}_N}{e_N} \right] \tag{15.30}$$

The balance of payments involve imports of working capital given by (15.28), exports X as a function of the real exchange rate $X = X(e_R)Y$, and short-term capital inflows F which are determined as follows:

$$F = f(d - d_w - \left(\frac{\dot{e}_N}{e_N}\right)^*)PY \tag{15.30a}$$

where d_w is the nominal interest rate abroad. Hence the nominal change in net foreign assets ($\dot{R}$) can be written as

$$\dot{R} = PX - e_N K_{wf} + F \tag{15.31}$$

Money consists of high powered money H, foreign assets R and loans L.

This model has three target variables, e_R, ω and π, and three policy variables, d, μ and e_N.

The principal additional economic insight obtained from the open economy model is that it may not necessarily be optimal to devalue to the full extent needed to get equilibrium in the balance of payments. It might be optimal to let the real exchange rate e_R drop during the transition period.

CONCLUDING COMMENTS

In this chapter we have examined some models of economic growth suitable for developing countries. We discovered that financial repression has been inimical to the growth prospects of developing countries. Fry (1988) provides an exhaustive survey of growth models relevant to developing countries.

NOTES

1 The Tobin model ought to be contrasted with the work of Foley and Sidrauski (1971) who show that money is superneutral: the rate of growth of the economy is unaffected by changes in the rate of growth of the money supply.
2 If this assumption is not made we may have problems of instability.

16

A postscript

This book has attempted a broad survey of the macreoconomic issues confronting developing countries. We learnt that there is considerable disagreement among the mainstream and alternative schools of thought. The latter, we discovered, have attained considerable respectability of late and can no longer be regarded as peripheral. Macro problems of developing countries are all the more pressing, however, since a concern for stabilisation in the standard sense of the term must necessarily be tempered with one for quick and equitable growth of economies that are economically very deprived. To quote Arida and Taylor (1989)

> The short and long run(s) have always avoided integration. The dilemma is most poignant in the Third World, where there is no agreement about an adequate vision of long-run circular flow and short-run stabilization problems led through orthodox policy into contractionary solutions.
>
> (Arida and Taylor 1989: 880)

In this book we have highlighted the differences between the mainstream and alternative approaches. However, we have also tried to find common ground, especially with regard to important policy questions. With regard to the problem of the international indebtedness of developing countries, for instance, there is almost complete agreement that debt relief for the most severely indebted countries is required. Similarly, there is some agreement on the need for financial liberalisation to stimulate economic growth in developing countries.

In key areas, however, there is deep disagreement. Most variants of the alternative model argue that devaluation in developing countries leads to stagflation whereas mainstream theory would have us believe that such devaluation is needed to bring LDC currency values more in line with their 'true' international worth. Some variants of the alternative model argue that credit and demand restraint in developing countries leads to shortages of working capital and, therefore, stifles industrial growth, whereas mainstream economists argue that such restraint is necessary to curb inflation and promote growth. Some supply-oriented versions of the alternative model agreed with some conclusions of the mainstream model – particularly with regard to the effect of demand restraint. Structuralists argue that the policy prescriptions of mainstream economics not only lead to stagflation in the short run but also dampen growth prospects in the long run apart from causing considerable suffering to the most vulnerable sections of LDC societies – the working poor. Empirical evidence seems to suggest that the IMF stabilisation packages have tended to reduce inflation and balance of payments difficulties at the cost of some sacrifice of the rate of economic growth in the short run. We have also discussed models that have tried to form an eclectic view and combine elements of mainstream thinking and the alternative model – in particular, structuralism.

This considerable difference of opinion between the two schools has generated many empirical studies. However, cross-country comparisons are hampered by paucity of reliable data (Gylfason 1987) and country-by-country analyses are not very revealing since both schools of thought can garner support for their points of view from the experiences of different countries. Leff and Sato (1980), for instance, consider a standard IS–LM model, with some features of LDCs. The countries studied were Argentina, Brazil, Chile, Costa Rica, Israel and Taiwan over the period 1950–73.

They discovered that growth in these economies easily leads to inflation and balance of payments deficits. Investment is very responsive to changes in economic conditions but savings are rather sluggish. Along a growth path, the gap between investment and savings leads to increases in the price level and balance of payments difficulties. But, except for Taiwan, the ensuing inflation does not equilibrate the goods market. Reduction of credit and other stabilisation measures would, therefore, be stagflationary. It would retard growth and lead to greater external indebtedness as the economy would not grow rapidly enough to pay off the loans taken to tide over balance of payments difficulties. Similar evidence along these lines was put together in a volume edited by Killick (1984). IMF-type stabilisation programmes of Indonesia (1966–70), Jamaica (1972–80) and Kenya (1975–81) were studied in that volume.

However, Dervis and Petri (1987) study a large number of developing countries over a long horizon and come to conclusions that are very different from those mentioned above. Developing countries that have been 'successful' have adopted realistic exchange rates – thus underscoring this policy prescription of the IMF. They also argue that outward orientation of the economy has been crucial to rapid development. They also point out that low external debt and high exports are closely linked to rapid economic growth in cross-sections of developing countries. To be sure, these authors also emphasise the importance of prudent supply-side policies such as improving the efficiency of investment in a programme of rapid economic development.

These conclusions are very much in line with IMF thinking on development issues. Similar conclusions were advanced by Fischer (1991) and, as has been noted in Chapter 12, by Gylfason (1987).

In this book we have tried to lay out carefully the basic analytical structures and policy prescriptions of both schools of thought. In instances where there is some agreement between the schools, e.g. the assignment of instruments to targets, the mutually acceptable theoretical formulation is also presented. We have also tried to present eclectic versions, combining elements of both approaches, whenever possible.

It may be the case that short-run stabilisation poses a dilemma for most developing countries. Credit restraint and devaluation by restricting demand may lead to a drop in the industrial growth rate with inflation adjusting only slowly and with considerable lag. The resulting stagflation may cause considerable hardship in economies where most people are poor and there are hardly any social insurance or welfare schemes. Reforms of output and factor prices (by reducing taxes and reducing subsidies) may be necessary to improve efficiency of supply but may cause considerable industrial restructuring. Nevertheless, there can be little doubt that such adjustments are necessary to ensure balanced and steady growth in the long run. Such are the choices that exist for developing countries. An immediate task of meaningful policy research in this area is to strike a balance between the requirements of short-term stabilisation and long-term rapid and equitable growth.

At the transnational level considerable work needs to be done to lower tariff barriers in developed countries. We have noted the severe problems with regard to both tariffs as well as dumping clauses that developing countries face in the markets of most developed economies. As has been stressed in Chapter 13, considerable work needs to be done with respect to the problem of developing country debt reduction. In this and other aspects of transnational policy (aid for structural reforms in developing countries) the activities of multilateral agencies such as the IMF and the World Bank need to be coordinated better.

The economies of many LDCs are in crisis today. However, there appears to be considerable scope for long-term growth if home and transnational policies are better coordinated. In this coordination lie hopes for healthy long-term growth in both developed and developing countries.

Bibliography

AFL–CIO Executive Council (1986) 'The International Debt Problem', statement of the AFL–CIO Executive Council, 5 August 1986.

Aggarwal, V. (1987) 'International Debt Threat: Bargaining among Creditor and Debtors in the 1980s', *Policy Papers in International Affairs* no. 29, Berkeley, University of California, Institute of International Studies.

Ahmad, S. (1986) 'Rural–Urban Migration – Policy Simulations in a Dual Economy Model of Bangladesh', *The Developing Economies* 24 (1): 26–43.

Akerlof, G.A. and Milbourne, R.D. (1987) 'The Short-run Demand for Money', *Economic Journal* 90 (3): 885–900.

—— and Yellen, J. (1985) 'A Near Rational Model of the Business Cycle with Wage and Price Inertia', *Quarterly Journal of Economics* 100 (supplement): 176–213.

Alexander, L.S. (1987) 'Three Essays on Sovereign Default and International Lending', Ph.D. thesis, Yale University.

Altonji, J.G. (1982) 'The Intertemporal Substitution Model of Labour Market Fluctuations: an Empirical Analysis', *Review of Economic Studies* 49 (5): 783–824.

Ando, A. and Kennickell, S.M. (1986) 'How Much (or little) Saving is there in Micro Data', in R. Dornbusch and J. Bossons (eds) *Macroeconomics and Finance: Essays in Honor of Franco Modigliani*, Cambridge, Mass.: MIT Press.

Argy, V. (1970) 'Structural Inflation in Developing Countries', *Oxford Economic Papers* 22 (1): 73–85.

Arida, P. and Taylor, L. (1989) 'Short-run Macroeconomics', in H. Chenery and T.N. Srinivasan (eds) *Handbook of Development Economics*, Amsterdam: North Holland.

Arrow, K.J. (1959) 'Towards a Theory of Price Adjustment', in M. Abramovitz (ed.) *The Allocation of Economic Resources*, Stanford: Stanford University Press.

Bailey, M.J. (1956) 'The Welfare Cost of Inflationary Finance', *Journal of Political Economy* 64 (2): 93–110.

Balassa, B. (1982) 'Disequilibrium Analysis in Developing Economies: An Overview', *World Development* 10 (12): 1027–38.

Ball, L. (1987) 'Externalities from Contract Length', *American Economic Review* 77 (4): 615–29.

Barro, R.J. (1972) 'A Theory of Monopolistic Price Adjustment', *Review of Economic Studies* 39 (1): 93–110.

—— (1974) 'Are Government Bonds Net Wealth?', *Journal of Political Economy* 81 (6): 1095–117.

—— (1977) 'Long Term Contracts, Sticky Prices and Monetary Policy', *Journal of Monetary Economics* 3 (3): 305–16.

—— and Fischer, S. (1976) 'Recent Developments in Monetary Theory', *Journal of Monetary Economics* 2 (2): 133–67.

—— and Gordon, D.B. (1983) 'A Positive Theory of Monetary Policy in a Natural Rate Model', *Journal of Political Economy* 91 (4): 589–610.

—— and Grossman H. (1976) *Money, Employment and Inflation*, Cambridge: Cambridge University Press.

—— and Hercovitz, Z. (1980) 'Money Stock Revisions and Unanticipated Money Growth', *Journal of Monetary Economics* 6 (2): 255–67.

Baumol, W.J. (1952) 'The Transactions Demand for Cash: an Inventory Theoretic Approach', *Quarterly Journal of Economics* 66 (2): 545–56.

Begg, D. (1982) *The Rational Expectations Revolution in Macroeconomics*, Oxford: Oxford University Press.

Benassy, J.P. (1975) 'Neo-Keynesian Disequilibrium Theory in a Monetary Economy', *Review of Economic Studies* 42 (4): 503–23.

Bernheim, B.D. (1987) 'Ricardian Equivalence: an Evaluation of Theory and Evidence', *NBER Macroeconomics Annual* 2 (1): 666–89.

Beseler, J.F. and Williams, A.N. (1986) *Anti-Dumping and Anti-Subsidy Law: The European Communities*, London: Sweet and Maxwell.

Bhagwati, J. (1978) *Anatomy and Consequences of Exchange Control Regimes*, Cambridge, Mass: NBER.

—— (1986) *International Trade in Services and Its Relevance for Economic Development*, Geneva: Pergamon Press.

Bhalla, S. (1981) 'The Transmission of Inflation in Developing Countries', in W.R. Cline and S. Weintraub (eds) *World Inflation and Developing Countries*, Washington, DC: Brookings Institution.

Black, F. (1975) 'Bank Funds Management in an Efficient Manner', *Journal of Financial Economics* 2 (2): 323–39.

Blanchard, O.J. (1988) 'Why does Money Affect Output? A Survey', in B.M. Friedman and F.H. Hahn (eds) *Handbook of Monetary Economics*, Amsterdam: North Holland.

—— and Fischer, S. (1991) *Lectures on Macroeconomics*, Cambridge, Mass.: MIT Press.

—— and Summers L.H. (1986) 'Hysteresis and the European Unemployment Problem', *NBER Macroeconomics Annual* 1 (1): 15–78.

Blinder, A.S. (1981) 'Retail Inventory Behavior and Business Fluctuations', *Brookings Papers on Economic Activity* 2 (1): 443–505.

—— (1987) 'Credit Rationing and Effective Supply Failures', *Economic Journal* 97 (2): 327–52.

—— and Fischer, S. (1981) 'Inventories, Rational Expectations and the Business Cycle', *Journal of Monetary Economics* 8 (2): 277–304.

—— and Solow, R.M. (1974) 'Analytical Foundations of Fiscal Policy', in A.S. Blinder, G. Break, D. Netzer, R. Solow and P. Steiner (eds) *The Economics of Public Finance*, Washington, DC: Brookings Institution.

Boskin, M.J. (ed.) (1987) *Private Saving and Public Debt*, Oxford: Basil Blackwell.

Branson, W.H. (1986) *Financial Capital Flows in the U.S. Balance of Payments*, Amsterdam: North Holland.

—— and Rotemberg, J. (1980) 'International Adjustment with Wage Rigidity', *European Economic Review* 13 (3): 309–32.

Bray, M.M. and Savin, N.E. (1986) 'Rational Expectations Equilibria: Learning and Model Specification', *Econometrica* 54 (5): 1129–60.

Brock, P.L. (1981) 'Optimal Monetary Control during an Economic Liberalization: Theory and Evidence from Chilean Financial Reforms', Ph.D. thesis, Stanford University, Stanford, California.

Brunner, K. and Meltzer, A.H. (1971) 'The Use of Money in the Theory of an Exchange Economy', *American Economic Review* 61 (3): 784–805.

Bruno, M. (1979) 'Stabilization and Stagflation in a Semi Industrialized Economy', in R. Dornbusch and J.A. Frenkel (eds) *International Economic Policy*, Baltimore, Md.: Johns Hopkins University Press.

—— and Sachs, J. (1985) *Economics of Worldwide Stagflation*, Cambridge, Mass.: Harvard University Press.

Bulow, J. and Rogoff, K. (1988) 'The Buyback Boondoggle', *Brookings Papers on Economic Activity* 2: 675–98.

Cagan, P. (1965) *Determinants and Effects of Changes in the Stock of Money, 1875–1960*, New York: Columbia University Press for NBER.

Cardoso, E. (1981) 'Food Supply and Inflation', *Journal of Development Economics* 9 (2): 269–84.

—— (1987) *Inflation, Growth and the Real Exchange Rate*, New York: Garland Publishing Company.

—— and Dornbusch, R. (1989) 'Foreign Private Capital Flows', in H.Chenery and T.N. Srinivasan (eds) *Handbook of Development Economics*, Amsterdam: North Holland, pp. 1387–439.

Chenery, H.B. and Srinivasan, T.N. (eds) (1989) *Handbook of Development Economics*, vols 1 and 2, Amsterdam: North Holland.

Cho, Y. and Khatkhate, D. (1989) 'Lessons of Financial Liberalisation in Asia', *World Bank Discussion Papers* no. 50.

Cline, W. (ed.) (1981) *World Inflation and the Developing Countries*, Washington, DC: Brookings Institution.

—— (1987) *Mobilizing Bank Lending to Developing Countries*, Washington, DC: Institute for International Economics.

—— (1989) 'The Baker Plan and Brady Reformulation: A Reformulation', in I. Husain and I. Diwan (eds) *Dealing with the Debt Crisis*, Washington, DC: World Bank, pp.176–93.

Cohen,B.J. (1986) *In Whose Interest? International Banking and American Foreign Policy*, New Haven, Conn.: Yale University Press.

—— (1989) 'Developing-Country Debt: A Middle Way', *Princeton Essays in International Finance*, no. 173.

Cooper, R.N. (1971a) 'Currency Depreciation in Developing Countries', *Princeton Essays in International Finance* no. 14, Princeton, NJ.

—— (1971b) 'Currency Devaluation in Developing Countries', in G. Ranis (ed.) *Government and Economic Development*, New Haven, Conn.: Yale University Press.

Corden, W.M. (1974) *Trade Policy and Economic Welfare*, Oxford: Clarendon Press.

—— (1988) 'An International Debt Facility?', *International Monetary Fund Staff Papers* 35 (3): 401–21.

Cox, J.C., Ingersoll, J.E. and Ross, S.A. (1985) 'A Theory of the Term Structure of Interest Rates', *Econometrica* 53 (2): 385–408.

Crawford, V.P. (1987) 'International Lending, Long-term Credit Relationships and Dynamic Contract Theory', *Princeton Essays in International Finance* no. 59.

De Gregorio, J. (1993) 'Inflation, Taxation and Long-run Growth', *Journal of Monetary Economics* 31 (2): 271–98.

Dell, S. (1985) 'Crisis Management and the International Debt Problem', *International Journal* 40 (2): 655–88.

Dervis, K. and Petri, P. (1987) 'The Macroeconomics of Successful Development: What are the Lessons?', in S. Fischer (ed.) *NBER Macroeconomics Annual*, Cambridge, Mass.: MIT Press.

De Vries, M.G. (1987) *Balance of Payments Adjustment 1945 to 1986: The IMF Experience*, Washington, DC: International Monetary Fund.

Diamond, P.A. (1965) 'National Debt in a Neoclassical Growth Model', *American Economic Review* 55 (5): 1126–50.

Diaz-Alejandro, C.F. (1963) 'A Note on the Impact of Devaluation and Distributive Effect', *Journal of Political Economy* 71 (2): 577–80.

—— (1975) 'Less Developed Countries and the International Economic Order', *Princeton Essays in International Finance*, no. 108.

—— (1984) 'Some Aspects of the Brazilian Payments Crisis', *Brookings Papers on Economic Activity* 2 (2): 515–52.

—— (1985) 'Good-bye Financial Repression, Hello Financial Crash', *Journal of Development Economics* 19 (1): 1–24.

Dobb, M. (1937) *Studies in the Development of Capitalism*, Cambridge: Cambridge University Press.

Dornbusch, R. (1973) 'Devaluation, Money and Non-Traded Goods', *American Economic Review* 63 (5): 871–80.

—— (1976) 'Exchange Rate Expectations and Monetary Policy', *Journal of International Economics* 6 (3): 231–44.

—— (1981) *Open Economy Macroeconomics*, New York: Basic Books.

—— Fischer, S. and Sparks, G. (1985) *Macroeconomics*, Toronto: McGraw Hill, Ryerson.

—— (1992) 'International Debt and Economic Instability', *Federal Reserve Bank of Kansas City Economic Review* 12 (1): 15–32.

Drazen, A. (1979) 'The Optimal Rate of Inflation Revisited', *Journal of Monetary Economics* 5 (2): 231–48.

—— (1980) 'Recent Developments in Macroeconomic Disequilibrium Theory', *Econometrica* 48 (2): 283–306.

Duesenberry, J. (1949) *Income, Saving and the Theory of Consumer Behavior*, Cambridge, Mass.: Harvard University Press.

Dunn, R. (1983) 'The Many Disappointments of Flexible Exchange Rates', *Princeton Essays in International Finance*, no. 154.

Eaton, J., Gersovitz, M. and Stiglitz, J.E. (1986) 'The Pure Theory of Country Risk', *European Economic Review* 30 (2): 481–513.

—— and Taylor, L. (1986) 'Developing Country Finance and Debt', *Journal of Development Economics* 22 (1): 209-65.

Economic Policy Council of the United Nations Association of the United States of America (1988) 'Third World Debt: a Reexamination of Long-term Management', report of the Third World Debt Panel.

The Economist (1987) 'The Limits of Cooperation', Survey of the World Economy, 26 September 1987.

Edel, M. (1969) *Food Supply and Inflation in Latin America*, New York: Praeger.

Edwards, S. (1984) 'The Order of Liberalization of the External Sector in Developing Countries', Washington, DC: World Bank.

—— (1986) 'Are Devaluations Contractionary?', *Review of Economics and Statistics* 68 (3): 864–73.

—— (1988) 'Exchange Rate Misalignment in Developing Countries', *World Bank Occasional Papers* no. 2, Baltimore, Md.: Johns Hopkins University Press.

—— and van Wijnbergen (1989) 'Disequilibrium and Structural Adjustment', in H. Chenery and T. N. Srinivasan (eds) *Handbook of Development Economics*, Amsterdam: North Holland.

Erzan, R. and Karsenty, G. (1987) 'Products Facing High Tariffs in Major Developed Countries: An Area of Priority for Developing Countries in the Uruguay Round?', Discussion Paper no. 401, Institute for International

Economic Studies.

Ethier, W. and Bloomfield, A.I. (1975) 'Managing the Managed Float', *Princeton Essays in International Finance* no. 112.

Fama, E.F. (1975) 'Short Term Interest Rates as Predictors of Inflation', *American Economic Review* 65 (3): 269–82.

Farber, H. (1986) 'The Analysis of Union Behavior', in O. Ashenfelter and R. Layard (eds) *Handbook of Labor Economics*, Amsterdam: North Holland.

Fethke, G. and Policano, A. (1986) 'Will Wage Setters ever Stagger Decisions?', *Quarterly Journal of Economics* 101 (4): 809–20.

Finance Ministry of Japan (1988) *Statement by the Alternate Governor of IMF and World Bank for Japan*, Press Release #12, 27 September.

Fischer, S. (1972) 'Keynes–Wicksell and Neoclassical Models of Money and Growth', *American Economic Review* 62 (5): 880–90.

—— (1977) 'Long Term Contracts, Rational Expectations, and the Optimal Money Supply Rule', *Journal of Political Economy* 85 (1): 191–206.

—— (1982) 'Seigniorage and the Case for a National Money', *Journal of Political Economy* 90 (2): 295–313.

—— (1988) 'Recent Developments in Macroeconomics', *Economic Journal* 98 (2): 294–339.

—— (1991) 'Editorial' in O.J. Blanchard and S. Fischer (eds) *NBER Macroeconomics Annual*, 1990, Cambridge, Mass.: MIT Press.

Fisher, I. (1930) *The Theory of Interest*, New York: Macmillan.

Fleming, J.M. (1962) 'Domestic Financial Policies under Fixed and Floating Exchange Rates', *IMF Staff Papers* 9 (2): 369–79.

Foley, M.J. and Sidrauski, M. (1971) *Monetary and Fiscal Policy in a Growing Economy*, New York: Macmillan.

Frenkel, J. and Johnson, H.G. (eds) (1976) *The Monetary Approach to the Balance of Payments*, London: Allen and Unwin.

Frenkel, J.A. (1985) 'Portfolio Crowding out Empirically Estimated', *Quarterly Journal of Economics* 100 (4): 1041–65.

—— Dooley, M.P. and Wickham, P. (eds) (1989) *Analytical Issues in Debt*, Washington, DC: International Monetary Fund.

—— and Razin, A. (1988) 'The Mundell–Flemming Model a Quarter Century Later', *IMF Staff Papers* 35 (2): 246–61.

Friedman, M. (1957) *A Theory of the Consumption Function*, Princeton, NJ: Princeton University Press.

—— (1971) 'Government Revenue from Inflation', *Journal of Political Economy* 79 (3): 846–56.

Fry, M. (1988) *Money, Interest, and Banking in Economic Development*, Baltimore, Md.: Johns Hopkins University Press.

Gandolfo, G. (1980) *Economic Dynamics: Methods and Models*, Amsterdam: North Holland.

Gelb, A.H. (1989) 'Financial Policies, Growth and Efficiency', *World Bank Working Paper* no. WPS 202, Country Economics Department.

Gemmel, N. (ed.) (1987) *Surveys in Development Economics*, Oxford: Basil Blackwell.

Gilbert, C.L. (1987) 'The Impact of Exchange Rates and Developing Country Debt on Commodity Prices', *Oxford University Applied Economics Discussion Paper* no. 30.

Goldstein, M. and Montiel, P. (1986) 'Evaluation of Fund Stabilization Programs with Multicountry Data: Methodological Pitfalls', *IMF Staff Papers* 33 (2): 304–44.

Goode, R. (1984) *Government Finance in Developing Countries*, Washington, DC:

Brookings Institution.

Granger, C. (1980) 'Testing for Causality: A Personal Viewpoint', *Journal of Economic Dynamics and Control* 2 (4): 329–52.

Gray, J. (1976) 'Wage Indexation: A Macroeconomic Approach', *Journal of Monetary Economics* 2 (2): 221–35.

Gupta, K.L. (1984) *Finance and Economic Growth in Developing Countries*, London: Croom Helm.

Gylfason, T. (1987) 'Credit Policy and Economic Activity in Developing Countries with IMF Stabilisation Programs', *Princeton Studies in International Finance* no. 60.

Haggard, S. and Kaufman, R. (1989) 'The Politics of Stabilisation and Structural Adjustment', in J. Sachs (ed.) *Developing Country Debt and Economic Performance*, vol. 1, Chicago, Ill.: University of Chicago Press for NBER.

Hahn, F.H. (1969) 'On Money and Growth', *Journal of Money, Credit and Banking* 1 (2): 172–87.

—— (1977) 'Keynesian Economics and General Equilibrium Theory: Reflections on Some Current Debates', in G. Harcourt (ed.) *The Microeconomic Foundations of Macroeconomics*, London: Macmillan.

Hansen, B. (1973) *A Survey of General Equilibrium Systems*, New York: McGraw Hill.

Harberger, A.C. (1963) 'The Dynamics of Inflation in Chile', in C. Christ A. Goldberger and A. Zellner (eds) *Measurement in Economics: Studies in Mathematical Economics and Econometrics in Memory of Yehuda Grunfeld*, Chicago, Ill.: University of Chicago Press.

—— (1974) *Taxation and Welfare*, Boston, Mass.: Little Brown.

Hayek, F.A. (1932) 'A Note on the Development of the Doctrine of "Forced Saving"', *Quarterly Journal of Economics* 47 (1): 123–33.

Helleiner, G.K. (1986) 'Balance-of-Payments Experience and Growth Prospects of Developing Countries: a Synthesis', *World Development* 14 (8): 877–908.

Hicks, J. (1932) *The Theory of Wages*, London: Macmillan.

—— (1939) *Value and Capital*, Oxford: Clarendon Press.

—— (1965) *Capital and Growth*, Oxford: Clarendon Press.

—— (1969) *A Theory of Economic History*, Oxford: Oxford University Press.

—— (1973) *The Crisis in Keynesian Economics*, New York: Basic Books.

Hirschman, A. (1981) 'The Social and Political Matrix of Inflation: Elaborations on the Latin American Experience', in A. Hirschman (ed.) *Essays in Trespassing: Economics to Politics and Beyond*, Cambridge: Cambridge University Press.

Holley, H.A. (1987) *Developing Country Debt: The Role of the Commercial Banks*, Chatham House Papers no. 35, London: Routledge and Kegan Paul.

Husain, I. and Diwan, I. (eds) (1989) *Dealing with the Debt Crisis*, Washington, DC: World Bank.

IMF (1987) 'Theoretical Aspects of the Design of Fund-supported Adjustment Programmes', *IMF Occasional Papers* no. 55.

Intrilligator, M. (1971) *Mathematical Optimization and Economic Theory*, Engelwood Cliffs, NJ: Prentice Hall.

Inter American Dialogue (1989) *The Americas in 1989: Consensus for Action*, Washington, DC.

Islam, S. (1984) 'Devaluation, Stabilization-Policies and the Developing Countries', *Journal of Development Economics* 14 (1): 37–60.

—— (1988) *Breaking the International Debt Deadlock*, Critical Issues Series no. 2, Council on Foreign Relations, New York.

Jha, R. (1982) 'Aggregate Output, Growth and Inflation under Adjustment Costs', in A. Chikan (ed.) *Inventories in the National Economy, Proceedings of the*

Second International Symposium on Inventories, Amsterdam: North Holland.
—— (1987) *Modern Theory of Public Finance*, New Delhi: Wiley Eastern.
—— (1988a) *The International Economic Order*, New Delhi: Commonwealth.
—— (1988b) *Essays in the Theory of Aggregate Supply*, New Delhi: Commonwealth.
—— (1991) *Contemporary Macroeconomic Theory and Policy*, New Delhi: Wiley Eastern.
—— and Lachler, U. (1983) 'Inflation and Economic Growth in a Competitive Economy with Exhaustible Resources', *Journal of Economic Behaviour and Organization* 4 (1): 113–29.
—— and Sahni, B.S. (1993) *Industrial Efficiency: an Indian Perspective*, New Delhi: Wiley Eastern.
—— Sahu, A.P. and Meyer, L.H. (1990) 'The Fisher Equation Controversy: a Reconciliation of Contradictory Results', *Southern Economic Journal* 57 (1): 106–13.
Johnson, G. and Layard, R. (1986) 'The Natural Rate of Unemployment: Explanation and Policy', in O. Ashenfelter and R. Layard (eds) *Handbook of Labor Economics*, vol. 2, Amsterdam: North Holland.
Johnson, H.J. (1972) *Further Essays in Monetary Economics*, London: Allen and Unwin.
—— and Frenkel, J. (1978) *The Economics of Exchange Rates*, Chicago, Ill.: Addison Wesley.
Joyanovic, B. (1982) 'Inflation and Welfare in the Steady State', *Journal of Political Economy* 90 (3): 561–77.
Kahil, R. (1973) 'Economy of Brazil', *Economic Journal* 81 (4): 1012–15.
Kahler, M. (ed.) (1986) *The Politics of International Debt*, Ithaca, New York: Cornell University Press.
Kalecki, M. (1943) *Studies in Economic Dynamics*, London: Allen and Unwin.
—— (1952) *Theory of Economic Dynamics*, London: Unwin University Books.
Kaletsky, A. (1985) *The Costs of Default*, New York: Twentieth Century Fund.
Kapur, B. (1974) 'Monetary Growth Models of Less Developed Economies', Ph.D. thesis, Stanford University.
—— (1976a) 'Alternative Stabilization Policies for Less Developed Economies', *Journal of Political Economy* 84 (4): 777–95.
—— (1976b) 'Two Approaches to Ending Inflation', in R.I. Mckinnon (ed.) *Money and Finance in Economic Growth and Development: Essays in Honor of Edward Shaw*, New York: Marcel Dekker.
—— (1983) 'Problems of Indexation in Financially Liberalized LDCs', *World Development* 10 (2): 199–209.
—— (1986) *Studies in Inflationary Dynamics: Financial Repression and Financial Liberalization in Less Developed Countries*, Singapore: National University of Singapore Press.
Kaufman, R. (1986) 'Democratic and Authoritarian Responses to the Debt Issue: Argentina, Brazil, Mexico', in Kahler (ed.) *The Politics of International Debt*, Ithaca, New York: Cornell University Press.
Kenen, P. (1983) 'Third World Debt: Sharing the Burden: A Bailout Plan for Banks', *The New York Times*, 6 March.
Keynes, J.M. (1936) *The General Theory of Employment, Interest and Money*, London: Macmillan.
—— (1973) *The Collected Writings of John Maynard Keynes*, ed. D. Moggridge, London: Macmillan.
Khan, M.S. (1987) 'Macroeconomic Adjustment in Developing Countries: a Policy Perspective', *World Bank Research Observer* 2 (1): 12–24.

—— and Knight, M.D.(1982) 'Some Theoretical and Empirical Issues Relating to Economic Stabilization in Developing Countries', *World Development* 10 (9) : 709–30.

—— and —— (1985) 'Fund Suported Adjustment Programs and Economic Growth', *IMF Occasional Papers* no. 41.

Kilborn, P. (1989) 'Debt Policy Shift Set on Third World', *The New York Times*, 11 March.

Killick, T. (1981) *Policy Economics*, London: Heinemann.

—— (1984) *The IMF and Stabilization*, New York: St Martin's Press.

Kouri, P. (1976) 'The Exchange Rate and the Balance of Payments in the Short Run and in the Long Run: a Monetary Approach', *Scandinavian Journal of Economics* 78 (2): 280–304.

Kraft, J. (1984) *The Mexican Rescue*, New York: Group of Thirty.

Krueger, A. (1978) *Liberalization Attempts and Consequences*, Cambridge, Mass.: NBER.

—— (1987) 'Debt, Capital Flows and LDC Growth', *American Economic Review* 77 (1): 159–64.

Krugman, P. and Taylor, L. (1978) 'Contractionary Effects of Devaluation', *Journal of International Economics* 8 (2): 445–56.

Krugman, P.R. (1988a) 'Market Based Debt Reduction Schemes', Working Paper Series no. 2587, NBER, Cambridge, Mass.

—— (1988b) 'Financing vs. Forgiving a Debt Overhang', *Journal of Development Economics* 29 (2) : 253–68.

—— (1989) 'Private Capital Flows to Problem Debtors', in J. Sachs (ed.) *Developing Country Debt and Economic Performance*, vol. 1, Chicago, Ill.: University of Chicago Press for NBER.

Kuczynski, P. (1987) 'The Outlook for Latin American Debt', *Foreign Affairs* 66 (1): 129–49.

Kydland, F. and Prescott, E. (1977) 'Rules Rather than Discretion: the Inconsistency of Optimal Plans', *Journal of Political Economy* 85 (3): 473–92.

LaFalce, J. (1987) 'Third World Debt Crisis: The Urgent Need to Confront Reality', statement prepared in Washington, 5 March.

Laffer, A. (1981) 'Government Exactions and Revenue Deficiencies', *Cato Journal* 12 (1): 1–21.

Layard, R. (1986) *How to Beat Unemployment*, Oxford: Oxford University Press.

Leff, N. and Sato, K. (1980) 'Macroeconomic Adjustment in Developing Countries: Instability, Short run Growth, and External Dependency', *Review of Economics and Statistics* 63 (1): 170–9.

Lipschitz, L. and Schadler, S. (1984) 'Relative Prices, Real Wages, and Macroeconomic Policies: some Evidence from Manufacturing in Japan and the U.K.' *IMF Staff Papers* 31 (2): 303–38.

Lipson, C. (1986) 'Bankers' Dilemmas: Private Cooperation in Rescheduling Sovereign Debts', in K.A. Oye (ed.) *Cooperation under Anarchy*, Princeton, NJ: Princeton University Press.

Lucas, R.E. (1988) 'On the Mechanics of Economic Development', *Journal of Monetary Economics* 22 (1): 3–42.

—— and Stokey, N. (1987) 'Money and Interest in a Cash-in-Advance Economy', *Econometrica* 55 (3): 491–514.

Mahalanobis, P.C. (1953) 'Some Observations on the Process of Growth of National Income', *Sankhya* 30 (3): 378–405.

Mann, H.B. and Whitney, D.R. (1947) 'On a test of Whether One of Two Random Variables is Stochastically Larger than the Other', *Annals of Mathematical Statistics* 18 (1): 50–60.

Mathieson, D.J. (1977) 'Portfolio Disequilibrium', *Journal of Money, Credit and Banking* 9 (3): 491–506.

—— (1979) 'Financial Reform and Capital Flows in a Developing Economy,' *IMF Staff Papers* 26 (3): 450–89.

—— (1980) 'Financial Reform and Stabilization Policies in a Developing Economy,' *Journal of Development Economics* 7 (3): 359–95.

—— (1982) 'Inflation, Interest Rates and Balance of Payments During a Financial Reform: The Case of Argentina', *World Development* 10 (9): 813–27.

—— (1983) 'Estimating Models of Financial Market Behavior During Periods of Extensive Structural Reforms: The Experience of Chile', *IMF Staff Papers* 30 (2): 350–93.

McKinnon, R.I. (1973) *Money and Capital in Economic Development*, Washington, DC: Brookings Institution.

—— (1979) 'Foreign Trade Regimes and Economic Development: a Review Article', *Journal of International Economics* 9 (2): 429–52.

—— (1981) 'Financial Repression and the Liberalization Problem within Less Developed Countries', in S. Grassman and E. Lundberg (eds) *The Past and Prospects for the World Economic Order*, London: Macmillan.

—— (1984) 'Financial Liberalization and the Debt Crisis in LDCs: The International Misregulation of Commercial Banks', Stanford, Center for Research in Economic Growth, Memo no. 265.

Milner, C. and Snowden, N. (1992) *External Imbalances and Policy Constraints in the 1990s*, London: St Martin's Press.

Mundell, R. (1963) 'Inflation and Real Interest', *Journal of Political Economy* 71 (3): 280–3.

—— (1968) *International Economics*, New York: Macmillan.

—— (1971) *Monetary Theory*, San Francisco, Calif.: Goodyear.

Muth, J.F. (1961) 'Rational Expectations and the Theory of Price Movements', *Econometrica* 29 (2): 315–35.

Nam, C.H. (1986) 'Export Promoting Policies under Countervailing Threats: GATT Rules and Practice', Discussion Paper, Report Number VPERS 9, World Bank.

Nichols, D.A. (1983) 'Some Problems of Inflationary Finance', *Journal of Political Economy* 83 (2): 423–30.

Niehans, J. (1987) 'Classical Monetary Theory: New and Old', *Journal of Money, Credit and Banking* 19 (4): 409–24.

Nowzad, B. (1981) 'Debt in Developing Countries: Some Issues for the 1980s', *Finance and Development* 19 (1): 13–16.

O'Driscoll, G.P. (1985) 'The Ricardian Non-equivalence Theorem', *Journal of Political Economy* 95 (1): 207–10.

Page, S. (1993) (ed.) *Monetary Policy in Developing Countries*, London: Routledge.

Pasinetti, L. (1974) *Growth and Income Distribution*, Cambridge: Cambridge University Press.

Patinkin, D. (1965) *Money, Interest, and Prices*, Evanston: Harper and Row.

Pease, D. (1988) 'A Congressional Plan to Solve the Debt Crisis', *The International Economy* 2 (1): 98–105.

Phelps, E.S. (1961) 'The Golden Rule of Accumulation: a Fable for Growthmen', *American Economic Review* 51 (4): 638–43.

—— (1965) 'Second Essay on the Golden Rule of Accumulation', *American Economic Review* 55: 251–65.

—— (1969) (ed.) *Microeconomic Foundations of Employment and Inflation Theory*, New York: Norton.

—— (1972) *Inflation Policy and Unemployment Theory*, New York: Norton.

—— (1979) *Studies in Macroeconmic Theory*, New York: Academic Press.
—— and Taylor, J.B. (1977) 'Stabilising Properties of Monetary Policy under Rational Expectations', *Journal of Political Economy* 85 (1): 163–90.
Phillips, A.W. (1958) 'The Relation between Unemployment and the Rate of Change of Money Wage Rates in the United Kingdom 1861–1957', *Economica* 25 (1): 163–90.
Polak, R.J. (1957) 'Monetary Analysis of Income Formation and Payments Problems', *IMF Staff Papers* 6 (1): 1–50.
—— (1989) *Financial Policies and Development*, Development Centre Studies, OECD.
Porter, R. and Ranney, S.I. (1982) 'An Eclectic Model of recent LDC Macroeconomic Policy Analyses', *World Development* 10 (9): 751–65.
Poterba, J. and Rotemberg, J. (1987) 'Money in the Utility Function: an Empirical Investigation', in W. Barnett and K. Singleton (eds) *New Developments in Monetary Economics*, New York: Cambridge University Press.
—— and Summers, L.H. (1987) 'Finite Lifetimes and Effects of Budget Deficits on National Saving', *Journal of Monetary Economics* 20 (2): 369–92.
Prachowny, M.J. (1984) *Macroeconomic Analysis for Small Open Economies*, Oxford: Clarendon Press.
Ranis, G. (1989) 'Analytics of Development: Dualism', in H. Chenery and T.N. Srinivasan (eds) *Handbook of Development Economics*, vol. 1, Amsterdam: North Holland.
Rasche, R. (1987) 'Velocity and Money Demand Functions: Do Stable Relationships Exist?', in K. Brunner and A. Meltzer (eds) *Carnegie Rochester Conference Series*, Princeton, NJ: Irwin.
Rattso, J. (1989) 'Macrodynamic Adjustment Mechanisms in a Dual Semi-Industrialized Economy', *Journal of Development Economics* 30 (1): 47–69.
Renshaw, G. (ed.) (1989) *Market Liberalization, Equity, and Development*, Geneva: International Labour Office.
Robinson, J.D. (1988) 'A Comprehensive Agenda for LDC Debt and World Trade Growth', *Amex Bank Review*, Special Papers Series no. 13, American Express Bank, London.
Robinson, R. (1953) *Essays in the Theory of Employment*, Oxford: Basil Blackwell.
—— (1960) *Collected Economic Papers of Joan Robinson*, Oxford: Oxford University Press.
Robinson, R.M. (1988) 'Duration Analysis – Managing Interest Rate Risk', *Journal of Banking and Finance* 12 (1): 162–6.
Rohatyn, F.G. (1983) 'A Plan for Stretching out Global Debt', *Business Week*, 28 February 1983.
Romer, D. (1986) 'A Simple General Equilibrium version of the Baumol–Tobin Model', *Quarterly Journal of Economics* 101 (4): 663–86.
Romer, P. (1986) 'Increasing Returns and Long Run Growth' *Journal of Political Economy* 94 (5): 1002–37.
Rose, H. (1966) 'Unemployment in a Theory of Growth', *International Economic Review* 7 (3): 260–82.
—— (1967) 'On the Non-linear Theory of the Employment Cycle', *Review of Economic Studies* 34 (1): 153–73.
Rotberg, E.H. (1988) 'Towards a Solution of the Debt Crisis', *The International Economy* 2 (1): 42–8.
Rothschild, M. (1971) 'On the Cost of Adjustment', *Quarterly Journal of Economics* 85 (2): 605–22.
Sachs, J. (1979) 'Wage, Profits, and Macroeconomic Adjustment: A Comparative Survey', *Brookings Papers on Economic Activity* no. 1: 269–332.

—— (ed.) (1989) *Developing Country Debt and Economic Performance*, vol.1, Chicago, Ill.: University of Chicago Press for NBER.

—— and Huizinga, H. (1987) 'U.S. Commercial Banks and the Developing Country Debt Crisis', *Brookings Papers on Economic Activity* no. 2: 556–606.

Sah, R.K. and Stiglitz, J.E. (1989) 'Sources of Technological Divergence between Developed and Less Developed Economies', in G.A. Calvo, C. Diaz-Alejandro and C. Federico (eds) *Debt, Stabilization, and Development*, Oxford: Basil Blackwell.

Saini, K.G. (1982) 'The Monetarist Explanation of Inflation; the Experience of Six Asian Countries', *World Development* 10 (10): 871–84.

Salop, S.C. (1979) 'A Model of the Natural Rate of Unemployment', *American Economic Review* 69 (1): 117–25.

Salter, W. (1959) 'Internal and External Balance: The Role of Price and Expenditure Effects', *Economic Record* 35 (1): 226–38.

Samuelson, P.A. (1947) *Foundations of Economic Analysis*, Cambridge, Mass.: Harvard University Press.

—— (1958) 'An Exact Consumption-loan Model of Interest with or without the Social Contrivance of Money', *Journal of Political Economy* 66 (2): 467–82.

Sargent, T.J. and Wallace, N. (1975) '"Rational" Expectations, the Optimal Monetary Instrument and the Optimal Money Supply Rule', *Journal of Political Economy* 83 (2): 241–54.

—— and —— (1987) 'Inflation and the Government Budget Constraint', in A. Razin and E. Sadka (eds) *Economic Policy in Theory and Practice*, London: Macmillan.

Seers, D. (1964) 'Inflation and Growth: the Heart of the Controversy', in W. Baer and I. Kerstenetzky (eds) *Inflation and Growth in Latin America*, Homewood, Ill.: Irwin.

Selowsky, M. and Van Der Tak, H. (1986) 'The Debt Problem and Growth', *World Development* 14 (9): 1107–24.

Sengupta, A. (1988) 'A Proposal for a Debt Adjustment Facility', prepared for the IMF Executive Board Seminar, 88/3, 9 February 1988.

Shaw, E.S. (1973) *Financial Deepening in Economic Development*, New York: Oxford University Press.

Snowden, P.N. (1989) 'The Interpretation of Market Discounts in Assessing Buy-back Benefits: Comment on Dooley', *IMF Staff Papers* 36 (3): 733–5.

Solow, R. (1956) 'A Contribution to the Theory of Economic Growth', *Quarterly Journal of Economics* 70 (1): 26–41.

Squire, L. (1981) *Employment Policy in Developing Countries*, New York: Oxford University Press.

Streeten, P. (1987) 'Structural Adjustment: a Survey of the Issues and Options', *World Development* 15 (12): 1469–82.

Taylor, L. (1981) 'South–South Trade and Southern Growth: Bleak Prospects from the Structuralist Point of View', *Journal of International Economics* 11 (2): 589-602.

—— (1983) *Structuralist Macroeconomics*, New York: Basic Books.

—— (1985) 'A Stagnationist Model of Economic Growth', *Cambridge Journal of Economics* 9: 383–403.

—— (1987) 'Macro Policy in the Tropics: How Sensible People Stand', *World Development* 15 (12): 1407–35.

—— (1988) *Varieties of Stabilisation Experience: Towards Sensible Macroeconomics in the Third World*, New York: Oxford University Press.

Tobin, J. (1947) 'Liquidity Preference and Monetary Policy', *Review of Economics and Statistics* 29 (1): 124–31.

—— (1955) 'A Dynamic Aggregative Model', *Journal of Political Economy* 63 (2): 342–57.

—— (1958) 'Liquidity Preference as Behavior Towards Risk', *Review of Economic Studies* 36 (2): 312–34.

—— (1965) 'Money and Economic Growth', *Econometrica* 33 (4): 671–84.

—— (1982) *Asset Accumulation and Economic Activity*, Oxford: Basil Blackwell.

Tun, W.V. and Wong, W. (1982) 'Determinants of Private Investment in Developing Countries', *Journal of Development Studies* 19 (2): 246–61.

UNCTAD (1986) *Trade and Development Report (1986)*, Geneva, Switzerland.

van Wijnbergen, S. (1983) 'Credit Policy, Inflation and Growth in a Financially Repressed Economy', *Journal of Development Economics* 13 (1): 45–65.

—— (1986) 'Exchange Rate Management and Stabilization Policy in Developing Countries', in S. Edwards and L. Ahmed (eds) *Exchange Rate Policy and Structural Policy in Developing Countries*, Chicago, Ill.: NBER and the University of Chicago Press.

—— (1988) 'Monopolistic Competition, Credibility, and the Output Costs of Disinflation Programmes: an Analysis of Price Controls', *Journal of Development Economics* 29 (2): 375–98.

Vogel, R. (1974) 'The Dynamics of Inflation in Latin America, 1950–1969', *American Economic Review* 64 (1): 102–14.

Whitman, R. (1975) 'Global Monetarism and the Monetary Approach to Balance of Payments', *Brookings Papers on Economic Activity* no. 2: 491–536.

Williamson, J. (1983) *The Open Economy and the World Economy*, New York: Basic Books.

—— (1985) 'On the Question of Debt Relief' *Statement of the Roundtable on Money and Finance*, New York, 13–14 December 1985.

—— (1988) *Voluntary Approaches to Debt Relief*, Washington, DC: Institute for International Economics.

Williamson, J.H. (1965) 'The Crawling Peg', *Essays in International Finance* no. 50, Princeton University.

Woolmer, R. (1977) *Monetary Policy in Nigeria*, mimeo, University of Nigeria, Lagos.

World Bank (1987) *World Development Report*, New York: Oxford University Press.

Index